T0271506

BETWEEN FRIENDS

BETWEEN FRIENDS

*Letters of Vera Brittain
and Winifred Holtby*

Edited by Elaine and
English Showalter

virago

VIRAGO

First published in Great Britain in 2022 by Virago Press

1 3 5 7 9 10 8 6 4 2

Typeset in Goudy by M Rules
Printed and bound in Great Britain by
Clays Ltd, Elcograf S.p.A.

Papers used by Virago are from well-managed forests
and other responsible sources.

Virago Press
An imprint of
Little, Brown Book Group
Carmelite House
50 Victoria Embankment
London EC4Y 0DZ

An Hachette UK Company
www.hachette.co.uk

www.virago.co.uk

Winifred Holtby

Vera Brittain

CONTENTS

DRAMATIS PERSONAE

VERA BRITTAIN AND HER FAMILY

Brittain, Vera (1893–1970): spent her childhood in Macclesfield, Cheshire and Buxton, Derbyshire; in 1914 went up to Somerville College, Oxford to read English; left in 1915 to serve as a Voluntary Aid Detachment nurse in Buxton then London; became engaged to her brother's schoolfriend Roland Leighton; posted in 1916 to Malta for eight months, and then Étaples in France, near the Front in 1917–18, followed by a further spell in London; suffered the loss in the war of her fiancé, her brother Edward and two close friends; returned to Oxford in 1919; there met fellow student Winifred Holtby. In 1925 Vera married George Edward Gordon Catlin, professor of political science at Cornell University; they had a son, John, in 1927, and a daughter, Shirley, in 1930. Her novels, *The Dark Tide* (1923) and *Not Without Honour* (1924), had only modest success, but in 1933 she published her memoir *Testament of Youth*, a bestseller in both Britain and the United States, and now regarded as a classic. In 1936 Vera oversaw Winifred Holtby's posthumous novel, *South Riding*, to publication, and in 1940 published an account of their lives together as *Testament of Friendship*. In 1960 she edited a limited edition of her correspondence with Winifred, *Selected Letters of Winifred Holtby and Vera Brittain*.

Brittain, (Thomas) Arthur (1864–1935): Vera's father, prosperous director of a family paper manufacturing business; committed suicide in the summer of 1935.

Brittain, Edith, née Bervon (1868–1948): Vera's mother; one of four daughters and two sons of an impoverished musician.

Brittain, Edward Harold (1895–1918): Vera's brother, educated at Uppingham School; volunteered in 1914; awarded the Military Cross for his bravery on the first day of the Battle of the Somme; killed in action in Italy on 15 June 1918.

Brittain Catlin, John Edward Jocelyn (1927–87): son and eldest child of Vera and Gordon Catlin. Later a businessman and author of a book about his family, *Family Quartet* (1987).

Brittain Catlin, Shirley Vivian Teresa, later Baroness Williams of Crosby (1930–2021): daughter and second child of Vera and Gordon Catlin. Cabinet minister in the Labour government 1974–9; co-founder of the Social Democratic Party 1981; Professor of Electoral Politics, John F. Kennedy School of Government, Harvard University.

Bervon, Florence (1865–1936): Vera's aunt, her mother's eldest sister; with her partner Louise Heath-Jones ran St Monica's School at Kingswood in Surrey, which Vera attended, and where both Vera and Winifred later taught.

Catlin, George Edward Gordon (1896–1979): Vera's husband, son of a Congregational minister who later became an Anglican clergyman, won distinction in an abbreviated history course at New College, Oxford; converted to Catholicism; taught briefly at Sheffield, then took up a post at

Cornell University in Ithaca, New York, where he continued
to teach after marrying Vera; knighted in 1970 for his work on
Anglo-American relations. He preferred to be called George,
but because that was also his father's name, he went by the
name Gordon until his father's death in 1936; in the letters
between Vera and Winifred, he is always called Gordon, and
that name is used in this volume.

Catlin, Reverend George Edward (1858–1936): Vera's father-in-
law, a clergyman, initially a Congregationalist, then in the
Church of England.

Brittain, Muriel, later Groves (1879–1971): Vera's aunt, youngest sibling of her father; married Henry Leigh Groves.

Groves, (Henry) Leigh (1880–1968): Vera's uncle by his marriage to her aunt Muriel Brittain; wealthy heir of a brewing
family, lived at Holehird near Windermere.

Chard, Standish (1880–1953): a distant American cousin of Vera
Brittain, who lived in the New York area.

VERA BRITTAIN'S FRIENDS AND ASSOCIATES

Brett, Jr, George P. (1893–1984): publisher, president of the
Macmillan Company; welcomed Vera to the USA in 1934,
when she arrived for her first lecture tour.

Heath-Jones, Louise (c.1869–1931): partner of Vera's aunt
Florence Bervon; the two women ran St Monica's School.

Latham, Harold (1887–1969): editor in the London office of
Macmillan, he read part of *Testament of Youth* and accepted it
for American publication before Victor Gollancz had accepted
it for British publication.

Leigh, Colston (1901–92): founded the Leigh Bureau in 1929, a
speakers' agency still in existence, with a distinguished list of
clients; he handled Vera's American tour in 1934.

Leighton, Clare (1898–1989): artist; daughter of Robert and Marie Leighton, sister of Vera's fiancé Roland.

Leighton, Marie Connor (1867–1941): a successful novelist, married Robert Leighton in 1889, mother of Roland, Evelyn and Clare.

Leighton, Robert (1858–1934): editor and author of boys' fiction.

Leighton, Roland Aubrey (1895–1915): son of the writer Robert Leighton, schoolfriend of Vera's brother Edward, engaged to Vera in 1915. Enlisted at outbreak of war; left for the Front in March 1915, mortally wounded in December 1915.

Notestein, Wallace (1878–1969): distinguished professor of English history; he was at Cornell University in the early 1920s and supported Gordon Catlin's career.

Richards, Grant (1872–1948): notable London publisher, who launched his eponymous company in 1897; he published Vera's first two novels.

Stamford, 10th Earl of, Roger Grey (1896–1976): friend of Gordon Catlin from New College, Oxford, who served as best man at the wedding of Gordon and Vera.

WINIFRED HOLTBY AND HER FAMILY

Holtby, Winifred (1898–1935): daughter of a prosperous Yorkshire farming family, educated at Queen Margaret's School in Scarborough, showed literary talent when young; went up to Somerville College, Oxford in 1917; enlisted in the Women's Auxiliary Army Corps in 1918, was stationed at a WAAC camp near Abbeville in France. When she was demobilised, she returned to Oxford and met Vera Brittain in 1919. Published her first novel, *Anderby Wold*, in 1923, with moderate success; followed with *The Crowded Street* (1924), *The Land of Green Ginger* (1927), *Poor Caroline* (1931), *Mandoa,*

Mandoa! (1933) and *South Riding* (posthumously in 1936), as well as volumes of short stories, poetry and non-fiction. In 1924 she became friends with Margaret, Lady Rhondda, who invited her in 1926 to become a director of *Time and Tide*, an important feminist periodical. She died at the Elizabeth Fulcher Nursing Home, Devonshire Street, London, on 29 September 1935.

Holtby, Alice, née Winn (1858–1939): mother of Winifred and Grace Holtby, wife of David Holtby; a woman of strong character, she was elected in 1923 to the East Riding County Council and in 1934 became the first woman to serve as alderman in the district.

Holtby, David (1860–1933): father of Winifred Holtby; until the First World War, a prosperous farmer in Rudston, Yorkshire; gave up farming in 1919 when conscription had made farm labour scarce.

Holtby, Grace, later Tolmie (1896–1928): Winifred's elder sister and only sibling; married Dr Peter Tolmie in 1923 and died soon after the birth of her second child.

Coundouroff, Edith de (1888–1956): the wife of a Russian man, George de Coundouroff (1892–1919), who came to England to study agriculture in the pre-War era, and was taken in by the Holtbys; he was reported missing during the Russian Revolution, and Edith remained with the Holtbys for the next twenty years.

WINIFRED HOLTBY'S FRIENDS AND ASSOCIATES

Archdale, Helen Alexander (1876–1949): feminist, suffragette, first editor of *Time and Tide*.

Halls Dally, John Frederick (1877–1944): doctor, authority on high blood pressure; treated Winifred in her last years.

Hamilton, Cicely Mary (1872–1952): actress, writer, journalist, feminist, part of the inner circle of *Time and Tide*.

Keun, Odette Zoé (1888–1978): Dutch novelist, journalist, artist; from 1924 to 1933, partner of H. G. Wells, and in that same period a friend of Winifred's.

Leverkus, Dorothy Nellie Louise (1900–60): doctor based in the village of Chinnor, treated Winifred when she was at Monks Risborough.

Mannaberg, Edith, later Smeterlin (1898–1982): schoolfriend of Winifred; married in 1925 the Polish concert pianist Jan Smeterlin (1892–1967).

McWilliam, Jean, called 'Mac' (1881–1963): Winifred's superior in the WAAC, later headmistress of Pretoria High School for Girls in South Africa; regular correspondent of Winifred's, co-edited with Alice Holtby Winifred's letters to her, published in 1937 as *Letters to a Friend*.

Millin, Sarah Gertrude (1889–1965): South African novelist who became a friend of Winifred's.

Obermer, Edgar (1895–1958): Austrian doctor, specialist in blood pressure, treated Winifred, diagnosed Bright's disease, and in 1932 apparently told her she might only have two years to live.

Pearson, Harry (1897–1976): childhood friend and neighbour of Winifred, an occasional but erratic suitor, assumed by Vera to be Winifred's love interest.

Rhondda, Viscountess, Margaret Haig Mackworth (1883–1958): businesswoman and active suffragette; founded *Time and Tide*; funded that periodical and other feminist and progressive organisations like the Six Point Group; met Winifred in 1924 and in 1926 made her a director of *Time and Tide*.

FRIENDS AND ASSOCIATES OF BOTH
VERA BRITTAIN AND WINIFRED HOLTBY

Benson, Stella (1892–1933): novelist and world traveller.

Bentley, Phyllis (1894–1977): prolific and highly regarded novelist from Yorkshire; her best-known novel, *Inheritance* (1932), is a portrait of the textile industry in the West Riding.

Blackwell, Basil Henry (1889–1984): son of the founder of Blackwell's bookshop and publishers in Oxford. Took over the family business in 1924.

Brailsford, Henry Noel (1873–1958): a prolific left-wing journalist in the early twentieth century; lived with Clare Leighton from 1928 to 1937.

Burnett, Amy and Charles: Amy, née Francis, was employed by the Brittain-Catlins as a maidservant in September 1930; she married Charles Burnett in 1934 and he joined the household as butler and general handyman, while she was promoted to cook-housekeeper. They gave 'unstinting and loyal service' for over thirty years.

Dakers, Andrew (1867–1966): after success as a non-fiction author, Dakers became a publisher and literary agent.

Gollancz, Victor (1893–1967): the leading left-wing publisher and humanitarian. Gollancz founded his publishing company in 1927; in 1933 he published Vera's masterpiece, *Testament of Youth*.

Gray, Dr: a female doctor who treated Vera and her children, and also Winifred, in London.

Jameson, Margaret Storm (1891–1986): a prolific and highly regarded novelist, originally from Yorkshire.

Kennedy, Margaret (1896–1967): a successful novelist, whose most famous work was *The Constant Nymph* (1924).

Reid, Hilda (1898–1982): a Somerville contemporary of Vera and Winifred, and the author of four historical novels.

Scott-James, Violet (1885–1992): journalist who worked for the *Manchester Guardian* and the *Yorkshire Post*; Vera and Winifred often relied on her to publish their articles in the 'Women's Column', of which she was editor.

West, Rebecca (1892–1983): the celebrated writer, she was a director of *Time and Tide*, and is mentioned simply as 'Rebecca' in the letters between Vera and Winifred.

CHRONOLOGY OF THE LIVES OF VERA BRITTAIN (VB) AND WINIFRED HOLTBY (WH), 1919–1935

Biographical details are taken from the two major biographies: *Vera Brittain: A Life* by Paul Berry and Mark Bostridge (1995) and *The Clear Stream: The Life of Winifred Holtby* by Marion Shaw (2000).

1919

April	VB returns to Somerville College, Oxford; changes subject to history
October	WH returns to Somerville College, Oxford
	WH and VB meet at a tutorial with C. R. M. F. Cruttwell, the dean of Hertford College
Near end of Michaelmas Term	VB humiliated in a Somerville debate organised by WH

1920

April–July	VB briefly engaged to Roy Anthony
summer	WH writing often to VB and to Jean McWilliams
July	VB and WH on holiday together in Cornwall
summer–autumn	VB an editor of *Oxford Poetry*
August	VB makes first visit to Bainesse, the Holtby home at Cottingham

1921

winter–spring	VB and WH both writing novels, 'Daphne' and 'Anlaby Wold'
January	WH writes to VB that Harry Pearson, her erratic suitor, has become engaged while en route to South America
July	VB and WH sit their final exams in the last week of July
	WH writes and WH and VB act in the Somerville 'Going Down Play'
	VB and WH go to the Brittain family home at Oakwood Court, London
	VB and WH go to the Holtby family home at Cottingham, hear exam results there; both have seconds

August–mid-October	VB and WH spend six weeks in Italy and France, go to Milan, Venice, Florence, visit Edward Brittain's grave at Granezza and Roland Leighton's at Louvencourt
autumn	VB begins giving lectures at St Monica's
October–November	VB ill with jaundice and a gall-bladder problem
November	VB and WH, with their families, attend Oxford degree ceremony
December	VB visits WH in Yorkshire before Christmas
	VB and WH move into a flat at 52 Doughty Street, London, on 30 December

1922

January–December	VB and WH both lecturing at St Monica's, also for the League of Nations Union and the Six Point Group
March	VB and WH both complete drafts of their first novels
August	VB and WH attend the League of Nations school in Geneva
	WH's novel *Anderby Wold* accepted by John Lane. VB disappointed that WH will be published first
September	VB and WH move to the top-floor flat at 58 Doughty Street

VB and WH meet Percy Harris, Liberal candidate in Bethnal Green, and work for him

1923

January–December	VB and WH both lecturing at St Monica's
February	VB's article on 'Whole Duty of Women' in *Time and Tide*
March	Alice Holtby, WH's mother, elected to East Riding County Council
	WH's novel *Anderby Wold* published by John Lane
April	VB's novel *The Dark Tide* accepted by Grant Richards with subsidy paid by WH
July	*The Dark Tide* published on 16 July
	VB receives a letter from George Edward Gordon Catlin, known as Gordon, beginning a regular correspondence
	WH visits Rudston with her mother
autumn	VB's second novel, *Not Without Honour*, accepted by Grant Richards
	WH hired by Oxford University Extension to give lectures in the Lake District
September	Grace Holtby, WH's sister, marries Dr Peter Tolmie

WH and VB attend the League of Nations assembly in Geneva

November | VB and WH move from Doughty Street to 117 Wymering Mansions, Maida Vale

VB shifts her political support from the Liberal to the Labour Party

1924

months not certain | WH gives lectures and teaches to earn income

February | VB's second novel, *Not Without Honour*, published

WH's article 'The Human Factor' published in *Time and Tide* on 22 February – her first journalism; WH begins friendship with Margaret, Lady Rhondda

March | WH's novel *The Crowded Street* accepted by John Lane

WH writing new novel, 'The Runners', about John Wycliffe

April | VB goes on League of Nations speaking tour in Scottish border towns

VB stops at Aunt Muriel's in Windermere, flirts with uncle Leigh Groves

before summer term | VB and WH go on a fortnight's holiday at Whipsnade

June	VB delays seeing Gordon Catlin on his return from the USA on 10 June; he proposes 15 June, she delays reply, falls ill
July	VB goes to Oxford to see Gordon, agrees to marry him on 5 July
July–August	VB continues to write and lecture
August	VB refuses to have sex with Gordon before marriage
	WH's article 'Ladies First' published in *Time and Tide*
September	Gordon sails for America on 10 September
	VB and WH go to Geneva to report on the League of Nations for *Time and Tide* on 12 September
September–November	VB and WH travel in Germany, Hungary, Austria and Czechoslovakia

1925

June	VB marries Gordon Catlin at St James's, Spanish Place on 27 June; they depart for a four-week honeymoon in Europe
July	WH declines offer to be headmistress of St Monica's
	VB appoints Andrew Dakers as her literary agent

	VB working on an autobiographical honeymoon journal
August	WH goes to Yorkshire to help her family during an epidemic
	WH uses time in Yorkshire to read Wycliffe and work on 'The Runners'
early autumn	WH invites VB to meet Stella Benson
September	VB and Gordon sail for America on 11 September and WH goes to Geneva the same day
autumn–winter	VB increasingly unhappy as a 'faculty wife' at Cornell
October	WH spends a weekend at Stonepits in Kent with Lady Rhondda, meets St John Ervine
November	WH's novel 'The Runners' rejected, and is never published
	WH meets J. B. Priestley
December	WH spends time with VB's family in London
	WH with her own family at Cottingham over Christmas

1926

January–August	WH on a lecture tour in South Africa

March	VB and Gordon go to New York City for five months for his research; VB acting as his typist and assistant
May	WH planning new novel, *The Land of Green Ginger*
July	WH lands at Tilbury, spends a night with Brittain family in London, goes on to Yorkshire
summer	VB tells Gordon she will not return to the USA next year
August	WH has a holiday in Yorkshire
	VB arrives Southampton without Gordon, met by WH, 13 August
August–September	VB and WH go to Geneva for League of Nations meeting
September	WH invited to become a director of *Time and Tide*
autumn	WH writing *The Land of Green Ginger*, and is much in demand as a journalist
	WH and VB return to Wymering Mansions
December	VB and WH at *Time and Tide* party given by Lady Rhondda at Boulestin's

1927

January	VB and WH stewards at Lady Rhondda's debate with G. K. Chesterton

	WH meets with Arthur Creech Jones about South African trade unionism
February	WH still receiving rejections for 'The Runners'
March	VB sails with her mother to the USA, WH sees them off, 28 March
April	VB realises she is pregnant
	WH meets and interviews Storm Jameson
May–summer	WH, Ballinger, and other left-wing politicians welcome Kadalie from South Africa
June	VB and Gordon return to London
September	VB, Gordon and WH move from Maida Vale to 6A Nevern Place in Earls Court
autumn	WH's novel *The Land of Green Ginger* published
December	VB gives birth to John Edward Jocelyn Brittain-Catlin, 19 December

1928

month not certain	WH lectures in Halifax, meets Phyllis Bentley
January–April	VB has post-partum depression
January	VB left with baby as Gordon returns to America
March	VB left alone as WH goes to Yorkshire; WH's sister Grace dies on 11 March

late spring–June	WH and VB attend memorial services for Mrs Pankhurst
	WH returns to London, leaves again quickly for a motor tour of Ireland with Stella Benson
	VB's treatise *Women's Work in Modern England* published
summer–autumn	WH holidays in Monte Carlo
	WH publishes *Eutychus; or the Future of the Pulpit*
November	VB called as a witness at the prosecution of Radclyffe Hall for obscenity in *The Well of Loneliness*
December	VB sees *Journey's End*, at the beginning of a big year for war memoirs and fiction

1929

February	VB engaged by Kegan Paul to write *Halcyon, or the Future of Monogamy*; it is published in September
March	VB responds to Gordon's letter in which he says he wants to have an affair
April?	WH goes to Paris with Dot McCalman and Jean McWilliam at Easter
May	WH and VB campaign for Monica Whately in the general election

WH publishes *A New Voter's Guide to Party Programmes*

August   WH goes to Monte Carlo with Jan and Edith Smeterlin

September   VB goes to Geneva with Gordon for the League of Nations

VB speaks at World League for Sexual Reform

WH looks after John Edward Catlin while VB and Gordon go to Vevey and Geneva

WH working on *Poor Caroline*

Autumn   WH making weekend trips to Yorkshire to care for her ailing father

November   VB begins working on *Testament of Youth*

VB, WH, and Gordon look for a larger house

December   VB learns she is pregnant again

1930

April   VB and family move to 19 Glebe Place, Chelsea

April–May?   WH writes play *Judgment Voice*, not staged, revised as story *The Voice of God*

June?   WH writes play *Efficiency First*

July   WH works on novel *Poor Caroline*

VB gives birth to Shirley Vivian Brittain-
Catlin, 27 July

August   WH takes first plane flight to visit Lady
                  Rhondda at Agay in the South of France

                  WH goes from Agay to Geneva

autumn   WH very active as a journalist

1931

January–June   VB rereading diaries and letters for *Testament
                  of Youth*

January   WH publishes *Poor Caroline*

spring   WH leaves Jonathan Cape and signs a three-
                  novel deal with William Collins

summer   WH on holiday in France

                  WH writing a study of Virginia Woolf

                  WH stays with Lady Rhondda at St Lunaire

August   VB settles on title *Testament of Youth*

                  WH stays with Violet Scott-James at
                  Abondance, Haute-Savoie, has headaches

                  WH goes to Cap Ferrat with the Smeterlins

August–   VB takes her children to Rustington in Sussex
September?
                  VB and Gordon go to St Raphael, WH cares
                  for their children

September–October	VB and Gordon's holiday cut short by his candidacy in election on 27 October
	WH canvasses for Gordon, unsuccessful Labour candidate in October general election in which the National Government came into office
	WH falls ill with the first symptoms of renal failure
November	WH convalesces with Clare Leighton at Monks Risborough, Buckinghamshire, 7–13 November
	WH collapses, goes into a nursing home in Earls Court, 22 November until after Christmas
end of the year	WH begins writing *Mandoa, Mandoa!*

1932

January	WH convalesces at Sidmouth with VB
	WH ill in Monks Risborough, Gordon in the USA
February	VB and children have chicken pox
February–April	WH still on a rest cure at Monks Risborough, has a revelation of her impending death
March	VB and Monica Whately drive to Monks Risborough, 11 March
	WH has a visit from Harry Pearson, c. 17 March

April	VB invites Phyllis Bentley to stay with her in Chelsea
May–summer	VB invites Phyllis Bentley again; they quarrel
	WH diagnosed with renal failure; sees a specialist, Edgar Obermer, who tells her she will die soon
	WH returns to London, first to the Earls Court nursing home and then Glebe Place
July–August	VB, WH and the children, and later Gordon and his father, holiday at Sidmouth
	VB visits St John Ervine at Sidmouth
	VB's father gives her an annuity of £500
	WH's *Virginia Woolf* accepted for publication, 28 July
	Between visits to Sidmouth, WH visits family at Cottingham
autumn	VB and WH visit St John Ervine at Seaton, E. M. Delafield at Cullompton
October	*Virginia Woolf* published on 7 October
November	VB gives a lecture in Halifax, visits Phyllis Bentley, but cuts visit short due to illness
December	VB quarrels by post with Phyllis Bentley; they patch it up for a while
	WH feeling better; conceives novel *South Riding*

1933

January	VB shows *Testament of Youth* to Harold Latham of Macmillan, who buys it
	WH publishes novel *Mandoa, Mondoa!*
February	WH called to father's bedside in Yorkshire
	VB finishes writing *Testament of Youth*
	VB learns that Victor Gollancz has accepted *Testament of Youth*, 16 February
	VB attends party at Rebecca West's
March	WH briefly in London, sees *Cavalcade*, writes an article on it
	WH's father David Holtby dies on 9 March
	VB finishes revisions of *Testament of Youth*, delivers manuscript to publishers
April	VB takes children to Worthing for Easter, receives letter from Gordon critical of *Testament of Youth*
	WH back in London working at *Time and Tide*, has to return to Yorkshire for family
May	WH publishes *The Astonishing Island* on 1 May
summer	VB quarrels with Phyllis Bentley over *Testament of Youth*

June	WH and VB spend a week at Painswick in Gloucestershire
July	VB, WH and Gordon holiday at Hardelot in France
August	*Testament of Youth* published by Gollancz, 28 August
autumn	VB warmly received at Somerville College, Oxford
	WH feeling better; agrees to write monthly review for *Good Housekeeping*
October	*Testament of Youth* published in the USA by Macmillan
	WH and VB visit Dame Ethel Smyth
December	VB signs contract with the American agent Colston Leigh for lectures and broadcasts

1934

January	WH and VB attend Dame Ethel Smyth concert and reception, 6 January
February	WH publishes *Truth Is Not Sober*, a volume of short stories
March	VB gives talks in Hull, visits WH
March–May	WH in Withernsea, Yorkshire, sees Harry Pearson

	WH's work on *South Riding* interrupted by other demands
	WH's mother Alice Holtby elected alderman, 18 March
April	VB ill, but leaves for holiday in Italy with Gordon on 11 April
May	VB visits Beatrice Webb at Passfield Corner
	WH publishes article about attending Fascist meetings
June	VB visits WH in Yorkshire
summer–autumn	WH very active, gives talks on political causes
autumn	VB working on novel *Honourable Estate* when she goes to America to lecture
September	VB sails to America with Gordon; WH sees them off on the *Berengaria* in Southampton, 15 September
	VB arrives in New York on 21 September and stays with George Brett in Connecticut; Gordon goes to Cornell
	VB honoured at Macmillan reception, 29 September
October	WH's study *Women and a Changing Situation* published, 5 October

VB begins speaking tour at Wheeling, West Virginia, 5 October

November | VB goes to Massachusetts and Toronto, back to New York on 6 November

VB spends Armistice Day with Gordon and the Bretts

VB attracted to George Brett, her American publisher

VB resumes tour on 16 November, has passionate farewell with Brett

VB spends Thanksgiving in New York with Gordon

WH courted by James Anderson

December | VB concludes tour, returning to New York on 4 December

VB sails for England on 14 December

VB arrives in England on 21 December, brief reunion with WH, who goes to her family in Cottingham. VB's father is ill and her mother house-hunting and demanding; the children have mumps

WH writing play *Take Back Your Freedom*

WH with her family in Yorkshire for three weeks

WH catches mumps from VB's son John

1935

January	VB and WH both at Glebe Place, WH has mumps
January–March	VB misses Brett, works on *Honourable Estate*; Gordon returns
February–April	WH in Hornsea, Yorkshire, finishing *South Riding*
	WH sees Harry Pearson intermittently
March	VB lecture tour from 11 March in the north of England; sees WH in Hornsea
	Gordon leaves for two months in Russia, 23 March
	VB lovesick over Brett; Gordon decides to resign from his job at Cornell and stand for Parliament
April	WH joins VB at Tenby, Pembrokeshire
	WH, despite illness, planning to go to Africa again
May	Gordon returns from Russia
	WH and VB attend celebrations for the Silver Jubilee of George V and Queen Mary, 6 May
June	VB meets George Brett in London for business, 6 June

July	VB says farewell to Brett, with no sign he shares her feelings
	VB and Gordon go to Staffordshire for research on her novel *Honourable Estate*, visit Buxton
	WH reviews T. E. Lawrence's *Seven Pillars of Wisdom*
	WH goes to Malvern Festival with Lady Rhondda, meets George Bernard Shaw
	VB and children go to Wimereux on holiday, 31 July
August	VB's father, Arthur Brittain, commits suicide in London by drowning on the night of 1–2 August, WH goes to France to bring VB the news
	VB goes to her family in London; Gordon falls ill; WH stays with the children in France
	WH returns from France, goes to visit her mother
September	VB takes Gordon to convalesce in Brighton
	WH completes *South Riding*
	WH moves from Glebe Place into the Elizabeth Fulcher Nursing Home, 9 September
	WH dies of Bright's disease, 29 September
October	VB attends WH's memorial service at St Martin-in-the-Fields, 1 October
	WH's funeral at Rudston, 2 October

1936

March   *South Riding* published

1937

April   Publication of *Letters to a Friend*, edited by
               Alice Holtby and Jean McWilliam

November   Publication of *Pavements at Anderby*, short
               stories by WH, edited by VB and Hilda Reid

1938

January   Film of *South Riding* released in London on 4
               January

1939

July   Alice Holtby dies on 31 July

1940

January   VB publishes *Testament of Friendship: The Story
               of Winifred Holtby*

NOTE ON SOURCES AND METHODS

The holographs of the correspondence between Vera Brittain and Winifred Holtby form part of the Winifred Holtby Archive, formerly housed at Hull Central Library and now at the Hull History Centre. In preparing the present edition, we have not been able to visit the archive, but we have had access to scans of the letters, generously supplied to us by Martin Taylor, the City Archivist.

Vera Brittain assembled the correspondence soon after Winifred's death in 1935, and left occasional notes on the manuscripts. She used the letters in writing *Testament of Friendship*, which appeared in 1940. In 1960, in collaboration with Geoffrey Handley-Taylor, Vera published a limited edition of five hundred copies of *Selected Letters of Winifred Holtby and Vera Brittain*, to which we refer in the notes as *SL*.

This is the second modern edition of Vera Brittain's correspondence, following the publication of her First World War letters in 1998 as *Letters from a Lost Generation*, edited by Alan Bishop and Mark Bostridge. It would require several volumes to reproduce the full text of the Brittain-Holtby letters. As Vera's original title states, she published only part of the total correspondence. Furthermore, she edited the individual letters, often heavily. As Vera explained in her introduction to *Selected Letters*, she was reluctant to publish 'the forthright and sometimes intolerant judgments passed on persons still living and others recently dead by two eager and ambitious literary apprentices'. Consequently, she cut many striking passages, but we did not find any places where she had altered the text to change the meaning.

One of the 'persons still living' was Vera's husband, George Edward Gordon Catlin. Some of the most fascinating letters in the collection are the ones written in the early years of their marriage, in which Vera described to Winifred both her appreciation of her husband's intelligence and good character, and her many problems in adjusting to married life. On several occasions Winifred consoled Vera or counselled her on how to deal with the situation. Mr Catlin preferred the name 'George', but it was also his father's name, and so until his father's death in 1936 he went by 'Gordon', the name Vera and Winifred use consistently, and which we also use in our notes and discussion. Gordon would surely have objected to having many of the passages relating to him made public during his lifetime, but they provide a moving and illuminating view of a young woman's intimate thoughts about marriage, sex and her role as a wife, mother and professional woman.

As Vera did in *Selected Letters*, we have omitted many letters and parts of letters, in which the two friends described their day-to-day activities, their opinions on politics and fellow writers, their relations with their families, and their plans for the immediate future. In general, we have focused on the themes of Vera's and Winifred's relationship to each other, their experiences as young professional women and their growth as writers.

We have attempted to identify the less-known people, places, publications and events mentioned in the letters in the endnotes. In many places, Vera and Winifred used initials for familiar names, not only 'G.' for Gordon, but 'Y.P.' for the *Yorkshire Post* and

'L.N.U.' for the League of Nations Union; rather than oblige the reader to refer to endnotes, we have given the full names in the text at the first occurrence in each letter. We have provided a list of the people who appear most often, arranged in groups: the two writers' families, their separate circles of friends and their mutual friends. And we have provided a chronology, giving a month-by-month list of notable events in the two friends' lives.

In rare instances, no manuscript of the letter was found in the scanned copies we had. In such cases we have explained the source of our text in an endnote. The notes also call attention to occasional references to missing letters. Similarly, when there are significant breaks in the continuity, the situation is explained in the introductions and in the notes.

PART I

1920–1925

A Working Partnership

INTRODUCTION

'It has been a wonderful time . . . and we will go again. There are heaps of lovely places to see and things to do. Never doubt that I want to see and do them, and that I ask no better travelling companion than you.' On 20 September 1921 Winifred Holtby wrote enthusiastically to her friend Vera Brittain at the close of their six-week tour of Italy and France. Winifred's parents had thought a trip abroad would renew her energy and buoyancy after her final exams at Oxford, and Vera had long planned a trip to see the First World War battlefield graves of her brother Edward on the Asiago Plateau in Italy, and her fiancé Roland Leighton at Louvencourt in France. She thought there was no one with whom she 'would rather share this pilgrimage' than Winifred, and she remembered it as 'the most perfect holiday of all my experience'.

That wonderful trip was the start of what Vera called a 'shared working existence'. After Oxford, Vera and Winifred decided to live together in London and embark on their literary careers. Unlike many young women graduates after the war, they did not plan to teach. Supported by their proud mothers and prosperous fathers, they could afford to pursue their fierce ambitions to be novelists and journalists. They wanted to be independent, to make their own rules, choose their own friends and give each other the encouragement and support they would need to risk criticism, competition and rejection.

Their ideal was a partnership of equals, and these first five years of living together were the closest Vera Brittain and Winifred Holtby came to achieving it. They were equals in talent, ambition, education and determination to succeed. Both were single, although Vera expected to marry and have children someday, and their relationship was flexible enough to allow for many separations, including daughterly duties, lecture tours, illnesses and travel, and to deal with emergencies. That initial stage lasted until Vera's marriage in June 1925, and with bold experimentation, and some stresses and strains, the relationship lasted until Winifred's death in 1935.

When they were apart for long or short periods, they carried on an exuberant correspondence. In their letters, they found a flexible medium, a long conversation open to musings about love, work, sexuality, marriage, politics and the literary market. They tried out literary styles, plots for novels, feelings about friends, family and each other, and the fluctuations and challenges of their daily lives. In addition, the crises in their lives over those fifteen years shaped a narrative as moving and complex as an epistolary novel, and a plot as dramatic as a three-act play.

Their 863 surviving letters (Vera said some may have been destroyed during the war) are housed in the Winifred Holtby Archive at Hull. While some have been quoted in biographies and scholarly articles, most of the letters remain unknown and unavailable to the general public. In 1960, Vera, with Geoffrey Handley-Taylor, published a heavily edited selection in a limited edition of five hundred copies. In her introduction, Vera explained that she had first intended to leave the letters unpublished during her lifetime out of concern that they might offend living people. But as the twenty-fifth anniversary of Winifred's death approached she changed her mind, because looking back 'it seemed to me that the correspondence of two young women deeply interested in life, and in their work, does have a special value'. In their day, unmarried daughters were regarded by their parents 'as heaven-sent conveniences upon whom "duty" laid the combined functions of nurse, companion, secretary and maid-of-all-work'. They had both been pressured to be dutiful and available. Although young women of the 1960s were no longer bound by these despotic expectations, she thought the correspondence might still be relevant. Accordingly, she emphasised their work together, but omitted the affectionate salutations and endearments that mark the correspondence, and excised the most candid passages.

In this edition, we have included 234 of the letters in whole or in part, restoring the addresses and the censored material. Almost all the letters are handwritten. Winifred typed a few of her letters written on trains in South Africa in 1926, because the motion made her handwriting illegible, but Vera made clear immediately that she preferred them handwritten and more personal. Their epistolary styles are very different. Winifred was often funny and self-mocking. Vera called Winifred 'a gay, grateful, infinitely responsive letter writer, whose correspondence suggested a long vivid, unbroken conversation'. Vera's own letters were more of a monologue than a response. She wrote about her ambitions and frustrations as a writer, and used Winifred as a therapist, adviser, sounding board and second self. She was also wary – as she had long been – that people might read excessive endearments as evidence of a lesbian relationship.

Vera said that although they did not grow up together, they 'grew mature together, and that is the next best thing'. When they met, they were already young adults, shaped by their wartime experiences as well as their families. Vera had spent her teenage years in Buxton, the fashionable spa town in Derbyshire. Her younger brother Edward was her dearest companion, but she also realised from an early age that he received better treatment because he was a boy. Although less academically gifted, he was being prepared for Oxford at his public school, Uppingham, while she faced 'provincial young ladyhood' at St Monica's in Surrey. At school, however, a suffragist teacher loaned her Olive Schreiner's pioneering classic *Woman and Labour*, and Schreiner's call for women's right to work and education inspired her desire to go to Oxford too. But her parents insisted that she return to Buxton, make her debut and take up the round of social activities that would present her to eligible bachelors. Pretty and attractive to men, she nonetheless became increasingly alienated by the town's 'provincial narrow inhabitants' and began studying on her own for the Oxford entrance exams. Then, at an Easter holiday dinner at their home in 1914, she met Edward's schoolfriend Roland Leighton and was entranced both by his intellectual seriousness and by his bohemian and literary family. They corresponded, and when she went to Uppingham Speech Day, she saw him again. She looked forward to getting to know him.

War was declared on 4 August 1914. Roland, Edward and their friends wanted to enlist at once. In early October, Roland became a second lieutenant in the 4th Norfolk Regiment. In the same month Vera went up to Somerville College, Oxford to read English literature, joined the university society for women's suffrage and made a few friends, although she far preferred the company of men: 'Strange how one can feel as I do about some women and be an ardent feminist still!' she wrote in her diary. 'A feminine community is always appalling to anyone like me who gets on so much better in the society of men.' She felt that being at Oxford made no sense during a war. At the end of her first year at Oxford, in the summer of 1915, she signed up to be a nurse in the Voluntary Aid Detachment and left to do her hospital training in Buxton and then London.

On 15 March 1915, she had said farewell to Roland before he

left for the Front. Their correspondence started out as lofty and romantic, but gradually he became angry and disillusioned. On his leave in August 1915, Roland and Vera became engaged 'for three years or the duration of the war'. By Christmas Roland was planning to come home on leave, and Vera went to stay with his family to await his arrival. On the morning of 26 December the telephone rang and she ran eagerly to answer it, only to hear a message that Roland had died two days before, in France. He was only twenty years old; she was just twenty-two.

They did not have time to know each other well; when he died, they had met only seven times, for a total of seventeen days. But Roland was the lost romantic hero whose idealised memory occupied Vera's emotions for years. For the rest of the war she worked as a nurse, in 1916–17 in Malta; 1917–18 on the Western Front, seeing the carnage close up and tending even to badly wounded German soldiers. Edward and his friends were still fighting in Europe, and she had hopes that they would survive. But one by one they were wounded or killed; Edward lived until five months before the Armistice, killed in action on the Asiago Plateau in northern Italy on 15 June 1918.

When the war ended on 11 November 1918, Vera felt emotionally dead. She had no one left to love, and 'only ambition held me to life'. For about six months, through the influenza epidemic, she worked at hospitals in London. In April 1919, she went back to Somerville College to read History instead of English Literature, in an attempt to understand the causes of the war. Her tragic war experience influenced her later pacifism. She was also a passionate feminist. By the time Vera returned to Oxford her central values had been established. Although she still supported a Liberal candidate in 1923, the next year she joined the Labour Party, believing it to be more effective in working for feminism and peace, the causes she cared most about.

Winifred Holtby was almost four and a half years younger than

Vera. She had grown up in the village of Rudston, in the East Riding of Yorkshire, the younger daughter of a well-to-do farmer. Both her father and her vigorous, active mother, who would become the first woman alderman in Yorkshire, encouraged her to explore and play as freely as a boy. Because she had no brothers, Winifred was not made constantly aware of male privilege, and did not think of herself as a feminist. Educated at home by governesses and at the village school, she did not have access to many books, but she started writing her own plays and poems. In 1911, her mother surprised her by printing twenty-five of her childhood poems as a pretty gift book. By then Winifred had been sent to boarding school in Scarborough, where she was a poor student, always untidy and a terrible speller, but irrepressible in her confidence and humour. One of her school reports admonishes that 'she must be careful not to allow herself to become too critical or give her opinion too freely'.

In contrast to Vera, Winifred's mother was keen for her to go to Oxford. Indeed, as Winifred later told Vera, she was one of the rare women who actually went to Oxford to please her mother. She passed the entrance examination for Somerville College, but first she went to work as a probationer in a London nursing home. Then, after a brief time at Somerville in 1917, she left to join the Women's Army Auxiliary Corps. Most of her service was near Abbeville in France, on 'the fringes of the war'. Winifred enjoyed her experience and became close to the head administrator, Jean McWilliam, and she suffered no tragic personal losses. After the war, although her father had retired and moved the family to a large handsome house in Cottingham, a village outside Hull, she prepared to pick up her life in Oxford where it had left off.

In October 1919, when Winifred returned to Somerville, she was excited and enthusiastic. She did not expect to be a great scholar, but she was ambitious to become a journalist and a poet. Unlike Vera, she had no serious political ideas, and joined all three of the major Oxford political clubs – Labour, Liberal and Conservative – explaining 'How can I know which I like best until I've tried them all?' She sang in the choir, wrote or acted in almost every play, and was president of two debating societies.

The grieving Vera Brittain who returned to Oxford at twenty-five was much older than the other undergraduates, and she felt that she was the ageing remnant of a lost generation, 'a piece of wartime wreckage'. She consoled herself by thinking of her moral superiority to the frivolous younger students. But the first months were lonely and difficult. By the autumn she was deeply depressed, hallucinating that she was growing a witchlike beard. Whether a symptom of survivor's guilt or post-traumatic stress, the beard was perhaps the projection of conflicts she could not confront or discuss.

When the popular extrovert Winifred and humourless introvert Vera first met, sharing a tutorial in modern European history with C. R. M. F. Cruttwell at Hertford College, they did not get on at all. They were very different physically and in their feelings about their looks. Vera was dark-haired, five feet three inches tall, delicate and confident in her attractiveness to men. Winifred was blonde, five feet nine inches tall and always felt clumsy and lumbering. She made fun of herself, imagining her mother's friends pitying her for being so 'gawky and weird'. She hated dressing up for the wedding of her pretty sister Grace, and looking like 'a stuffed Amazon'. When she tried to find fashionable shoes to wear to Vera's wedding, the shop assistant said 'Not in *that* size, madam.' She weighed eleven stone and her shoe size was a non-gigantic 8, but she defensively exaggerated her size and awkwardness. In plays she always took male roles.

Vera later celebrated the moment when Winifred burst into Cruttwell's study, 'superbly tall, and vigorous as the young Diana with her long straight limbs and her golden hair'. In that telling, Winifred seemed to embody the youthful energy Vera felt she had lost for ever in the war. Yet, she added, Winifred's 'vitality smote with the effect of a blow upon my jaded nerves'. She was relieved to find that Winifred hadn't done all the reading for the seminar, and that Cruttwell criticised her writing. For several weeks, she admitted, 'the contrast between Winifred's gay, stimulating popularity and my own isolated depression provoked me to barely concealed hostility'.

When the Somerville debating society chose to take up the motion 'that four years' travel is a better education than four years at the University', Vera saw it as a great opportunity to display the wisdom of her wartime experience. But Winifred crushed her in a witty speech, ending with a quotation from one of her favourite plays, As You Like It: 'I had rather have a fool to make me merry, than experience to make me sad; and to travel for it, too!' The audience vociferously sided with Winifred.

Embarrassed and upset, Vera kept her self-control until she got back to her room, where she broke down in tears, certain that the confrontation had been an intentional humiliation. Only later did she learn that Winifred too had served in the war. To her surprise, Winifred sent her a warm letter of apology and visited her in her room when she was ill, bringing a bunch of grapes. From then on, they became inseparable, taking long walks, sharing a room and exchanging their stories and poems. From these 'ironically inauspicious beginnings', Vera wrote in 1933, came a friendship that 'in thirteen years has never been broken and never spoiled, and today remains as intimate as ever'. Yet they had met as rivals, and Winifred had won.

Their correspondence began during the summer vacation of 1920, when they visited each other's families and then returned home to study for exams, Winifred to Bainesse (an Indian word for welcome) in Cottingham, and Vera to her parents' flat in Oakwood Court in London. Winifred sent Vera a story she had just written; Vera responded months later, during the Christmas vacation, passing on belated praise of the story by Roland's father, Robert Leighton, and mentioning Harry Pearson, Winifred's childhood friend, neighbour and sometime boyfriend. Harry continued to pop up in Winifred's life at random moments, a handsome, erratic figure with whom she had an on-again, off-again relationship, but whom Vera saw as her destined romantic partner.

After their European trip, Vera and Winifred took their final exams at Oxford and started to write their first novels. That autumn, each took small jobs to make money. They were tired of being the available unmarried daughter for their parents, and on 30 December gathered up their clothes, their books and their manuscripts, and moved into a flat at 52 Doughty Street in Bloomsbury. There, close to the British Library and its Reading Room, they launched what Vera called their 'strenuous, independent, enthralling London existence'. They were not financially independent; indeed, their parents gave them allowances of two hundred pounds a year; and for two pounds twelve shillings a week they were able to hire a housekeeper who brought them breakfast on a tray. Neither of them knew how to cook or would ever learn. But they knew that they were privileged to live their dream.

Over the next few years as they launched their careers, they had to face the reality of competition with other women. Deborah Gorham, one of Vera's biographers, sees the acceptance of professional rivalry between women after the war as a sign of modernity. No longer feeling that sisterly bonds were incompatible with competition, 'educated women of the post-war period . . . welcomed the fact that they would compete for success' in the literary market. Vera and Winifred understood those dynamics very well, and even relished outdoing some of their rivals. But they found it much harder to confront, even acknowledge, the subtexts of competition and envy between themselves. The unspoken tensions of living with a beloved rival came up strongly in 1922, around the publication of their first novels.

Vera was trying to sell her Oxford-themed novel, *The Dark Tide* (originally called 'Daphne'), but more than a dozen publishers turned it down. Then, on 19 August 1922, John Lane accepted Winifred's Yorkshire-themed novel *Anderby Wold*. She was eager to use her new publishing contacts to help Vera, but they didn't seem to work. As she wrote to Jean McWilliam, 'The really awful thing has happened. I took [*The Dark Tide*] to John Lane and made them interested in it and her, but they won't publish it. They returned it yesterday. I've got the MS. She doesn't know yet. It's a horrid thing, for her book's miles away better than mine, only Yorkshire stories just happen to be in fashion and college ones aren't.'

Vera was shocked and shaken by Winifred's early success, and painfully revised her assumption that she would be the first to be published. She was older; she had survived tragedy; and she thought she was a better writer. Suddenly she had to acknowledge that Winifred had outdone her. When she wrote to Winifred that 'we are not equals any more', Winifred declared that indeed Vera would always be the superior artist. That became the credo, or perhaps the self-fulfilling prophecy, of their relationship. Whatever the judgement of the world, between them Vera was the star, and Winifred, as her biographer Marion Shaw put it, 'was the satellite'.

Anderby Wold had few reviews and sold modestly, but it introduced Winifred as a promising new figure on the literary scene. At last Vera's novel was accepted by Grant Richards, thanks to a subsidy of fifty pounds paid, or at least advanced, by Winifred, and it was published on 16 July 1923. *The Dark Tide* turned out to be a controversial and even scandalous book which received seventy-three reviews. Some were outraged at the author's harsh treatment of Oxford personalities, but others, including the *Times Literary Supplement*, were impressed and admiring. The most savagely treated character, clearly a caricature of Winifred, was

Daphne Lethbridge, the clumsy, loud and garishly dressed rival of the tasteful, beautiful, erudite Virginia Dennison, clearly Vera.

And yet Winifred accepted or forgave the mockery. On 25 July she started signing her letters to Vera 'v.s.v.d.l.', which stood for 'very small, very dear love'. This pet name made Vera's size an endearment. Soon Vera started using the acronym as her nick-name, and sometimes as her own signature.

But even little Vera needed room to work. In September 1922 they moved to 58 Doughty Street, then in November 1923 to a more spacious flat in Maida Vale, with both a housekeeper and Winifred's old nurse to help them out. Their social life expanded too. They became more sophisticated, particularly about forms of sexuality. 'Amongst our friends,' Vera noted, 'we discussed sodomy and lesbianism with as little hesitation as we compared the merits of different contraceptives, and were theoretically familiar with varieties of homosexuality and venereal disease of which the very existence was unknown to our grandparents.'

They were both wary about marriage, for different reasons. Winifred had realised that marriage 'was not for me, nor ever, for me, those romantic hopes ... of postponed fulfillment'. But she was determined to make a fulfilling life on her own. Vera, however, felt sure that she did want to marry eventually. Ten years later, she would explain that she wanted to have children, and she believed that the feminist movement needed some lead-ers who were also wives and mothers in order to appeal to a wide segment of women.

Then, in August 1923, Vera received a letter from a twenty-seven-year-old university professor who admired *The Dark Tide* and wanted to meet her. Gordon Catlin was a political scientist, educated at Oxford and now teaching at Cornell University in Ithaca, New York. He had seen Vera at Oxford. He wrote her intense, intellectual fan letters, which caught her interest, and they began a regular correspondence. When her second novel,

Not Without Honour, came out in early 1924, she sent Gordon a
presentation copy. He responded with a lengthy critique, taking
the book very seriously but also mocking her 'intellectual pretensions'. He had hit on the perfect combination of admiration
and argument.

And his timing was lucky. Vera turned thirty on 29 December
1923, and was not immune to anxieties about spinsterhood.
When he told her of his plans to come to London, she agreed
to meet him. On Friday 13 June, he took her to a production of
Shaw's *Saint Joan*. They spent the following day walking in Kew
Gardens. Then, on Sunday, he proposed. Vera was so shocked
by the three-day courtship that she had an attack of colitis. She
wrote to him that marriage would have to be subordinate to her
primary commitment to an independent life of feminism, the
League of Nations and literary work. She warned him that Roland
Leighton's death had frozen her nascent sexuality and she had not
been physically attracted to any man since his death. But Gordon
persisted, and on 5 July she accepted his proposal. On that day,
Winifred wrote 'Ave atque Vale' in her own copy of *Saint Joan*.

They were both virgins. Gordon wrote that he wanted to have
sex before the wedding but Vera refused, and they avoided facing
the issue by postponing the wedding for a year. Gordon went
back to Cornell while Vera and Winifred carried on as usual.
The engagement was devastating for Winifred, but she concealed
her pain. 'In June, Vera will go,' she wrote to Jean McWilliam;
'. . . how shall I live? One thing I am determined on, that I will
not fall into the common error of circumstantial victimization.'

On 27 June 1925, Gordon and Vera were married in a Roman
Catholic ceremony at St James's Church in Spanish Place. Vera
wore an ivory satin gown with a long veil. Winifred was the only
bridesmaid, wearing their favourite colours: a blue dress and a
mauve shawl, and carrying a large bouquet of blue and mauve
delphiniums. After the ceremony she went back to the empty flat

alone. 'I like, respect [Gordon],' she wrote to Jean McWilliam, '... and I'm very happy, though it means losing Vera's companionship.' And to Gordon she wrote: 'When you return to England you will find I have effected quite a neat and painless divorce.'

Vera's marriage meant drastic changes in the friendship. Winifred had thought she could gallantly hand her over to Gordon. She expected to be the dependable mutual friend. Gordon, however, wanted to establish a triangular relationship with Winifred as quasi-parents to Vera, a precious and fragile child. On his wedding night, before the couple left for a hectic four-week honeymoon to five European countries, Gordon wrote to Winifred from Dover, promising her that he would take great care of Vera and declaring that 'the child ... looks amazingly well ... Having a husband at present seems to agree with her.' In reality, although Vera was more than four years older than Winifred, and three years older than Gordon, she enjoyed being cherished as a child. Roland had used the term as well, and Winifred herself had addressed Vera in some letters as 'child'. So to some degree, the language of parenting worked.

But the power balance of the friendship was altered, with Winifred initially the odd woman out. Gordon assumed a natural husbandly authority over Vera's desires and needs, and expected primary rights to her time. Vera felt that she had senior status as a married woman, sexually experienced and worldly wise. When Winifred welcomed the honeymooners home to London at the end of July, she was uncharacteristically cross and depressed, and left after two days, claiming she had to nurse Yorkshire relatives with mumps. Vera was concerned by the muted reception, but she did not wonder if her marriage might have anything to do with Winifred's mood. By the end of the summer, she was calculating the right time to have a baby.

At the end of September, Vera and Gordon left for Cornell and a large apartment on the edge of the campus. At first Vera was very busy, spending hours each afternoon in the library. The apartment had no stove, so she did not have to cook, and they got plenty of exercise walking up and down the hills for breakfast, lunch and dinner in town. But she soon became annoyed by the social customs of an American academic community. The wives of Gordon's colleagues called on her intrusively and incessantly, and were shocked that she had kept her maiden name. From Vera's point of view, they were dreary provincial housewives who did not recognise her intellectual status; no one in Ithaca knew she was a writer or had read her work. Socially awkward and on the defensive, she did not make a single woman friend at Cornell.

Meanwhile, Winifred was having a very good time in London. She enjoyed going to the theatre, making new friends and even spending a weekend at the country house of Margaret, Lady Rhondda, the wealthy founder and editor of *Time and Tide*, the major feminist journal of the post-war period. That autumn Winifred was going to meetings, building her own professional and social network, and teaching in order to make money for a lecture tour of South Africa. In a reversal of their expectations, she was the one giving Vera advice about succeeding in the literary world.

LETTERS

1920

WINIFRED TO VERA

Summer Vacation 1920

Dear Vera,

Here's the story. It's a loathsome thing; but I *had* to write it. It came into my head when I was in London, sitting in the lounge of the Regent's Palace Hotel, and has been worrying me ever since. I had to write it – but I think it should be burned only as you wanted me to slang an amateur I've let you see it. Why does one write beastly things? I want to write happy, jolly songs, and I write 'The Dead Man'. I want to write clean spacious stories like 'Anlaby Wold' and I've just finished 'The Amateur' – and it's bad as well as unpleasant. Only real cleverness could save it – and I doubt that.

Don't overwork. I've done two hours today but have been

packing and rewriting the story and washing up. I'm just going to do some economic history and it's twenty to twelve – so goodnight.

love from Winifred

VERA TO WINIFRED

10 Oakwood Court, London W14 | 15 December 1920

My dear Winifred,

Mr Leighton has just been here and as he said a good deal more about your writing (not having seen me since I left your story with him at the end of last vac.). I thought you would like to hear it before I forget it. As it happened, I did not introduce the subject at all but Mother showed him the copy of *The Outlook* with my 'All Souls' Day' in it – which incidentally he was immensely pleased with – said it was original and could hardly have been improved upon, except that it did not make it clear until half way through whether the person telling the story was a man or woman. He said if he'd known about it he would have made me send it to *Chambers' Journal.* Then he read your two poems – without my pointing them out at all – and said, 'These poems are very good – especially the first. Aren't they by the friend whose story you showed me?' Then he went on, 'She's capable – she writes well, with pleasantly unexpected little turns of phrase. And her psychology is unusually good – she seems to have a great feeling for what is in people's minds. It was good even in that story you showed me, but I shouldn't think that was a typical example of her work. Do you know if she intends to take up a literary career?' I said I thought so and I believed you were going to write a novel sometime soon about the Yorkshire wolds. He said,

'Good – that's splendid.' So I asked, 'Can you tell me what she particularly lacks?' He said, 'It's much easier at present to say what she has than what she lacks. Speaking generally I should say the chief thing she lacks is a knowledge of life. And of course every day will remedy that. Her work's interesting. I should like to see more of it.'

Much love, Vera

WINIFRED TO VERA

Bainesse, Cottingham, East Yorkshire
[Christmas Vacation, 1920–1]

My dear,

Your letter was so sympathetic and beautiful and encouraging, that it would be far the most artistic thing to leave the whole matter there and never allude to it again except perhaps in poems! But then I should feel such a hypocrite and it would be so unfair to Harry if we ever met him – as it's very probable we may when he comes back to England – that I feel compelled to do the inartistic thing and reply – and even explain a little more at the risk of showing you even further what a really hopeless sort of person I am to have any romantic fancies about. (I like people having romantic fancies about me, too.)

If there's been any disillusion in the past affair, it was on Harry's side, not mine. He never gave me any sign that he cared for me beyond other people, except the poems and one conversation with Mother about four years ago. These I deliberately laughed at – told him to his face he was soppy – and quite firmly and definitely quashed any romance that might hang round me. Even then I knew, you see, in my heart of

hearts, that what he loved was a dream woman whom he called
by my name because he knew no one else. And I would not
accept his identification of me with his dreams until we had
both proved ourselves; for, if he was uncertain of his love for
me, I was still more uncertain of mine for him. And we have
proved ourselves.

I've seen a photograph of Irene, the girl in Guiana, and she
is far more like the girl he dreamed of than I could ever be –
not only because she is small and slim and dark and wistful,
but because, from what I have heard of her, she is brave, and
gay, and filled with a passion for all beautiful things, an artist
to her finger tips (she is a pianist) and has travelled into the
strange places of the world. I do not know much about them
both, except from his mother, but as far as I can judge, she loves
him as I should never have done – as a wife should – not as a
rather patronising and superior friend, who, while she reserves
the right to criticize, still harbours a secret desire for all the
romantic trimmings of life.

He was right – he had a perfect right to love whom he liked.
I set myself at work to leave him perfectly free from the first
moment I knew he loved me. The most incriminating thing
I ever did was to send him that poem, and by the time that
came he had been rendered invulnerable by a real love, not a
broken dream.

And (I'm not saying this because I'm proud, but because
I daren't accept a sympathy which I don't deserve) I am not
hurt. The only thing I am disillusioned about is my power of
holding others – not about him a bit, for the girl fits in with my
conception of him far more than I ever should. She is penniless
and needs looking after. I am independent, and should have
looked after him. I'm glad he has struck out for himself, glad he
has made his own choice, not one which his family and friends
were always encouraging him to make. They thought I was

so suitable! Glad most of all that I did not spoil his life – as I should have done. We were too much alike in lots of ways, and both too independent.

And I realise now what I suspected before, that I had no more love for him than for a friend – and that I still have, only stronger because it is clear of all illusions – about myself, not him. I only wanted romance. I felt a bit 'Dead Manish' so played with the most romantic thing that ever happened to me, until I almost believed it was real – almost, not quite.

All the same, I meant my poem, and I'm glad you like it.

What a screed and what an egotistical one. You don't know what a temptation it was, though, to let your letter pass and pretend that I deserved it, I was the brave, strong-souled person it makes me out to be. I'm not, dear; it isn't brave not to cry about something that doesn't hurt. I shed far more bitter tears over a Richard paper that I wanted desperately to do and which came out as heavy as dough that wouldn't rise i' the baking.

My new black dress has come, and I wear it this evening to go dazzle the aunts in Driffield. Grace and I are on show tonight. It will be 'dear Grace!', 'dear Winifred' – and when we've gone – 'My dear – that younger girl of Alice's grows more gawky and weird every day. I don't know why Alice lets her go to this Oxford; she never did do her duty by her children!'

I'm not nearly through with my one volume of Charters, let alone the rest – I am trying to make up my mind to eschew festivities. I've given up one dance in Hull already. There are *three* more in the offing and the opera in Hull – the *best* Carlo Rosa straight from London and *Samson and Delilah* on Monday. Was ever woman in this workaday world so set about with temptations?

Yours, tempted but determined, Winifred

1921

WINIFRED TO VERA

Bainesse, Cottingham, East Yorkshire |
Easter Vacation 1921 [c. 27 March 1921]

My dear –

There never was a game so well worth playing as the one
where the fates play against you with loaded dice. It looks as
though they'd put on no end of weight this time, but you've
got the brains and you've got the pluck, and you *shall* win
out. Never mind about the old books. I'm nothing like ready
yet. Keep them as long as you like to snatch at in between
gargles. You once said – or you said several times – that you
would rather be a woman than a man, because the man has no
disadvantages to fight. It was a gallant wish – and it rather looks
as though life had taken up the challenge. But you'll do it. With
every disadvantage from the beginning, lack of preparation,
weariness of effort, disturbance during term and the vacation,
your own health – or the lack of it – and now this. It's a kind
of obstacle race, with each obstacle growing more fearsome; but
you'll win, all the same. Thank goodness it isn't solid knowledge
they need, so much as ability to use it.

I do hope that by this time either your mother is better, or
has got a nurse, even if not. I think you can do it. If you come
back very tired, we'll go straight on to Boar's Hill. We could
take a few books there, and do questions. And do remember
that most people haven't started proper revision yet.

Don't get flu – but if you do, get better quickly. Even that
won't be the coup de grace, if you don't let it. There's something

in you – burning fiery furnace or whatever you please to call
it – stronger than any circumstances that ever arose yet. I'm not
going to say 'poor Vera. I'm so sorry.' I'm not sorry. I'll only be
sorry when it's all over, if you have not pulled through to the
top. I'd say 'Good hunting, old Sportsman . . .' and mean it with
every ounce of me.

   Good luck to you, Winifred

VERA TO WINIFRED

10 Oakwood Court, London W14 | 27 June 1921

I do love your letters. They're just like broken-off conversations.
   I enclose a copy of my scheme for International Relations
lectures, partly because I want your criticism of it, partly
because I think it may help as a basis for your reading on
the subject, and the order of it. I showed it to Mr Leighton
yesterday. He seemed very impressed with it – both as to
arrangement and subjects, also as to the amount I knew. He
said, 'But this is *General* History – and absolutely on the right
lines. It takes a wide and comprehensive view and yet has a
thread of consistency to hang everything on.' (The Leightons,
as I think I told you, have always been inclined to think I spent
two years learning lists of English battles and their dates, tho'
Mr has been better than Mrs in this respect.)
   He's terribly afraid that I am going to forsake fiction for
Academe. Why is it that all my university mentors want me
to do research work at the expense of fiction, and my literary
mentors fiction at the expense of History? I wish I hadn't both
tendencies; it makes things so complicated. Mr Leighton,
though, is more sensible than most; he thinks they can be
done concurrently and that's what we both want, isn't it? But

he says I mustn't forget that Fiction is always greater than scholarship because it is entirely creative, whereas scholarship is synthetic and depends largely on the work of other people. On the other hand one has people like Maude urging one on to the ideal of historical truth and the world's need of more and more enlightenment. How is one to reconcile the two ideals? Are they compatible or not? Can both of them be true at once, and each at different times matter more than the other?

'*Potterism*'s a great book! What Potterists we all are!' I am much more of one than you – with my thralldom to anniversaries, and last times, and goodbyes, and love of posing and situations! But even you – though so much freer from cant – can't quite escape from the tyranny of tradition and superstition. (Don't let that remark turn you on to one of your old inward endless dark journeys in the thorny search for truth!) Do you know, I think Harry is rather like a mixture of Arthur Gideon, and Peter in *The Lee Shore*. What a contempt Rose Macaulay has for mere success as such.

I always wonder whom you are most hard on – Harry or yourself! You haven't really much mercy on either. I always feel certain that you and he will come together in the end. You may not marry, but you'll come together mentally. But not yet. At present you both suffer too much; you wouldn't help each other. I can guess how he suffers – and I know how you do – in spite of the strain of philosophy and mysticism which Hilda says is so strong in you which makes you take things as they come and put them aside, and which I sometimes think I am too modern and too ambitious to appreciate as I should.

Au revoir, my dear, and much love, Vera

WINIFRED TO VERA

Bainesse, Cottingham, East Yorkshire | *[30 June 1921]*

My Dear –

You asked whether Maude or Mrs Leighton are right – or
both. In my humble opinion both are right and wrong. The
use of literature, whether academic or artistic, seems to be in
a new interpretation of life. It's the old saw. There are no new
things, only old ones seen differently. History and fiction both
offer new interpretations of life, only viewed from a different
stand point. I believe the best history to be as creative as
the best fiction. If historical writing is 'largely synthetic and
borrows from the work of other people', bless you my dear, so is
fiction! – merely a synthesis of the things people see and hear,
with constant plagiarisms from the conversation and characters
of their friends and enemies. In the best history or fiction, the
value is the same – the value of the ideas they enshrine and
the perfection of their expression. In the mediocre stuff, you
can take your choice between the creation of worthless ideas,
or the reproduction of the results of other men's historical
research. Personally I prefer the latter. It is possibly grounded on
a certain amount of solid scholarship and may contribute to the
enlightenment of people who have not had sufficient education
to be worried by its mediocrity or bored by its poverty of
thought. That is why I always said – though you scorned me for
the saying – that if I found I was going to be no good at writing
fiction, I should turn to purely academic or administrative work.
Either of these are useful, even if only mediocre. Mediocre
fiction is worse than useless. It may be positively harmful.

I am glad George Eliot liked straw hats with blue flowers
and strings. It makes one feel that she had a real feeling for Mrs
Tulliver, who wore fan shaped caps, which, forty years ago at

St Ogg's, were considered 'sweet things' – also for Aunt Glegg, whose perturbation when forced to choose between spots or sprigs, was only equalled by her usual imperturbability. Mr Leighton must be a fascinating raconteur. Oh, and talking of raconteurs, I must interrupt this rather high brow letter to tell you two good stories I picked up at a tennis party the other day, which might amuse Miss Heath-Jones.

A Scotch boy decided he wished to marry. He went to his father.

'Dad, I wanna marry Janet Campbell.'

'Nay lad, dinna do that. She's your sister.'

He abandoned the courtship of Janet, and turned to Jeannie Macgreggor.

'Nay lad,' said his father. 'Ye canna wed Jeannie. She's your sister.'

A little later he asked leave to marry Maggie, and Katy, and Helen, and was met by the same objection. In despair he went to his mother.

'Mither,' he said. 'What shall I do? I want to get wed, and father says ilka lass in this village is my sister.'

'Nay lad,' said his mother. 'Dinna fash yourself. He's no thy father.'

Yesterday, when Mother was in Whitby, Grace in Hull, six men from the *Carysfort* descended to play tennis – only Captain Carpenter, V.C., one of the nicest men I ever met, came to the rescue, took the young men in hand, sat me down on a seat and talked to me till all the shyness went away. He looks fifty-five, and is forty – blue eyed, white haired with charming manners, and an amazing gift for setting people at ease. He has a daughter of sixteen. He thought I was nineteen – so you see how shy I must have been! He has just come back from escorting the King and Queen to Belfast. He was present at the opening of Parliament there, and says, that of all the incidents in his career – and that

includes such trifles as Zeebrugge, and escorting Queen Victoria
on her Jubilee procession, and delivering 98 lectures in 95 days
on a triumphal tour through Canada after he got the V.C. – the
Belfast Parliament was the most impressive. And he's asked me
to go over the *Carysfort* – and he's coming again on Saturday.
I almost think I was a success! But I forgot all about the young
men! I can always get on so much better with the old ones.

My dear, I must go. It's tennis at the Rectory this afternoon.

Love, Winifred

VERA TO WINIFRED

The Manor House, Crantock, Cornwall | *5 July 1921*

I showed your syllabus to Miss Heath-Jones last night. She was
much impressed with it and says your problems are excellently
put, and ought to make a good set of lectures or classes.

Miss Heath-Jones says there are heaps of good History posts
going but she thinks we are very wise to refuse the 'safe' jobs
(which tempt at any rate me with the prospect of a quiet life –
but do I really want a quiet life!) until we have first tried the
literary work we prefer. People with our qualifications, she says,
can always procure the 'safe' jobs if they want them. Like Mr
Leighton, she emphasizes the necessity of being in London
(or abroad) for a literary career. The provinces, she says, are
hopeless until one is known, because a literary career depends
so much on meeting literary people socially. I think we hardly
need to be told that.

Miss Heath-Jones thinks rooms near the British Museum
an excellent idea. I think I shall give 3 days a week to money-
making of some kind, and the other 4 (including Sunday) to
literary work. That seems about the right proportion, I think.

She is very anxious to see you and wants me to bring you over to St Monica's one day during the autumn term. I think it would be quite worth your while for as you know you are always extremely attractive to women. If you would spend a day or two with me when we return from Italy or when you come up for the degree, we might manage it quite well. I told Miss Heath-Jones you are tall and fair and rather beautiful, with a charming speaking voice, and a brilliant mind – much better than mine, though as yet not quite as mature, but capable of achievements which you yourself as yet scarcely realise, but which other people do. I told her that your gifts were only exceeded by your humility and that you wouldn't believe anything you did was any good. She said that it was very rare to find humility combined with such qualities as yours, and she very much wants to meet you.

So much for business! I am being very lazy and getting extremely sunburnt. Schools results still hang over me like a cloud, but I feel too torpid in this place to worry as much as I did. It's as hot as it can be and more like Malta than ever; the sea and sky are almost tropical. Miss Heath-Jones has lots of Bernard Shaw here; I have just been reading *The Doctor's Dilemma* to her. It's about the best of his I've struck so far and full of delightful epigrams, such as 'Morality consists in suspecting other people of not being legally married.'

Au revoir, my dear, always your loving Vera

WINIFRED TO VERA

Bainesse, Cottingham, East Yorkshire |
Between Viva and Schools July 1921

My Dear – If it consoles you at all – though if you're made like me, it probably won't, I'll confess that the parties and tennis and

young men are all very well, and sometimes I enjoy them a lot
at the time, and always I make a good deal of fuss about them
and pretend I enjoy them tremendously; but more than often I
am a little resentful about them, because I have so much to do,
from which they keep me; because there is a table here, covered
with books waiting to be read, and Italian to be learnt and
'Anlaby Wold' waiting to be written and heaven knows what
else waiting to be done. I'm busy with my old game of snatching
minutes, and hours, and half mornings, to do the things I want
to do, while the parties that sound so gay, and are often rather
boring, though I pretend even to myself they are glorious, crowd
upon me like the surge of a tide from which there is no escape.
Happiness is a strange, elusive creature. I'm not sure quite what
it is, though I know well enough what it is not; but I certainly
think that, such as it is, it is to be found more fully even among
'death and blood and sickness' than among Cottingham tennis
parties – just as you found it more in France than in Buxton.
Anyway, don't run away with the idea that I shan't want to
come to London. You always rather tend to believe what I say,
you know; which is rather bad luck for you, and certainly more
my fault than yours. Of course I am having a good time now;
and I am intensely grateful for it in so far as it has thoroughly
banished all thoughts of schools and all except in dreams,
where they return in most ridiculous forms – but such a time
does not unfortunately bring with it satisfaction for 'hungry and
impatient ambitions', now, any more than it did in the term
of Mr Cruttwell's coachings, when I used to boast to you and
everyone about my parties, and then go and howl in my room
because I was not the talented young woman I had hoped to be!

I am looking forward *most awfully* (There's slang for you,
which you'll hate!) to the London business visits and agents,
even in a sort of queer way to the vivas.

Au revoir, my little Bat. I'll try and give you lots of tennis parties when you're here, and you shall wear the little white frocks and look ten at most.

Yrs, Winifred

VERA TO WINIFRED

10 Oakwood Court, London W14 | *16 August 1921*

My dear,

I have just been to tea with the Leightons and they have said such nice things about you that I am writing to tell you before some of them go out of my head. When I announced I had only a Second, Mrs Leighton said 'So much the better – and I should be better pleased still if you hadn't got a degree at all!' However, later on when I told her how much better you had done than I and described the examiners' squabble over you, she said 'I am not surprised they were impressed with her; she's a girl who will always make people interested in her. She gave me a tremendous impression of mental power.' Mother said something about your being good-looking and Mrs Leighton said firmly, 'No, she's not in the least pretty but she's got something much better than mere prettiness. She has the kind of face that people will always want to look at twice.' Then she said 'She gave me the impression of a person very much given over to intellectual things. I don't mean in an academic way, but someone who realises the value of a mind and is sensible enough not to waste her time on unnecessary things, like fretting unduly about her personal appearance. She'll spend enough time on it, but never too much, because she'll realise that Nature has endowed her with sufficient personal attractiveness to carry her a long way without unnecessary additions.' She went on 'I liked her so much – I liked her especially for the laughter in her. And what's more she knows when to laugh; she'll never laugh at the wrong things.'

She was very surprised to hear you had been so delicate; she said you impressed her as being so full of energy and strength and vitality – a regular young Viking.

I meant to do Italian this morning; instead I drifted into 'Daphne' and wrote the 2nd half of Virginia's last speech. Tell me first if you like it, and secondly if you think it's true.

Much love, Vera

Bainesse, Cottingham, East Yorkshire | *18 August 1921*

I like the speech of Virginia; it is true. I read it through two or three times, and finally took it downstairs to Mother, told her vaguely enough of the plot to make the speech intelligible, and then read it to her. I cannot tell you how much she liked it. We talked a lot about you, and about your work when I had finished reading. Mother thinks you are going to write great things – whether you yourself become famous or not. Any suffering that you have borne, from the really big things down to a second in schools (though that in its way was big) is only the penalty to be paid for your gift. – And you don't pay just in the way of compensation. You pay because you can't write until you've paid.

She said she thinks you will be great – greater ever than I shall be, unless undreamed of things happen – because you have paid already a high price, and, in the end, in life as well as in business, we get our money's worth. It may not lie in a transitory or even a lasting fame; but it will lie in a power that only suffering can give – a courage and understanding and inspiration, that is a greater gift to the world than anything, even greater than joy.

'Daphne' is going to be a fine book – but that's not the end of it. You will be a finer person for having written it – but that's not the end, either. The world may possibly be a better place because you wrote it – and, if there is, as I believe, immortality of all things that are good and beautiful then even that is not the end.

My dear – go on and prosper. You have earned your right to be great. If there is yet a higher price to be paid, you will pay it; and if the achievement is worthy of the promise of 'Daphne', then no price will have been too high. You will say, I know, that the price can be too high, that a time comes when suffering defeats its own end, and becomes a corrupting, not a stimulating force. Your own work shows that for you the time has not come yet, and there is every reason why it should never come.

You are to have a good time now, if human effort can make it possible. Anyway, we'll enjoy ourselves in Italy – to descend to more immediate and mundane things.

I must wrap this up and go to bed. I've been out all day, lunching at Dowthorpe and having tea with Mrs Jameson. She was very nice, keen that I should begin my novel, and terrified of the attractions of an academic life; but when I told her I was going to share digs with a girl who was far more literary than I, and described you a little, she became reconciled. She said I hardly knew my luck, having someone with whom I could work who shared my tastes and ambitions. But I think I do know my luck a little.

Goodnight. Take care of yourself. Don't blow away before August 31st. There's such a little of you, I sometimes fear that in a high wind, an extra gust will waft you right beyond our reach.

With love, Winifred

VERA TO WINIFRED

10 Oakwood Court, London W14 | 19 August 1921

My Dear,

I wish I believed that what you say about my literary power is true. I do think at present that you're much more of a scholar than I, which may mean that I am more literary, but I believe this to be only a phase with you, due to (what we're always forgetting) your extreme youth! The scholar phase is often only a young one and many literary people have it to begin with – George Eliot, for instance, had it for 20 years. But you wouldn't always want to write so much, and often succeed in writing so well, if you weren't born a writer. You've got the writer's temperament absolutely – all the catholicity and the sympathy and the intense vitality and interest in things – and the writer's mind is only a question of time and experience.

Much love, Vera

WINIFRED TO VERA

Bainesse, Cottingham, East Yorkshire | 20 October 1921

My dear little heart,

It has been a wonderful time, dearest. But you know, the best thing of all was finding out from day to day how dear you are. The journey would have been pleasant in most circumstances, and interesting in any, but because you were there, it was wholly delightful. Whatever things may happen in the future of good or evil, at least we have had one perfect time which nothing can take away.

'Our actions all have immortality;
Such gladness gives no hostage unto death.'

Thank you, thank you, thank you, for being so completely
satisfactory, you most sweet woman.

And we will go again. There are heaps of lovely places to see,
and things to do. Never doubt I want to see and do them, and
that I ask no better travelling companion than you.

Goodnight. May that god whom you and I both in our
different ways worship, bless you and keep you, and let the light
of his countenance shine upon you, and give you Peace.

Goodnight, Winifred

VERA TO WINIFRED

10 Oakwood Court, London W14 | 4 November 1921

Tomorrow I shall have been in bed a week and wonder if there
is some chance of being allowed to sit up a little, but I suppose
not, until some of this orange dye clears off. I want very much
to get back to 'Daphne'. I'm afraid the thought of lectures
rather bores me at present. I wish I could write something good
enough to justify my sticking to 'that one talent' . . . it's the only
thing in the way of work that really absorbs me. Only I feel in
despair when I read Sheila Kaye-Smith and Rose Macaulay and
find how good they are.

Don't be depressed if Grace thought 'Frederick' dull – she
thinks all History dull, whereas at least 10% of your audience
will be interested, even if they are not specially talented. I
trust your magnificent brain, which I know so well and believe
in so much and hope everything from, to produce something
stimulating and comprehensive in the way of lectures. You won't

trust yourself at all or believe how grand you are – your very chaos of ideas sometimes proves you to be so. You get lost in your own tremendous vision. You're big – like the Wolds and your Viking ancestors and their wide sea spaces.

London is cold and wet and full of fog; I don't seem to be missing much by staying in bed.

WINIFRED TO VERA

Bainesse, Cottingham, East Yorkshire | *5 November 1921*

Little Girl my Dear,

You absolutely are forbidden by your friend and guardian critic, to talk about your 'petty, parochial' talent. I simply will not hear a good thing abused. I admire it, and look up to it so much that such discourtesy to it sounds like sacrilege. I don't think it matters a brass button, except to your own most private feelings, how old you are. For the matter of that, you are a chicken. Think of Jane Austen and George Eliot and Charlotte Brontë. All the greatest women writers start late. The 'clever' modern ones begin early and burn themselves out young. Your particular kind of talent only attains perfection through experience. You must write of what you know, therefore you must have lived before you can write. Your chronicle is memory, your legend, joys and sorrows of your own experience. How could you write before you lived?

10 Oakwood Court, London W14 | *11 November 1921*

My dear,

I have just been listening to the guns going for the two
minutes' silence. It's the first Armistice Day since the original
one that I haven't spent with you in the Cathedral at Oxford. It
was funny, wasn't it, how in the 1919 one our mutual hostility
drew us into the Cathedral in spite of ourselves. I wonder if
even then the gods were laughing at us and planning to turn
our rather foolish rivalry into something really blest. Today I
cannot go out and stand at the Cenotaph or pay homage to
Unknown Warriors or anything. I don't know that I really
mind. It was better to go to Asiago and Louvencourt. And I
don't require two minutes' silence to think of the dead. They're
with me always; it's like putting two minutes aside in which
to breathe.

Much love, my dear one, from Vera

1922

10 Oakwood Court, London W14 | *21 August 1922*

My dear,

My family were quite excited about your book and most
delighted. I am trying to make myself believe that a book of
yours will really exist, with your name on the cover, and we

shall perhaps stand outside Bumpus and look at it on the shelf
of new novels. I couldn't take in the fact on Saturday at all.
I know the reviews will be nice. It is a kind book as well as
a clever one, and has always inspired me with a secret envy.
I think I pretended that it bored me mainly because it gave
me a despairing sense of my own inability to reach the same
level – not so much of English, which is a detail, but of thought
and vision and psychology. You make me feel very humble –
one who talks but never achieves, while you yourself achieve
and don't talk. You will be quite famous by the time you are
my age – and one rare thing will make your success the more
distinguished and that is that you cannot get any success so
great as the success you deserve. I really agree with Maude
and Dot and Hilda all the time, only I never admit it because
I have the kind of second-rate mind which enjoys the exercise
of domination, instead of your first-rate sort which is quietly
content with the fact.

Do hurry up and finish 'The Wallflower' – I believe it will be
even better than 'Anderby'. It will be a new experience to live in
close contact with triumph – and one I look forward to. I shall
be glad really to know someone intimately who succeeds – just
because all my best friends so far have either died before they
could achieve anything, or else are held up for lack of funds.

Don't know why I really seem to have nothing to say.
Somehow the whole world seems subtly changed by your book
getting taken. I suppose it's like what I said in 'Daphne' about
crossing the gulf between aspiration and achievement; once
people have done it they are never quite the same again. I
don't know whether better – certainly not worse – but quite
as certainly different. Almost I think of you as if you were a
stranger; we are not equals any more.

WINIFRED TO VERA

22 August 1922

My beloved,

You must not really talk such nonsense, you know. All about
first-class and second-class minds – when all the time down in
your heart you must know – or else, because of your perverse
humility, have forgotten – how infinitely better you are than
me. You are perfectly right in saying that we are not equals. We
never were and never will be. I have always known how much
keener and clearer and finer your mind is than mine – you,
who have the daring to go steadily to the point – I, who deviate
blindly until I fix myself half-reluctantly on to some track,
more by chance than anything. The mere accident of someone
being rash enough to take my book without alteration, while
someone else wants to take yours after a purely arbitrary piece
of alteration, makes no difference. It may even depend on the
quite superficial circumstance of my book being in one part,
while yours is in two, for I have come to the conclusion, after
your experience with Blackwell and Collins, that if a publisher
can get you to alter a book, he will. And as we both of us know
perfectly well, acceptance is no criterion of merit. I still think it
is a toss up which book comes out first, and even if mine should
come out first, that is far from saying that it will bring me fame.
Acceptance and approval are very different things, and I never
thought 'Anderby' particularly arresting – which 'Daphne' – in
either version – is!

My little dear, I do not think that the time is far distant
when you will really 'live in close contact with triumph' – your
own. I seem to be lucky, but I doubt very much my capacity
to take the best advantage of my luck. You are not lucky; your
success is not a ripe fruit that will fall easily into your lap; but

remember that the best fruit of the tree has to be climbed for, and windfalls are generally a nest of earwigs.

My love to you, Winifred

VERA TO WINIFRED

10 Oakwood Court, London W14 | 24 December 1922

My dear,

I cannot resist writing to you again this morning, because it is such a lovely morning, and my mind, instead of being occupied with Christmas, is full of imagined scents and sounds of an Italian spring – of azaleas blossoming at Siena, and the walls of the Carceri at Assisi all bright with flowers. To make matters worse Mr Leighton has given me a calendar showing Siena Cathedral in spring, with the Lizza and the deep Valle all covered with pink and white blossom. I don't feel as if I could wait 18 months to see Italy in April. If only some fairy godmother would drop a couple of hundred pounds at our feet! Nobody else could, because I am not a lucky person, and therefore that would be too romantic a fashion for sorrow to be turned into joy. My dear, I feel it is so mean to you that I am not lucky; the wail about disappointment is that it won't even confine itself to the disappointed person. Therefore I feel mean because I not only never give you any pleasant, thrilling surprises, but I don't ever permit you to enjoy your own luck in the gay, whole-hearted way that I know you would if I were not perpetually with you, fighting against fate.

Such a splendid solution for the problem of that insidious rivalry flashed across my mind last night – splendid and obvious. I will hereafter write as Hilary Deane. Nobody will compare Winifred Holtby and Hilary Deane, even though they really know that Hilary Deane is Vera Brittain, simply because it is not an obvious association of ideas. You weren't at college with Hilary Deane, you don't share a flat with her, or lecture with her on the League of Nations Union. Therefore she'll be an independent identity and you another.

Now as Vera Brittain, lecturer, and speaker for the League of Nations Union etc., I feel quite able to hold my own with Winifred Holtby, and to tell you the honest truth, I don't care a damn if I can't. I don't really care for a thing but writing, and merely making up my mind to stop doing it would never prevent me from going on. I always know that at once as soon as I get out of the racket and can sit in my room in the morning sunshine with leisure to think and dream (just as I could sit at Doughty St. in the evening sunshine if I weren't so foolish and so ridiculous as to burden myself with crowds of second-rate work). Not that writing isn't a bitter business. Yesterday I read bits of Barbellion, whose life seemed to be filled, like mine, with rejected manuscripts. Then I made up my mind that even though our flat was choked with the returned manuscripts of 'Daphne' and probably 'Little Dog', I would nevertheless put all I know into the 'Man on the Crucifix' – a thing which, as you well know, I have never done yet at any time. And then, if he gets finished, to try to publish him under the name of Hilary Deane. At any rate no past shadow of unsuccessful effort clings to Hilary Deane, even though she lent her name to camouflage someone else's sad story.

So I set to yesterday evening and wrote the first draft of the difficult first page of the first chapter. I immediately hated it. I wanted to produce on myself the same effect as Hugh Walpole and 'Elizabeth' produce on me, and I found I couldn't do it. Then I cursed myself because I couldn't write. But perhaps that's a better way of doing it than rising from the table complacently content at having 'got through' half a chapter. I wonder whatever made me do that, for I don't labour under the illusion that things are easy, as a general rule. I can't remember, but I

believe that a year ago I had a sort of idea that I'd only got to
finish a book to get it published; Mr Leighton's rather insidious
form of encouragement after all did rather suggest that, didn't it?
And wasted years had shut out any other means of knowledge.
At any rate, perhaps hating what I do, being a least a new
method, may produce a different result.

I am feverishly and discontentedly yearning for Italy in
the spring and with you. What a discontented creature I
am, always longing for something I haven't got. I must really
go out into the sun, try not to see the prosperous, well-fed,
unimaginative inhabitants of Kensington, and pretend that I
am in Siena in April.

My very dearest love and mind you come for dinner on
Friday. (Mother is 'treating' us out of the housekeeping so
there's nothing to worry about.)

from Vera

1923

VERA TO WINIFRED

10 Oakwood Court, London W14 | 25 July 1923

My dear,

So many thanks for your two postcards and your letter. I have
been dead to the world since Monday, or would have written. I
am so glad everything at home is so pleasant, and that you are
pleased with your clothes and Grace's. I am longing to see the
bridesmaids' dress. Do they like the hat?

It is a relief that your Mother likes *The Dark Tide*. I am quite

out of concert with my poor child at the moment and feel I
simply can't pick it up and look at it.

The American girl I met at Lord Waring's has asked me to
lunch with her at the American Women's Club in Grosvenor
Street on Friday. She rang up twice; I was out both times, so
she then wrote. Is this the beginning of 'lionization'? Having
striven all my life for publicity, I am frightened of it now that
it may come.

I am re-reading 'The Prophet' before continuing it – I feel a
little less depressed; it has the effect of making me indifferent to
The Dark Tide. I think it is really better; the psychology is much
less crude. I hope he will take it.

Much love, dearest heart, from your V.S.V.D.L.

WINIFRED TO VERA

Bainesse, Cottingham, East Yorkshire | *25 July 1923*

Little dear,

It would do your heart good if you could hear the things
that people here are saying about *The Dark Tide*. Mother hasn't
words enough for it. I heard her yesterday telling Dr Jackson – a
medical doctor friend of Tolmie's – about it. She said that in her
life only one or two novels have stood out with real strength,
getting to the heart of life. This is one of them. I told her how
it had been refused. She said, 'It's too strong meat for babes.
The publishers might be puzzled by it. It's always the case with a
really strong, great thing. People are frightened of it. The public
now may not think as much of it as they should. But the few
who really know and who care for good things, they will be able
to appreciate it.' She laughed when I told her that Sylvester had
been considered impossible. She says that she has known plenty

of men like that, and plenty of women who, like Daphne, made sacrifices for them that no one ever heard of nor cared about. I have rarely known her so excited or pleased about anything.

My dear, dear love, W.

VERA TO WINIFRED

10 Oakwood Court, London W14 | 28 July 1923

My dear,

I had the strangest time last night. I went to Portland Place at 7.00, and found myself at an exquisite but completely tête-à-tête dinner with Lord Waring. He then motored me to the Regent, and we saw *Robert E. Lee* in the stalls in the midst of about a dozen M.P.s, including Sir Harry Brittain. (I don't like Sir Harry Brittain; he seems to know everyone in the world worth knowing, but he is the kind of person who starts squeezing your hand five minutes after you've been introduced.) I was then taken back in the car all the way to Oakwood Court. He wanted me to go out with him again before I went for my holiday, but I said firmly that I was going early on Monday morning and was engaged every moment until then. So he then said he would write to me in September when I came back. In the taxi he urged me most strongly to find a constituency and start 'nursing' it; he said I should be an immense influence in Parliament, and that I ought to get in *soon*, while I was still young and could look forward to a long career in which to become a power. He intimated that he would gladly associate himself (although one of Lloyd George's Conservative friends!) with any effort I made to get into Parliament as an Independent Liberal, and when I said it wasn't worthwhile working up a constituency until I had made enough money to fight an election, he merely remarked that when the time came the money was generally forthcoming too! Altogether an amazing evening. I must say he behaved like a perfect gentleman throughout, but that he should continue to do so seems too much to hope for. I do wish I were not attractive to men; it is such a curse; one never knows when they cease to be interested in one's sex and begin to be interested in one's intellect. I must say that as far as conversation goes it seems to be my brains at present, but naturally people have to start on those. He discussed my book and said that the chief thing about it that interested him was how a person as young as I could know things by intuition about politicians and political life which I could not possibly have learnt yet from experience. He seemed to think my account of them as valid and correct as it could be if written by someone who had had a long political career, and was interested and amazed at the coincidence of the Divorce Bill.

Oh dear! What a chance – and ought I to go on taking it? And think how useful his good will might be if we wanted to furnish a flat! What a hard world it is for a woman especially for a 'v.s.v.d.l.'!

You must go to *Robert E. Lee*. I will take you again; I was so much occupied in preventing Sir Harry Brittain from squeezing my hand (especially when the guns went off, which they do frequently) that I couldn't give it half the attention I wanted to.

Best love, sweet heart, your V.S.V.D.L.

WINIFRED TO VERA

Bainesse, Cottingham, East Yorkshire | *28 July 1923*

My own little dear,

This is the first installment of Oxford opinion, which I think may amuse you. For the *Oxford Chronicle* I suppose that this is

all fairly high praise. As for *Time and Tide*, I expect that they
have decided to wait another week before publishing a review
of *The Dark Tide* – or possibly two – which certainly won't
kill the book.

I hope that your dinner on Friday amused you. It should
have been great fun. Dear and sweet, don't hide your pretty
head. People like you and love your book and the other
nonsense never was more than nonsense and is dead. I think
that the Bumpus display means quite a lot. You never see bad
books there, nor quite unsuccessful books. I am so *longing*
for it to reach the 2,000 and Grant Richards to have to pay
you that 12%.

My proofs of the University Extension syllabuses have come
and rather scare me. They look so very formidable. I shall have
to read a lot. I am not trying to write here – but three things
dance in my head all the time – 'The House in Raymond
Passage', for which I am still in search of a form – 'The Crowded
Street', and more and more 'The Creditor' – *your* book,
although it won't be about you exactly. I am too different, my
dear, to try to draw anyone just like you. I should not succeed
as well as you succeeded with Daphne. All the same, it is to be
your book.

I am reading Brailsford's *War of Steel and Gold*. It was
published in June 1914 and is strangely interesting for
its absolute ignorance of coming events, as well as for its
remarkable wisdom on the interpretation of past ones.

I wish I did not get so irritable when you aren't there – just
cross like a spoiled child, because I can't tell you things when I
want to. And also I feel guilty the whole time, thinking of times
when I might have been nice to you and wasn't.

au revoir, my v.s.v.d.l. W.

VERA TO WINIFRED

Holehird, Windermere, Cumbria | *31 July 1923*

My dear,

I can't, of course, believe that there really are no more reviews than you have sent; I suppose all the time that there's indignation raging behind my back of which you have told me nothing. The *Oxford Chronicle* notice was very nice, but I feel sure it is one gem amid a heap of mud. I suppose I must go on sending for them though. I may as well know the worst sometime or other, so will you please tell Durrants to keep sending them. I am sorry to trouble you, but I have no reviews here and forgotten their address. I curse myself sometimes for having had the audacity to publish a book – especially a book about Oxford.

I wonder if *Time and Tide* will give me a review this week – and if it will be decent. I shan't see it here, so please let me know when you write on Friday, whether they have or not. I wish the beastly book didn't make me so miserable and so apprehensive.

I ought to feel happy, for there is the loveliest view from the window of my bedroom where I am writing, of mountains and woods and sky, and though it has been pouring hard all morning, there are fitful gleams of sun over the hills and a rainbow mist half veiling one of the highest peaks. In the garden, though it has been too wet to go into so far, there are the loveliest flowers on earth, and I can see some of them from my window.

What a morbid person I am for a friend! I think I am suffering from the feeling of flatness which comes from having finished 'The Prophet', and wondering whether it is good enough for Grant Richards to contemplate.

I will try to have a real holiday. I hope it won't be too wet, as there is tennis, and we are going for a motor drive if it keeps fine.

This house is heavenly and the fever and fret of my everyday life seems very far away. Perhaps at the end of a week the fever and fret in my mind will go to sleep too. I wish someone would write and say something nice about *The Dark Tide*. Here no one has either read or seen it, which is a great relief.

My very dear love, I look forward to next week. I expect I shall let you get to the flat before I arrive.

Your V.S.V.D.L.

Don't say your writing is inefficient – it isn't – but it is like you in being without bitterness – so doesn't upset either you or other people. I seem with mine to have a talent for doing both even when I don't intend to.

VERA TO WINIFRED

10 Oakwood Court, London W14 | 24 December 1923

My dear love,

Mr Catlin has sent me his copy of *The Dark Tide* all the way from America for me to put my signature on; I do call that enthusiasm, don't you? All over the front he has stuck cuttings of Grant Richards' little notices in the *Times Lit. Supp.* The book looks well read and well handled; it was bought at Blackwell's; there is a Blackwell label inside, so the gentlemen evidently stocked them in spite of Basil having refused to publish it! We had Basil on the wireless the other night on the subject of children's books. He has just had *another* daughter!

My very best love – V.S.V.D.L.

VERA TO WINIFRED

10 Oakwood Court, London W14 | 27 December 1923

My dear love,

I have had another long letter from Mr Catlin – intimate
and amazingly interesting. Isn't it queer that I don't even know
what he looks like. He knows me all right though; he has
seen my photo in *The Bookman* and calls it a 'libellously bad
reproduction'. Here are one or two strange extracts from his
strange letter. 'I confess to a little sorrow that you are not too
fond of Virginia (as I am) to throw her over. If you do not know
what happens to her, I do, and will tell you someday, for I have
met her.' He proceeds to do so – at length and very interestingly
and ends with: 'She is an admirable type of the "modern
woman", because in her I think I can foresee the collision
between the temporal demands of sex and (in a woman who is
no nun) the eternal demands of idealism, between the human
and the mystical emotions – she would not call them mystical,
of course.'

Is this a description only of Virginia? It seems to strike
home somehow. The letter (3 pages of his microscopic writing)
includes a biography of himself and a long dissertation on
marriage – interesting, I will show it to you. It reveals a splendid
mind – better than mine, which is unusual enough to be
thrilling.

More letters from Leigh Groves – and today, from a shop
in Bond Street, a box of 100 cigarettes of obviously a most
expensive variety – lovely cigarettes, in a wooden box.

You know, I feel vaguely uneasy and rather miserable. I do
hope that, after this lovely period of peace, some devastating
male is not going to push into my life and upset it again. Just
when things look so promising, too. Dear heart, you must exert

yourself as a bulwark and protect me from them. (I can see
you smile sorrowfully and a little resignedly.) I haven't really
anything to feel uneasy about – what after all are a letter from
America and a box of cigarettes? And yet I do feel it. Please
write and laugh me to scorn.

Forgive this foolishness – but I feel pent up and irritable, and
the near approach of thirty doesn't seem to make me as safe
from my horrible personality as it ought to do.

Your V.S.V.D.L.

WINIFRED TO VERA

Bainesse, Cottingham, East Yorkshire |
29 December 1923

Dearest child,

Mr Catlin is right, that the demands of sex are temporal, and
the demands of idealism eternal; but both are inevitably part
of a woman's life, and neither should be completely ignored. I
for one do not believe that it is right to leave the upbringing
or the bearing of children to the mediocre. Just at the moment
there are too many people in the world for perfect comfort,
and the ultimate issue is postponed to a later generation; but
that is just fortuitous. Neither sex nor marriage as its social
expression are wrong, I think. What is wrong is this collision
between the institutions of domesticity and public service, and
the reason for this collision is not unavoidable. It has occurred
because we live during a transition period. Women, who have
hitherto concentrated their idealism upon the sex functions,
have just learnt that they can exercise them upon society
at large. Because this is the wider spiritual adventure, the
'admirable type of modern woman' has completely reversed her

old mentality, and in her 'social' idealism has left no force for
the 'domestic'.

Further, society, moving even slower than individuals, has
not yet adjusted the domestic conventions to the needs of the
modern citizen woman. Indeed, far from that, convention still
demands that she shall conform to institutions hammered
out by generations of the domestic type. Hence the enormous
difficulty of making a success of both sex life and public life.
Hence the 'collision' of Mr Catlin's letter. But I do not agree
that the conflict lies between the *emotions* nearly so much
as between the social environment of those emotions. When
two or three generations have learnt how to manage their
lives according to the wider sphere of action, then the smaller
will not 'collide' with the greater nor the temporal with the
eternal – any more than eating collides with thinking, though
the anchorites of primitive or slow developing races thinks so.

My dear, how often have I warned you not to put your trust
in being thirty? I never could think where you got hold of your
absurd idea that thirty years constituted an invincible armour
against the attacks of sex-attraction. Forty won't with you. I
should still walk cannily at fifty.

Dear child, I also hope that you are not going to allow another
male to prove himself devastating after this period of peace. But
I cannot help thinking that you can yourself prevent them being
devastating, though I admit that you cannot help their being
difficult. Mr Catlin sounds more than a little interesting. Perhaps
it is a pity that you have not seen him. He may be fat and greasy.
I sometimes wish that you were! Anyway, he is still in America,
so I don't think that there is any need to worry, and it is a relief
to hear of somebody intelligent and interesting. Jean McWilliam
told me that she feared I was becoming anti-man, because I
hardly ever mentioned one without some deprecating remark.
I told her that I would give worlds to meet a few who gave me

a better opinion of the sex. I thought that they were all in the colonies or in their graves, except a few old and middle-aged ones. So if only Catlin is interesting and is nice, it will be such a blessing for a world that needs nice men enormously.

As for the personal side – he does seem to be a good deal intrigued, but then it's all rather from a distance, and he's probably quite safe. Time enough to worry when he comes to England to tell Virginia what happens to her. Perhaps his theory may be mistaken after all.

My dear love, I'll be your bulwark for as long as you want me.

As for Leigh, I think that he is a pretty good bulwark too, if you use him as one. The best thing to do with a dangerous rock is to use it as the foundation for a lighthouse.

I love you, my blessed little child. I love your stories. I do think that they can be good.

Bless you my little lovely one.

WH v.s.v.d.l.

1924

WINIFRED TO VERA

Bainesse, Cottingham, East Yorkshire | *1 January 1924*

Dearest child,

Today the York Rescue worker is coming over, and I am to have a long talk with her. They have all been having a most exciting time here because a girl at Driffield murdered her baby, and two years afterwards confessed to the matron of the rescue home for which I am speaking. The police found the skeleton of

the baby in a barn, but the matron refused to make a statement
of what had been told her in confidence. The girl had pulled
herself together and lived a straight life since, and she would
not have her prosecuted.

The police were furious. The bishop, who employs her,
reprimanded the matron. The county chief of police, a Major
Dunlop, gave her a public reprimand, which was printed in
the local papers and even mentioned in the London ones. He
demanded her dismissal as an unfit person to be in charge of a
home. Mother backed the matron, who was legally within her
rights and psychologically beyond reproach. The whole case,
with Mother as witness, came into court, but fortunately Dr
Jackson (*your* Dr Jackson) was there and by a clever argument
placed the matron in the right. But the whole thing has caused
immense excitement. I am looking forward to some rousing
meetings. People here have been refusing to have the subject
discussed in their drawing rooms, and consequently I only have
about half-a-dozen meetings – but I feel thoroughly on the
warpath about the few that I have got.

I am going to lecture on 'The Social Work of the League',
officially. Actually, I am going to begin with the need for an
awakening to the moral danger to young girls, which exists
largely from the apathy of public opinion, the laxity of the
law, and the ignorance about morality and hygiene, especially
in villages. Then I am going to talk about the world-wide
movement to a greater feeling of responsibility, as shown in the
social work of the League, and finally to point to the part which
they ought to play, in the world by membership of the League of
Nations Union and at home a more active support of the work
that has been begun.

Take care of yourself, my very dear. Because I love
you always –

v.s.v.d.l. WH

VERA TO WINIFRED

Holehird, Windermere, Cumbria | *3 January 1924*

My dear love,

Bless you for your letters. Mind you fight gallantly for the rescue home to keep its pictures and Indian mats, and also the nice matron who realises that if 'fallen' women are to cease to be 'fallen' one must first keep one's word to them as to anyone else. But don't work too hard.

My lecture (partly your lecture) on the importance of foreign policy went down quite well yesterday at the Women's Institute; at least Aunt Muriel seemed quite pleased. Leigh came in to listen and sat at the back, but in the hop that followed (valses, lancers, Sir Roger de Coverley, all of which I danced in with the women and thoroughly enjoyed) he absolutely refused to dance with me. One or two of the 'better class' pro-French ladies of this district were inclined to get a bit dusty in question time; I am afraid I settled one of them afterwards with more neatness than politeness.

Leigh has given me a heavenly blue-green scarf to wear under a coat – the sort of hand-woven silk that they make here on special looms – for my birthday; also *Hassan* and a book on History in Education. The situation here continues interesting, though indeed I am still very far from making up my mind what the situation *is*; consequently all the time I am not sure whether I am doing right or wrong. It wants the observation of a clever psychologist.

VERA TO WINIFRED

Holehird, Windermere, Cumbria | 10 April 1924

Many thanks for forwarding all my letters, none of which were
interesting except Catlin's, which would have entranced you
as much as it did me! Apart from the fact that he enclosed
his photograph (nice-looking, much gayer and less pedantic
than his letters sound, dark, slim, looking on the tall side of
middle-height tho' that's difficult to tell, clothes neat and well
cared for) he spent the best part of eight pages in telling me
in discreet and carefully chosen but quite unmistakable words
that he has never had sex relations of any sort with anybody.
Starting of course from John Donne and his relief that I took
the receipt of him as I did. Silly boy – if he was anything
but a Puritan he would never have dared to send *Problems
and Paradoxes* – as if I didn't know that! I really think he is
rather nice. He wants a photograph in return which Leigh
has promised to take for me – thereby scenting a romance and
dragging from me all details about Catlin except his name,
which I refused to give! He – Catlin – says he will be in London
during the first fortnight in July. He sent me a good many other
photographs – of Ithaca and Cornell University.

WINIFRED TO VERA

16 April 1924

Dearest Heart,

I hope that your letters are coming all right. Mine were
forwarded to me today quite safely. One from the Von Gerlach
girl, written in Paris, to say that her father has got safely out

of Germany, and that if the elections go all right he may not
be tried for high treason even now. Poor things! What a hell
of a time most European countries give their best citizens.
The liberals in Hungary, the anti-fascists in Italy, the pacifists
in Germany, the liberty-loving in Russia – and all for what?
I still see the little Von Gerlach girl leaning across the table
at Pinoli's, with her big, tear-filled eyes and her fierce little
voice. 'Oh you in England don't know what Europe is! how can
you? You're so *safe!*' I thought of her as I came up in the train
yesterday, riding along the side of a tranquil sunset over this
dull, placid, strangely untroubled country that lies from London
to the Humber.

I was interviewed by Cicely Hamilton on Monday, and was
not impressed favourably. She kept me waiting and then never
apologised – which Lady Rhondda always does. She spoke
to me as though I were an office boy. She wore the filthiest
Whiteman's shirt under an old sweater that I have ever been
unfortunate enough to see on any self-respecting woman –
altogether she was not prepossessing. However, she gave me a
free hand with my notes, but whether she'll print 'em or not is
a different affair. Vera darling, when you become eminent, treat
the little worms nicely. They like it.

I do love you, my dear. v.s.v.d.l. W.

VERA TO WINIFRED

10 Oakwood Court, London W14 | 19 April 1924

Dearest child,

I have just received, by this afternoon's post, what I can only
describe as an amazing letter from Mr Catlin, containing a
criticism of my book that should raise me to the seventh heaven

if it were not rather too agitating. 'Let me collect my thoughts and see if I can say anything not too obviously absurd. The first thing is that you have raised me again for a while onto those levels on which one would desire to live out all one's experience. Once again, as I turn the pages, life, to which one has learnt in bitterness to adopt the attitude of a harsh refusal to believe that as ordinarily lived it will yield anything entirely and purely valuable, becomes something quite worthwhile – not for the pleasantness but for the keenness . . . I put down your book feeling a very small man. And I find it difficult to continue a correspondence in which I find it difficult to convince myself that I can be of any use . . . No one who is not quite something – it matters less what – can be of use to another. It is for this reason that I venture upon the impertinence of writing thus frequently in order that you may the more speedily discover what kind of person I am and how little capable of being of any use to you . . . Next time I will try in my insolence to see what the surgeon's scalpel can do, if only to display the perfection of the anatomy. But as anaesthetic take this: rest assured that we are as much in love with Christine as a girl as with Virginia as a woman . . . ' And so on, for 3 sheets.

I have written – I had to – some kind of an answer. As for writing anything but letters – why, how can I, for all life seems suddenly to be tumbling about my ears.

I have decided – after half a morning's and a whole afternoon's relentless walking – that I must deal Leigh a more or less knockout blow. It will be (in fact it *is*, I have already written it) in the form of a letter which I will not trust to the post but will leave here for him to read when I have gone. It need not be a completely knockout blow unless he chooses it shall be, but after Wednesday night (as I can make you see) I must state quite clearly not only what my position is, but also what it cannot be and never in *any* case could have been, with regard to him.

Dear, dear child – most desperately I want you, selfish little pig that I am.

Many thanks for your Good Friday letter which has just come. I'm glad they think *Not Without Honour* was well reviewed. Catlin says: 'I should disregard the *Times* reviewer who is clearly a damn fool; he appears to desire you to treat a girl of nineteen "more maturely" than a woman of twenty-five. But, as we grow older, we realise – do we not? – that there is less and less value in any passion, more and more in wisdom.'

Do we? I really sometimes wonder.

The best of Easters, my love. Here it is gloriously warm and spring is beginning at last.

I love you. Your V.S.V.D.L.

WINIFRED TO VERA

Bainesse, Cottingham, East Yorkshire | *22 April 1924*

Dearest Heart,

A most interesting development with Mr Catlin. He sounds to be extraordinarily attracted and somewhat attractive, for that is not the letter of a fool. My dear, it seems that one must choose between stagnation and agitation in this world, and that for some people the choice is taken out of their own hands. Life may be quite an interesting affair for you this year. I see no reason why it should 'blow up' as you say. That all depends upon yourself, I think.

Wednesday night was a risk with anyone in any world. It was also a test, and it seems as though your relationship had come to a point when a test was necessary. I write in the dark, but probably you are doing the wisest thing. If the man cannot be content with what you are able to offer, and contact with you only increases his discontent, makes him wish for impossibilities and then to regard his wife and domestic surroundings, which are, after all, his own affair, as the only bar to what is in any case an impossibility, and so comes to hate what before he tolerated, better end the whole thing. You did not give him his domestic ties. If he cannot face his own responsibilities, then he certainly cannot go further. You have given him everything that was in your power to give. The last gift possible for you may be cruelty. Knowing you, I fear that this may cost you most. Sometimes it is the kindest gift. The rest depends upon him. If he is really decent he will undertake to bear his own burden of responsibility. As Catlin says, 'we cannot really help other people unless we are *quite* something', and I would add, unless they also are *quite* something they cannot be helped.

I am delighted that Catlin has seen what I think to be the real merit of *Not Without Honour*. So few of the criticisms seem to have realised what I think to be the extraordinarily advanced maturity of the book nor its psychological power. Knowing how often my taste has been in error, I have sometimes wondered whether it was I who could have been wrong in thinking its fineness and power as well as its literary technique miles away beyond *The Dark Tide*. It is always difficult for me in my heart of hearts to believe my judgment to be better than that of others. From the very first reading of the m.s. I thought your study of Christine exquisitely fine in its freshness, its humanity, its tenderness. She is so real, so genuinely young, rather like Turgenev's study of Elena in *On the Eve*. Your restless mood would persuade you that you 'are not getting it', can't write, etc. I believe that you have great ability – far greater perhaps than either you or I realise now. The proof is your power to influence other people, even so far removed from you geographically as Catlin, spiritually as Leigh Groves. If I did not think this of your spirit, I would not love so much your restless mind nor your small, beloved body. There are times when I feel very humble by you, very 'small' as Catlin says, and unadventurous. But if, even so, I may serve you, I will. You say that you want to talk to me. You shall, and you shan't think that you are 'selfish'. To serve where one may also worship is joy, not hardship, as the medievalists discovered. The only hardship lies in finding that one can do neither.

I shall be arriving Friday at 1.55. I can't write more now. Mother is still rather poorly. The house is full and there are a thousand messages arriving from her admirers every hour. I am exceeding well and fat and getting lots of buns.

I love you, W.

WINIFRED TO VERA

St Monica's, Burgh Heath, Surrey | *[c. 10 May 1924]*

My own little dear,

I am sorry that my theories on the rôle of the husband annoy you – or rather, not my theories but my preferences. My theory I think agrees with yours – at least it has always been my cry that no one should impose upon others a rule of conduct that they themselves would not choose to follow.

Remember that I speak as one who has nearly all experience upon the debit side of fortune. I still owe to life much more than I have paid, and if there were any way to rid myself of my debt without calling upon others who have already paid too dearly to share it with me, I would do so. It may be pride, but it is neither selfishness nor callousness that urges me. It is an instinct which is inevitably alien to you, who have never played my rôle.

As for the rest – do I seem cold to you? Oh, my dear love,

I am torn between the exacting demands of love, and my invincible belief that no one person should lay too heavy claims upon another, to let each one of one's beloveds feel completely free, even the most beloved of them all, to interpose no barrier of pity or tenderness between them and their destiny, that needs a little careful schooling. If I have taught myself too well, then I am sorry – and yet I would not that it were otherwise.

Did you write last night? Dear heart, one day when your work has been recognised for all that it is – its rare honesty, its lucidity, its high fineness of vision all praised as one day they will be, will you then look back with half-regretful amusement upon the despairs of your sterile periods, or will you still fear for the sterility of the future?

Good night, dear love. I believe you know I love you. Do you want me to say I know that you love me? Sweet child, do you think I dream for a moment that you could have endured my limitations all these years if you had not loved me? That would be setting a high premium upon my value!

Goodnight. v.s.v.d.l. *WH*

Vera and Gordon became engaged in the summer of 1924.

WINIFRED TO VERA

Bainesse, Cottingham, East Yorkshire | 20 August 1924

Dearest Little Love,

I am here and well. We travelled up in great comfort, to find that Grace and Peter had just arrived before us, brown as berries from motoring, and very tweed-and-leathery. Harry telephoned up to say that he is coming over tomorrow, so the first lesson shall then begin.

I found a letter from Dawes awaiting me in which she says: 'I saw Miss Brittain's photo in the *Daily Express* announcing her engagement to Professor Catlin. It is a fine photo yet scarcely does her justice, although a friend of mine declares her to resemble the Madonna. And that, I think, is about the nicest thing a woman could have said of her. I am so glad to hear of the coming marriage. Please convey my very best wishes to Miss Brittain.'

So I have, you see.

I have Grace's bedroom, and am luxuriating in plenty of space. They have given me a large table to work at and tomorrow I hire a type-writer.

Take care of yourself, sweet dear little girl, most beautiful, v.s.v.d.l. W.

VERA TO WINIFRED

10 Oakwood Court, London W14 | *27 August 1924*

Dear Sweetieheart,

Your literary activity overwhelms me; you are a rising star and I sometimes feel I am no star at all. I wonder when – or if ever – I shall be in a writing mood again. Probably not till I am married – unless I can forget about Gordon sufficiently while he is away. Queer to think that according to the first idea we might have been getting married today. I have not written anything except letters, because at present my mind is occupied with the queer physical relationship set up even by an engagement; I mean when the two are lovers and especially when the man is the more active lover of the two; if the woman is the more active I don't believe any such relationship is set up. How am I to understand this queer mixture of a

brilliant boy and a lonely man, who quite consciously and
deliberately follows his instincts to lengths which would
frighten most men – and certainly most women – before
marriage, and then, when I protest, cries out that I want to
shame and humiliate him and make him feel his purity to be
an unclean thing, that only thus can he overcome a strong
sense of shame in all matters of sex and that only when
physical desires and acts (apart from the one act which has the
'utilitarian value' of producing children and therefore comes
into a different category) become so instinctive that we no
longer feel self-conscious or even think about them, are we
released from them, and become free to concern ourselves
with the more interesting things of the soul and the mind?
The superficial explanation of course would be that all men
are sensualists, that some are frank blatant sensualists, and
others explain and justify their sensuality by philosophy,
but that the ultimate result of either amounts to much the
same thing. But I feel this explanation is much too easy. It
is not thus that one accounts for the queer clash between
the lover and the priest, the sensualist and the ascetic, the
Epicurean and the Stoic. Sometimes I feel that in a sudden
panic I may break off this engagement, not for the usual
reason that married life would be too easy where it was not
too troublesome and in any case completely uninteresting,
but for the cowardly one that it would always be too difficult
and too interesting for either placidity or passivity ever to be
possible. Is *The Lay Anthony* any help for the understanding
of this child, who writes that he is 'always tacking up and
down in search of things half seen, not steering straight for a
perceived port'. Tell me where to seek an explanation of him.
Certainly not in the last century, nor yet in the 18th with its
full-blooded coarseness, nor in the 17th with its clash between
hot licentiousness and chill Puritanism, nor in the 16th with

its rich, care-free adventurousness. Shall I go back for him
to Ancient Greece, or shall I look for him in the queerly
sexual spirituality of the Middle Ages? Have Wycliffe and he
anything in common?

Au revoir, sweetieheart, your V.S.V.D.L.

VERA TO WINIFRED

10 Oakwood Court, London W14 | 29 August 1924

My darling girl,

Your dear letter this morning, I have not time today – owing
to an overwhelming correspondence this morning and Gordon's
arrival at Paddington after lunch – either to read it or to answer
it with the care it deserves, but I will later.

You and Gordon both make me feel a little, superficial,
suburban thing; something that has never really thought and
felt, something immature and childish in spirit, mind and body.
Sometimes I think it is that I am the opposite of what Harry
Scott Stokes called Gordon: that I am a person with a very
simple mind but a complicated nature. Sometimes I fear – as
when I read both your and his letters – that my mind is not
really simple, nor lucid, but merely small and insufficient. How
strangely you understand him, while I have spent a week in
bewilderment though partly through what he has said, partly
through what you have said, and partly because I myself have –
how rare the occasions are – tried to think, there is more light
now. Some time I will tell you about the queer crises of this
week; a worse crisis than any we have both been through,
though now that it is almost past I love him – and think he
does me – better even than before; better than either of us
thought possible.

My reason, based upon my education (my education which
has never let me down and preserved me inviolate through all
the dangers of the war) bade me resist his worship of my body,
as I told you. At first – you have my last letter – he cried out,
almost wept, that I made an unclean thing of his instinctive
purity, his attempts to free his mind of his body by allowing
his body to express itself without shame. After he had gone I
wrote him a long explanation of what my resistance was and
why my reason approved of it. He has read my letters, and has
given in to me completely; admits his methods mistaken since –
however unintentionally – they gave me pain, and says that,
since I do not want a sensual affection, he will show me that
he has another and far better love to offer me. As if I did not
know that, and as if I had not had it already. He humiliates me
by imputing in me to righteousness that which may only have
sprung from ignorance and fear.

Yet the strangest thing is that, now he has yielded to my
resistance, even humbled himself before it, my reason approves
of it no longer. I feel that my body is only the bread and wine
of our love; it is no more the whole sacrament than the bread
and wine alone is the whole of the Mass. The body is not the
essence of love; the essence lies in that of which it is but the
symbol. Am I right, and is this what you meant?

Dear child, I will answer you more anon, when perhaps –
so quickly does my experience increase – I shall understand
better. I feel as though I had never loved before – or rather,
that I have loved only as a child and not as a grown-up person.
Perhaps it is so. Perhaps the two loves are not two different and
antagonistic things but the later is made the sweeter and fuller
because of the earlier. Thus shall she belong to them both at
the Resurrection.

Adieu, my sweetieheart, your V.S.V.D.L.

Gordon returned to Cornell for the academic year, while Vera and Winifred continued living together in London. Their correspondence resumed after Vera's wedding in London on 27 June 1925, when Vera and Gordon went on their honeymoon.

1925

VERA TO WINIFRED

Lord Warden Hotel, Dover, Kent | 28 June 1925

Darling sweet,

Saying goodbye to you even for six weeks nearly made me weep. I wanted to take you with us – I *did*, even at that moment. I never thanked you half enough for making my wedding the success which – though at the end it all seemed like a dream – I believe it really was. That it *was*, was entirely due to you. Do write me a long letter to Vienna and tell me all about the church and the reception and the many things I had no time to ask you about. At the reception I scarcely saw you.

One or two bits of inevitable business!

Gordon's, of course, not mine!

1.) Can you possibly retrieve his light gloves, which he left with his silk hat, and send them to Vienna?
2.) Can you also retrieve his pen, which he left in the pocket of his morning coat, and send that with the papers to La Grave? He will not have it sent anywhere before that, as it is too precious to be risked.
3.) The hat box you sent here arrived smashed by some

idiot, so I shall have to get something else to send my
going away clothes back in. If I can't get a hat box I
shall have to send the clothes in a parcel, and take the
hat with me.

4.) Will you please send a copy of Monday's *Times* to: Mrs
H. Shaler Williams, 318 Highland Rd., Ithaca, N.Y.

5.) Lord Stamford informed us that all the bills at the
Church had been settled by someone except 13/6 for
the Registrar. Gordon is a little concerned lest Father
should have done this. I don't think so for a moment;
I suspect Lord S., but you might tactfully discover
whether Father did or not. If he didn't, Gordon does
not care who did.

We have been treated with amazing tact all through. On the
train we had a little private Pullman, for which (as we paid no
extra) I again suspect Lord S. – who saw us off – though he says
he didn't. Here we have been given a little curtained alcove in
the window looking straight on the docks and the sea. This
hotel is typical and pleasant enough; it is right on the docks so
we have only to walk onto the Ostend boat. Yesterday there was
a high wind, but today it has dropped and is calm and dull, and
the waiters say it is likely thus to continue for some days – so we
should have a good crossing.

Gordon is being a dear. You would laugh to see him 'doing'
the married man, with a manner which is a mixture of
academism, nonchalance, and solicitude!

Darling sweet, I do love you. I have my suspicions that,
though others are capable of being loved in ways that you are
not, the something in you that I love I shall always love best.

Bless you, and a thousand thanks, my sweetieheart,

Your v.s.v.d.l.

WINIFRED TO VERA

117 Wymering Mansions, Elgin Avenue,
London W9 | 29 June 1925

My Very Dear,

I was so glad, so very glad to have your letter. I love you
indeed for your delicate honesty, and I am happy and much
mentally relieved to hear all that you say. I should like to write
you in reply an adequate letter; but that must wait, as the more
complete description of your wedding must wait, until I have
become a person again. At present I am not a person, but a
List. It is an exceedingly diverse and attractive List, and I have
been living in this incarnation for about five days, and have
on the whole rather enjoyed it. It is a painless, rather fatiguing,
but most entertaining experience, wherein one lives, not in
a coherent and organic life of growing human relationships,
and expanding thoughts, but in a singularly inorganic series of
incoherent trivialities, which one performs, then crosses out,
and so has done with them.

The whole Six Point Group – alone among our
acquaintances – pays you the exquisite compliment of being
apparently exceedingly sorry for me (who need no sorrow
a) because of the reasons given in my little poem; b) because
I am enjoying being a List) and has been loading me with
attentions. Miss Mayo pleaded with me to come and hear Lilian
Barker on Child Assault. Miss Moore asked me to come and see
her sister in *Mary, Mary, Quite Contrary*. But Lady Rhondda
did even better; for when I went round this morning to see
about *Time and Tide* notes – somewhat hot and dishevelled,
in exceedingly dirty gloves – she whisked me off in a taxi to
some Soho restaurant, to lunch with Cicely Hamilton, Olga
Lindo (from *Rain*) and the Women's Rotary Club, a select but

formal gathering chiefly of Time and Tide Publishing Co., with a few photographers, journalists, advertisers and hotel proprietors added. I know what they were, for a roll-call is read to which one replies by saying one's profession. Lady R. is a 'Coal owner' – which seems to me not a profession but a misdemeanour. I am an 'Author' – not my choice, hers.

The wedding. Yes. The wedding. I am to write a long letter and describe it all – and I do not think that I can. For me too, it is at present an experience in two layers. The top layer is again lists, full of trifles about whether the sacristan would put his chair on your veil, and whether everyone had champagne correctly, and the receipt for your bag, and the number of people's rooms and so forth. The under layer is still a dream-like pool of fluid impressions A little space of tranquility would enable them to crystallise and achieve definite form, whereon I could sketch them in some way for you. I can only now offer you disjointed and fragmentary pictures of quite external things ...

At the door I found Harry Scott-Stokes with whom I renewed an all-too-brief acquaintance. A nice person, Harry Scott-Stokes. And you were there almost before I could think. After that, it is all rather confused. I know that the Church is very long, and dark at the entrance, but lit with a subdued and coloured radiance round the Chancel. I know that it seemed to be singularly well-filled for the number of people whom I knew to be there and that your white veil rippled in front of me up a very long aisle. I know that you stood between two tall banks of greenery and pale pink peonies; peonies so softly pink that they were like roses that have grown beyond their form and become transfigured, exquisite peonies, exactly the colour of your pink-shadowed gown. I know that a young priest with a very beautiful face and voice came and spoke the service intimately and graciously, as though he spoke solemn words to people whom he loved; and that he spoke a short, but admirable,

dignified address; and that your responses were both low and
clear; that you were white as marble as you went up the church,
but smiling and pink as your roses in the sacristy; and that
Gordon kissed me in the Sacristy with charming propriety, and
looked so happy and so young and so much beside himself that
as you both walked down the Church the whole congregation
fell in love with him, and that I have heard nothing but his
praises ever since. I know too that the organ was beautiful, and
that the 'Ave Maria' rolled up and through the Church like
a benediction. And that your father stood like a soldier, with
every button on his waistcoat doing its duty, and that Stamford
lost one of Gordon's gloves and was horribly worried over it,
and that he insisted on staying behind in the vestry to 'settle
accounts' – therefore your theory may be true, though I have
not had time to ask your father – and that there were besieging
legions of photographers on the steps.

Eh, well – and the upshot of it all, of telephone messages and
receptions, of cake stands and arranging presents, of letters and
wires, is that you are married. These others I realise. They are
quite comprehensible and vivid. This I shall grasp by degrees.

May you be happy, oh my very dear, and if not happy, well,
that seems to me to be inessential. For these things which are
sweet and these things which are painful are so closely akin
that I, for one, do not know which is preferable. I only feel that
there are some things which make for life, and some which
are merely a negation of it; and whether those that make for
life bring tears or laughter, whether they are exquisite through
suffering or through joy, that they are to be desired. And of
such, surely of such, shall this your marriage be.

Thank your husband for his letter, I will write anon; but now
it is two in the morning and tomorrow I have still a diversity of
things to do, so that I may not answer it yet.

But all my letters for you are of course for him as your wife. I feel completely at rest in the thought of him, so he will perhaps pardon a delay in an individual letter for I am rather weary, quite pleasantly so, but I only feel capable of supervising his more mundane requests.

1. His gloves I will send.
2. His pen I will retrieve.
3. His three *Times* I have sent according to his directives.
4. About the wedding fees I will make tactful inquiries.
5. His tie pin, socks and so forth I will seek.
6. His spoons I will take to the jewellers.

Au revoir, sweet child, dear heart, beautiful and belovéd creature, friend, lover, comrade, v.s.v.d.l. W.

VERA TO WINIFRED

Hotel Tegetthoff, Vienna | 2 July 1925

Darling girl,

So many thanks for your nice little note, which caught me at Dover just before I left. So far I have had nothing else from you though a long letter from Mother has just arrived. She seems very well content with everything.

Before I forget, we are of *course* having to send back (having had to pay 8/ excess for it at Vienna) Gordon's large and cumbersome leather suitcase, which was anyhow almost empty. I believe I was guilty of saying: 'I told you so'! Anyway, an agency is sending it back from here direct to Wymering Mansions. As they did not know the weight of it when we made the arrangements, it will have to be paid for on delivery – so will you once more be an angel, and settle for it, and I will

refund on my return? It should arrive alright before the end of
this month.

It is true that one gets accustomed with remarkable speed
to this marriage business. Nevertheless I cannot get rid of my
impression of it as an interlude – an intermezzo – an experience
set apart, and quite unconnected with the real business and
the fundamental importance of life. Gordon merely remarks
that if he had been le bon Dieu, he would have found a way of
showing affection that was both prettier and kinder. Personally I
am beginning to find a queer fascination in it, but I still cannot
understand why for this cause wars have been fought, and great
houses wrecked, and great purposes betrayed. Frankly, I don't
think passion or lust or whatever you call this particular aspect
of love is *in* it with ambition for power. Much as I love my
husband, I would not sacrifice one successful article for a night
of physical relationship. I find words quite inadequate to describe
my impressions. What surprises me more than anything is the
way in which its more disgusting aspects produce as nothing
else in the world for me at least has ever done, an instantaneous
indifference to disgust. One simply does not mind. And another
surprising thing is the amazing physical effect upon one,
combined with an almost complete absence of psychological
effect. In spite of a sex relationship now complete, I no more
feel married than I did a week ago – and yet I look prettier than
I have ever known myself, and feel more physically fit than I
have ever been since my school days. As for Gordon, the change
in him is so remarkable and so immense in five days that I tell
him it is a good thing we have gone abroad, as otherwise people
would be making obscene remarks. A queer world, my dear! I
look forward to getting to La Grave and plunging into my novel.
Meanwhile I still have the persistent feeling that my beloved
husband is a mere accessory and that you, not he, belong to the
real essentials of my life. Write soon, dear heart, and write often.

Through it all I am enjoying myself immensely. Gordon has
become at the moment more bewitched than devout – a sudden
descent from the Virgin Mary to the Venusberg! And in all
circumstances it is quite impossible to quarrel with him!

My love, Dearest heart, Your V.S.V.D.L.

VERA TO WINIFRED

Hotel Tegethoff, Vienna | 4 July 1925

Darling sweet,

At last your most welcome letters have come. We all seem to
have put upon you dreadfully; someday, somehow, I will try to
make up for it. I like your description of the wedding: anything
too finished and complete would have been unreal. My own
impressions were even more fleeting and dream-like; they gather
chiefly round that contrast during the service between my own
surprisingly unmoved self-possession, and Gordon's condition
of an emotion so speechless that he could scarcely make the
responses at all. I wish I knew what it was to feel like that about
a person. Perhaps in the old days I may have felt something like
that about Roland, but that was almost a child's emotion and
anyway it is too long ago to remember clearly and reliably.

Sweetieheart, I miss you quite badly, daily and hourly; I
wonder what you make of that? A man's devotion, however
ardent, is singularly inept and unintelligent compared with a
woman's; it appears to know neither when to begin nor when
to stop, though such knowledge can, I suppose, only come by
practice. And anyway for this I should blame, not him, but my
own inability to love either with his abandon or his continuity
of affection. Apart from physical love – which in my case
is much less vigorous than I thought and much more easily

satisfied – I am sure beyond doubt that I love you best, and that your companionship is more adequate. But life brought me to a strange pass in which you alone were not enough; yet this by no means implies that *he* alone is enough. He is not. Consequently I need you more than ever, and the ideal life which this world never quite gives, seems to me that in which I come into daily contact with *both* him and you. You supply everything that he lacks; he supplies what you lack in the formation of me, because where you tend to spare my strength, he makes demands upon it, and demands upon my understanding such as you, being less complex and more completely en rapport with me, never need to make. Which is excellent for me.

If you asked my advice – which of course you would not; one can judge only for one's self on these matters – as to whether to marry yourself, my advice (after a week of marriage!) to you, would be, on the whole, I think, *not* to marry. That does not mean that I regret my own, except in so far as at times one regrets anything whatever that one has done. But even for me a little physical satisfaction goes such a very long way that probably for you one occasion would go as far as you ever needed – which would make you in this direction an even more unsatisfactory wife than I feel myself to be! Our complete relationship of last Wednesday evening, queerly and intensely attractive as it was at the time, has left us in a state of perpetual flight from any more for the present, coupled with attacks of conscience because my husband makes such a flight all too easy, asking nothing, but waiting only to be given just what I choose and no more. You, I think – unless you happen to find a man whom for other than physical reasons you love more than you have loved me (which without compliment to myself I think unlikely, simply because a clever woman has all the sensitive intelligence of a man and so much else besides) – would find that a week of marriage would last you all your life!

Does this seem a rather sinister letter? It is not so intended;
it is part of long soliloquy which I have been having by myself
all this week, and which endeavours to do as much justice
to the disadvantages as to the advantages of a situation.
Somehow you must endeavour to see my husband, and not
only me, before we go to America. A long talk between you
and him would probably be far more helpful to him after a few
weeks of marriage than it ever was before. Don't let this letter
depress you. It simply means that I am too old in experience,
too critical, and too analytical to be 'eblouie' by any given
situation. Meanwhile I look forward to an ideal life, perhaps not
more than a year or two ahead, in which you and he play an
equal part. You may marry yourself, but I venture to say – the
likenesses between us justifying me in so saying – that even if
you do, you will continue to feel the same persistent need for my
companionship and my understanding, as I now feel for yours.

Keep this letter, for in five weeks' time – or when I see you
again; when is it? – I shall probably have many comments to
add which will make it more intelligible. At present I am feeling
my slow way through a fog to a light ahead, which at present
is too vague and dim to provide more than the minimum of
illumination.

All love, my sweetieheart, your v.s.v.d.l.

WINIFRED TO VERA

117 Wymering Mansions, Elgin Avenue,
London W9 | 7 July 1925

My very dear,

Your letter of July 4th, saying that mine have reached
you – and other things, no, my dear, not, I think, a sinister

letter in any way. Nor one which surprises me, except in that
it confirms my idea of you – and of myself – more than I had
thought to be confirmed. For it seems to me that the truth
lies in this queer immunity to magic which you and I possess.
We were so made that our eyes remain open, even when our
nerves and our bodies and even our hearts may be momentarily
enchanted. That is why I can't join a political party, or
a church or a lover, except perhaps after most deliberate
weighing of the pros and cons, and then perhaps with infinite
regrets. I think, in spite of what you say, that I might one day
marry, simply because detachment is negative and contacts,
experiences and so forth, the stuff of life. I believe that life is
intended to be corporate as well as individual – only I think
with you that marriage is probably no more enchanting than
any other great emotion – religion, the early days of the War.
I used to be somewhat enchanted by religion. It is an ecstasy:
a thing which in itself captures and contains the universe.
Gordon now has an ecstasy over you. You haven't over him.
I think that the reason why you and I may always be able to
love, to rest in one another, is because neither of us can be, or
expects to be, carried away by an experience of love. We have
the same personal measure to bring to the relationship. *Les
Désenchantées?* Yes. Perhaps.

And I do not know that I expected anything different. I
only wondered if there was a compelling magic here. I am
neither glad nor sorry that there is not, nor do I think that
your remaining open-eyed should spoil your marriage. I still am
glad of it.

For one thing, here is something which has come off – in
spite of circumstance and time and accident.

Then it is an enriching rather than an impoverishing
thing at least. I do not mean that it is all the things that the
sentimental nor even the sincerely entranced say of it, but it is

experience, completion. And without it there would have been regrets always that one had not known.

Then Gordon. My dear, do you remember how clumsy I was at first, how maddening in my slowness of mind, my insistence that I was right in my limitations? You must measure Gordon not by me now, whom five years of close contact have shaped into something which fits in with your personality, but with me after one year of knowing you at Oxford.

And then, of course, here I am. And, if I ever should marry, which is improbable but possible, here I always shall be. And the ideal life will probably be, as you say, when you return to England and we are both here, Gordon and I. I don't think that close contact will really mean personal rivalry.

Well, it comes to this, I suppose, as it always did. That for you and me there is no complete satisfaction this side death – only a search, a gathering of experience, a demand for service. We cannot blind our eyes to imperfection – no, not for the least fraction of an hour. And I am glad that it is so.

Meanwhile, I hope that you enjoy your tour. And your brilliant, englamoured, loveable husband whom I love more than I thought I could love a young man of his – or indeed any type (an odd confession to a wife on honeymoon. Odd and true as yours to me.)

Of course I shall keep your letter. I keep them all. And when you return, oh, my dear love – I send you my love.

Draw all happiness and pleasure that may be drawn from this. It is good. And the rest may be added onto you.

My dear love, v.s.v.d.l. W.

VERA TO WINIFRED

Albergo Roma, Vicenza | 14 July 1925

Darling girl,

My dear, in my opinion a honeymoon (at least a honeymoon abroad) exists in order to provide a married couple with all possible disillusionments in the minimum of time, to avoid disappointment later. When you have seen each other at your tiredest, dirtiest, untidiest, most hot, most hurried, and most bug-bitten, what disillusion remains? It seems to me that if (as is the case), after all that, you retain a large degree of regard for each other, there must be some hope for your marriage. Daphne at least is amply avenged for *The Dark Tide*, for if I have not been bitten on my face, I have been bitten everywhere else, while Gordon has gone scot free! I have found nowhere, not even Trieste or Venice, too hot, but ye gods, the animals! There were fleas in Buda, bugs in Jugo-Slavia, God knows what of a poisonous variety that bit me yet further in the train, and here and in Venice, mosquitoes. Or rather, it is truer to say that in Venice there were few mosquitoes and a very adequate net, whereas here there are millions of mosquitoes and no nets at all. At least none in the *single* rooms! and I was so badly bitten last night that I have actually been reduced to consenting to share a double room with Gordon for the remaining two nights here in order to acquire a mosquito net! Mon Dieu – and Gordon suggests I should write a book about a honeymoon. Well, perhaps I may; we have had between us a rather brilliant idea about one, of the 'letters from England' type – a mixture of philosophising about marriage, local description, and international (or rather national) politics. Incidentally, I can now add a perfectly good lecture on Jugo-Slavia to my collection. Well, tomorrow we spend a quiet day here for which

I breathe a sigh of relief. The strange thing is that I am not
more tired than I am after such a racket; and it is not due to
what the lawyers call 'cohabitation', for there has been none of
that since the second evening in Vienna. It requires a degree of
energy of which such rapid travels deprive one. No, I must be
getting used to travelling in all weathers and circumstances.

The Plateau to-day was definitely more sinister than when
I went with you. Incidentally, you were nicer to go with than
Gordon, though he asserts that he never loved me so much as
on our return from it – mainly I think because he had made
up his mind that I was going to cry, and I didn't! Men have no
small change, no half-way houses; they are either completely
preoccupied or ardently in love, and their love is of much too
ardent a variety to permit them to assist one in bandaging a
mosquito-bitten hand; no, no, that is a 'job', an 'interruption!'
Father naïvely remarked in a letter to me to-day that he
'hoped we liked marriage life as far as we had got' – to which
I replied that I liked married life well enough, as it seemed to
me extraordinarily much the same as being single – and that I
found Gordon a charming travelling companion, but was not
prepared to say that he was a better one than Winifred. To
return to the Plateau, it was canopied with heavy clouds, dark,
menacing, and rainy – later when we were down in the Brenta
Valley again, we saw it blotted out by clouds in a storm that
must have broken after we left. The Plateau is further from
here than from Bassano, yet the run is cheaper; I did this for
£2.10.0 instead of £5. What a climb, and what terrors of hairpin
bends, for which Gordon scorned me, not sharing my terror
and therefore not being, like you, sympathetic in both senses! I
took some red and white carnations – rather poor but the best
obtainable here, and two roses, now so much faded, from my
wedding bouquet. Thus I introduced my husband to all that
remains of my dear, dear brother, and whether the future suffers

by comparison with the past or vice versa, I am not prepared to say. But some day perhaps, my husband will help me to create another Edward, and thus perhaps the end which Nature and le bon Dieu have in view for all these strange things will be fulfilled.

Adieu, sweetheart; it grows late. Write soon and write often.

Toujours à vous – Your V.S.V.D.L.

Gordon's own remark about marriage in relation to the rest of life, is that it is 'pleasant, dangerous, and quite unimportant!'

WINIFRED TO VERA

117 Wymering Mansions, Elgin Avenue,
London W9 | 20 July 1925

My Sweet,

I love your letters. You are right about the experience. And surely with such a husband more worth while than ever.

I have been spending the weekend at St Monica's. Your aunt was very sweet, a little tired but full of vitality. She besought me again with tears in her eyes to consider the possibility of taking on the school. My dear, how could I explain to her that it is one of my intentions to remove such schools, however admirable, from England all together? I could only say 'Impossible', and be very sorry. The place looked lovely. I find you, Sweet, in all small and lovely things, in the little fishes like flames in the green water, in the furred and stupid softness of bumble-bees fat as laughter, in all the chiming radiance of warmth and light and scent in the summer garden. I love you for all small and silly things.

My darling, I do not think that I can see you before

September. I am leaving here on July 28th and going to
Bainesse. Remember this for cables, please. But you see, darling,
I must go home. Mother is not very well. I am going to take her
up to Aunt Jane's and try to keep her there a bit. She has been
wrestling with the heat, her work, and Edith. Edith is having
a passionate love-affair – is having it – and it's all difficult and
unsuitable, and full of heart-breaking complications. And they
want me – and I want to go to them too.

But I am looking forward so much to seeing you here, and for
our short time together. – There is indeed so much that I want
to say, to hear – everything.

Give my love to your husband.

Oh, Hilda is here intermittently. She is charming and
pleasant and has introduced me to Edith Sitwell, to my very
great delight. *Bucolic Comedies* is a work of most rare and
delicate genius, a fantastic and enriching imagination and a
very perfect and exquisite technique. But the Georgians are
damned as well as lovely. They have eschewed morality in order
to gain the potent beauties of a small, significant Hell of their
own invention. Subtle but devastatingly unhappy is their talent.

Au revoir, love of my heart. I am happy. In a way I suppose I
miss you, but that does not make me less happy. When a person
that one loves is in the world and alive and well and pleased to
be in the world, then to miss them is only a new flavour, a salt
sharpness in experience. It is when the belovéd is unhappy or
married or troubled that one misses with pain. But even pain
is perhaps not wholly undesirable. I feel of pain as Plato felt of
death. You remember in the *Apology*: 'For to fear death, sirs, is
simply to think we are wise when we are not so; it is to think
we know what we know not. No man knows whether death is
not the greatest of all goods that can come to men; and yet men
fear it as though they knew it was the greatest of all ills.'

This alone is to be feared – the closed mind, the sleeping

imagination, the death of the spirit. The death of the body is
to that, I think, a little thing. I do not know whether the spirit
survives the death of the body, but I do know that the spirit
can be killed while the body lives, and that most men walk the
world as skeletons. Their skulls are hollow, save for fibre and
sinew and gristle. Their bones are overlaid and filled within
only with that which is corruptable. And this is a hideous
thing. I believe in the communion of saints, and in the life of
the spirit. Amen.

Hilda has told me what is admirable for my soul. I have a
woolly mind. Well, well. One can card wool and spin it, and dye
it with rare colours. One can make it into ropes for strength,
and garments for warmth and carpet for beauty and elegance. I
may have a woolly mind, but it is not to be fleeced.

Sweet, what nonsense I write you. I love you.

v.s.v.d.l. w.

VERA TO WINIFRED

117 Wymering Mansions, Elgin Avenue,
London W9 | 28 July 1925

My darling sweet,

I hope you got home quite alright. I do *hate* you being
miserable. I hate it so much, that an argument with a quite
benevolent ticket collector, who told me that according to
my ticket I ought to have changed at Baker Street and not at
Paddington, all but reduced me to tears on the spot. What was
it really, my most dear? Was it the thought of going home into
the mumps, when you had hoped for complete peace and quiet?
Or your hair not pleasing you and costing so much more than
you had intended? Or that an invasion of the flat gave you more

work to do than you ever said and made you tired? Or that
Harry went off so unkindly without telling you and without
realising, after all your efforts on his behalf, that whatever it
was, you would have understood – and contrasted with this the
absurdly shameless way in which Gordon is in love with me (the
sweet selfishness of it enough to drive a third person to fury) –
or something so ridiculously impossible as that you feel yourself
no longer *the* person to me, after having been it almost since
you grew up?

Well, there is something to be said about them all (and I
expect it was a mixture of them all, wasn't it? One is seldom
miserable for any *one* reason, unless it is some especially
tremendous reason.)

Mumps, after all, don't last long and anyhow are not serious;
while a small regular amount of cooking takes less time up
than a bevy of insistent and loquacious visitors. As for your
hair, I am sorry it cost so much and if only you will allow me
to will be so pleased to pay half – as a coming home present?
And partly my fault, because I persuaded you to have it done.
As for feeling pleased with it, when you have time to arrange
it as you wish, I am sure you will like it. I was anxious about
my shingle all the way home, but now I have brushed and
combed it out it looks perfectly charming, especially as I have
discovered that by putting in two of the four little combs
I bought to set it with (which hardly show and look much
prettier than slides) I can keep it completely in order while it is
soft, and can probably remove them altogether when it stiffens
and gets used to itself.

As for Harry, I feel sure there is some explanation which
he will give you and you will be able to scold him for being
so idiotic as to think you would not understand. At least you
enabled him to keep himself respectably and live fairly happily
for a year, and to show his parents he could do it if he liked.

While Gordon – well, he is in love with me, yes; but he is far,
far more in love with the discovery that life is not a cold, grey
desert full of bitter winds, but a thing which holds sunlight
and warmth and joy, and that, even if he loses them one day,
nothing can take from him the rapture of the knowledge that
they were, after all, there. He is like a man born in a dark
forest who suddenly, after many years, discovers that there is a
golden day outside. I do not underrate myself so absurdly as to
say that almost anyone would have done, but I do say that if
half the joy is in me, the larger half is in the situation. As for
myself, if I do become complacent and even a little delirious
(as, with the utmost contempt for things and the fullest
intention to remain sane and sardonic, I am sure I sometimes
do) it is not because I feel self-satisfied in that Gordon loves
me, for love is only one of the satisfactory things that may
befall one, and to fulfil the least of one's ends means infinitely
more, but it is the sheer astonishment and wonderment to find
a love that is warm flesh and blood and caressing hands and
brilliant shining eyes, instead of a few newspaper cuttings and
a grave and some faded flowers and a memory. When I say
'love' here I mean love of the sexual sort – which leads me to
say that you are quite wrong if you consider yourself any less
the person than you were before. Gordon brought along a new
set of experiences of great value, but he has very little part in
the old kind (old because they came first, not because they
are past, for they never pass) which belong to you. A relation
based on some fact of sex – whether of husband, or of parents,
or, I strongly suspect, of children, is not *necessarily* to me the
best or most interesting sort of relation. About such matters I
am quite unprejudiced, and though Gordon has come to play
so important a part, and deeply as he interests me, and much
as I love him, I think I speak the truth when I say that a world
with Gordon, but without you, would be much more lonely

than a world without Gordon but with you. I mean this as much as I meant it when I once said that if I had been given the choice whether to keep Roland or Edward, I would have kept Edward. And then I can never forget that you were *my* conquest – I sought you out and won you – whereas Gordon is merely the person who conquered me! I am sorry if I *have* after all been complacent, but the essence of it is not in being loved at all, but in the joyous surprise that the real end for which I married Gordon appears to have come off for, as you know, I accepted him last year, not because I loved him so very much, but because he touched my pity and wrung my heart more than anyone I had ever met, and I wanted him to have a little happiness and a little warmth, if only I could give it. Our joys, unlike our sorrows, are short-lived and none can say how long each one shall endure – but what he in his abyss of pessimism and defensiveness needed was not so much an enduring joy as the knowledge that joy existed, and that some men and women at least *wanted* to be good. And such knowledge has come to him at least as much through you as through me. He read most of the letters you wrote me abroad – they all touched and delighted him.

Be happy, my sweetieheart; I can only repeat G's naïve remark to me, and say that you give so much happiness to other people that you surely must receive something in return. There are the Harrys, of course, but then we are not all Harrys; some of us are – not better – but luckier.

Au revoir, darling girl; I write again very, very soon.

My love and all greetings to your family.

Ever your V.S.V.D.L.

WINIFRED TO VERA

Bainesse, Cottingham, East Yorkshire | 29 July 1925

Darling little sweet,

How horrid of me to make you unhappy by being cross. And how humble and sweet you are in your reasoning.

Dear Love, all your reasons but one were wrong – Harry, I think – and the few hours of what was a very real suspense until I heard that he was safely in existence – perhaps tired me more than I knew. You see, with people like him, I always dread the ultimate despair and destruction. But today even that is past, with a really charming letter from him – all apologies and thanks and full of happiness. He says 'You know how a moose gets its head up after a sultry night when it smells dawn – well, that is how I feel now.' Curious how, though I do not love nor respect as lovers love, I yet feel my personality so strangely linked to him. I do not particularly want to see him, and in his company I am a little bored. But the thought of disaster to him oppresses me beyond words, and for the three days since the Friday when he should have telephoned me, till the time when I went seeking him in a sort of comic nightmare from Leicester Square to Peckham and back to the Air Ministry, I was more terrified than my sane senses let me realise.

All the rest, I think, was the pains of the enceinte. I wanted to write. I have for two or three months been heavy with notions. But today I have written undisturbed all morning, and I have the evening before me, and am completely happy, and fearfully apologetic for making so much fuss over nothing.

Darling, I do love you. But you are quite, quite wrong if you think that either you or Gordon are complacent, or that I find your happiness painful. Why, my dear love, what matters is that happiness – the golden day – should exist in the world – not much to whom it comes. For all of us it is so transitory a thing, how could one not draw joy from its arrival? I have known no greater pleasure – complete and soothing – (not like the wild dark joy of literary composition, which is more painful than agreeable) – no greater pleasure than in the knowledge that you and Gordon might be happy. This is not a sort of altruistic benevolence. It is a necessity. I can't enjoy my own pleasures so well if my beloveds are not enjoying theirs – and positively, I can warm myself very comfortably at their fires. I like to be with you both – you give me exquisite joy. I never knew anyone who could make me giggle as Gordon can. They are chuckles of pure content without a backward thought. And as for you, my heart, do you not realise that I don't care twopence whereabout in the scale of your loves I come, provided that you love me enough to let me love you, and that you are happy? I don't want you to tell me whereabouts I come, to define and weigh and analyse – because a) one can't do it; b) I don't care. I simply don't care. I love you in a way that part of me has become part of you. When you are troubled, so must I be, whether I like it or not. When you are happy, part of me is happy, whatever else befalls. Only be happy, my sweet. Fulfil yourself, as you must with joys and pains and enriched experience. I who am part of you, can only gain by your gains. This you must and shall believe. I do not want a shadow of doubt to cross your mind about this – for it would be a false doubt.

For myself, I have one of my own peculiar little private joys today – flowers in profusion, a lime tree outside my window, a broad, clear table, and a ream of new paper.

Darling sweet, I love you. I also think that your husband is very nice. Give him my love. Of course he may read any of my letters that interest him sufficiently.

My sweet my pretty, I kiss your clear head. W.

VERA TO WINIFRED

117 Wymering Mansions, Elgin Avenue,
London W9 | 31 July 1925

Darling girl,

I was so glad to get your letter. I hardly like to say that I
was pleased to hear that it was *only* Harry, as that sounds like
underestimating things, but at least I am glad that since it
was Harry, it was nothing more. But you should have told me
more about how worried you were. As it was, I had no reason
to suppose that his forgetfulness about Sunday was any more
than his frequent forgetfulness about coming to lunch and
never letting us know. You *should* have said. Things like that
don't worry other people in the way that they worry you, while
talking about them is a relief. It is exactly like the troubles I
used to have over my family; you could sympathise over them
without worrying, because whatever happened they could
scarcely be *your* troubles. You don't say what explanation he
gave for treating you so shabbily. The fact that he likes what
he is doing and feels cheerful over it, is scarcely an adequate
recompense for his failure to explain.

The flat really does look charming, and Gordon gets more
and more pleased with it and its working atmosphere day by day.

Of course I don't show my husband all your letters. He sees
some and gets occasional extracts from others!

All love, dear sweetieheart, your v.s.v.d.l.

VERA TO WINIFRED

117 Wymering Mansions, Elgin Avenue,
London W9 | 15 August 1925

My darling girl,

I have just written to Andrew Dakers to ask if he will deal
with the honeymoon book, and Gordon has written to Dutton's
in U.S.A. to ask if they would like to see what we now call
'Herakles, or Certain Commandments Reconsidered'. I have
told Andrew Dakers that you will always act on my behalf if he
wants to consult someone when I am in U.S.A. My articles are
having no luck. I have not heard from the Weekly Westminster.

Gordon and I had a long discussion the other night about
future plans. We will tell you in more detail when you come.
Briefly, he has definitely decided to finish his two years at
Cornell, but that he wants a political rather than an academic
life. If anything rather good in England in the academic way
should turn up during those two years he will take it, but in any
case he will not remain in America longer than June 1927.

As for myself, I want if possible to stand as a candidate in
1928; whether as Liberal or Labour I don't much care. It rather
depends on the state of parties then. I am not interested in
parties, but in feminism and peace, and I will throw my weight
on to either party which seems mostly likely to work for either
or both of those things effectively. (A really dying party,
however meritorious in itself, cannot effect one's ends, but time
alone can show whether the Liberal party will really die or not.)

As for a family it is of course manageable as soon as we return
to England where an income of £800 a year will not be half
spent on journeys and the deficiencies of American civilisation.
As I want to make myself conspicuously political in 1928 (and
even if I could not get adopted, this could still be done over the

1928 elections, by speaking, etc.) I mustn't have a baby then. We both think that, if nature proves accommodating, the best time would be the late summer of 1927 – August or September or even July, by which time one would hope to be settled in some place in London where one could stay.

Well, all plans of course are subject to the Almighty, but it is a great relief to have some clear idea as to what one means to do, and it is, I expect, of some use to you also. We really have decided things as far as they can be decided; it was not just a vague discussion. On the strength of such a definitely limited stay in U.S.A. Gordon cabled getting rid of the bungalow, and also to friends about rooms; and we have had a reply saying that rooms are at our disposal which are in part of another person's very nice house, and which G. says are both charming and comfortable. It is a great relief as I shall not have to take out half so much luggage; also expenses are cut down a good deal.

Best love, my sweetheart, Your V.S.V.D.L.

VERA TO WINIFRED

117 Oak Avenue, Ithaca,
New York | 24 September 1925

My Sweetieheart,

The crossing was even worse than I had imagined. Owing to the strike the boat was sailing with all inexperienced firemen, and on the day that we had the storm, and the 80-mile-an-hour gale, they all went sick, and struck work – and the Captain, so my informant says, was quite put to to know what to do to get the boat out of danger, and had to appeal to the engineers and the crew to do the stoking! Don't tell the family this! Especially as it is not a circumstance which is likely to arise again. At any

rate we *did* arrive all right, but it was a dreadful day, and my
head is still dizzy at intervals from the swinging of the boat –
though I feel better already for the pure clear air here and the
wonderful cleanliness of everything. We put in a somewhat
dismal Sunday at Montreal, as it was cold and raining and there
was nothing whatever to do that could be done in comfort.

We left by train in the evening; we arrived here about
midday. 'Here' is not so much lodgings as a small flat, called in
America an 'apartment'. More than anything it reminds me of
our top flat at 58 Doughty Street; it is the whole top floor of a
three-storey house (built, like most American houses, of timber,
not brick or stone) shut away from the rest by a glass-fronted
door which in England would have a Yale key, but which in
America is left, like all front doors, unlocked. The three rooms,
however, are about the same size, and much better furnished
(with big desks and large armchairs) than Doughty St. There is
no kitchen, but a much better bathroom, with lavatory, basin,
bath, and unlimited hot water; also a marble-topped cupboard
with a grill where I can make tea.

The place is lovely, up hill and down dale; the University is
on the steep hill (like our rooms, which are in the University
area) built on either side of a deep gorge; and the town is in
the long valley, with the lake at one end; and town and gorge
and University are full of immense drooping trees with dark
trunks – maples and poplars and limes – just beginning to
turn yellow in the brilliant September sunshine. Tonight we
stood on the campus and looked down to the town; lazy smoke
curving blue against the dark hills up to a sky of pure turquoise
and orange. I suppose it is the nearest American equivalent to
Buxton, but much, much lovelier; the shopping capacity of the
town is about the same. Americans are amazingly kind; one
lady – of the Ithaca élite – met us in her car and took us out
to lunch, and afterwards sent in an enormous basket of fruit,

biscuits, and sweets; another and her husband sent in a box of exquisite pink roses, and then in the evening the girl who found us these rooms took us out to dinner in her car. Two people called this afternoon, and I am going out to lunch tomorrow.

These are only crude impressions, as I have been unpacking for two days and have scarcely been about at all. To sum it all up, the place is beautiful and so healthy that it is bound to do me good; I think I shall enjoy it immensely for a short time, but I could not do with it indefinitely; it would be too much like a return to Buxton. I don't know what will happen about lectures; I *may* get some, but the distance from any big town is a disadvantage.

Well, I do miss you, my sweetieheart; I wish you were here seeing all this. Why is it that the companionship of even the most charming man is so much less adequate than that of a woman? It is queer, marriage satisfies me physically and temperamentally, but intellectually (only this?) and socially it leaves me a little lonely and unsatisfied. In other words I want Gordon at night, but you during the day!

I am straight at last and hope to begin work again tomorrow. Much love, my dear heart – more later. Ever your v.s.v.d.l.

VERA TO WINIFRED

117 Oak Avenue, Ithaca, New
York | 28 September 1925

My darling sweetieheart,

This place grows on one in some ways and is tedious in others. The little 'apartment' is now straight and is extremely easy to keep in order, with its polished floors and its large, few pieces of furniture. It was all done this morning by 9.30. Gordon helps like a Trojan, assists me with the bed, and does the floors with a mop and the rugs with a carpet sweeper, while I tidy the bathroom and dust! We have each made a study of our bedrooms, as the sitting room, which looks north, is the least pleasant to work in, and is very useful to keep tidy in order to receive visitors. One gets plenty of exercise. Apart from going out to meals (to a restaurant which is near, warm, and friendly, and has quick service and good food), the town is at the bottom of a steep hill, about twenty minutes distant, and if one has no other excuse for exercise one can walk down into it for lunch or supper for a change.

The people, however, who are beginning to call thick and fast, are really rather boring; from this I except one or two of Gordon's men colleagues. The women, though, are pretty deadly; they all talk local gossip or about each other; that part of it is just like Buxton. One can of course pick up various useful bits about America from them if one can only switch them off each other on to even their households. A little elderly lady, Mrs Williams, who has a large house and a charming daughter, is giving an 'At Home' for me next Saturday. She has the appearance and all the notions of Queen Victoria, and is the 'grande dame' of them; nevertheless she seems quite to have taken to me, and to think I have almost thrown myself away upon my beloved Gordon because he is only an Assistant and not a full Professor! It is all very amusing, and, especially if I can write in these beautifully quiet and pleasant rooms, will quite provide me with experience for nine months; I am glad, however, that I am not faced with the prospect of it always. Gordon is a dear, and not only appears not to mind if I do not come over the whole of next year, but says I need not come next year at all if I find that my work demands my staying in London. I may quite well take advantage of this, especially as he is very tired of America, and says he will not stay after next academic year, whatever he comes back to. At any rate I think you can count on having me for most of the autumn.

Meanwhile it is important that Gordon should if possible get his book on Politics out before the election; he has done almost all the first draft of it, and with luck and comparative peace should finish it by next April. I am at present finishing the first draft of 'Herakles', and when that is done we shall leave the revision till later, as G. does not want it to come out before his big book as it might give the impression that he only meant to publish small popular studies instead of more serious works. When the first draft is done I shall start in on the 'honeymoon' book. I am leaving articles for the present, but after various experiences I have quite an amusing one in mind on 'Married Women's Names'. I wonder if *Time and Tide* would like one on this; if you get the chance you might inquire tactfully. It is not topical, so could be sent in any time.

No more now, my sweetheart, as I have my dress to change, some distant calls to return, and then several more notes to write. How goes the flat? I hope you have found a pleasant lodger.

Au Revoir. All love. Your V.S.V.D.L.

VERA TO WINIFRED

117 Oak Avenue, Ithaca, New York | *1 October 1925*

My darling girl,

It seems absurd to talk of life being a rush in a small American town, especially after London, but I do not know when the days have been so full. The continual problem is how to do a reasonable amount of one's own work, and at the same time get as much out of this place as its very great possibilities permit. Start with the initial fact that there are half a dozen desirable courses of lectures going on, all within ten minutes' walk and all on subjects

that one feels one ought to know. Go on with the other fact
that almost at one's door (not an hour's journey by Tube!) is one
of the best libraries in America, full of all the things one ought
to have read, and distinguished particularly for its War library,
its law library, and its periodical room! And finish with the fact
that every person who calls on one, however dull or narrow in
themselves, *may* be the source of valuable introductions, and is
certainly a source of useful indirect information about America,
even if it is only household information. Voilà! I came here
uncertain whether to limit the number of my acquaintances and
social functions. I find that to do so involves infinite possibilities
of offence with very little saving of time – so one plunges in, and
hopes one's clothes will last the year, and that the fruit of it all
will be a novel (I have already been asked by Professor Prescott of
the English School 'Are you going to write us all up?') or at least
some useful and amusing lectures.

A lady is giving a tea for me on Saturday and another the
following Friday; this is quite unusual; it is not generally done
for newcomers and Gordon is terribly impressed by it! Yesterday
I was at an 'At Home' given by one of the 'lion' families of this
place, where also I had dinner the previous evening; I wore my
going away dress, and met everybody. The 'grande dame' of
Ithaca was there, who is giving the tea for me on Saturday, and
seemed quite disconcerted to find that I had already been taken
up the other 'lions' before she got in!

It is all enormously amusing, exactly like a little play in a
theatre, outside which is the wide world – as represented by the
lake and the mountains and the long valley with its smoke and
twinkling lights at sundown, and the blue spruce-covered hills,
and the orange and turquoise sky of twilight. These people gape
a little at the 'Miss Vera Brittain'; half reserve judgment, and
half decide to sympathise. The 'grande dame' is inviting people
'to meet Mrs G. E. G. Catlin', and the other (wife of Professor

Cushman, head of Gordon's department) 'to meet Miss Vera Brittain!'

Much love, dear sweetheart, this would be such unmitigated fun if only you were here. Gordon never will be quite the same, never quite my second self in exactly the same and dependable way.

Ever your V.S.V.D.L.

We discussed starting to have a baby this year if I remain in England next – but decided against it for the time being. Gordon, however, suffers from a perpetual terror of being quite alone again and is more anxious than he cares to admit to have a child as a guarantee against being left once more with no one to work for and be interested in. He is a being of queer complexes. The strain of his parents' quarrels and his Civil Service years rooted in him an even deeper pessimism, and fear of life and people, than I realised ever before. It comes out here in a perpetual fear that something will go wrong with his personal circumstances, and that this will paralyse his ability to work. He really is extraordinarily like Barbellion – only with a slight disease of the mind instead of a disease of the body.

WINIFRED TO VERA

117 Wymering Mansions, Elgin Avenue,
London W9 | Monday [5 October 1925]

My dearest Heart,

Your first letter from Ithaca came, my heart. I rang up your mother and she had got hers too. We were both very pleased with our posts this morning.

I am glad that Ithaca is lovely and the people are kind. It will be an experience – useful if not permanent. I think that South Africa will be very much the same from all accounts. These things are good for a time. Certainly I think it bad to spend too much time in London. One must keep the provincial life in mind, because the majority of people in the world are provincial and it is with the provincial mind that one has to deal. London gives one a false sense of the intelligence of the world.

Lady Rhondda has asked me to spend the weekend at Stonepits on the 30th. She and Mrs Archdale are being quite charming to me. I really think that it is niceness, because they know that I miss you.

And so I do – and don't. I cannot describe it. I am, as I said, very, very happy, but it's a sort of autumn empty happiness. I miss the feel of your small fingers round my left arm when I walk out through the evening streets, and the lamps are golden flowers among the sycamore trees. But I enjoy the trees and the lamps and London and Bond Street shops and the theatre and my work no less. Besides – we will soon meet again, if the gods are kind – most sweet of women, most small and dear. Only be happy and well.

Au revoir, my sweet life, my dear heart, my very small, very dear love. I kiss your pretty fingers tip by tip, and wish you all the fortune in the world.

Winifred

VERA TO WINIFRED

117 Oak Avenue, Ithaca, New York | *11 October 1925*

My darling girl,

If you can carry on for this year I do not suppose that I shall ever have to leave you by yourself, and do without you myself,

for so long again. Gordon and I have definitely decided that
I am not to come out here next year unless some unexpected
opportunity for me this side opens up before next June.
Everything of value about America that I need to know I can
learn in a year and another year would only be redundant. Of
course it will be devastating to part for another nine months
but as Gordon says (and the remark was quite unprompted by
me) there is no reason at all why I should come out with him
next year except pure sentiment, and neither of us can afford
to sacrifice things to pure sentiment at this juncture. He also
swears that nine months alone is no great strain on a man's
fidelity unless he is abnormal. To separate would also enable
both of us to save, and me at any rate to make more money
towards keeping the infant when it comes.

Gordon has just received 20 dollars (about 4.4.0) for his
review in the *New Republic*. I *rather* suspect it is the first money
he has ever made by writing, as *Philosophical and Pol. Sci.
Reviews* don't pay their contributors and I don't suppose that
Thomas Hobbes was lucrative. He came and dropped the cheque
on the table in front of me without a word, with such a pretty,
deprecating gesture, as though he were laying it at my feet!

We hope to go to New York for a few days next month. I
expect Gordon will go with me, as he wants to see a Statistical
Society there, and then return earlier, as I have so many more
people to see than he has.

Only a short note to-day, as I have people coming in to tea.

Au Revoir, my sweetieheart, All love from us both, Your
V.S.V.D.L.

WINIFRED TO VERA

117 Wymering Mansions, Elgin Avenue,
London W9 | 21 October 1925

My dear Beautiful,

Your letter of Oct. 11th has come, in which you say that you do not think you will go back to America next year unless something unexpected transpires. Well, we can all just wait and see. There is no need to make plans ahead. I personally like to ride loosely in the seat of circumstance and take what comes as it comes.

I am so glad about Gordon's 20 dollars. It was a witty, good review and deserved it.

I am just back from Liverpool – two meetings there, but neither very large. Mr Macdonald most interested in you and Gordon – made me retell the whole story of the engagement etc. He also let fall in the course of conversation that at different times he specially approached Webster, Philip Baker, and another Oxford don whose name unfortunately he could not remember but who comes from Exeter, to ask what they thought of *The Dark Tide*. Apparently everyone had read it and had definite opinions. Mr Macdonald loves Philip Baker, who is apparently not only a fervent quaker, but captained the last British team at the Olympic Games and created the Cambridge record for half or quarter mile – I forget which. I have had that young man's praises sung to me in a sort of antiphon to mine of Gordon. I have an idea that J. Macdonald had an undercurrent of advice to me to 'Go thou and do likewise', but unfortunately I have never been introduced to this paragon!

Friday

Yesterday I worked solidly all day at 'The Runners'. I have got to the stage of not knowing whether it is good or despicable, but it is perfectly insistent.

v.s.v.d.l. W.

VERA TO WINIFRED

117 Oak Avenue, Ithaca, New York | *25 October 1925*

My darling sweetieheart,

I have been feeling indignant to-day; this faculty suffers from a pronounced under-current of anti-feminism, which comes, as one would expect, from the older professors plus all the more stupid wives, who are capable of nothing but domesticity themselves, and don't want to see anyone else capable of something different. North-Oxfordism at its worst, I imagine. Gradually the under-current creeps to the surface as people get to know one a little better. Yesterday at a tea a woman – the one 'advanced' feminist here – told me that the one sure way to be unpopular in this place was to be interested in intellectual things; anything but bridge and gossip is called 'highbrow'. (Oh joy! if only one can become unpopular so easily and be left alone – un-telephoned to, uncalled-upon – what a relief! Seems too good to be true!)

A typical example of the kind of spirit that is rife here (not, however, among the younger members much) is the so-called History Club. This institution falls between two stools; it is neither a good research club nor a good social institution. It is open to faculty members of the History and analogous (e.g. Pol. Sci.) Departments, graduate students in those departments, and, by courtesy, *wives*! The other evening (I was not present; I have not yet attended this club) a meeting took place at the house of a certain Miss Hull, an elderly, very conservative lady whose brother is a Professor here. I was told this last night at dinner by Mrs Preserved Smith, a very cultured woman who has done a good deal of reviewing of history books, and is only incidentally the wife of Professor Preserved Smith, the historian. Someone read a paper, and when it was over Miss Hull approached Mrs P. Smith and said to her and the other woman: 'Now we'll go into the next room; the men want to talk about the things that really interest them,' and shepherded Mrs P. Smith indiscriminately along with other 'wives' into another room, and then began 'Have you been playing any bridge lately, Mrs P. S.?' The point is, if I had been there, what should I have done? Gordon says: 'Be damned to the club – it's so little, so unimportant. Don't trouble your heart about it. Don't go.' And yet, is it so little? Is not this one of the occasions when the general is mirrored in the particular? Shall I stay away? But if so, I merely appear to come in to the general conservative opinion here that women ought to 'keep out' of 'intellectual' pursuits. (The trouble of course with this particular club is that it ought to be elected on a basis of qualification – in which case Mrs P. Smith and I would belong as historians, not as 'wives', and mere wives wouldn't belong at all – or it ought to be a social club to which, if women are invited, they remain as they would at any party.) But if I go, and the same thing happens again, what should one do? Should one, out of courtesy to the hostess, consent to be shepherded without protest? Does one sacrifice principles to courtesy? Surely not – when did any would-be reformer? Then should one say 'No, I won't go. I have a History degree and have been lecturing in History these four years; if I have not quite the same title to membership as the Faculty, at least I have a far better title than the graduate students.' Or

does the diplomat compromise by smiling sweetly and saying:
'Oh, thank you – I really only came to hear the paper and join
the discussion; if I am not to have any more of it, I must be
getting along home'?

Tell me, O wise young sage, what does the good feminist do
on this occasion?

I laugh often – for this place is divided between those who
refuse to call me anything but Mrs Catlin though I repeatedly
sign my letters to them 'Vera Brittain', and those who without
really approving call me 'Miss Brittain' on every possible
occasion because they have a vague notion that it is 'smart',
'advanced', or somehow or other 'the thing' – I only give you
such a full account of the History Club because it is typical
of the atmosphere of this university (and, I suspect, of North
Oxford and many others). No wonder so many University
women become extreme feminists.

Gordon says that one person has no right by marriage to
impose an unsuitable social environment upon another, and
that I must not return here next year. Certainly I doubt whether
there is much to be gained from this place tho' of course there
is a great deal to be learnt in the wider America outside it. But
here I could, I think, produce nothing more than another *Not
Without Honour*, and I don't really want to repeat that. But you
and I might come here for *part* of the year, and travel about
a good bit.

Well, sweetieheart, at the moment I can no more. Yesterday
nearly finished me off – an engagement for breakfast, another
for lunch, horse show in the afternoon, an 'At Home' 4 to 6,
a dinner party 7 to 10, then treated to tea and toast by two
Commonwealth scholars at a restaurant. Eheu! I must cut all
engagements henceforth with a drastic hand. For a month,
in order that an English woman may not appear to come
to America full of prejudices and swollen with a superiority

complex, I have bowed and scraped and eaten their teas and uttered pleasant phrases. Henceforth I cease to bow and scrape, and when asked the universal question 'How do you like Ithaca?' instead of uttering amiable platitudes about the scenery and the weather, I shall begin to give my real opinion of its people!

Much love, dear heart, Your V.S.V.D.L.

VERA TO WINIFRED

117 Oak Avenue, Ithaca, New York | *6 November 1925*

My darling one,

Gordon still follows me round like a dog, and likes always to be in the same room with me whatever I am doing, even if it is typewriting on the noisiest of tables! Not that we see as much of each other as this sounds, for we are both out continually, and separately. But he is getting much less rigid and less serious, and his sense of humour is developing enormously. He tells me I 'corrupt' him, but the process is excellent for him. *Shall* I leave him all next year, I wonder? Part, perhaps; the rest depends on opportunities here, which seem likely to develop gradually; things move slowly in this great country.

We are arranging to return on June 12th (D.V.!) either on the *Leviathan* (U.S. Lines) or the *Homeric* (White Star), according to which gives the best 2nd class berths for the money. Both are huge and quick boats; both arrive at S'hampton on June 18th. And you? Try to be back by end of June, as we shall probably travel in August; shall certainly go to the Hague and Geneva. Why not suggest to the Six Point Group that I speak at one of their summer Monday meetings on the Problem of Married Women in America, or American Women's Societies or something.

I really must stop and go early to bed before to-morrow night's journey.

Much love, sweetieheart, and thank you so much for being nice to my family. They do so appreciate it.

Your V.S.V.D.L.

VERA TO WINIFRED

New York | 9 November 1925

My darling girl,

Behold me in New York! Gordon has been here for the week-end, but returned this evening by the night-train. It is a queer feeling to be alone in the largest hotel in the largest city in the world – a city like no other city, full of terrestrial monstrosities, which at night appears like the grim ghoulish worlds imagined in some of the novels of H. G. Wells.

Well, I must stop and get to bed in this comfortable room with its own bath and lavatory, limitless soap and towels, telephone, writing desk, note-paper and electric lamps – one big one on the ceiling, and little ones on the dressing table, the desk, and the head of my bed! American standards of comfort demand these things even in the 'inexpensive rooms' – which however are 4.50 dollars a night (=18/6) without food at all!

Wish you were here; I miss Gordon whom I have just seen off by the night train. It sounds too terribly trite to say that marriage with him gets better and better every day; I can only say that it is so because he identifies himself with my work, and my interest, and all my thoughts, as well as with my love of frivolous things; he has just left me ten dollars to buy for my Christmas present (if I can find them here) two tiny jewelled

combs to wear when I wear evening dress in the place where
I always wear combs! In fact it seems amazing that the world
can hold *two* persons of such understanding as you and he.
Oh, if you were but here too, sweetieheart, in New York and
everywhere.

    your v.s.v.d.l.

WINIFRED TO VERA

10 Oakwood Court, London W14 | 19 November 1925

My dear Love,

    Dear love, I enjoyed immensely your letter from New York.
You are so small that I hope you did not lose yourself in that
large city. I should hate to think of Mrs Catlin returning
distracted to Ithaca having mislaid Vera Brittain in 24th
Street East 7590 – or was it 396th South Street 4994? These
arithmetical directions would undoubtedly undo me. My dear,
I cannot come to New York until it rechristens its streets. I
cannot! Away with mathematics! Certainly I should stay away
from the solemn meeting, because I should have sought it
in 745 Street instead of 475 Street. What a barbarous age of
materialism must that be in which men call their habitations
by numbers, like stocks and shares or prison convicts. Myself, I
have never been able to associate numbers with godliness. They
stand for me among the devices of the evil one. I cannot think
of any goodly thing which needs a number, save the Cherubim
who had six wings, and they kindly separated these into
couples. No, in my heaven, there shall be no more numbers.

    Eh well, my own, I love you. 'My dear love! my dear love!' –
Also my very small and very dear love. W.

VERA TO WINIFRED

117 Oak Avenue, Ithaca, New
York | 29 November 1925

Darling heart,

Your lovely letter has come about the numbers of New York streets (which gives me an idea for an article on the subject). It really is a *lovely* letter.

I have just been reading a *T. and T.* article which I am sure is yours on 'Arbitration'. They have taken my article on 'America and the Marriage Problem' but alas! as a leader, so I don't propagand my name. In a day or two I will send you the one on 'Married Women's Names', and I hope they will be induced to sign *that*!

Letters like your last make me miss you more than ever. One of the few things Gordon has never understood – I suppose, in the nature of things, he could not understand – is how much I love you. One could hardly expect one's husband to understand the queer link that makes me able to give a freer devotion of the mind where there is no sexual connotation – just as I loved Edward better than Roland, though I didn't know it until I found, when they were both dead, that I missed him more. He gives delight to a side of me which is biologically beyond you – yet somehow to the rest of me you give more than he; we share more secrets, as it were. He hasn't your love for silly things, and he never says 'Tell me some more!' He is a most stimulating companion, yet it never does me as much good to discuss my books with him as with you, for instead of letting me tell him what I want to put and then commenting, he starts off by telling me what he thinks I ought to put! Much of it is good and useful, but it doesn't help me to develop my ideas in the same way. In all things political he is of course absolutely sound.

VERA TO WINIFRED

117 Oak Avenue, Ithaca, New York | 27 December 1925

Darling sweetieheart,

I will try one more letter to England and then I will send to the first address you gave me in S. Africa. If this is the last letter you get before you sail, you know how much you have all my love and wishes for a good voyage on those vile winter seas.

Do take care of yourself, sweetieheart; never doubt how much you are to me, and that no one in the world can ever take your place. The only person who could possibly have meant the same to me would have been a sister whom I loved as I loved Edward, and that I can never now acquire. As for a daughter, it would take at least 25 years from now before I could be as fond of her as I am of you!

Ever and ever your V.S.V.D.L.

PART II

1926–1930

Semi-Detached Marriage

INTRODUCTION

On 14 January 1926, Winifred sailed from London to Cape Town, travelling first class but fascinated by the third-class passengers, including doctors from Rhodesia, emigrants from eastern Europe and single women. She was also delighted by the dolphins and sharks she could see from the deck, the magenta houses, flame-coloured flowers, straw hats and pink biscuits at Tenerife and other tropical ports. Her vivacious, funny letters, illustrated with sketches and cartoons, displayed her *joie de vivre* and ability to adapt.

She landed in Cape Town on 9 February, and from then until mid-June lectured on the League of Nations in Kimberley, Durban, Pretoria, Bloemfontein and Johannesburg. Wherever she went, she easily made new acquaintances and friends, whether black, white, male, female, Boer, Indian or Jewish. Enamoured by the climate, landscape, exoticism, natural beauty and drama of South Africa, she also rapidly grasped the problems of the different political groups, social classes and races. As Vera was a born feminist, Winifred was a born anti-racist. By the time she left South Africa she had become dedicated to fighting the oppression of the black population. The issues of racism would engage her for the rest of her life.

In sharp contrast, Vera came to hate Cornell, and her new role as a faculty wife, an antipathy that would extend to everything American. Increasingly, Ithaca reminded her of Buxton, but colder, and she associated winter, small towns and influenza with marriage. Inevitably her resentment of the icy weather, the remote university and the intrusive society turned into resentment of Gordon, too busy with his own writing and professional status to give her the time and encouragement she needed. She poured out her grievances to Winifred, and in February described a 'queer dream about going back to live with you for a long time'. During her time in Ithaca, the word 'queer' came up several times in her letters – not to connote lesbianism, but to indicate her struggle to define her feelings about Winifred.

In March, to her relief, Gordon was granted a five-month leave of absence from Cornell to take up a research appointment in New York. In their cramped apartment, she laboriously retyped her honeymoon book with two fingers, and also typed and edited Gordon's manuscript. His book would be published by Knopf, and secure his academic reputation in the US, but her writing career had stalled. Both British and American publishers rejected the honeymoon book, and her efforts to establish a career as a journalist in the United States failed. *Time and Tide* turned down her application to cover the Geneva Conference of the League of Nations that autumn. Meanwhile, Winifred was planning a new novel, *The Land of Green Ginger*; writing and placing articles about her experiences in South Africa; and thinking of taking a trip to China to visit a new friend, the novelist Stella Benson.

The competition for literary success, always difficult for them to admit and address, was exacerbated by the differences in their social status, contentment and general optimism. Vera was sure that marriage hadn't changed *her*, but she thought South Africa had changed Winifred, whose letters were less intimate, and somewhat impersonal. Had Winifred moved ahead of her professionally? Would she have to compete for Winifred's friendship? The dimly glimpsed possibility that she needed Winifred more than Winifred needed her sent her into a panic. Much as Vera detested Ithaca, she was afraid of what she might find when she came back to London.

By the summer of 1926, Vera had begun to express her anxiety that Winifred was withdrawing, that indeed she might not want to share their flat again. With long gaps between their letters – some could take two months to get from Ithaca to Cape Town – their communication slackened. As Vera became more insecure, Winifred either missed the hints or responded with her customary brisk good cheer, which Vera took as indifference or coldness. She thought that Winifred was departing from South Africa in late May, instead of late June, and therefore began sending her letters to Yorkshire to await Winifred's return.

When Winifred got back to England in July and read the pile of letters, she was flooded with emotion, and in a great outpouring of ardent feeling she wrote the most passionate and intimate letters of the entire correspondence. A relieved Vera began to cheer up about returning to London, and to set out her ideas about the inevitable unhappiness of traditional marriage. Winifred pointed out it might be true that marriage in general was an unhappy state, but so was being single.

On 13 August, Vera landed at Southampton alone, having persuaded Gordon that she would spend autumn and winter in London to work, and rejoin him the following spring. Winifred met her in an emotional reunion, and in September they went together to Geneva for the League of Nations meeting. By the end of the month they had returned to the flat in Maida Vale. All autumn they were together, so there are no letters. They were both moving forward with their journalistic careers. Winifred had accepted Lady Rhondda's July invitation to become a director of *Time and Tide*, and would become one of its most important and productive writers. Vera went back to journalism with renewed energy, getting articles accepted by the *Manchester Guardian*, *Foreign Affairs* and the *Nation and Athenaeum* among others.

But Gordon was miserable. In theory he had consented to Vera's demand that she had to spend most of the year in London, where she could do her own work. But he was horribly lonely, and wanted her to come back immediately. They argued all autumn, as Vera realised that Gordon really wanted a conventional married life and a devoted wife who put him first. She felt that she was fighting not only for her own independence but for the freedom of wives in general. In a poem she sent him in November she declared:

> *Meek wifehood is not part of my profession;*
> *I am your friend, but never your possession.*

Eighteen months later, in an article for the *Evening News*, she would outline her full argument for 'semi-detached marriage', an agreement between husband and wife to live apart when necessary for the wife's career. 'Our grandparents,' she wrote, 'were wont to boast that they had been married for thirty years and had never spent so much as one night under different roofs.' But 'under such circumstances marriage soon becomes a bondage, with mutual jealousy for chains'. Instead, Vera envisioned regular separations and intermittent reunions. (Children would stay in the care of their mother.) She conceded that semi-detached marriage might not be appealing to many men, but she believed that 'more advanced' men would be willing to sacrifice their comfort because they were aware of the costs to women of giving up their professions. She did not, however, suggest that there should be a third person in the marriage.

Long before the article was published, Vera knew that Gordon was not sufficiently advanced to accept living across the ocean from her for six months of the year. In December 1926, he had told her that he was on the brink of a nervous breakdown and insisted that she rejoin him at once. She was horrified at the prospect of going back to dreary Ithaca, and appalled by his emotional fragility, for 'to carry a weak man on my back for the rest of my days was no part of my scheme of life'. She threatened a formal separation. At this dire juncture, Winifred stepped in, cabling Gordon's doctor for more information about his condition, and calming him down with affectionate flattery about his importance to Vera. With her mediation, Vera and Gordon reached an agreement: she would join him at the beginning of April.

Saved from a collapse of her marriage, Vera wrote Gordon a loving and conciliatory letter; she had been 'stupid not to realize how ill you were; I have not understood; forgive me, and pardon my bitter letters. For you are the greatest joy of my life.' And there was an advantage to joining Gordon in Ithaca: she was nearly thirty-three, and time to start a family was running out. They could use the reunion to 'produce a baby at Christmas time' and 'prove that work and maternity' could co-exist. If their semi-detached marriage could be seen to work and if she could also have a child, they would be an example to the world that motherhood could successfully be combined with a career.

On 28 March 1927 Vera left for America, accompanied by her mother. Winifred saw them off, having promised to take care of Vera's father Arthur Brittain, and Gordon's father, the Reverend Catlin, while they were away. On 1 May, right on schedule, Vera realised she was pregnant. Winifred was quietly ecstatic at the opportunity to be really useful, while Vera felt more and more convinced that maternity should not be an obstacle to women's public and political work. Yet when *The Land of Green Ginger* was accepted by Cape that spring, she felt the old pangs of envy. She too must quickly write another novel, and pregnancy was turning out to be more of an obstacle than she had expected. At last in June, at the end of the academic year, they all returned to London. Clearly the Maida Vale flat was too small to raise a baby, so in September Vera, Gordon and Winifred moved into the two upper floors of 6 Nevern Place in Earls Court.

On 19 December, Vera gave birth prematurely, without anaesthetic, to John Edward Jocelyn Brittain Catlin. It was a difficult delivery; she stayed in the nursing home for three weeks, and then suffered from post-partum depression for several months. Gordon returned to Cornell in January, and despite various nursemaids and visits from relatives, Vera was overwhelmed. In March Winifred's sister, Grace, died after childbirth, leaving two small children, and Winifred went home to Yorkshire for several weeks. Just as she came back to London to help Vera, they were all exposed to smallpox through a charwoman, and had to be vaccinated. John Edward had a fever of 105 degrees.

At last Vera hired a capable nurse. Winifred was able to travel with friends to Paris and Monte Carlo, and Vera felt jealous. Later, she confessed that 'many times during the early part of 1928 I was moved by an unworthy envy of Winifred's success, popularity and freedom'. In 1928, war novels and memoirs were beginning to appear; Vera studied several and began to think about writing a memoir of her own. In July, as the right to vote was extended to women on the same terms as to men, she published a feminist treatise, *Women's Work in Modern England.*

But her main work was writing weekly book columns for *Time and Tide*, seventy-five in all over this period, commissioned by Winifred. The most significant was a review of Radclyffe Hall's *The Well of Loneliness*, on 12 August 1928. Vera called it 'a plea, passionate, yet admirably restrained and never offensive, for the extension of social toleration, compassion and recognition to the biologically abnormal woman, who because she possesses the tastes and instincts of a man, is too often undeservedly treated as a moral pariah'. Although calling lesbians 'biologically abnormal' women was hardly the most liberal view of the case, in November Vera was asked to testify at Radclyffe Hall's trial, one of forty witnesses summoned by the defence along with Leonard and Virginia Woolf, E. M. Forster and Vita Sackville-West.

Of course, her own living arrangement attracted a lot of attention. From the beginning, there was gossip that she and Winifred were lesbian lovers. Vera was always defensive about these rumours. 'I am a markedly heterosexual woman,' she told her friend Sybil Morrison, while in a note left in her papers, quoted by her authorised biographers, Paul Berry and Mark Bostridge, she declared that she was 'wholly a heterosexual person without an atom of homosexuality in my makeup'.

Twentieth-century scholars and biographers have disagreed about the importance of a sexual element in their relationship. In *Vera Brittain and Winifred Holtby: A Working Partnership*, Jean Kennard argued that anyone writing about an intense female friendship must raise the question of whether it was a lesbian one, although there is no evidence that Vera and Winifred ever had a physical relationship, and much that they did not. Kennard concludes, however, 'the partnership between Holtby and Brittain was one of primary intensity, whether or not one is willing to call it lesbian'. But Deborah Gorham, in her biography *Vera Brittain: A Feminist Life*, insists that the term 'lesbian' should 'be reserved for overtly erotic relationships between women'.

Today the lesbian question seems much less urgent and meaningful. Definitions of gender and sexuality are so fluid that no simple label can account for the complexity of the Brittain-Holtby bond. Neither woman, moreover, placed a lot of emphasis on sexuality. Although she was attracted to men, Vera was candid about her own lack of sexual desire: 'My predominant concern always was, and always has been, ambition.' Winifred took a more complex view. In *Women and a Changing Civilisation*, she declared we did not know 'whether the "normal" sexual relationship is homo- or bi- or heterosexual'. She described herself as asexual, and having read Freud, suggested that her sexual drive had been sublimated into work.

But Winifred had grown up feeling that she was too large and unfeminine to be desirable to men. She fetishised Vera's smallness, and there is also an erotic element in the pleasure she found in serving Vera. In a letter of 14 May 1927, she claimed that she was happiest when she could 'sit down at the feet of the people whom I best love, and look with the eyes of a handmaid towards the hand of my masters'. Stella Benson grew so angry at the one-sidedness of their friendship that she told Winifred to her face that Vera was her 'bloodsucking friend'. But Winifred was unperturbed. Perhaps, Benson noted in her diary, Winifred 'liked having her blood sucked'.

Both Vera and Winifred knew that sexuality was much more complicated than a simple binary division could encompass. They hoped that human sexuality would evolve. In February 1929, the London publisher Kegan Paul invited Vera to write a book for their series 'Today and Tomorrow'. Her contribution, *Halcyon, or the Future of Monogamy*, was a feminist allegory in the genre of Charlotte Perkins Gilman's *Herland*. She predicted that by the end of the twentieth century men would have learned how to exercise voluntary restraint of their sexual desires, and monogamy would prevail. But real life did not follow her ideals. In March 1929, Gordon told her that he was 'sexually infatuated' with a young Russian woman, and wanted to have an affair with her. Vera was shocked. She couldn't 'imagine anything that will more quickly make me feel our relationships were smirched and spoiled'. Gordon did not pursue the Russian woman, but over the next decade would begin to have discreet affairs. In his mind, the terms of 'semi-detached marriage' gave him the right to have extra-marital affairs, as long as he told Vera about them.

Their menage continued to challenge conventional expectations of marriage, but had reached a kind of equilibrium and calm. In December 1929, Vera learned that she was pregnant again, and they looked for a larger residence, inspecting seventy-six houses in Chelsea and Kensington. In April 1930, they moved to 19 Glebe Place in Chelsea, and in due course hired new staff, who would make their lives much more manageable: a couple who served as cook/housekeeper and butler/handyman for over three decades years; a German nurse for the children; and a secretary for Winifred and Vera. On 27 July 1930, Shirley Vivian Brittain Catlin, named for the 'gallant cavalier' of Charlotte Brontë's novel, was born, and Winifred insisted on being present at the birth, 'in case she ever had to describe a childbirth in a novel'.

The household arrangement worked for all of them, each in their own way. Gordon came to appreciate being semi-detached and liked the calm and unemotional tone of their home, with Winifred a buffer between husband and wife. 'How tremendously we gain,' he wrote to Vera in 1929; '... How Winifred supplies a cooler, detached element when our own relations grow too emotional and "nervy".'

He had noticed that Winifred was semi-detached as well. In an article for the *Manchester Guardian* on 26 October 1929, she wrote about the advantages of the modern maiden aunts who were connected to a family and children: 'Some of us live alone. But those who prefer family life may still enjoy it ... living with their self-chosen families, as independent equals, satisfying their natural instincts for domesticity. And are they not portents of the family as it may be? A small community of equal, independent citizens, related either by blood or by affection and common interest, living together by choice, not by necessity.'

Vera was the chief beneficiary of the arrangement. She had a large house, arranged to her specifications, servants, and in Winifred a devoted companion who understood her need for recognition, loved her children and enjoyed playing with them, and had an infinite capacity to forgive her self-centeredness. Looking back, she wrote that their time in the Chelsea house 'was the nearest thing to complete happiness that I have ever known'.

The children benefited too. Shirley Williams fondly remembered that 'for my brother and me, Winifred was the source of unending pleasure: stories, games, wild fantasies, exotic visitors and carved wooden crocodiles from South Africa, the country she had come to love after her visit there in 1926 . . . John and I loved Auntie Winifred. We were also aware how much her friendship meant to our mother. For Winifred was life-affirming, one of those blessed people who find the world a constant source of delight, excitement and laughter.'

LETTERS

1926

VERA TO WINIFRED

117 Oak Avenue, Ithaca, New York | 10 January 1926

My darling one,

   I am suffering from the usual depression which accompanies
a desire to write plus complete inability to do so. I haven't
wanted to write so much for ages. Gordon says that according
to Freudians it is not the artistic but the social devotions
which most successfully achieve the sublimination of sex, and
that is why health visitors, political workers, and 'committee
women' are so largely composed of either unmarried women
of uncertain years, or married women whose marriages are
either unhappy or uninteresting. Gordon's mother was a typical
example. I believe I knew this, but had forgotten it. Perhaps
this is why I have become so suddenly bored with my League of

Nations Union work – and perhaps it is not; through reading
the *New Leader* regularly, I am perhaps becoming a little
suspicious of the League, and a little unduly keen about the
Labour Party. Certainly the Labour Party has all my allegiance
now, without reservations; I am done with Liberals who include
Captain Henderson-Livesey and the Eighty Club and 'now won't
one of the ladies give us a little talk'.

But writing! I find it so easy and so quick to write stuff which
is good – mediocre; so difficult and so painful to write what is
just better than that. Gordon is a most valuable critic, with his
high and exacting standard of verbalism, his quickness to seize
nuances of meaning, and his immediate detection of clichés and
commonplace phrases.

Gordon wears your handkerchief as a scarf because – vanity
of vanities – he knows it brings out the blue of his eyes. The
knitted grey silk scarf that I gave him last Christmas is now
worn only on very wet or very dirty days!

We want a house in Campden Hill – like the Boswells –
not St John's Wood which is too far out and barely served by
tubes. Campden Hill would be much easier for you, too, to live
near us – there are many more rooms, and tiny flats, in that
neighbourhood. I am longing to return to England and live in
pretty surroundings, furnished by myself. The chief disadvantage
of this apartment is that, though it is warm and comfortable, it is
so ugly that no covers, pictures, woodcuts, Chinese embroideries,
or even flowers (which are almost unobtainable here) make it
look any different. The lady who owns the house is a widow; her
husband who was a schoolmaster and a recluse, seems to have
had all the say in the matter, and expressed his soul in dark olive
green wallpapers and browny-yellow ceilings! The result is that
unless you actually sit in the window (where there is always a
draught) the rest of the rooms are almost too dark to read in!

All love, my dearest, from your own V.S.V.D.L.

I have discovered – without telling him – really only Gordon didn't like *The Harp*. It is because it was about failure. He suffers from a dreadful failure complex. Seeing what a chaos both his parents made of their lives, it is scarcely surprising.

WINIFRED TO VERA

24 January 1926

Today we saw Cape Verde. (Look at your atlas, please.) Because the weather was so perfect and navigation easy, the Captain took us a mile or two out of the course to go right in to the coast.

Now I have seen Africa.

The third-class people are on the whole much more interesting than the first-class. There are doctors from Rhodesia, a woman veterinary surgeon who wears man's clothes always, French, German, Russian and Polish emigrants, some delightful young farmers, two schoolmasters, my nice Captain Collender, wives and unattached young women to match. I shall never again hesitate about going third in a Union Castle boat.

Oh, darling, I wish you could see all these lovely things and have this warmth and sunlight. I am wearing cotton frocks all day and at night your black shawl over an evening dress.

[WH lists her best friends, ending with:]

The Skipper. One night when I was watching the moonlight by myself, and he had had, I imagine, one glass of whisky too much, he made what the papers call 'improper proposals' to me – to my intense astonishment. He of all men, and I of all girls. Well, well. I suppose that I appeal always to the older ones. He said it was my figure. Now we smile and say 'How do you do', but walk no more together. A pity, because I did enjoy talking to him, and now I can only remember that he wants to stroke my legs. It seems so frightfully silly and undignified for a really fine-looking oldish man, who has travelled so much, and is a good commander. I was not angry, only astonished and emphatic.

Otherwise, as you see, I am most decorous in my friendships. There are a lot more. I know heaps of the third-class people, but apparently I am the only first-class passenger who has the free run of both decks. These people are individually charming but collectively snobs.

Jan. 26th

We are somewhere about the Equator and it is glorious – hot, soft winds, flying fish, porpoises, and long sunny days reading novels. All very agreeable.

Jan. 29th

I won the first prize at the fancy dress ball last night. I went as The Sheik – three sheets, bronze paint, a peaked beaker and some scarves. For ages no one recognised me, and as I refused to speak they thought I was a man. The chief flirt of the ship was irresistibly coy with me, and I had a wonderful time. I really looked quite handsome, though blue eyes in a dark face have a quite uncanny effect.

VERA TO WINIFRED

117 Oak Avenue, Ithaca, New York | 24 January 1926

My darling girl,

We still don't know our arrangements for next year. Gordon has sent in his formal application for the Social Science

Research Fellowship, for which applications close in about a week. If he doesn't get it, and has to put in another year here, for all but sentimental reasons he is not particularly anxious that I should come with him. He says that the last thing he wants to do by marrying me is to make me a less worth-while person, as this would be not only detrimental to me but to himself. He really does feel that I am rather mistreated here; one gets no new contacts after the first two or three months, only a repetition of the old ones, and he fears that by being marooned out here I am losing the opportunity of making social contacts which would be invaluable to us both. It is also exceedingly difficult to work here. The trouble is that in every provincial community – like Buxton, like Cottingham – there are too many women with nothing to do but kill time, who simply cannot grasp the fact that there are any women whose work is of more importance than theirs. One is bothered perpetually by social trivialities, which waste time and introduce one to no new people. Gordon suffers almost as much as I do as nearly everybody here being married, the invitations are usually à deux. I don't think he realised how much society would feel that it had, so to speak, a stake in him by the mere fact of his getting married.

If the Social Science thing – which would involve travelling and be useful – fails, I shall have to think very carefully. Even though we – you and I – lived modestly as we did before, I think a very profitable nine months could be spent in deliberately cultivating useful people. It sounds dreadfully utilitarian! but that in fact is what we have to do! The mere fact of *my* being married makes it easier to some extent to ask the people we want. Certain people – e.g. interesting and eligible creatures like Jonathan Cape – are very difficult for unmarried women below a certain age to invite to anything. By the early spring of 1927 Gordon will know whether he gets Glasgow or not – and as Glasgow only involves October till March, with the Christmas

vacation in between, the first thing to do then is to look for a
house in London with a room in which we can entertain. A
house with two rooms capable of being made into one would be
ideal, and if he got Glasgow we could afford it, as between us we
should have £1,000 a year. The ideal thing of course would be
to get it taken, furnished, and all ready before he returned from
America. We could share it till he returned, and then, if you
wouldn't stay, find you a little flat or rooms as near as possible.
But all these are chimera until we know something more.

Au revoir, dear heart. I am thinking of you as halfway
through your journey. Come back in June.

All love, dear sweetheart, Ever your V.S.V.D.L.

VERA TO WINIFRED

117 Oak Avenue, Ithaca, New York | 28 January 1928

My darling love

I am dreadfully sad to think what an age it must be before
I hear from you again; at least a month, I suppose, even if you
can write from Teneriffe or St Helena. Literally you are half a
world away.

I am very well, but we are both bored with winter, especially
Gordon, who has had three of them. One of the most trying
things is that even when it is fine, the roads and pavements
are sheets of ice, which is impossible to walk on – so that one
never gets quite enough exercise. So we sit and write! – which
is perhaps as well! But Gordon (who is pushing his Social
Research Fellowship as much as possible) definitely doesn't want
me to come out next year if he is here, as he feels it is a waste of
life for me and of opportunity for us both.

I have had another very nice letter from *Harper's* asking me really to send something else so they must have liked the article they had to send back. I shall later but I want first to get on with my honeymoon book and finish it by June.

Best love, my dear sweetheart, Always your V.S.V.D.L.

WINIFRED TO VERA

Train, Kimberley to Durban | *18 February 1926*

Darling Heart,

I know that you do not like type-written letters, but people in South Africa are so hospitable that the only time to write letters is in the train, and the trains are so energetic that hand-writing is illegible, mine at any rate. And to my joy, I have discovered that the little tables which let down over the wash basins make admirable typing tables. An empty carriage becomes an office, where one can work at leisure through the long warm journeys. The country here continues as between the Cape and Kimberley, except that the ground is not quite so parched, the grass, a curious cactus grass with long runners, replaces much of the tufted scrub, and the bushes when they appear, are greener. There are the same low, sinister hills crouching like beasts above the hot plain. The same fierce sun swoops down on the winding train, and seems to snatch with fiery winds at the wan travellers through the shutters.

But I still like the heat. My face is no redder, nor does my appetite fail, to the astonishment of my friends, who on the one hand expect me to be prostrate, and on the other, arrange for me programmes of such congested effort that if I were not in rude health I should already be dead. At Kimberley I went just to see Bridgewater. I was entertained to Jewish receptions, to British Empire dinners. (One each, to be accurate. The

plural is for euphony.) I was taken to meet Alan Cobham at
a Cabaret and danced fashionably with the élite of the town,
beautiful brown young men, who dance divinely, and do not
show the English attitude of dumb hostility towards a reputed
'clever' woman. I went to see Pavlova dance, to see an enormous
Kaffir stoking engines in the De Beer works, on an eight-hour
shift at a temperature of something like 110–120! I could only
put my head in the roaring, blazing boiler-room for about two
minutes; but his huge figure, perfectly made, outlined in black
against the glow of the furnaces, as he stooped and shovelled,
naked, rhythmic, beautiful, was one of the unforgettable and
unanticipated beauties. I went over De Beers diamond works.
I watched the yellow uncut diamonds falling over the rollers
on to a sloping table spread with vaseline, down which the
stones and garnets and crystals roll quite casually but on which
the diamonds stick. I was allowed to handle the astonishing
creatures, and was given a packet of garnets to take as a souvenir.
I have motored round Kimberley with an ultra-imperialistic lady
to whom some friends introduced me under the happy delusion
that the League of Remembrance and the League of Nations
were the same thing. She was frightfully kind, because I came
from England and had been in the army; but I ate her admirable
ice pudding, and lounged in her luxurious car under pretenses
so false that I blush to think of them. Her husband was one of
Rhodes' greatest friends, and certainly a very interesting man. I
never knew that Rhodes and you had just the same tempers!

Kimberley is an interesting example of the autocratic
principle in government. De Beers own the very atmosphere
breathed by the people. They control the schools, amusements,
politics, and social life of the town. The resulting inertia,
kind stupidity and mental deadness must be experienced to be
believed. The people are reputed to be, and I think must be, the
kindest in South Africa. They are also the only town of any size

that has no League of Nations Union. I got hold of the editor of
the local paper, some clergy, and a few social lights of the town,
and they have promised to form a branch if I will return to start
it – or send somebody else. I shall see what can be done.

Feb. 20th

The sound of your literary activities fills me with shame. I
can think of nothing to write. With floods of priceless copy
all round me, I am dry. I may try to do something about Mrs
Millin. That was so kind of you to suggest it. But do you know
that when I arrive at places I am confronted with type-written
slips containing time-tables of terrific congestion. Sometimes
four lectures and an at home or two per day, and the local
papers here beg me to contribute little potty propaganda
articles, which are good publicity, and good business for
the Union, which badly needs publicity here, but take time
without any more lucrative result and certainly won't add to
reputation. Here is, I believe, much like America. I smiled
over your delightful description of the evils of good fellowship.
Kindness here is so overwhelming that visitors have no time to
think. Even in train the conductors are full of information, the
passengers full of friendliness, and the first touch of real insight
I have encountered is at this house, where they have given me a
little office to work in, with a lovely big desk.

VERA TO WINIFRED

117 Oak Avenue, Ithaca, New York | *24 February 1926*

My darling girl,

I am writing to you at a most unwonted time – 11 o'clock
on Wednesday morning – because I am furious and miserable,

having just concluded, without finishing, a discussion with
Gordon on the subject of my next novel which ended in – as
the result of many such quite unprofitable discussions – an
angry and hopeless argument. It is probably not a good mood
to write in, but by this afternoon he will be again his usual
charming, disarming self, and I shall forget, or see less clearly,
the problem of isolation from fertilising contacts which must be
overcome, or at least compromised with, if ever I am to do any
good work.

The instance was simply this. You know the mood in
which one wants to grope, by means of informal discussion
at the particular moment when one is in the humour for it,
towards ideas which one is not quite certain one has or not –
moods when one wants to talk one's self into having ideas,
not simply loud quarrels who will carry a point at the finish.
Well, Gordon's response was thus: when I had put forth a few
remarks – vague, I admit – but helping me to turn my own
mind towards some dimly understood ideas, he picked up the
N.Y. *Times*, and began to read some perfectly unimportant
article about the Klu Klux Klan. I said really pointedly 'Why
can't I perhaps do occasionally what I want to do?' To which
his reply was to say: 'Don't you think we'd better reserve an
important conversation like yours to some afternoon when
we're both free,' and put up his paper again. And then he was
surprised that this form of reception put me off and stopped me
having any further ideas. He still doesn't understand why it did.
Need I say more?

I shouldn't say anything if this were an isolated instance, but
it is only one of so many. When I want to talk about my novels,
I am met with one of three forms of obstructiveness—

1. A desire to, so to speak, schedule the discussion for a
    future occasion and put it down on the time-table, and

allot, say, 1½ hours to it as if it were a class with his students. (Do you remember the time-table we once made for the honeymoon: '9.00 Breakfast 9.30 Discuss the League of Nations. 11.00 Make notes for next chapter. 1.00 Lunch. 2.00-3.30 Discuss the League of Nations again etc.') Well, all his life is rather like that; it is crowded with 'things to do' at, and by, a certain time; a sort of personal college time-table.

2. The information, rather heavily and dictatorially expressed, that if I *had* any ideas worth considering, they would be 'bubbling up', and that above it all is that nothing met his condition that they be worth his 'spending time' on.

    My remark that if they were 'bubbling up' I would simply write them down, and should not need a listener, simply meets with a blank stare of non-comprehension. And how can one explain one's needs further while one is still uncertain exactly what it is that one needs?

3. Instead of listening to what *I* say I want to do, and making comments about that, he always has (for *my* book!) an opposing scheme about what he thinks I ought to do – so that instead of letting me work out my scheme, he forces upon me an argument as to the merits of his own.

    Well, all this we foresaw last year, but now I see little chance of ever getting this sort of help from him; for one thing, he does not *want* to understand: he simply wants to 'put over' to me his own notion that the scientific and artistic method of creating a thing ought to be exactly the same!! The result is that he sees no difference between a book that is competent in method and a book that is great in conception;

between, for instance, my honeymoon book, which
is largely a skillful interweaving of comments,
observations, and descriptions, and the really great
novel that I want to write before I die.

Now all this has a practical conclusion; because the help
I cannot get from him, I must therefore still have from you,
as I have always had it ever since I knew you. You are more
necessary to me than he is, because you further my work,
whereas he merely makes me, for most of the time, happy;
happy about everything except the one thing that matters most.
He is useful over articles, and a good critic of a finished piece
of work; but in the vital period of 'working out' he is of no use,
because fundamentally, his mind is scientific and analytic, not
imaginative.

He still derides imagination – 'that intuition nonsense!' I
suppose, if ever I am old enough to look back upon it, I shall
perceive a marriage with Gordon to be but one more instance of
my long hesitation between literature (real literature as distinct
from political journalism) and politics. The more we talk, eat,
and breathe politics, the more acutely do I desire to be a really
good novelist. Novels, as you know, are my real mainspring; if I
turn in the end mainly to politics, it will be as a second chance,
as a faute de mieux.

The one thing of which I am becoming more certain is
where I want to do well – and here I need you badly, both in
the vacation and perhaps later. I had a queer dream last night
about going back to live with you for a long time – and with
such a sense of relief. Fortunately, my honeymoon book (which
is mainly a matter of competence and for which Gordon's
limited power of criticism is quite adequate) will occupy me till
that vacation; then I want long discussions with you.

Do let us arrange to go down to Devonshire or Cornwall

together in August and spend most of the time without
Gordon who, if he is there, will only engage you in perpetual
philosophical discussions instead of allowing you to have
any time with me. I want to reciprocate at the same time.
(This letter is egotistical, but my intentions are not so purely
egotistical as they sound!) by reading your first draft of Wycliffe,
and hearing, if you will discuss them with me, your ideas of how
to alter it. I daren't think how much I look forward to some long
days alone with you.

This letter probably sounds more depressed than the occasion
seems to warrant. Seeing how thoroughly obtuse most men are,
the average person would say I was exceedingly lucky to have
married Gordon, with his sensitiveness and his high standards
of both conduct and achievement. So I am, if I really needed to
marry at all. And misunderstanding from a person with whom
one has most things in common is so much more painful and
infuriating than misunderstanding from someone (like say,
father!) from whom one expects nothing in any case. My love,
you have spoilt me (as my aunt foresaw) for the companionship
of anyone else. Truly there is no one like you in the world.

Best love, my Darling – my one certainty in this strange
existence of experiment and mistakes.

Always your V.S.V.D.L.

WINIFRED TO VERA

*355 Musgrave Road, Berea,
Durban | 26 February 1926*

My darling,

Your literary activities sound tremendous, and I from my
barren wanderings, sigh. I have not even the energy to keep up

my diary properly. After giving five lectures a day in different parts of the town to totally different audiences, writing numbers of the business letters inseparable from a tour where everyone alters arrangements at least twice, I have no vitality left even to write proper letters.

I am meeting Gandhi's son Manilal, tomorrow. Today I interviewed Champion, the extraordinarily dignified, efficient and moderate Zulu Trades Union Secretary. I was present at the Natal Indian Congress, and stood up to pray (as a Parsee, Mohamedan, Hindoo and Christian) for wisdom and enlightenment to be bestowed upon the South African government. An interesting occasion to see four thousand 'heathen', praying that a Christian government may see light. And I have broadcast, which is simply a business of sitting down at a table and reading a paper for quarter of an hour. I have a thousand things to tell you, and all, I feel sure, interesting; but I must go to bed. I am so sleepy that the words won't come. Indians, natives and Europeans dance through my mind in a sleepy mist. If you were here I could talk till next Christmas.

Sweet heart, I love you and love you. I am very well and happy and having a time full of astonishing interest.

My dearest love v.s.v.d.l. W.

VERA TO WINIFRED

117 Oak Avenue, Ithaca, New York | 28 February 1926

My darling girl,

I am feeling so much better since I wrote my last letter. The day after I wrote to you I got so angry with Gordon that I scolded him until he retired to bed and wept! He has

been perfectly charming ever since. So have I. It is a dreadful
temptation to 'treat him rough', because he is always so very
nice afterwards.

I am feeling quite excited because yesterday and to-day I had
a great inspiration for what will, I think, be my next novel –
partly because I can write it very quickly and without having
to look up anything except my own letters and diaries: partly
because it depends largely on scenes and events of which my own
recollection fades more and more as the years go by; partly because
it is, far more than *The Dark Tide*, the good-selling type – and
I do want to produce a good seller, as soon as possible, because
once you have done that you are freed from the endeavour to be
profitable to your publisher, and can write what you like.

Gordon says that my title 'The Incidental Adam' ought to
be a fortune in itself. The enclosed simple scheme (which will
probably be the secret scheme that I shall put in the book) will
tell you more about it than volumes of explanation. Of course
it will be dreadfully autobiographical as usual (from the very
names that I have given to the people, apart from their dates,
you will probably be at once able to fit them on to the right
originals) but in Gordon's opinion I do autobiographical work so
much better than any other that he is probably right that it will
be safer to keep to it for the next book or two until I am ready
to experiment with 'The Springing Thorn'. Of course it could
also be a very cheap Sadducee woman-with-seven-husbands sort
of book, but on the other hand it could be made a fine book
too; everything depends on the impressionistic treatment of
a very historically important decade. It should be interesting
because each chapter – which will be long and divided into
sections, gives you 1) a different period of a girl's development;
2) the psychological portrait of a different man; 3) a different
chronological period of contemporary history; 4) a different
social and local background. A woman's development through,

roughly, a decade, shown by means of vignette sketches of her contacts with different men, who are only incidental to what she believes to be her chief purposes in life.

Best love, my dear sweetie heart, Ever your V.S.V.D.L.

WINIFRED TO VERA

c/o Mrs Lewis, 26 Lock Avenue, Parktown
West, Johannesburg | 8 March 1926

Darling Heart,

It seems so long since I wrote to you. I seem to have done so many things since. Durban, Maritzburg, Ladysmith, Johannesburg, Pretoria, and now Johannesburg again. I have driven into the heart of a gold sunset towards Spion Kop among the battlefields of Ladysmith. I have wrestled in spirit with eight fat ladies of the Johannesburg rich at a Country Club. I have seen Jean McWilliam again and very happily smoothed away the irritations of our correspondence last year. I have met timid secretaries, complacent women's societies, active and excited schools, individuals of a hundred stories and types. A little strange journalist sent to interview me poured out instead the tale of her divorce from a husband whom she still loved. If I had time, time, time, I could write down notes for a hundred novels or articles, but my days pass in a whirl of more or less useless activity. I shall have much to say about the utility and non-utility of lecture tours when I return. Here in this town organisation is buried beneath social snobbery.

The Nationalist Party may be outrageously selfish and crude in its conception of native policy. But the South African Party which now so bitterly condemns it enjoyed five years in office of almost unbroken inaction. Labour here is simply a white workers' protection agency, with all the autocracy of Trades Unionism and little of its compensating security. Labour, afraid of unequal competition, allied with a Nationalist Party imbued with the Dutch notion of the serf-native, makes an unholy combination. Africa is being panicked into what now appears the most ghastly blunder. Some people say that a native rising would be the only thing to shock people awake to the true situation. I don't believe that good can come from violence. I talked to Champion, the Zulu Trades Union leader, and told him of the early history of the English Trades Unions, begging for patience. He is reasonable, courteous, patient beyond description; but he has upon him the burden of millions of men, still uneducated, brought into contact on the very worst possible lines with western civilisation, taught the crudest elements of Communism with a dash of militant Bolshevism, and then abandoned to find their own salvation.

Later.

Oh my love, the insects! Moths as huge as bats, or so they seem to me. One invaded my room last night. I chased it with newspapers, but could not slay it. Its powdery wings prevented me.

I love you so. I love you. I want to have you here in the sun. My love to Gordon and best luck to his book. It sounds good. I want to read it.

v.s.v.d.l. W.

VERA TO WINIFRED

277 Park Avenue, New York | *8 March 1926*

My sweetieheart,

Since Wednesday I have been here in New York staying with

the Chards, and dashing about in the absurd way that one does when one lives in the country and comes up to a city for a few days. I remember I used to do the same thing in London when we lived in Buxton ... Mon Dieu, why is Ithaca in all respects so much like Buxton, and why do I feel that I am repeating in another country the experience of a dozen years ago, and that I have to fight to get Gordon and myself away from it now, just as I had to fight to get away from it then?

Well, I have given my lecture to a select little circle at the Cosmopolitan Club, and have been to three theatres, one of them a good performance of *Hedda Gabler*, except that the Hedda was too old, and overacted somewhat. Finally I ended up by getting a slight attack of what is known in this country as 'grippe' – aches, pains, a temperature, and a slight cough. So instead of returning on Saturday as I meant to do, the Chards, who are most charming people and kindness itself, persuaded me to stay over the week-end and spend Sunday in bed. So I did, and probably shall not return to Ithaca till Wednesday to be on the safe side, though I am up again to-day and much better. Poor Gordon is, I fear, a little restive, and would have come racing up to New York (350 miles and £5 return!) if I hadn't stopped him late last night on the telephone by telling him that really nothing serious was wrong.

I shall surely hear from you soon; it is nearly five weeks since you landed. I do look forward to getting your letters again. It is really very good for Gordon to be without me for a week. Last night on the phone he said 'Oh, when *do* you think you can come back!'

Au revoir, darling girl, Ever your V.S.V.D.L. V.

VERA TO WINIFRED

117 Oak Avenue, Ithaca, New York | *13 March 1926*

My own darling sweetieheart,

I have just had your first two letters from S. Africa – the one written on the *Grantully Castle* after Teneriffe, and then the first one written from Cape Town. It was sent on Feb. 11th and arrived here on March 11th, so after all the letters do not take so long – only a month instead of the six weeks that I expected. It is so lovely to be in touch with you again. Your programme sounds so gorgeous and exciting. Your description of the voyage excited me beyond words.

I am going to keep all the letters you write from Africa and bring them back with me, because you really ought to write a book of African sketches, or at any rate a series of articles – and you may not always have time to keep a very full diary.

But sometimes I get such a fright lest you come back quite different. (I wonder, do you ever get that same feeling about me? That a year of marriage will have changed me in a way that two months hadn't time to do? Never believe it.) I am so afraid that your lovely time in Africa, the adventure, the widening of the world, may quite change you towards me. I think I could bear better that anyone – even Gordon – should change towards me, than that you should. I have always believed in you so absolutely – been so sure of you for so long.

Come back safe and well, sweetieheart.

Always your v.s.v.d.l.

WINIFRED TO VERA

In the train to Pretoria | 15 March 1926

My dearest little one,

I have had a funny week. Last night was most terrifying. I have
rarely been more diffident and more alarmed. I had to talk to a
small drawing room meeting of about twenty distinguished South
Africans. I had not to make a speech, but to extract from them
opinions on the League. I have got out a sort of memorandum
about S. African attitudes and shall be able to make some kind
of report at the end of the tour. Last night helped me, but I felt
stupid and impotent, partly the result of a bad cold in my head,
and I still feel as though I had wasted an opportunity. I have
helped myself. I don't think I did much good for the League.

I had one extraordinary experience one night. I was whisked
off in a car about 9.30 p.m. to an address supposed to be
unknown, but which I managed to observe and remember,
and was there interviewed by a masked and disguised group of
five men, the chief executive of a semi-secret society organised
against the Jews. It is a sort of Klu Klux Klan. They wear black
and white robes and masks right over their faces. They told
me that their numbers run into over 5 figures and that among
those present were members of parliament and people whose
names would make me jump. The effect was rather spoilt by the
bourgeois little sitting-room in which we met, with embroidered
table mats and dyed grass in a vase. Also by the dilemma of
Honourable Brethren 13 and 4, when they tried through their
inadequate mouth holes to drink the tea, brought in at about
eleven o'clock. It is fearfully difficult to drink tea through a Klu
Klux Klan headdress!

I was not frightfully impressed by anything except the
childishness and possible peril of it all. Anti-Semitism horrifies

me, especially after what we learned in Hungary. They talked
for ages and then asked me to give my impressions of them. I
told them pretty much what I thought, but it was difficult at
that short notice to express anything except a vague distrust
of the whole movement, so since then I have been preparing a
statement which they have promised to read. It is done now –
and I was quite outspoken, I think. But I do find little patience
with these semi-lawless, semi-secret organisations for the purpose
of fanning all too easily aroused prejudice. South Africa probably
is on the eve of a big crisis – but it will be a colour crisis, and
for Gentiles and Jews to be thwacking at one another just now
seems to me to be the height of irresponsibility.

Yesterday I saw Clements Kadalie, the leader of the Zulu
Bolshevists. He works in the I.C.U. office, a queer mixture of
self-respect and squalor is the office. I have copies of his paper,
The Workers' Herald, all sorts of documentary stuff that will
interest you. This colour question is rather fierce just now.

At the Bantu Social Centre I was speaking about the
League last night to natives and had shrewder questions than
in any former audience. They understand the constitution of
the Mandate System, but have hitherto failed to perceive its
advantages. I can hardly accuse them of blindness!

Much love always, vsvdl. W.

VERA TO WINIFRED

117 Oak Avenue, Ithaca, New York | 28 March 1926

You are wrong to envy my literary activities, for though I am
in the last chapter of my honeymoon book I am *very* much
dissatisfied with it.

I suppose my own two chief triumphs have been *The Dark*

Tide with its little sensation, and Gordon – who from the point of view of the average person is, I suppose, a triumph indeed; there are so few happy marriages. Yet I suppose no two things ever made me more thoroughly upset. *The Dark Tide* worried me so much I never had any time to be pleased about it; as for Gordon, I still alternate between being in raptures over his sweetness and intelligence and unselfish patience, and wishing to goodness I had never met him, and linked my competent, efficient plans with the adventures of someone else.

I am in a perturbed state of mind at the moment. I don't know if I told you in my last that Gordon was going up to New York for the week-end for an interview with the Committee (of professors, govt. officials, etc.) who are arranging a big investigation into the whole question of the effects, success or failure, etc., of Prohibition – an immense social investigation all over U.S. They were interested in Gordon and got into touch with him through one of the Professors here because of (a) his experience of very similar types of investigation on the Liquor Control Board during the War; (b) he is also an Englishman and therefore impartial; (c) he is a social scientist, yet not head of a Department, so is able to leave it conveniently.

He rang me up from N. Y. last night to say that they have offered him the job of preliminary investigation to prepare for the big investigation which begins on September 5th. If he accepts, it means that we have to clear off immediately, this week, and go either to New York or Washington where G. will be in charge of a small office with two or three stenographers, etc. He is considering whether to accept (subject to the permission of Cornell, which I think would be quite easy to get owing to the prestige of the job) and we shall discuss the matter when he returns late this evening. It is an important piece of work, and they have offered him 2,000 dollars (£420) for the 5 months, which is 2/3 of his present annual salary, or £220 more than he would get by finishing the year here, and all expenses, travelling etc. except actual board and lodging. He would have to write a preliminary report which would be published with his name, but of course the disadvantages are that he couldn't get over to England this summer (unless he cld just run over to see his father for ten days in Sept. between the ending of the job and the beginning of the autumn term here) and his father would nearly have a fit.

Now what about me? We are both of course agreed that I must spend several months in Eng. some time soon on account of my work (and also his English contacts.) I don't think it is fair to leave him for more than the 6 winter months and I don't want to, but he is quite ready to spare me for that on account of work.

Sometimes I wish Gordon had never turned up at all to involve me in such complications – but it seems foolish to wish that when he is so sweet, and has made me so happy, and has taught me what I never believed – that it is possible for a young man to be as considerate, and patient, and tender, and full of gratitude for the least sign of real love, as any nice woman.

And I suppose that when one has children the claims are a dozen times more conflicting still!

Well, I suppose that this is all experience, and these are the responsibilities that marriage means, and that understanding them from the inside makes one a completer human being. But oh! how simple life *was* when I was just an intelligent, independent female with only my own plans to consider! Mon Dieu, why can't one love one person at a time, instead of being always in a perpetual ache because somebody or other isn't there!

Don't get blown up in thunderstorms, sweetieheart – and don't *please* get overtired and ill.

All my best and dearest love, Ever your own, V.S.V.D.L.

WINIFRED TO VERA

High School for Girls, Pretoria | *5 April 1926*

My darling,

Your letter of February 24th – about writing. Of course it is possible that Gordon may never be able to 'talk out' novels very well – not being a novelist. Seeing that he has almost every other quality desirable in your husband, it would be unreasonable to expect this too, and possibly to the analytic mind, 'talking out' is not a legitimate form of composition. But fortunately, from my memory of your work, it is not a long process with you. There is no reason why we should not have as you suggest a holiday in Cornwall or Devon or somewhere and 'talk out'. I should love it. I want to discuss my play too. Wycliffe is vieux jeu. Then you may be ready for writing if you decide to go back for the autumn to America. I suppose it depends partly on your health. My plans are quite plastic, and wait to be moulded to a large extent this year by yours, I have written to see if I can get a passage on May 25th from Cape Town and should be back only a few days after you. Any plan you want to make, make it. I am leaving myself as free as I can to fit in. I must, of course, see my family as soon as possible. They have been having a wretched time, what with one thing and another; but I shall certainly manage three weeks convalescence with you unless some unforeseen accident occurs. And Geneva, if you are well enough. It would be fun. And if you do decide to spend the autumn in England, then perhaps I'll go out to America with you after Christmas and take that route to China.

I love you so much. Take care of yourself, and of Gordon, and come home safely.

v.s.v.d.l. W.

VERA TO WINIFRED

Westminster Hotel, 420 West 116th
Street, New York | 11 April 1926

My sweetieheart,

I am all alone this week-end. We had only been here 24
hours before Gordon was telegraphed for to go at once to
Madison, Wisconsin (1,000 miles from here – London to
Moscow!) for a Conference to-day on the Prohibition question
with Professor Merriam of Chicago, the head of the National
Social Research Council. I was not at all happy about it, as the
poor child was still struggling with the remains of a very bad
cold, and was thoroughly tired out with packing and removing.
Moreover, after we had both spent a hectic 24 hours in trying
to find an office and a secretary (Gordon interviewing about
20 of them one after the other in one room while I answered
their applications on the telephone in the other!) and had
practically engaged the latter, the telegram instructed him to
make no commitments on office or secretary until he had seen
the Nat. Soc. Research Council! These University Professors
are just like that, authorising you to do a thing one moment
and then wanting to alter it the next; they have no more idea of
business than a flea. He sent me a telegram from Chicago this
morning saying 'All well', so I hope he slept the previous night
on the train and is not too tired. I suppose he will leave again
to-morrow and be back there about Tuesday.

Meanwhile I have nothing to do, having no books, no M.S.,
no papers, and only the clothes I stand up in! Gordon is going
to wire me from Madison to say whether to unpack or not. It
is annoying to be able to do nothing when as soon as we begin
there will be such a tremendous press of work on hand.

When Gordon goes away I miss him so much that I begin to

wonder whether work is really my own mainspring. The world
is glorious with both him and you in it, and with either him or
you, life could be very happy (as it always was with you before I
had him) but without either of you, though I suppose I should
go on with my work faute de mieux as I did in 1919, I doubt
very much whether I should really care whether it succeeded
or not. Being away from you and sometimes from him makes
me understand why he wanted to marry me so badly; however
valuable the work may be, one lacks the necessary incentive
to carry it through if no one understands it or cares how one
does it. He looks so pathetic when he is tired that I don't know
how I shall tear myself away from him for six months, but he
says it is the fact of *having* me, rather than the fact of always
being with me, that makes his work worth while to him – and
for my part I have begun to think last fortnight that, it won't
be at all a bad thing to have a quiet winter in London, and
get some of my *own* writing and lecturing done! If two people
are both actively occupied, it is impossible for each to avoid
being occasionally swept into the whirlpool of the other; the
only way to avoid it is to separate the whirlpools occasionally.
Also I want to get out of the academic atmosphere for a time.
Professorial society is an excellent intellectual tonic for a time;
it raises one's standard of mental exertion and exactitude, but
after a time it is a little oppressive to be always with people
who think that no work is worth while unless it is associated
with a university appointment of some kind, and no book
worth writing unless it contributes a meticulous iota to the sum
of human knowledge.

Au revoir, my sweetieheart, Ever your V.S.V.D.L.

WINIFRED TO VERA

55 King Edward Road, Bloemfontein | 20 April 1926

My little Heart,

I feel that you have had very scrappy letters, and that I owe you a much better one this week. My apology for it lies in my programme. I have given eleven lectures in the past three days, interviewed innumerable people, attended two tea parties, and sat up till one and two, after an all-night journey. Bloemfontein is strenuous. But I am immensely well, and this is almost the most interesting of the South African towns. It is the heart of the Dutch element, and here the strong Nationalist feeling is most prominent. Here are men who openly hate the English. The principal of the University Senate declared *me* to be imperialist British, because in the course of a speech about disarmament and security I had not mentioned the 'menace of the British navy'. The intensity of the political feeling has to be experienced to be imagined.

Later

Since I wrote this I have given four lectures! I am going round the big schools and colleges, and this morning have spoken in a Dutch medium school for boys, in very slow English, remembering that it was a foreign tongue. I have to go in ten minutes to meet a certain Dr Dryer, president of the senate of Grey University College, an ardent Nationalist, who is to be my chief opponent at a debate which I am most incautiously holding at the Town Hall. Having promised to speak there, I am overwhelmed by the rashness of my venture. Here Nationalism = anti-League, and anti-contact with any outside states. The thing that amazes me most is the fact that the Africanders hate the Hollanders as much as, if not more than, they dislike the English. By the way, they never say 'a Dutchman' but 'a Hollander' when mentioning an inhabitant of the Netherlands. Here comes my scout. Au revoir again.

Next day

You see how I write. This was interrupted last night by a conversation which lasted until 3.30 a.m., in which I heard domestic revelations of the stress of life on an isolated farm community enough to fill a novel – but one alas, which I can never write without greater certainty of background. It embraced passion, tuberculosis, suicidal mania, neurasthenia, lack of sanitary accommodation and stifled creative desire (artistic, not pro-creative, though this exists too.) 'The healthy, sane life of God's out-of-doors.' Poppycock. This was true enough.

My dear, I love you, my very small very dear love. Winifred

WINIFRED TO VERA

*Oriel House, Rhodes University College,
Grahamstown | 26 April 1926*

My darling,

I have just got your letter of March 13th, the first in answer to mine since I got here, and I feel 'linked up' again. It is so nice. My dear, you say that you sometimes fear that you will find me changed. If you saw the way that I ran to my mail and kept your letters, hardly daring to open them, between joy of hearing from you and fears that some evil should have befallen you, you would not fear.

My time in Africa is being lovely and yet very difficult in many ways. The intense political feeling of this country presses in and in upon one, belying the superficial cheerfulness and hospitality. I was happy at Lovedale, because I was at rest. In spite of the strangeness of a mission station and 700 native students, I felt, 'These are my friends. Here I can speak as I really feel.' Which was curious. All the same, the missionaries here do seem to fit in with one's own conception of life better than anywhere else. But I have come to dread that approach of a hostess: 'Oh, do let me introduce Mr —. He is *so* much wishing to talk to you.' For I know that a smiling gentleman will be led across who will forthwith proceed to tell me what I ought to think about the Dutch, or the Natives, or the Imperial question, and always expect me to agree with him. And I can't say much because being a stranger it would at once be rumoured: 'Oh yes, Miss Holtby. Only been in the country three months, and of course she think she knows *everything.*' And then they would not come to my meetings, where at least I am allowed my own opinion about the League of Nations. Up to a point, anyway. Some of the more ardent Nationalists would hardly allow me that. So that sometimes I find myself beating and beating against prejudice and ignorance unbelievable.

However, it is intensely interesting. And the experience is not all political. Staying in other people's houses is a perpetual source of surprise. I spent the whole of one night beseeching an almost complete stranger not to betray her husband and go off with a lover . . . A case where this would have meant real betrayal. She is a fine woman but I did not anticipate these very intimate personal relations.

I wish that you had had more sunshine. I feel so greedy having it all, though today my conscience is a little soothed by a cold bleak wind from the hills, a grey sky, and a huge mosquito bite on my right arm. I have not yet grown acclimatised to these creatures and I am told that there are some who always present irresistible attractions!

Au revoir, my joy and my dear v.s.v.d.l. W.

VERA TO WINIFRED

Westminster Hotel, 420 West 116th
Street, New York | 30 April 1926

My darling sweetieheart,

   My letters since we left Ithaca seem to be as scrappy and
once-a-weekly as you say that yours are. Last night I dreamt
that on our eventual return we quarrelled violently – which
must surely mean that we shall be very happy together again
next year. So Grace has a daughter and all is well! Will she
be pleased, I wonder, or did she want a boy? I imagine that
she will know much better how to manage a girl. Personally I
want to publish two more books before embarking on a family.
America – where nurse-maids and servants are prohibitive to all
but the very rich – gives me a dreadful idea of having children.
No kind of independence or freedom seems possible to any
but the well-to-do mothers; they are simply swamped by their
families, who are brought up in a sort of hullaballoo, have the
worst manners of any children I ever met in the world, and are
nothing but a trial and an anxiety to their parents as soon as
they become old enough to know their own minds.

   If you propose to return in the middle of June, I suppose it
won't be worth while my sending more than one or two letters
to Africa. Oh, sweetieheart, do meet me at Southampton – in
my mind's eye I have a picture of arriving in a big boat on a
summer day and finding you and Mother waiting for me on
the quay. Fancy not seeing you both for nearly a year! I am
looking forward to next autumn, and probably, indeed, to
next spring. I don't suppose I shall go out to Ithaca again, for
it is a complete waste of my time to be there, and certainly
not worth spending £100 and more to go there for 3 months.
Gordon does not want me to, any more than I want to, for

he knows as well as I do that love in marriage is too rare and
precious a thing to be endangered, and that nothing threatens
it so seriously as the sense of lost time and lost opportunity
due to that marriage itself. And again, nothing is so easily and
insidiously degenerated into as 'wifehood'; I find myself spoiling
him, petting him, furthering his interests much as you have
spoiled and petted me! – and while it is safe to do such things
for a friend, it is unsafe to do too much for a husband because
all the weight of tradition is there to drag a wife down to the
level of a 'helpmeet' – And, in the end, I know that what he
loves me for (in spite of his appreciation of the kind of spoiling
that he has never before had) is not what I do for him, but what
I do for myself; the more I am a person, the less I am a 'wife', the
more is my prestige, the greater my independence of him, the
more he loves me. I am keeping an article to show you from the
American *New Republic* called 'Confessions of an Ex-Feminist' –
a dreadful realistic account of the insidious ease with which a
professed feminist slipped into mere 'wifehood' – I have given
Gordon a year; I need next year with you and my own work
to redress the balance. After that, I hope, it will be possible to
have both work and him and you without any of you clashing.

Don't go as History lecturer *anywhere*. Academic life is
death to creativeness and enterprise; birth to complacency and
narrowness. I have seen so much of it this past year and I know.
Gordon knows it too. If he gets the Glasgow appointment he is
going to rent out rooms in Glasgow, and we will have a house
in London where I will live permanently and he spend all the
time that he is not teaching. The same if he goes to any other
university. The one thing for me to avoid is being a 'Faculty
wife' (as they are so flatteringly described at Cornell!)

I have so much to say to you about matrimony and other
things when we meet – not so long hence – but no time now.

Much love from Always your V S V D L

WINIFRED TO VERA

Oriel House, Rhodes University College,
Grahamstown | 2 May 1926

My dearest Heart,

I am afraid that 'The Runners' is no go. Cape has declined,
and as I imagine him – perhaps without reason – to be
interested in me, if he won't publish, I think that no one will.
Two years writing wasted, or possibly not wasted. I believe there
are some good things in it, and I may have gained experience
even if it never sees daylight. I have a vague idea for a new
novel, germinating at the back of my mind – a newish notion
for making use of any travel experiences I may have had
without moving the scene from Yorkshire. If I can borrow a
title of yours, I want to call it 'Hungarian Rhapsody'. It all takes
place at East Witton on the Wensleydale Moors, but its vitality
is to come from Hungary, Finland, South Africa, and China! It
is the love story of a woman, the daughter of a South African
missionary, taken back to Yorkshire in infancy, with a passion
for strange places. I want it to be crowded with colour and
bizarre foreign effects, yet all to take place in one very remote
district. It may be too mad.

I went to a dance last night and felt years younger; but all
my dresses are dreadfully tired after four months in suitcases.
However, my shingle looked sweet.

Oh darling, I wanted to curse over my book. But I feel better
about it now. I cheered myself up by buying a nice copy of the
Confessions of St Augustine, and going to a dance with my nice
shingle. What does one book matter, after all?

My dear love, take care of yourself, keep well. v.s.v.d.l. W.

WINIFRED TO VERA

c/o Mr Justice Benjamin, Somerset House,
Kenilworth, Cape Town | 18 May 1926

My Little Love,

Gordon's job sounds extraordinarily interesting, and the contacts that you may establish should be admirable for afterwards. And if you were to get into touch with the American papers and lectures, excellent financially, I should say. I am longing for the next mail, which will, I suppose, be forwarded here.

I am here in Cape Town with a really strenuous fortnight averaging 3–5 lectures a day – tomorrow I have *five*. But I shall live through it, and I think that it will be well worth while. I am going round to the oddest collection of societies. One day I had the united clergy, headed by the Archbishop, in the synod house. They made a rather dull audience, and their questions were not on the whole over intelligent!! But they were quite nice and overcame my natural bashfulness. Yesterday I talked to the Sons of England, in a marvellous patriotic atmosphere and a hall literally festooned with Union Jacks, where I was welcomed as 'a true daughter of England from the Old Country'. It seems that when South Africans are super-patriotic, they become American. On another occasion, proceeding by night up a very steep hill at the foot of the mountain, I was seized upon by a company of fifty boy scouts, who hailed me with war cries, dragged my bag for me, and escorted me making the appropriate noises of their patrol, up to the hostel where I was to speak. As the noises included bulls, bears, doves, lions, and wildebeests, the sound of my arrival must have been terrific. The only disadvantage about so full a programme is that it left no time at all for meeting interesting people, or visiting the House of Assembly, which is at present in session.

11.40 p.m. the same night

Just in from 4 lectures and a tea party. The latter of dons'
wives, all agreeable women, and mostly workers.

My host and hostess here are fervent Christian Scientists.
They are doing their best to make a convert of me. I think that
a good deal of what they say is most sensible, but I can not agree
with a sect which speaks of 'First Church of Christ, Scientist',
and talks an unutterable jargon about 'holding a right thought'
and 'the unintelligence of matter' and sings bright expurgated
Christian Science hymns. All these religions are so admirable
in many ways – and so impossible. I could join all or none. But
one is quite impossible and this one more so than most. My
hostess is also a Spanish Jewess – one of the old Spanish Jew
families that supplied physicians to the court of the Philips, and
other fine gentlemen of the fifteenth and sixteenth centuries.
She has admirable dark eyes, a penetrating voice, and a vivacity
which is apparently inexhaustible for her, but which would
exhaust me in half a day, did I not commonly leave the house at
9.30 and return at 4 p.m. But she is kind, generous, intelligent,
honest, an admirable worker and a sound feminist. And she has
given me a darling little posy of wool flowers in bright Russian
colours and she manages an invalid husband with immense
tact and courage. So that one feels churlish to protest against
her restless vivacity, which may be reaction against depression,
especially as she has been a most patient hostess.

Do take care of yourself, my little heart. I so much look
forward to August. I have arranged with your mother to go to
Southampton with her if possible to meet you. I love you so.

I have just thought of calling my new book 'The Land of
Green Ginger' after that lovely street in Hull. Don't you think it
sounds fascinating?

    v.s.v.d.l. Winifred

VERA TO WINIFRED

Westminster Hotel, 420 West 116th
Street, New York | 29 May 1926

My darling sweetieheart,

Your letters from Lovedale and Grahamstown came
yesterday; I am so glad that you had begun to have my answers
to yours and to feel 'linked up'. Your nice cable makes me feel
linked as it was still such a little time ago. And after all you
won't have to keep this letter waiting very long, as if you really
sailed on the *Beresina* on the 25th, you are already well on your
way home – in fact you have been on the sea as long as it will
take me to get more than half the way back to London. I have
booked my cabin on the *Berengaria* for Aug. 11th, and I should
arrive at Southampton on Aug. 17th. Oh, how much I do look
forward to seeing you and mother there! Now you are on your
way home, I seem to be within a reasonable distance of seeing
you again.

Gordon is away in Washington again. He never had any
complications after his measles and was quite all right when
he went; I only hope he won't catch something else! I never
can quite get over what a queer thing marrying him was – that
he should drop into one's lap, as it were, when one had never
sought him or any other man, and had ceased to expect, or even
to desire, any experience of the kind. When he is away and I
go for walks by myself in Riverside or Morningside Park (where
the lovely leaves are all golden-green unspoilt by smokeless New
York), I always think about him with a kind of light-hearted,
zestful tenderness – the feeling of having treasure in heaven. Yet
I can work just as well when he is away – he never interrupts
my work when he is here, nor draws me away from it when
he is not.

My honeymoon book is exasperating me, it needs so much revision; I drop so easily into the academic, 'leading article' jargon; find myself writing such atrocities as 'the domestic situation', 'racial improvement', 'a limited vocation for marriage', etc. etc. Good Oxford English, my dear, is the enemy of all true art. I am taking a diet of the best recently published novels to cure myself of the habit.

And all the time I am bursting to get to 'The Incidental Adam' – aching, at long last, to write about the War, all the glory and the grieving and the sacrifice and the struggle and the loss. Ah me! It is a book on which one ought to spend at least two years, and I want to finish it before I begin to have a baby! Perhaps, if one had got done the first draft, the baby wouldn't interfere too much with the revision.

Ever your own V.S.V.D.L.

VERA TO WINIFRED

Westminster Hotel, 420 West 116th
Street, New York | 4 June 1926

My darling girl,

Now about your book. I am sorry Cape has returned it, but still he speaks highly of it from every point of view but that of sales, and I see no reason whatever why you should waste two years' work. Try one or two other people first – let Dakers advise you – and then, if still no one takes it, why not subsidise it as I did *The Dark Tide*?

The other night we had here to dinner Mr C. K. Ogden, reader and editor of various series for Kegan Paul, and he gave me more insight into publishers and their methods than I have had for a long time. Ogden says he thinks it wrong that the

publisher should be able to stand between an author and his
public. Many scholars' books (e.g. the first two of H. J. Laski's)
are published on 'Foundations'; e.g. by publishers specially
endowed to produce such books – but in that case of course you
don't make a penny. Ogden said that Gordon would probably
have to pay partly for his, espec. if he wanted it out quickly.

But Ogden also knows Cape's well; he said that Cape started
excellently, but then damaged his reputation by producing a few
worthless books, and that now, though not exactly on the rocks,
he has to go carefully, and cannot afford to spend much on
advertising. Now if that is true, and I am sure Ogden knows, it
would be well worth your while to approach Cape, say you want
reputation rather than sales, and ask if, as he evidently thinks
well of the book in itself, he will be prepared to publish if you
guarantee him against loss. I have never for a moment regretted
paying for *The Dark Tide*; the incidental results of such things
are incalculable (look at Gordon, with whom a year of marriage
has been one of the most beautiful experiences I ever had!).
You did good work on your book; it is sound, Oxford will love
you for it, and it will be invaluable to students working on the
period. Why not get a few good notices and high recommends
if you can, rather than depression, disappointment and a sense
of waste? It seems to me far more worth while to spend £50 on
producing two years' work than on rushing off to China within
a few months after you return from Africa. I am not sure that
you can really afford again to be away from London so soon
and for so long. I agree with Sir John Marriott up to a point
about seeing things when you are young, but on the other hand
I think it is possible to do too much restless rushing round the
world without getting established in anything, and to come
back and find other people rooted in the places where one
wants to be. After all, once one is, for instance, an established
writer, invitations to travel and lecture come of themselves.

China won't run away if you wait till you have produced this book and written another.

Once I get permanently home I don't mean to go any more *long* trips abroad – only short expeditions of a few weeks, to the Balkans, Baltic, etc. – for about five years; not only because of babies, but because I want five years in which seriously to try to become an established writer on both sides of the Atlantic. I don't feel I have ever yet really attempted this. These last few months, when I have not had the opportunity to rush around as I did in London, I have had far more ideas, far more a sense of mastery over technique and certainty of what makes a good novel, than ever before. I don't say my honeymoon book will go; it is necessarily undramatic and has practically no story. But I feel pretty sure I can make the next novel a good one. Titles matter tremendously. Gordon says that if I had called *Not Without Honour* 'Adolescence' or even 'Growing Pains', it would have sold wildly; and indeed, if it is ever produced in America I shall probably rechristen it.

Don't be deceived by lectures. Lectures are narcotics – they bring immediate returns in congratulation, and they give one a sense of being tremendously busy and useful – but all the time they are merely vain repetitions of one another, and form a dreadfully good excuse for not facing the unpleasant, exacting, hard-thinking work of a book well done.

I don't suggest for a moment that you have acted unwisely in going to Africa; it was well to go, get a complete change, and gather fresh material while all your very excellent connections were still there. But it would have been a mistake to extend that experience too long; and it will be a still greater mistake if you dash off somewhere else before giving yourself a chance to translate your African experiences into writing.

I am longing for your return, and for your faithful reporting of 'business' both in letters and in the flesh. My angel Gordon has none of the reporter's art. The other evening the following conversation took place. He was talking to Knopf's agent about his book. I left them together after giving him precise instructions that after discussing his own book he should mention mine and ask if they were interested in that type of thing. When he came up I said:

'Did you mention my book to Mr Thomas?'

'Oh yes, we discussed it for about five minutes.'

'What did he say?'

'Oh – he seemed interested.'

'Yes, but what did he say?'

'Well . . . he put cogent questions.'

I ask you!

To-morrow I go down town to find you a birthday present, my precious, but I am afraid I shall not be able to equal your four, as New York seems to produce nothing which is not both cheaper and more plentiful in about every other part of the world.

Ever your own V.S.V.D.L.

VERA TO WINIFRED

Westminster Hotel, 420 West 116th
Street, New York | 16 June 1926

My darling girl,

Damned depressed. Not that anything of that importance has gone wrong, but a series of small rebuffs (all more or less explicable, but none the less discouraging) have almost the same effect.

To begin with, the enclosed letter from *Time and Tide* speaks for itself. I merely sent in the ordinary quite formal application; there was no other way of letting them know that I was going to

Geneva. I can quite understand that they took for granted that I was swallowed up in America, and fixed up with someone else; but why this curtness?

Gordon's explanations are:

1. Hurry.
2. The idea that I am permanently out of the running for such jobs (which means that whatever happens I must not be over here for more than a month or two next year.)

Mine are:

1. They had already arranged with you to do it again (which I still don't know) and imagined that I am trying to get it away from you while you are in Africa (as if I should if I desired!)
2. They have had enough League articles from me before and want someone else.

The trouble is that I can't get an American paper willing. This is the worst possible year to attempt such things, as it happens, because a World Conference of Journalists is taking place at Geneva at the same time as the Assembly; 600 journalists are going and of these about 300 are from America. Practically every paper of any standing in the U.S.A. is sending its own representative, who will of course do the Assembly stuff as well. It looks as if it will be almost impossible to get into an Assembly or Council meeting without a press ticket.

Then we are having a certain amount of trouble over Gordon's book – everyone who has seen it applauds its wonderful scholarship, fine literary style, etc. – but don't think it will pay them! Very probably he will not be able to produce it through an ordinary commercial publisher, but will have to have recourse to one of the institutions specially endowed to publish learned books, such as the Yale Press. After all Laski published everything of his this way before the *Grammar of Politics*, but such institutions don't advertise or pay you royalties, and it would have been nice if Gordon could have managed something else. There is of course no doubt whatever that it will be produced somehow, but the negociations are somehow the last straw when he has put three years' work into it, and I have worked on it almost night and day for two months, revising, correcting, and typing. (Don't tell anyone I did this for him. We both never intend it to happen again, but the Prohibition job coming so suddenly meant that if I did not do it, it would have to be postponed indefinitely, and his return to England partly depends on his producing it soon.) At the moment we are in negociation with Harcourt, Brace (the partner over here of Jonathan Cape). They are exceedingly pleasant and friendly, but, like Cape, are a young firm without too much capital.

Then, finally, I got a letter from Dakers saying that my contract with Grant Richards gives him the sole right to publish in all parts of the world, which means that I can't do anything about my honeymoon book over here, although I have made friendly personal contacts with several publishers. It is very annoying indeed, because my present publishing position in England is pretty hopeless.

Anyway I don't know if the honeymoon book is any good. Sometimes I think it is very bright and amusing and epigrammatic, and at other times it seems damned dull. It is hard to write bright stuff when small depressing things keep happening. Of course I finished the first draft long ago and am now revising, but that is just the time when you want to put in epigrams, and epigrams only come naturally when one is feeling

touched up. Damn this Prohibition country!!! Your lectures in
Africa, even when they are only to boy-scouts or sons of the
Empire, and allow you no time to think or meet people, at least
must be very good for you in that they keep you keyed up all
the time and full of vitality. (Do you get paid for any? If so, you
must be making a lot!) America is soaked, steeped, saturated in
lectures; and overdone, overwhelmed, indigestible with lions.
One of the Professors in charge of such arrangements at one of
the principal universities (I think Yale) said to him: 'If you sent
Lloyd George over I could perhaps just manage to fill the hall!'

I shall not send anything more to *Time and Tide* unless they
ask me. Gordon says (humiliatingly, but probably all too truly)
that I can only hope to succeed with an organisation where
there are no women on the staff. I fear that may be true; men
seem to know these things. He says I am prettier than ever, and
that people turn round to look at me in the street. If they do I
never see them, but if it is true, it is a damned nuisance, as it
seems to prejudice people against me, and make them think
me insincere. At any rate a meeting at Long Island the other
day didn't hesitate to state their disappointment (Americans
are very frank) because I didn't look older and more staid. They
said: 'We're not used to speakers who look about sixteen.'

Sometimes I am afraid to come back; I dread the autumn,
and that you'll be different after all these crowded experiences
in Africa – or that you'll go away at the last moment, and
leave me stranded in London without you or Gordon, fallen
between two stools. Why do I think this? Why should you be
different when I am not? These is no profounder psychological
experience than marriage; you get to know so much that you
can never unlearn whether you want to or not; it is more
profound than travel, much more profound than lectures. Yet
marriage has not changed me, I don't think. I count all the
things that I wanted before I was married; if anything I want

them more than ever. I can't think how people can regard
children as a substitute for work and experience. Children will
mean nothing to me unless I have the background of work
and experience to let them into. Even Gordon means to me
chiefly a person who will be pleased and delighted if I succeed
at something. And I am sure I should mean nothing to him
without my background of work and ambition.

No, marriage (and a year is a test) hasn't altered me; it has
only made me much, much more everything that I was before.
So why should Africa have altered you? Perhaps your letters
aren't as intimate? But then that's hurry, preoccupation. And
you never were a very good letter writer. I have just read your
letter of May 18th from Cape Town. Nice, but just a little
impersonal. Do time and distance really make a difference, and
are we too proud in imagining ourselves superior to them? At
least I haven't torn myself to pieces over you as I did last year
over Gordon during an even shorter absence. Yet he hadn't
changed at all. Why should I worry about you, remembering
that? But then you don't need me as he does. For him I am in
very truth the only person in the world. That is why I must
have children; it isn't good for anyone to put all their eggs in
one basket – though it means a nice safe feeling for the basket,
I must admit. (This metaphor, on re-reading it, seems somehow
rather improper!) But if you were to change I should cease to
believe in any kind of safety, even the right sort.

Adieu, sweetieheart. Yes, do come to Southampton if you
can. I have had a dream for so long of sailing in to that harbour
on a big ship, and you and Mother being there to welcome me –
my looking out for you as the ship moves in.

Ever your V.S.V.D.L

'Land of Green Ginger' v. good; much better than 'Hungarian
Rhapsody'.

VERA TO WINIFRED

Westminster Hotel, 420 West 116th
Street, New York | 29 June 1926

Darling sweetieheart,

I am so glad that you are really on the way back. I long
for you to be in England and within reach again. And I am
beginning quite desperately to look forward to coming home.
This country is experience, but it is also disturbance, crude,
noisy, and tiring; and after a year of such experience one longs
to get back to regular work against a background of mellowness
and peace.

My sweetieheart, is there any likelihood that for any reason
you won't want to keep Wymering Mansions (with me paying
half as usual) until at least Feb. or March? My whole plans have
been based on the assumption that you do want to keep it and
share it. I know – and it is only natural – that my family feels
that I am returning chiefly in order to pay a long-deferred visit
to them (and your family probably feels the same about you.)
But actually I am returning – and it is my only justification for
leaving Gordon so long, and the only reason why he accepts
the arrangement so sweetly – because I want to *work*, both for
him and for me. I *can* work; since I married, all my energy and
power of concentration has come back. I want to work like the
devil, and get the prestige of two years into one, so that we can
have a child next year without spoiling everything or feeling
unhappy about it or that it is a sacrifice. I want to love and to
want my child, and I can only do this with a solid background
of achievement immediately behind me. Does this sound
egotistical? Perhaps it does, but it concerns the immediate
happiness of three people and the creation of one. America
has been experience but not achievement (like Africa for you);

it has involved too much moving about, squashing into small spaces (and you know how tiring this is – one gets into the habit of *not* writing an article because one has to look for the material among piles of papers!), sudden spasms of urgency for us both which have left me a little flat and disinclined to settle to anything again for a month. I want to work solidly in the autumn, against the restful background of yourself (more restful though perhaps less stimulating than Gordon, with whom I argue perpetually and spend hours in getting, not producing on paper, ideas!)

Here they are, my red-hot irons, and the drawing them out with the best possible effect depends entirely on you.

Sometimes I feel anxious, because you said, 'I will meet you at Southampton if possible,' but 18 months ago you would have said 'I *will* meet you at Southampton.'

Is something very wrong at home, sweetieheart? Or is it merely that time and distance are making me apprehensive about you as I used to be about Gordon?

No more now. Let me know for certain about Wymering.

All love, dear sweet your v.s.v.d.l.

VERA TO WINIFRED

Westminster Hotel, 420 West 116th Street, New York | 7 July 1926

My sweetieheart,

Your nice letter from Pretoria has just come, I am now beginning to wait daily for news of you, as Mother is following your boat. I can't do that, as the American papers give no news of any but American-owned boats.

Before I forget, would you like me to return your letters before

I come or will it do if I bring them with me? It occurs to me
that you will probably use your five or six weeks at Bainesse to
write African articles; if so and you would like your letters I will
send them to eke out your diary. I would send them at once,
only somehow in a queer way I don't want to till I know you are
safe at home; they are all of you that I have to assure me that
you are still real.

What do you propose to do about Geneva? I suppose you'll *go*
with me. I hope you'll manage to come back before Gordon goes
as he will be bitterly disappointed not to see you and so shall I,
because curiously enough I always feel he likes you rather better
than you like him! and I do so much want you really to like
him. He always talks of you as 'My sister Winifred' – whether
as a term of affection or to reassure me I really don't know!
He asks me to thank you so much for the subscription to *The
Workers' Herald*, a copy of which has already appeared. He will
write when he gets back from Salt Lake City. At least he says
he will, but he is a terrible correspondent while he is doing this
job, as though it is interesting and full of prestige it doesn't quite
satisfy him intellectually (or else he is goaded by the sight of me
always writing things); at any rate whenever he has a moment to
spare he always wants to write an article or to review a book for
some learned monthly or quarterly. I have promised to correct
the proofs of his book (which are supposed to be ready for me
by Aug. 17th) in England, so as to save time and make sure of
December publication.

I have finished my honeymoon book and revised it; it now
only needs to be retyped, which I shall start at once. It is quite
short – about 220 pages of type – but long enough, I think, for
that kind of book. Sometimes I think it bright and amusing,
and sometimes it seems deadly; I feel that the last chapter,
on America, is a bit dull, but that may be only because I am
temporarily tired of America and find it dull myself. I wish I

could publish it as then I shan't feel the long winter months at Ithaca, during which I wrote most of it, were wasted.

By the way, if you are in communication with the League of Nations Union you might mention casually that I am returning in August and going to the Assembly; I don't want to write and inform them of this as it looks like asking for lectures. I don't want to ask, but to be asked, and politely; in any case I shan't have time to give many.

Ever your V.S.V.D.L.

VERA TO WINIFRED

Train, Springfield to New York | *16 July 1926*

My Sweetieheart,

I am on my way back from spending a week at the Chards' farm in Massachusetts – 5 hours, a long journey in England, here a mere bagatelle of a trip. You cannot have heard from me for some time, as I stopped writing about the end of April, thinking you were sailing in May. I have quite lost count of the number of letters I have sent to wait for you at Oakwood Court, but they must read like a serial story, and represent a dozen moods – glad, sad, triumphant, depressed, optimistic.

I am beginning now to look forward, more than I can say, to coming home. It has been a queer year, of mixed pain and pleasure, delight and disappointment. Two conclusions only I have so far brought out of it quite clearly (others will only come when I have been home and had time to think about it):

1. That I would not now for the world not have married Gordon, or want not to have met him.
2. That marriage in general is an unhappy state, and to

be avoided by anyone who is already quite happy single
unless they are *very* sure that it is what they want, and
have planned beforehand the conditions on which
they intend to live together.

I have come to the second conclusion because of the
marriages that I have seen. When you are married you get to
know much more of marriage than you did before; other women
confide little things to you – sometimes sordid, sometimes
merely pathetic – on the supposition that you too, being
married, are as unhappy as they are. I see my own happiness
(in marriage as such) as a very rare thing; a thing worth
even the long rustication and the bitter winter in Ithaca, and
certainly worth the crowded rough-and-tumble of New York,
the speeding, crude, garish uncomfortableness of noisy America
in general. The secret of my happiness with Gordon is, I think,
threefold – first and foremost that he is good, and considerate,
and unselfish, largely because, as your mother put it, he has
'worn the yoke in youth'. He is forever glad, forever grateful,
never taking me for granted; always telling me that he has never
felt so well and so able to do things as he has since he lived
with me. And for me too he has done something similar; added
colour to my too serious intenseness, and mixed sweetness
with my bitterness; above all practically destroyed the old
apprehension-bogie of unquiet nerves that we used to wonder
how to terminate. It will never go altogether; the dread of post-
time and shivering fear of telegrams is a heritage of the war, but
even that is better than it was.
    And secondly, it is because I did not marry early, and was old
enough to plan – psychologically, and as far as it can be done,
materially – the conditions of our life together, and to keep to
those plans.
    And thirdly, it is because circumstances are continually

separating us for short periods, always putting us in a state of
looking forward to seeing each other again, never allowing us to
become a habit to each other.

In so many of the marriages I have seen (especially the
University marriages) couples have been together year in,
year out, until it is too late to be anything more than a habit,
and they have grown tired of each other before they have
realised it. And I understand too why this need for separation
applies to husbands and wives, and not to friends of the same
sex; it is rooted in the sheer physical difference between men
and women, and the consequent slight perpetual demand for
imaginative understanding of another's bodily consciousness
which is different from one's own; so that in order to remain
one's self, and to retain sufficient energy and sympathy for the
constant give and take, one needs continual short periods alone
or in the company one's own sex. It is hard to explain what I
mean by 'understanding of another's bodily consciousness'; this
is not, of course, anything like so difficult as the understanding
of a different mental consciousness. I mean that Gordon and I
are so much the same mentally that the physical difference is
trivial, but still has to be recognised. It involves such things as
the recognition of fatigue when one is not tired one's self, the
taking into account slight temperamental differences, different
nervous reactions to different things; a realisation of a set of
circumstances which had led to a sexual need in the one which
the other shares only by sympathy. When we go away from
each other we both have the same experience – the first day
he enjoys what he calls 'the sense of recovered bachelorhood',
while I feel delightfully at ease and contented and my own
mistress. But on the second day the feeling begins to wear off,
and by the third we are each longing to see the other again
with a quite ridiculous fervour! That is why I am prepared to
swallow – though with a wry face – the bitter pill of parting

from him again for six or eight months. It will mean at the end a new marriage and a new honeymoon – better than the first, because there will be all the novelty and the relief without any of the strangeness and the embarrassment.

Why do I pour out all this on top of you? I don't know. I wanted to put it down and thought you might be interested to hear, after I have written so much of what I have been planning and doing, a little about what I have been thinking.

I long for news of you, my dear sweetieheart.

Always your own V.S.V.D.L.

WINIFRED TO VERA

SS Barrabool | *17 July 1926*

My dear, my little heart,

I am sitting on deck, wrapped up in a rug, watching through a calm silver afternoon the South Coast move leisurely past. Folkestone, Dover, Deal, Broadstairs – with a dado of white cliffs and green grass, and a flurry of gulls. This morning we picked up the pilot. His little black and red ship came chuffing up and down on the blue water. So calm a day, but with a bright wind. I waved my hand to Dover and to the Lord Warden Hotel. I saw France like a faint film on the horizon. Last night I saw the lighted ships, like constellations on a dark sky, shaming the stars. I stood till after midnight on the boat-deck, watching their green and red and golden lights steal past.

Tomorrow morning we land. I shall go straight to Oakwood Court to see your family and hear any news. I want your letters, and all about everything, and there is the flat to see about.

Oh, my dear, one more month. It seems centuries since I heard from you.

Oakwood Court. July 18th

My little Heart, I have arrived – and a million things to say.
Your Mother met me. Your mother has been a darling looking
after the flat, walking in the procession, and everything. She
looks so sweet and young and your father looks so well in a light
summer suit, and Oakwood Court looks so green, so green for
all its July dust, after the arid browns and yellows of Africa.

But first of all, your sheaf of letters, which I have read
through, with a heart growing heavier and heavier with shame.
For, my dear, my sweet, it never occurred to me that you could
doubt my feelings' remaining the same – my letters, my damned,
inadequate scrappy letters were the result of a state of racket
and strain that I only realised when I got aboard the ship. The
flu in Pretoria was really nothing but exhaustion, which I did
not realise because the sunlight was so heavenly and I felt well
enough. And I suppose that my cold letters – heaven knows
I did not feel cold – resulted from a total inability to express
myself. I feel all the more furious with myself because I had
vowed never to let you feel anxious for me when I was away,
except for acts of God, tempest and pestilence. And three of
your letters from Boston and from New York have made me
curse myself to fury for crass – what? Indolence, preoccupation,
lack of imagination – anything you like. Of course I have not
changed. How could I? Your small, fugitive figure goes with
me in my thoughts, is so much a part of me that I question
my feelings toward you as little as I question my own egotism.
Perhaps like a loving husband, I have grown stale in my
articulation. Oh, forgive me, sweet, if I have proved so dull,
so unworthy a husband. The fault lay in the pen, not in the
thoughts. How should I change? It is true that in one way I am
self-sufficient; I can love; I can enjoy my life; see colours, hear
music and voices; conceive ideas, taste new experiences, all

with true eyes and all alone. It is true that I love other people, Mother, Jean McWilliam; that I find interest in almost every chance acquaintance – the people whom I met in Africa, or on the boat. But you are you. And because you are you, there is part of me with which, in Margaret's words to Faust, 'I need thee every hour.'

Of course I am keeping on the flat – or rather, we are keeping it. Any other notion never occurred to me. And of course I am coming to Southampton, lest act of God again intervenes. My 'if possible' was only in answer to a certain scrupulousness that dreads to make promises which, even inadvertently, one cannot fulfill. I would rather lose my right hand than wittingly fail you. And I feel that even in letting you doubt me, I have in some measure failed, oh my little sweet. Oh, my dear, I have pictured so often going down to Southampton again, this time to meet my love, my love, my love, my ship coming in, my sweet from the sea, not yours, not Gordon's – mine.

It is absurd to write today; for tomorrow I shall have so much more to say of importance, about business especially. Don't worry about Nursie, or the flat or anything. I am seeing to all that, and will keep you posted. I can't stand feeling as I do – about your worrying. Tomorrow I shall send a cable. Oh, my little love – if you *knew* how I look forward and forward to this year's autumn. It will be spring.

About 'The Runners' – I will await developments. It is with Heineman. I want your opinion. My own, at a distance of six months, is that I have clipped its wings too austerely and the bird won't fly.

I could weep indeed, because my letters distressed you. My dear, but did you not know that nothing could change me except your changing? Not your attitude towards me, I mean, but towards life. Only I think I can explain what you call 'lack of intimacy' in my letters. You must remember that though superficially affectionate, my real nature is cold. I do not find demonstrative intimacy an easy thing. I had never thought to show such natural demonstrative affection as I find rises quite naturally now from my love for you. But expression of this love is only the outward and visible form. It is called from me when you are near, or when, as today, a long silence is broken by a series of letters that bring me poignantly near to you. Your presence breaks down a sort of inhibition that makes me otherwise unconsciously reluctant to show my feelings. I do not excuse it. I am only trying to explain. It is not that I love you less. I love you quite absurdly. But this inarticulateness, this inhibition against the expression of love, is always ready to rise up in me. The coldness is the insincerity, not the warmth. But I do not even recognise it myself for coldness, and, though I know I have no right to ask it, I must ask you to trust my love. My love for you is all gain to me. I think that all love is gain. Only at times, especially when tired or very full of business, an instinct beyond thought comes between me and the expression of love. This is badly expressed.

I have so much to say. Oakwood Court is full of you. I feel you, I need you every hour. Listen, my heart, I am too angry with myself, too weary to express exactly what I want to say; but you must believe these things – for they are true. I love you. I need you. I want to be with you. I have gained more from your companionship than I shall ever tell or know. What you mean to me, I can never make you see, for you are too humble beneath your thousand vanities. Marriage or non-marriage has nothing to do with it. Were I married too, it would be the same. I want you to understand this, because other separations might lead to similar apprehensions. If ever my letters get vague, scold me, but for heaven's sake don't worry about my feelings, my love.

Can't you see? I want so much to make you see, and I can only flounder stupidly in words.

My little love, if you doubt – ask Gordon if it could be possible, having loved you, to cease. His answer will be adequate, perhaps, as my intention.

We will make this winter a time of profitable work for you if we can. For me it will be pleasure. I wish that Gordon were to be here too.

Thank you for all your letters – and forgive me, my small, sweet love.

W.

WINIFRED TO VERA

Bainesse, Cottingham, East Yorkshire | *27 July 1926*

Small Sweet Heart,

I have just received your letter written in the train on the way back from the Chards. It seems so strange and so pleasant to be answering a letter written just ten days ago, instead of one written nearly two months past. It is all about marriage and Gordon. I readily endorse all that you say in your letter. South Africa taught me about marriage probably as much as the unmarried can learn. Things stand out more crudely in that hot, dry atmosphere where nerves are strung at tension point, and the reticence of women about their domestic affairs is broken by the greater loneliness. And I am inclined to agree with you that marriage in general is an unhappy state – but that so also, in general, is celibacy. The resigned loneliness and masked inferiority complex of most virgins who have no creative passion to sublimate their libido (I have been reading Freud, you may observe!) seems to me just as unfortunate as the disillusioned and often exasperated state of most married women. And I have been driven to the conclusion that most 'states' are unhappy. It is inconvenient to be an unmarried mother; it is soul-deadening to be a 'habitual' wife; it is embittering to be a virgin. (I use that word again because it is explicit. All spinsters are not virgins, though most virgins are spinsters. Not all.) Happiness then is not an affair of 'states' at all. It is for most of us an affair of moments. The most tragically married or unmarried enjoys ecstatic moments – from a sunset, a new hat, a Brahms symphony, a tennis match. A very few of us enjoy an individual personal relationship, rare, sweet and dangerous – you with Gordon, I with my friends, especially you, and my liberty for creation. Our 'states' are happy, because our source of happiness lies in our state. Most people win their happiness in spite of their state.

You and Gordon, thank heaven, had one of the rare adventures of finding the right person at the right time. And when that happens, 'states' may go to the winds. Is this all true, or nonsense?

Of Gordon, I was astonished by your suggestion that he likes me more than I like him. Apart from the fact that physically he has no appeal for me (who has? Harry did once, I think, but not now) I like him quite dangerously much, and find myself more and more inclined to use him as a sort of criterion for my masculine acquaintances. I nearly fell a little in love with a man on the *Barrabool* because he reminded me so much of Gordon. He was Oxford, and very Oxford. He knew J. B. S. Haldane, the Murrays, F. G. S. Schiller, and so forth. He held forth mightily upon the philosophic basis of the state. the material implications of birth control, and so forth. He was a Roman Catholic, and in spite of an admirable philosophic training and a scientific profession (he had read greats at Oxford, medicine at Trinity College Dublin), he was ingenuously pious,

and used, when the cabin became rowdy at night, to retire to
the bathroom to read Dante and say his prayers. He was kind
to all the wall-flowers, foreigners, women with children and
withal cynical-tongued and sceptically witted. And I found
myself continually criticising him, along the line of whether
he did or did not come up to a standard set by Gordon, leaving
myself with an open verdict regretfully inclined to the 'did not'.
Amusing adventure, but quite unimportant, as I shall probably
never hear of him again.

In spite of the wisdom of continual separations, I feel great
compunction in having you for the autumn instead of his
having you. I know the wisdom, and I long to have you – but,
my poor Gordon. Why can't I take you out for a weekend in the
middle of the time? Oh, how I wish that you had the inside of
cast-iron, my darling. We would fly off third class to visit your
husband. Well, well. I need not pour my compunction all over
you, where it will be nothing to yours, my dear loves.

I don't think that you need worry about the flat.

Dear Sweet heart – I love you – Less than a month now. I
count the days.

v.s.v.d.l. W.

VERA TO WINIFRED

Westminster Hotel, 420 West 116th
Street, New York | 30 July 1926

My darling girl,

I expect this is the last letter that I shall get through
to you before I leave, as the next big boat sailing after the
Leviathan is mine.

I have just been reading your long letter of July 17th. Darling

sweetieheart, it brings you all back to me. What an angel you
are, so much, much nicer than I; no wonder Lady Rhondda
loves you, and all the nice, nice people that I wish loved me,
and who never do. The wonder always is that you *do* love me –
that you see more in me than what most people see – which is
a combination of egotistical bitterness plus a kind of insincere
prettiness plus an intermittent (and, as they think, designing)
attraction for men.

Sweetieheart, I don't think in my heart of hearts I ever
doubted *you* weren't different; I really understood all the time
that you were engrossed and overfull of work and travel (did I
not go round Central Europe with you on a similar but much
less strenuous expedition, and even that strenuous enough to
make letter-writing, even to Gordon, a burden?) What really
started me wondering, I think, was little postcards from your
Mother forwarded by mine – and assumptions by mine that you
wouldn't go to Geneva, that you wouldn't keep the flat, that you
wouldn't fulfil the arrangement that I was basing all my plans
on. In normal conditions one would take no notice of such
things, but here, and after a year of facing assumptions on the
part of everybody that because one is married one won't want to
lead the same sort of life as one did before, it is different. One
begins to suspect that even the people who know one best will
take for granted that marriage *has* made a difference. (Unless
I am with Gordon, I never tell people that I meet for the first
time that I am married now. Over here, when people meet you
and think you unmarried, their first question always is 'What's
your job?' or 'What are you doing here?' But when they know
you are married they ask: 'What is your husband?') Personally
I don't feel a scrap more married than I did two years ago; I
still get a shock when the few people whom I have not trained
to call me 'Miss Brittain' address me as 'Mrs' and I have not
lost one jot of my desire to do any of the things I have always

wished to do, and I think – partly due to a fierce desire to flout America and its impertinent vulgarity (I don't mean that all America is impertinent and vulgar, I mean the part of it that is) – I am more ambitious than ever.

For all the real trouble – the real cause of apprehension and distrust and depression – is America. America is the kind of experience you are immensely glad to have had once, but hope you'll never have again – rather like the war in that way.

America is terribly noisy, terribly tiring psychologically, and terribly lonely. The noise consists not only in the automobiles and a peculiar kind of terrible iron drill which is part of the apparatus of building a skyscraper (they have been building one almost opposite to us since last week), but in the voices of the Americans themselves. Need I say more?

And it is tiring in many ways. For one thing, one leads a singularly arid life with regard to things that are small in themselves, but immense when added together. There is no early morning tea and no afternoon tea; one either makes it and drinks it with turned milk and a biscuit that has lost its first crispness (you can't buy a tin of biscuits here; they are all sold in paper packets), or else one wanders street after street looking for a restaurant that will condescend to serve it. Then there are no fires in winter; one stares at a black radiator that makes one stuffy rather than warm, and has to choose between keeping the windows shut and getting a splitting headache, or opening them and shivering with cold. Then it is tiring because one never 'gets' the psychology of the people. Every second person you deal with in the ordinary matters of life – shopping, eating travelling, taxis, servants – is a foreigner and a different kind of foreigner. In France you adapt yourself to the French, in Germany to the Germans, and so on. But in America you go into three shops and are served by, first, a Polish Jew, secondly an Italian, thirdly a Chinaman. You are waited on by Negroes,

and driven in taxis by Germans or Filipinos. And somehow all
this adds to the loneliness as well as to the interest of life. No
one understands you the first time; you have to say everything
twice to all foreigners and even then they don't understand you
because your English is not American English. You live also in
very small rooms with everything crowded on top of you. Half
the clothes I brought out I have never worn because they are in
drawers with others piled on top of them, or left in trunks; and
half the papers I brought I have never looked at for the same
reason. As for loneliness, one makes lots of acquaintances, but
gets intimate with no one. At first I thought that being English,
one was suspected and distrusted; now I think that intimacy is
not a characteristic which the American cultivates or needs.
His life is a rush; he doesn't like leisure because he doesn't want
to think. In other words, the only person with whom for a year
I have had an intimate conversation is Gordon, and it is good
for no one to be intimate with one person exclusively, especially
when that person by no means shares all sides of you (who
indeed can?). The fact that I still love his society and long for
him to come back whenever he is away in spite of this exclusive
intimacy, and that he longs for mine (for the situation is almost
the same for him, even after three years at Cornell) says perhaps
more for our marriage than anything else could. I doubt if even
you, with your gift for approachableness, could become intimate
with the average American.

If one is to enjoy America, two things (and by no means
easy things) must exist. First of all, one must be a 'lion'
already; America is so surfeited with lions that you must
bring your reputation over ready-made, and even then you
mayn't be successful. In the second place, one must have a
host of intimate friends who are prepared to push you for
purely personal reasons. The only other reason people will
do anything for you is if they think they are going to get any

money out of you. The people who are interested in personal things are a mere handful, an infinitesimal fraction, in the crowd of sensation mongers, dollar chasers, baseball readers, and the vast complacent indifference of the Middle West, the land of Main Street.

Well, dear sweetieheart, I seem to have got a long way from the subject of my doubting about you, but I haven't really. I know you will understand how here one is so far away, so alone, so overwhelmed by a strange, tiring, noisy so-called civilisation. At least I am thankful that I can keep separate, and see clearly, the different elements in the situation. There is nothing wrong with my dear Gordon, or with marriage – at least with marriage to Gordon. America is the problem – and America, as anything but a country to travel in when one wants to, like any other country – will soon, I hope, be done with for good for both of us.

Sweetieheart – must stop – I long and long to see you more than words can ever say – So sorry to have seemed to doubt you at all. I never will again.

Always your own V.S.V.D.L.

VERA TO WINIFRED

10 Oakwood Court, London W14 | *20 August 1926*

Darling girl,

I can't be sufficiently amused or sufficiently grateful to you for getting me in touch with the *Town Crier* people. They are the loveliest and funniest people in the world! To begin with, the paper is *very* arty and crafty and *very* highbrow, printed on *beautiful* paper, and with a lovely design of a red and green herald on the cover. I waited for the Editor in a little room

painted just like the most arty of the little shops in Church
Street. Half an hour later she appeared – a good-looking, grey-
haired woman in a beautiful black satin coat, very Irish, very
friendly, very vague and very excited. She took a fancy to me
at once, entirely because I was wearing my grey and blue dress,
and the blue happened to be exactly the colour of the office wall
and door, which was painted in blue and orange! As she said, I
might have dressed specially to come to see her. She didn't know
anything about Geneva, or how to get a Press ticket, was afraid
it cost a great deal, and was frightfully excited when I told her
that she could get one for nothing and it was merely a matter of
writing to the Secretariat to say I was their representative. So
she opened the door and called, and about three young women
came running in, and I had then and there to dictate a letter to
the Secretariat for them, telling them exactly what to say.

Then we had to decide what the article was to be about. She
said she wasn't interested in politics, and she wasn't a feminist,
and *Time and Tide* was too extreme for her, and she hoped I
wasn't a sex antagonist (at which point I informed her that I
was really married, and very much in love with my husband,
which charmed her almost to tears!), and she wasn't really
interested in celebrities but only in people who were doing
interesting and normal work, and what she really cared for
most was home crafts and industries and everything that makes
life more beautiful and is good for children! So eventually I
had an inspiration and suggested an article on Geneva and
beauty – you know the kind of thing – ugliness of war, things
of the mind and soul only grow in peace and leisure, League of
Nations the guardian of peace, therefore guardian of the beauty
of life – with one or two topical allusions to appropriate things
said at the Assembly. She thought this would be wonderful! and
then said: 'Can you do one or two of our Silhouettes as well? –
you know we have little paragraphs of 250 words, outlining

the personalities of women who are doing interesting work?' I thought of Anna Bugge-Wicksell and the law degree, etc., and said: 'Certainly; may I look at one of your past copies to see how you do them?' She said: 'Well, as a matter of fact, we haven't *had* any yet, but we thought it would be so *nice* to start them, and you must meet a great many people in your interesting life, and won't you send us paragraphs from time to time whenever you come across anyone? Oh, and could you do me an article for some future number on arts and crafts in America, and how the gift wraps are done there?' I said I thought I probably could – as I know someone to whom I could write for information.

She was most excitedly eager for ideas, and said she would pay me 10/6 a column while the paper is making its way, increased later when they can afford it, and about 5/ each for paragraphs. Really, it is quite a good thing to be in with, as it is on the upward grade. At present it is only published and printed from the office, but it is expanding so much that they are having to move into a much larger office further down Church Street.

I took my book and the stories to Andrew Dakers yesterday and had the most delightful talk with him, lasting about half an hour. I asked about your book, which apparently came back from Heinemann's and is now somewhere else; he didn't say where, but seemed to have every hope of finding a publisher for it. About mine, he seemed interested and said he very much wanted to read it as it sounded a change from the ordinary novel, one of those things that any publisher would be interested to see, that the title was a good one, and that such a book as it *might* be a great success if it caught on. I said that Rose Macaulay's reputation was just the kind I wanted, and he said, 'Well, why not? You've got plenty of time. She must be old enough to be your mother!'

Ever your V.S.V.D.L.

In early autumn, Gordon had returned to Cornell, while Vera remained in London with Winifred. In December Gordon suffered a kind of crisis, and insisted that Vera join him in America.

VERA TO WINIFRED

c. 6 *December* 1926

Sweetieheart,

Have had the most wretched week-end. The usual two miserable letters came from Gordon on Saturday, but this time they were worse than ever. Apparently Notestein has dropped his reserve a little, and has told Gordon

a) that we (he and I) have the reputation in England of being 'social pushers' and that there are people who will actually put themselves out to *prevent* our getting on.

b) that G.'s academic status in England is so low (at any rate cf. with what it is in America) that N. doesn't think there is any chance of his getting to Glasgow or London, and that he will 'ruin' his career if he tries to go back or do anything but quietly wait in America until promotion comes (and I gather that N. will see that it comes if he takes his advice)

Reading between the lines it is quite clear that N. is putting perpetual pressure on him 1) to abandon all efforts to get back; 2) to persuade me that it is my 'duty' to go to him in America – that people will 'say things' etc., etc. It must be very difficult for G. to stand up against this kind of pressure when he never hears the other side at all.

Marriage is the very devil. Ironically enough I got a letter (written personally) by same post from the Editor of the *Outlook* to say he was very pleased with my scheme and I was to get on with the articles. My career seems likely to work out all right now – it only depends on energy and industry on my part – but this 'left tick' is intolerable. How can one put in energy and industry when one is constantly torn by conflicting claims and principles? Is it surprising that ever since G. appeared in my existence I have been quite unable to write another novel, because some weight of misery connected with *his* perturbations, his career, has lain on top of me?

The 'social pusher' reputation does puzzle and perturb me. It would of course be ludicrous and laughable (does a 'social pusher' live in Maida Vale even for a time or leave influential Liberal friends to join the Labour Party, or cultivate the friendship of penniless teachers from Somerville while repudiating the society girls from St Monica's?) if it were not at the moment so dangerous. This must apply to me, because for the last 4 years poor G. has not been in England to push. It gives me again the desperately uncomfortable feeling, that I have from time to time, of having secret enemies, with some secret vague hostility, somewhere, who are trying to spoil things for me. I could understand being called 'ambitious' in the intellectual sense – what intelligent person worth their salt isn't? – but 'social pusher' baffles me – and is of course a much more damning accusation than that of ambition. Have you ever heard such an accusation? What sort of 'society' am I supposed to be trying to get out of – or into!

After thinking it over for 24 hours I wrote to Gordon yesterday (by *Leviathan* – sails to-morrow morning) and proposed that if Glasgow, London and Drink all fail, we had better agree to separate – at any rate for a time. I don't mean anything so cut and dried as a judicial separation, but one

sufficiently definite to enable us to announce it to our friends
and thus shut up these intolerable outside efforts to regulate our
private lives for us. If circumstances of themselves ever make
it possible that we should live together again we could do so or
not, as we wished. But if as Notestein says, it is true that G's
only good fortune is in America, I have no more right to spoil
his career than he has to spoil mine. On the other hand by
going out to America I should not only completely ruin my own
chances at everything (and even this is not a purely personal
matter – I do feel so strongly that every woman who 'gives in'
makes it a little harder for all the struggling women after her)
but should ruin even the marriage for which I had ruined it. I
am quite incapable of 'resignation' because intellectually I don't
believe in it; and if one has 'given in' the only alternative to
resignation is resentment, bitterness and at last vindictiveness.
It is better to treasure one's few months of happy marriage by
ending the marriage but keeping the memory intact, than spoil
even the memory by allowing the marriage to degenerate into a
bickering, bitter, mutually resentful relationship.

I told him that before we separated definitely I should like
to be sure of having a child – which I would support – because
the thought of losing him is unendurable unless I could have
something of his. I think he would agree to this. As to himself,
two years' absence on my part constitutes a formal desertion,
and if he wished he could then be free to divorce me and marry
someone who was willing to subordinate her life to his.

WINIFRED TO VERA

28 December 1926

My own Heart,

This is to wish you a happy birthday, my dear love, and a hundred more if it were possible. I don't see why it should not be happy either, in Olive Schreiner's sense of happiness. Great love you have, and much service you may give the world. At least, my Heart, were this birthday to be your last, you have known most kinds of pleasure and pain. You have been intensely and vividly alive. You have known pain and love and consummation of personal relationship, a little fame, the hot, pulsing joy of conflict, the tense, perverse rapture of release from fear.

My darling, next year I do hope that you will at least be about to have your hope of immortality. Bless us, what are circumstances compared to that?

I have been wondering, are we not perhaps fools to be deterred from what should be a supreme adventure of creation by considerations of nursemaids, rooms and prams? Surely these can be forced into our possession if we are content to take the kingdom of peace by storm?

I know that my advice would always be for caution because I love you and fear for you and am jealous of perils for you. But never be influenced by my caution, only by my love, which indeed would have you miss nothing of the richness of life. I don't believe that a baby would really bore you. Babies can, even while young, be charming, and your baby would have an appeal which I can imagine rather than describe. I would say, I think, be reckless. Get it somehow, and all these things, such as nursemaids and houses, shall be added unto you.

Babies are a nuisance, of course. But so does everything seem to be that is worthwhile, husbands and books and committees

and being loved and everything. We have to choose between
barren ease and rich unrest – or rather one does not choose.
Life somehow chooses. If I were you, I would be rich. Even if it
ultimately kills you, you'll have been alive and we all have to
die, even those who never lived.

So bless you, sweet of my heart. At least I have loved you,
and there's something in that.

And now I go to write an article on prophets and to visit my
relations at Dowthorpe, without much joy in it!

Bless you always, v.s.v.d.l. W.

1927

*After the December crisis, Vera agreed to rejoin Gordon in America
in the spring, and she sailed with her mother on 28 March 1927.*

WINIFRED TO VERA

117 Wymering Mansions, Elgin Avenue,
London W9 | 29 March 1927

My own darling,

It is a grey drizzling day, Deo Gratias, and it should be calm
on the high seas. I woke up to its merciful sobriety, and then
to your dear little letter written on board. I rang up your father
this morning and found that he had had one too.

Oh sweetieheart, I do hope that you don't hate it too much,
and that it stays calm, and that you aren't ill. I hate, hate,
hate your having to do things you don't like doing, and hate
still more the thought of your lying awake afraid. But it's no
use stopping doing things, I know, nor of encouraging other

people to stop them, which is even more tempting. And I
hope that it will keep like this, grey and calm – if it is grey and
calm with you.

I had such a charming letter from Sarah Gertrude Millin
last night. She says that her father has died and the business
of arranging for her mother's future and her two young
brothers has come upon her, and that lately she has had no
time for anything else. She says that she sometimes looks back
with wonder, and can't imagine how she or anyone ever had
the detachment of mind to finish a whole book. It is rather
consoling to know that even the great and the 'arrived' are not
immune from domestic complications – and yet infuriating to
reflect how the efficient must always be handicapped by other
people's dependence upon their efficiency. She is rather like
you, I imagine, abrupt and dependable and continually making
decisions for other people, and loves clothes and well-shingled
hair and all the rest of it.

I can't write the intimate sort of letters that I ought to write.
It's the bit of my father and mother in me which makes me
reticent and humdrum on paper. But I do love you. I shan't miss
you because I shall be too busy. But I think about you a great
deal, and with continual love and joy. The thought of you is
a pleasure to me which has no overshadowing of pain. Utter
confidence and tenderness in another brings rest and joy alone.
There is no pain, as in passion. Be happy. Give my salutations
to Gordon. Make lots of useful contacts.

Dear Heart. v.s.v.d.l. W.

WINIFRED TO VERA

117 Wymering Mansions, Elgin Avenue,
London W9 | 2 April 1927

Sweetieheart,

In a wee 'sma' while Nursie will bring the tea, and then I
must eat in haste with my loins girded and my notes in my
hand, and take my way – with a banner, steps, and a case of
cards and pamphlets, – to Hyde Park – to yell myself hoarse to
a Boat Race-day crowd. The only pleasant thing about it is the
consolation of feeling oneself a martyr.

5.10. Having worked myself up to a nice pitch of eloquence I
find that it is pouring with rain. Have just rung up the National
Union of Women Teachers and they say – 'No go.' So we shall
have no meeting. I am going out for a walk. I love you. I love
you. I am not lonely. I am not lonely. I am not. So there.

Oh, today I had to take my typewriter to be mended. It really
wouldn't work. So I found myself in the morning with an hour
in which to kill time. Mrs Scott-James had asked me if I could
do a 'Woman of the Day' of Storm Jameson. So I dropped
into Kathleen's office to ask if she knew anything about her.
She took me straight round to Heinemann's to meet Martha
Harris, who is young, and brusque and red-lipped and efficient.
She gave me quantities of stuff and then said, 'You'd better see
Storm Jameson.' Before I had time to say yes or no, she whipped
off the telephone, rang up Knopf's, and asked if Storm Jameson
could be interviewed then and there. Did you know that she
and her husband, Guy Chapman, are co-directors of the English
house of Knopf?

I went round, in the pouring rain, to Bedford Place – and of
course, it being so wet, in all my shabbiest things, and found her
in a large office with two youngish men at different tables. One

may have been her husband, I do not know. She is tall, slightish
fair, but not as fair as I, blue-eyed and untidy, though her blue
dress was very pretty. She is not pretty or smart, but downright
and pleasant and friendly in a business-like don't-waste-my-time
sort of way. She said that she never had any time to write all the
things she wanted to write, and that all her life was lived in a
hurry. That she hated speaking, cooking, and domesticity, and
she believed that all women really hated housework. She loves
ships, but not going in them, and loathes an Atlantic crossing.
And she is going to write two sequels to *The Lovely Ship*.

I don't suppose that I was there ten minutes. She was in the
middle of a letter, obviously anxious for me to go, and I was
dripping steadily on to her carpet! Also I find interviewing
a most perilous business. I never know how polite and how
truthful an interviewer should be. I'm much better at being
interviewed!

With all love, v.s.v.d.l, W.

WINIFRED TO VERA

117 Wymering Mansions, Elgin Avenue,
London W9 | 7 April 1927

Darling Sweet,

John Lane's have turned down 'Land of Green Ginger'. They
say 'it is a very fine piece of work extremely well written and
accurately observed', but they won't touch the consumption
part. Isn't it odd? I feel utterly at a loss to know what is
considered impossible.

The Debate incident repeated itself. I had a furious, but
curiously loveable, letter from Rebecca West, eight pages long,
exceedingly indignant about my article. I seem to be doomed to

insult inadvertently the women whom I most admire. Of course,
if it all ended as with you, I would walk around tomorrow firing
arrows into their sore spots intentionally; but in this case I was
as impersonal as a weather report and as full of admiration
as it is decent to be. She said that she had noticed in 'other
references' which I had made to her my hostility. I don't believe
that I have ever referred to her before excepting once to quote
her among women who could speak well. Perhaps she thinks
that I am someone else. Her letter was oddly much like your
outbreak after the debate. It made me like her tremendously –
a one-sided feeling, I fear.

Beloved, dear, sweet, I love you. You are the fragrance of the
spring to me.

v.s.v.d.l. W.

VERA TO WINIFRED

117 Oak Avenue, Ithaca, New York | 19 April 1927

My darling love,

I'm so sorry about 'The Land of Green Ginger', yet not
altogether surprised after what Andrew Dakers said about
consumption – although it is such a good book. It is *very* queer
how our fortunes run together – how we both got two novels
off in the days when no one would look at our articles, and
how, now that people actually demand our articles, no one
will take our books! Here is my advice for what it is worth;
you probably won't agree with it. I honestly think I should get
it back from Andrew Dakers and either remove, or modify,
the consumption parts. What matters now is to get a book
published, and soon; it is more important, at the moment, than
an obstinate determination to write exactly as one will. It is

bad psychologically to have *two* books in the air. There doesn't seem any doubt that, without the consumption parts, your book would go – and it is better to alter them now than to wait till ten publishers have seen it, and then have to alter it with your market much diminished.

Then, having altered it, I should be inclined to take it round to publishers yourself. Andrew Dakers can, of course, still fix your contract with you and get his 10%, but the time literary agents take, not so much to submit a book, as to get it back when submitted, is stupendous. It would be all right if we were immortal but not otherwise. Also I do think that personal interviews with publishers are valuable, especially any whom you happen to know a little already.

Gordon is in fine feather. The *Times Literary Supplement* review in England and Dewey's *New Republic* review in America have done for his book exactly what he wanted. He has several articles appearing in learned papers here, but better still *The Nineteenth Century* has written him a letter which he received this evening, asking him to write an article on 'Historical Mysticism and the Science of Politics' in reply to one by Mr G. Stirling Taylor on 'History and Politics' in their Half-Centenary Number which apparently was all about Gordon's book without actually mentioning it by name.

All love, dear sweetieheart – and do alter that book.

your v.s.v.d.l.

VERA TO WINIFRED

117 Oak Avenue, Ithaca, New York | 1 *May 1927*

My dear love,

I wish I had known that the Married Woman's Bill was

coming up in the House on April 29th, as I might have written three or four articles round it. But I can't do much out here; one is too far out of the stimulating contact of people who are doing things to have any ideas. I suppose as soon as I come back I shall have all kinds of brilliant ideas about what I *might* have done here, just as I did before. The notion of a popular sociological book on 'The Idle Woman' ('leisured' is not quite the correct description, as all women ought to be that for part of their time) still appeals to me – and also to Gordon – and there are a good many useful books on the subject in the library here which I shall probably look over during the next four weeks.

I suspect that I may just possibly be going to have a baby, though there won't of course be sufficient evidence to prove such a thing for some weeks, and I have certainly no intention of mentioning anything so hypothetical to anyone but you and Gordon. If only Gordon's plans were a little more certain I should be delighted to be told it was so; but I suppose that whenever or wherever such a thing happened, with people so full of plans as ourselves there would always be some kind of troublesome inconvenience.

This letter, needless to say, is entirely private from *everyone*. I don't want even the *rumour* of a baby to get round as long as I can possibly avoid it, because such things damage one's chance of earning money even among those people who believe on principle that they ought not to damage it.

I hope your family have forgiven us for leaving Father and spoiling your Easter holiday. It is never likely to happen again, and really I think has done Mother good; she is looking worlds better. So is Gordon; I am sure you will notice the change in him since last year.

All love and gratitude, my sweetieheart, ever your,
V.S.V.D.L.

VERA TO WINIFRED

117 Oak Avenue, Ithaca, New York | *5 May 1927*

My darling heart,

Mother says that there is no doubt that I am going to have a baby and it really isn't worth while my getting involved with one of the doctors here in order to make certain. I have all the orthodox and proper symptoms; what is more, it must have happened at once (i.e. 5 weeks ago) as I shouldn't otherwise be so sick in the mornings! I tell Gordon it is very tiresome of him to have led such a pure life! On the other hand it is really very well-timed, for though early January (a dreary and very satisfactory month to spend in bed) may be a little early in the year for the infant, it is just possible Gordon may come back here for the second semester (Feb. to June), in which case he will be able to sail with everything well over instead (as would have been the case if we had waited till June) of going off leaving everything about to happen. Cornell has told Gordon that if he *can* come back for that time they would regard it as a great favour and would raise his salary to 4,000 dollars (i.e. 2,000 for the half-year i.e. £400, of which he would be able to contribute quite £200 to general expenses.) This, if he gets nothing else but odd jobs, would of course considerably alleviate next year's financial situation. I think it is probable he will do this, and aim at a 1928–9 English job. He won't mind being without me for the Feb.–June months half so much as the Sept.–Feb.

It would also mean that we (you and I) could be entirely together again for the half-year if you thought you could endure my encumbrances and unless you want to go abroad. There is no need to alarm Nursie by telling her anything yet, and no hurry for anything, but between now and Christmas I must

find both another housekeeper and a somewhat larger (if even
only temporary) abode, as Wymering Mansions isn't big enough
and above all not sunny enough for a January infant, and at
Oakwood Court (though it is amply large enough) it would,
as you can well imagine and as Mother – rather reluctantly
admits – be impossible to have both Father and an infant under
the same roof even from Feb. to June. Besides, I must have
my books. It's no good having a nurse and then not writing
articles either! I gather that having a baby is a great upset for a
small household, so unless some exceptionally favourable set of
circumstances evolves, I expect I shall go to a nursing home or a
hospital in the end.

I hope I shan't be a great trial to you, my sweetieheart. I
feel – and I believe I am – quite good-tempered, only it's a
queer condition, which enslaves one in the most humiliating
way to little likes and dislikes. It's absurd to find one's self
fussy about food, just because such a very limited number of
things don't make one feel sick. It is even more absurd to be
intolerably revolted by certain smells; I have taken such a
dislike to the smell of the black fur on my purple wrap that I
would rather shiver than wear it, while the other day I bought
a new pot of face-cream that I found very agreeable last year
and hated the scent so much that I gave it straight away to
Mother. It is disconcerting to be the slave of such small things.
I am longing to get back to London, where people don't ask
one to meals that are an ordeal to sit through because of
the stuffiness and smells. I don't suppose I shall mind the
boat, as I probably shan't feel any more sick on it than I do
off it! Incidentally, my face is as brown as a berry and I look
disgustingly well.

Work is a little difficult when one is wrapped about in a kind
of encompassing languor, but on the other hand sitting and
doing nothing but wonder how soon one will feel sick again is

even worse, and as Mother says I probably shan't feel sick any more after another 6 weeks I am trying not to let anything drop. I think you had better not book any lectures for me for the present – i.e. until I am out of the sickness-miscarriage period – i.e. not before August. If all goes normally I wouldn't mind a few autumn ones in London; I mean a Six Pt. Gp. At Home Speech, for example. You can get me out of any summer ones by saying you are not quite sure whether I shall be in town – which wouldn't prevent my writing for anyone.

I really think Mr Catlin could be left alone now. I believe Mother is going to tell Father about the potential infant, as she thinks it may keep him quiet and stop him trying to send for her before we are due to sail, but do prevent him if you can from telling all sorts of people in confidence. You can always keep him quiet by talking about 'people who babble about their affairs' as compared with the wonderful people who (like himself!) mind their own business!

Gordon is angelic and seems rather afraid that if I step on the ground I shall break! (I rather think Mother has been putting the fear of the Lord into him!) He looks amazingly well, but rather resents being ribaldly addressed as 'Little Pa!' The Lord knows how he is going to get all his books packed, but I suppose they'll get done, as most of his things do in the end.

Again and again I am sorry you are having such a wretched time, sweetieheart, but at least I don't suppose it will ever happen that we are all away again. Mother being able to get over has really made all the difference to her as well as to me; and I think in a quiet way she quite enjoys it, and really feels very pleased to think that for once she is really useful to me! So at least you are doing a good work which she appreciates. Tell Father she is looking ever so much better for the change and the quiet here.

All love, Dearest girl Ever your V.S.V.D.L.

WINIFRED TO VERA

14 May 1927

My little Dear, my little Beautiful,

All blessings to you. And I hope that the physical
discomforts will not be sufficient to spoil all your pleasure in the
child which ought to be such a sauce of joy to so many people.
Do take care of yourself and don't spill it! I am so awfully glad
that your mother is with you. Darling, I have been amused
and pleased by my Two Old Men. They have given me much
entertainment and very little inconvenience. Your father has
loveable qualities, and a certain raciness, especially when he
gets a little bawdy, which make him at times most admirable
company, and I must have obtained from the two of them
material for a whole new novel.

But had it really been unpleasant, shouldn't I have been
fortunate to have the chance really to do something quite
useful for you for once? There is nothing in the world like the
happiness of being able to give something that they want to
the people whom you really love. The chance so rarely comes.
We dance about and protest our undying affection, and are
lucky if we escape being an encumbrance. Really to help you,
to serve you in some small way, to be of some quite mechanical
use to you. My trouble is always to allot nicely the attention
which I have to dispose of in the world. I should so much prefer
always to sit down at the feet of the people whom I best love
and look with the eyes of a handmaid towards the hand of my
masters. And I suppose that this purely personal devotion is
wrong. One ought to be more impersonal. But when a windfall
like this happens, when I can with a quite clear conscience
do something like this, I am happier than at any other time. I
don't know what life means if it does not mean loving, nor love,

if it does not mean serving – only to go and spend a pleasant
holiday at Brighton seems so silly a thing to make any fuss
about that I have not yet won my right to talk about serving
and other high-falutin' things. Anyway, I am glad. And so glad
that you will have a baby. And what fun it will be next year,
whatever the final arrangements are. Really, I am quite good
with babies. I will inquire about maisonettes and lets and have a
list waiting for you, my little Dear, my little Beautiful,
      v.s.v.d.l. W.

VERA TO WINIFRED

117 Oak Avenue, Ithaca, New York | *15 May 1927*

My dear darling girl,

Here are a few articles; do anything with them or nothing,
just as you like. One or more of the travel ones may do for
the *Manchester Guardian* Miscellany. I don't think 'The Myth
of the Weaker Vessel' is suitable for anything English, but it
may interest you to see it. I don't know that I am a very good
example of its main idea, but I don't suppose that matters much.
It is true of at any rate some people.

I am all alone today, as Mother and Gordon have gone off
to see Niagara, nearly 200 miles from here; they started at
7.15 this morning, and won't be back till 10 p.m. I should like
to have gone with them, but the faculty I have developed of
being suddenly and uncompromisingly sick at any hour of any
day makes me altogether too thrilling a companion for a long
excursion – just as it might have made me a rather too exciting
speaker at the National Woman's Party dinner! On the whole I
don't mind, as I am getting so used to it; though at times I feel
humiliated and annoyed with myself, and wish I could take it

all equably and competently. And yet I don't know. I hold to my
theory that those people are most entitled to an opinion who
keep it in spite of having faced the utmost disadvantages.

I still believe that complete physical fitness for all women
during maternity not only ought to but ultimately will be
possible. You and I were not brought up with the right attitude
towards sexual functions; we only adopted it long after being
grown up, which was too late to affect our physiology. In time
to come, girls will be brought up more sanely and normally, and
because they don't 'make a difference' during periodicity they
will find they don't have to for all but a few weeks of maternity.

But the Henderson-Liveseys have this much of sense in their
attitude, that the feminism of a woman who hasn't experienced
the sudden feeling of helplessness at being in thralldom to a
physical condition which she can't escape, must always remain a
little academic. All question of the peerage apart, it would have
done Lady Rhondda good to have a baby; it would have made
her feminism a little more human and a little more practical.
I don't of course mean that the prospect of a baby alters one
scrap the theories according to which you and she and I have
always worked; it only makes one realise the more fully their
implications. Nor do I mean that only mothers are entitled to
be feminists; that would be absurd. Some women don't marry;
some who marry don't have children, and even when they do,
to take three or four years off completely (if they have to) for
a job which if done competently is as useful to society as any
other (for how few problems there would be if everyone was
well-born and well-reared!), ought not to make a person less
valuable either to their profession or intrinsically as a citizen.

No one thinks less of a man because he takes four or five
years off from his normal work to fight in a war or sit on
a commission or go abroad on some special investigation.
Maternity, even if it takes up the whole of a woman's time

for two or three periods of a year each, is no more of an
interruption than many of the alternative jobs done by men.
It's absurd for maternity to be penalised as it is at present. It's a
penalty enough in itself, without lost jobs and lost incomes and
lost opportunities being added on. It seems self-evident that,
unless maternity is rewarded rather than penalised, the best
and most intelligent women in future will never be induced to
be mothers; yet education authorities and local boards go on
exactly the opposite principle.

I do hope you'll succeed before I come back either in pacifying
Nursie (for the next few months) or substituting Miss Dainty.
I don't want to be driven by her resentment to take refuge in
Oakwood Court – partly because Mother, for all her goodness,
and her very real services, irritates me a little all the time just
when I am in a state that is very easily irritated, and partly
because it will leave unsolved the problem of you and Gordon
together at Wymering Mansions (not that any of us would mind
but it might shock your family) and we can't at present afford for
him to have a separate abode, though he may go to Oxford for a
few weeks in the summer to break the back of his book. I don't
suppose I shall go unless I feel exceptionally well by then, as
you know the effect Papa Catlin has on me, and also I have had
about enough of lodgings and travels and packing under present
circumstances – or indeed under any circumstances.

I am counting the days (only just over a fortnight; we go to
N.Y. – the Shelton – on June 1st and sail the night of the 3rd–
4th) till I can get away from this place, as I live in perpetual
terror of uninteresting females ringing me up and asking me to
long, heavy meals. (A meal at the moment is rather like a visit
to the dentist; one is quite uncertain whether one is going to
get through it with dignity!) And this involves either enduring
tentatively and anxiously, the meal, or making an excuse which
becomes more suspicious the more it is repeated.

I have been too often bereaved to endure with equanimity inquisitive looks when I enter the room, combined with whisperings and a sudden, obvious change in the conversation. The nastiness of nature is merciful compared with the nastiness of certain human minds. I don't feel (not yet at any rate) an intense interest in my own situation. I want to forget it as often as I can, but once a certain type of woman knows, one is never allowed to do so. Even Mother keeps me perpetually and exasperatingly reminded of it; but that is probably because she is so really interested (and also so afraid of my 'being ill' before I get home).

The leaves are all out and little queer magenta flowers, a cross between a violet and a tiny iris, grow close to the ground in the wood. Here is one. They remind me a little, only they are neither so blue nor so beautiful, of the tiny irises that grew among the rocks on the seashore at Malta the spring that Geoffrey and Victor were killed. I wonder which of all the men I might have married would have provided me with the most gifted child. Probably Roland, though he would have been a much more difficult and trying husband than Gordon, who probably loves me more than any man I have ever known, though I doubt if any man's love equals a woman's love for a woman when it is healthy and genuine. Would any man have cared for Miss Heath-Jones as my aunt has done? Will Gordon ever be so good to me as you are? I doubt it. Fond as I am of him, I shall never, I think, have the same complete, unshadowed reliance on his benevolence as I have on yours. With men there is always a little arrière-pensée of their own comfort, their own convenience. So there is with many women (including myself), but I have never found it in you as regards me, or in my aunt as regards Miss Heath-Jones.

Dear, dear sweetieheart. More than I can say I long to get back to you. I suppose my longing is wholly selfish, but it isn't

a longing which wants to spoil anything you are doing, only
to have the stimulus of your presence. You warm me like a
beautiful summer day.

Ever, my darling one, your v.s.v.d.l.

VERA TO WINIFRED

117 Oak Avenue, Ithaca, New York | 19 May 1927

My sweetieheart,

I am absolutely delighted to hear about 'The Land of Green
Ginger'. It is a well-deserved award after you have done so much
for so many other people. Cape sounds an admirable publisher.
£30 down on the day of publication sounds excellent treatment
after people like Grant Richards. It will come out in the
autumn, I suppose – just the best time, and with all your articles
getting everywhere it ought just to assure your reputation.
It shows one need not be daunted in trying a publisher just
because he turned down a previous book.

I *must* write another novel. I feel I have been dreadfully
remiss and slack these three years. While you were writing your
book I was writing to Gordon or worrying about him. I could
easily have written a book in the time my letters to him took.
If only I can feel reasonably well, I ought to be able, by working
2–3 hours a morning, to get a novel written before the infant
arrives. Mother says she will see to all its clothes and enjoy
doing so, and I shan't be able to undertake much other time-
taking activity than writing. It's queer how it has been my fate
to get married, and now presumably to have children, when all
I really care for deeply is writing things and publishing them
and have so little *forte* for marriage and motherhood. You would
have done both so much better, and probably having a more

equable temperament, have written the books too. Sometimes I feel I want to cut all human relationships but yours and get back to the stage we were in at the beginning of 1923. At present I can't think of the prospective infant except as a tiresome reality which makes me feel sick when I want to work. How can one think of a thing as a human entity when the only indication of its presence so far are nausea and headache and fatigue? If only one's reactions could be psychological instead of so obsessively physiological!

So many thanks for all cuttings. This is just a scrawl to catch the mail, and to say how glad I am about 'The Land of Green Ginger'.

All love, my sweetest heart, Always your V.S.V.D.L.

VERA TO WINIFRED

117 Oak Avenue, Ithaca, New York | 29 May 1927

My darling sweetieheart,

This, I suppose, is the last mail I can catch before the one that brings me back myself. I am so glad – I am dead sick of this place, and have spent the last two weeks avoiding people who talk futilities and are damned inquisitive about Gordon's and my plans. It is Cottingham ten times worse because American, and therefore less reserved and restrained. People pursue one till one's only self-defence is downright rudeness, and even that doesn't always penetrate their skins. Surely even provincial South Africa is a little subtler and more sensitive than this!

I don't know, by the way, how anyone can postulate that maternity – whether actual or potential – is improving to one's moral character, for it seems to me to make one more selfish than one ever credited even one's self with being. I feel so physically slack that if anyone offers to do for me anything I don't want to do, I relinquish the effort to do it without a qualm of conscience! Of course I do think that this is as much the place as anything else.

The weather in May has been soaking, torrential rains sandwiched in between two days of thunderstorms. The only nice thing about the town is the tulips, which are pink and mauve and yellow and scarlet bubbles in front of all the houses. If people took as much trouble over their children as they take over their tulips, American families would be far more tolerable.

May 30th

We are all longing to get away from this place, and seem to do nothing but get on each other's nerves. As you know, more than a week or two of Mother at a time is always too much for me, and altogether for one reason or another I feel as if I had been in this place eight months instead of eight weeks. Every day seems like a week. However, I never intend to return to it. Too few years, even at the best, are left to me to waste them in this way. If Gordon has to return he must return alone; it is part of the risk of marrying a woman with her own work and individuality. I like him, but not enough to sacrifice everything else for. I don't like anyone enough for that, any more than you do. My one wish at the moment is that I had enough strength of mind and natural rudeness to tell one of the residents here what I really do think of the place.

But enough. In ten days or so I shall be home – to feel, I hope, as I did last year, quite different at once.

All love, my sweetieheart; I shall look for you at Southampton.

Ever your V.S.V.D.L.

In the year between the previous letter and the one that follows,
Vera's first child, John Edward Jocelyn Brittain Catlin, was born
in London on 19 December 1927. Vera, Gordon and Winifred
had all moved to a two-floor flat in a larger house at 6A Nevern
Place, London SW5, but Gordon spent much of the year at Cornell
University.

1928

VERA TO WINIFRED

The Falmouth Hotel, Falmouth, Cornwall | *1 July 1928*

Darling girl,

So many thanks for your letters. I do hope the child goes on
keeping well. I love him so much that I suppose the thought of
him will slightly spoil all holidays spent away from him for the
rest of my life!

I see by *The Observer* that George Allen and Unwin plus the
Houghton Mifflin Co. of New York are offering a prize of £5,000
and royalties for a novel with the War as a background. This
upsets a little my impulse to write a book on marriage before the
war novel. I don't mean that I shall go in for the competition (I
shall send to Allen and Unwin for the particulars, but I don't
think a chronicle of the kind mine would be would stand much
chance in a *novel* competition of the usual kind and to be turned
down heavily is a worse disadvantage than not to go in for it at
all), but it does look as if a large collection of war novels will be
published about fifteen months hence and therefore that if one is
to have any hope of acceptance one must get in before the rush.

I could do both this and the marriage book in a year if only I had a) physical energy; b) time, and freedom from interruption. The former I think this holiday, at least temporarily will supply. – enough to get started anyway; the latter depends largely on freedom from interruption on the part of the household. Do you think it would be a good thing for me, while we have a housekeeper who lives out, to use the little room for my study? It is simply devilish being the only person who has no room to go away to to work; it means I am fair game for anyone who has anything to ask – whether a telephone message, a parcel messenger who desires change, what I want for lunch, etc.

Somehow or other I *must* get more freedom from interruption; it is destroying all my work. How can it be done?

I sometimes really feel quite desperate when I think how time is passing and how much I could do, and then how little I actually get done even in time that is supposed to be work time.

Weather still rough – too windy to bathe – but doing lots of walks and meditation as well as a little reading. I expect *we shall* return on Friday as Gordon wants to go to the Anglo-American Relations conference – too many 'people of importance' to be missed.

All love, dear heart, V.S.V.D.L.

VERA TO WINIFRED

The Falmouth Hotel, Falmouth, Cornwall | *3 July 1928*

Dearest girl,

So many thanks for Monday's letter. I am glad the child is being agreeable.

There are very few people at this hotel and they all go to bed at 9.30! – *no* dancing, *no* wireless, not even a gramophone, and there seems to be no way of obtaining them in the town either. But it gives plenty of time for conversation, which in most ways is more valuable. Also, among the few people here are the Vice-Provost of King's College, Cambridge and his wife. They are both I should say near seventy, but a charming old couple – humorous, pungent, intelligent, tolerant and feminist – friends of the Webbs, Keynes, etc. – half the people one knows, or has heard of in the older generation.

Allen and Unwin sent the particulars of the war novel competition. It is financed from America and all the judges are American, and the winning novel is to be serialised (rights already acquired by the *American Legion Monthly*), dramatised and filmed; they apparently want something on the scale of Tolstoy's *War and Peace* combined with *The Dynasts* mixed with *The Four Horsemen of the Apocalypse*! Anyhow on a big scale. Had I four years' notice to think it out in, plus a year to write it in, I might have contemplated it, but in my interrupted life, with the necessity of earning fairly steadily by articles, it seems next to impossible – though the need to get quickly written any novel dealing with the war still remains.

So glad Clare liked the child. She is wise not to marry I think – the husband and children if rightly chosen are not really the trouble; it is the household they involve. I dread coming back purely and simply because it involves 'dealing tactfully' with Nurse and Mrs Walker and always having to give part of one's mind to this, instead of being able to allow one's self to drift into that state of complete preoccupation which seems to be the major necessity of good work. Nursie made it possible – I wonder if ever it will be again. Not, I suspect, until the child or children go to school.

All love, my sweetieheart, v.s.v.d.l.

WINIFRED TO VERA

Bainesse, Cottingham, East Yorkshire | *21 August 1928*

Darling,

I believe that we may perhaps make too much of this
'enrichment by sexual relations'. What if we find with Shaw's
Ancients that the true *adventure* is right outside sex, and that
the true *stability* is in one monogamous relationship? I'm all for
adventure. I fall in love with different minds yearly and know
no greater pleasure than to go hunting affections. I would hunt,
if I could, Shaw, Smuts and Lawrence – lovely minds, all of
them. I love Jan and Gordon. It amuses me to tease Andrews.
And Harry I shall love all my life. But it may be that you are
right and that sex is a force to be used for permanence – that
Aquinas was right and that it is a force to be used for children.
And that we have complicated life too much by mixing up
adventurous love and sex – by thinking that sex must enter
into every close relationship. It *must* in a natural – *i.e.* an
oversexed – state. Oversexed from the point of view of a more
intellectual civilisation. But shall we never escape the toils of
an animal nature, and reach a stage where we use sex as the
consummation of a peculiar relationship, towards the man or
woman from whom we want children, and as the memorial of
that desire with him or her; but that all other loves, though
far more intimate and adventurous than those which we dare
permit ourselves today are indiscriminate loves towards both
men and women? Like the angels in heaven, neither marrying
nor giving in marriage.

You must for your marriage book read Arthur Symons' *Life
of Blake*. Blake had the most extreme views about 'liberation of
the bodily desire' and so forth, but was one of the strictest and
most virtuous of men – like Henderson and other liberals.

It's a new thought to me, but not a new desire, that we should shake off this *tyranny of sex* – and use it only as the stabilising power towards the creature with whom we decide to continue the human race – if we do so decide.

I've written an article about 'Dancers and Inhibitions', based on Monte Carlo. At Monte Carlo everyone is so much afraid of complexes and inhibitions that they all run about having relations with men, women and both – and get more and more hot and bothered. Now when one watches the Russian ballet one realises that one's own body is full of inhibitions. I can't twirl on my toe or bend my head to my heels. But it is not restriction but lack of control that binds me. Discipline and training relaxes and liberates. Control liberates. Lack of control binds and makes clumsy in a thousand ways. Are we going all wrong in crying 'Less control'? Perhaps we are. Perhaps we need more control – more perfectly disciplined use of our bodies, but far, far greater adventurousness in our imaginations and affections towards another.

I must go and get lunch!!!

v.s.v.d.l. W.

Radclyffe Hall taught me a lot. She's all fearfully wrong, I feel. To love other women deeply is not pathological. To be unable to control one's passions is. Her mind is all sloppy with self-pity and self-admiration. She's not straight in her mind.

VERA TO WINIFRED

6A Nevern Place, London SW5 | *25 September 1928*

Darling –

So sorry you have had – as I am sure you have had – a trying

time. How terribly you are inundated with babies and their
ailments! John Edward at the moment is very well and has
just been having tea with Storm Jameson. He is beginning to
teethe so fast that Nurse thinks he may cut a tooth while I
am away, but she doesn't anticipate trouble and I am sure will
be quite capable of coping with him in any case. At the week-
end he began trying to climb out of his cot, so I had to rush
off to Harrods yesterday and buy him a crib and all the etcs –
£11! – but it is a lovely one; pale brown wood like the pen, with
nursery rhymes all written out and with blue pictures above
them. I took him down to the clinic and weighed him the same
afternoon; he is 17 lb. 3 oz. Storm Jameson said he was one of
the beautifulest children she had ever seen – loved his eyes and
the shape of his face.

The evening after the Treviglio lunch I had a *violent* bilious
attack – wrote the *Yorkshire Post* leader on folk-lore in the
intervals of being sick – and have felt surpassingly better ever
since! That night I had such a curious dream – thought we were
back at college and when I suggested to you, as I did, coming to
live with me in a flat in town you were dreadfully hesitant and
haughty, on the ground that you had so many other friends that
you liked as much if not better! I had a strange feeling all next
day that you and I now live week after week in the same house,
I so absorbed in adoring a husband and son in the intervals of
my work, and you so absorbed in running round with friends
of varying degrees of celebrity in the intervals of yours, that
we never really see one another at all. I don't know whether it
was the effect of my dream or whether it really is so. You are
much more self-confident and somehow louder (I don't mean
more vulgar but somehow more resonant) than you once were,
but then I am probably much more 'married' than I once was,
which is even more objectionable.

The Open Door Council have asked me to go on their

executive; I didn't much want to personally because of my book
but yet don't want to offend them because of the somewhat
delicate state of affairs. I rang up Lady Rhondda and neither
of us could make up our minds about it, so I finally decided to
go on for the present and to keep an eye on them; I can easily
resign after the winter if it involves much more work.

All love my sweetieheart, v.s.v.d.l.

VERA TO WINIFRED

6A Nevern Place, London SW5 | *26 December 1928*

Darling sweetieheart,

So sorry that a domestic upheaval is keeping you. As if
Christmas wasn't fuss enough without that. I suppose you will
be bathing and feeding not one but two infants for the next few
days. However I am doing it too – though at least the house and
the infant are mine. Yesterday I had him on my hands from 10.30
to 5.00; he knew it was Christmas or something and refused to
sleep at all. To-day I had housecleaning all morning and infant
again this afternoon and evening; however I believe in having
everything at once and then settling down, if one can, to work.

Your lovely coat was much admired at Oakwood Court last
night. Did you see the opal ring Gordon has given me – a
tremendous big one, about the size of a pigeon's egg? Gorgeous.
I am so disappointed that you will miss my birthday party on
Saturday; it won't be the same without you at all.

I am reading *Undertones of War*; grave, dignified but perfectly
simple and straightforward; why shouldn't I write one like that?

Lady Rhondda sent me a glorious bowl of blue hyacinths, the
bowl being of an opalescent blue glass – seven tall hyacinths,
smelling lovely.

No news as I have done no work!
All love, my heart, V.S.V.D.L.

Johnnie does nothing but ask for 'Auntie' – searched for you
yesterday not only in your room but in the coat cupboard!

1929

*In 1929 as in the preceding year, Vera and Winifred were living in
the flat at 6A Nevern Place in London, caring for the infant John,
while Gordon spent much of his time at Cornell. Most of the letters
between Vera and Winifred were written during their travels; Winifred
vacationed in France with Lady Rhondda, and Vera went to Geneva
for the League of Nations assembly.*

WINIFRED TO VERA

4 Rue de Chevreuse, Paris | *30 March 1929*

My small, darling love,

Your lovely scarf arrived yesterday night just exactly the right
time for Easter Day. I went down to the office and the nice
man there said, 'A letter for you,' and I saw the big envelope
and thought it would be crowded with tedious business letters
and sighed and said 'Oh no! No. I'm on holiday. I don't want
big envelopes full of letters to answer.' Then I took it and it
crackled deliciously and I thought 'Strange sound for letters
from the National Union of Societies for Equal Citizenship,
etc.!' Then I opened it and out came the scarf. I howled with
delight and the nice man clapped his hands and said, 'Un
cadeau, un cadeau!' and undoubtedly thought it was from my

lover! I just love it. With either my black or my grey things it looks *too* lovely, and the yellow *does* suit me quite a lot. My sweet child, how good of you to send it me, and you out away there, and I dancing here so gaily – not literally – I don't dance only walk. But I love it. And I love you for sending it. And I kiss your hands.

I have been hearing quite a lot of you today in strange ways. Both Lady Rhondda and Theodora Bosanquet arrived armed with *Good Housekeeping* and *Reality* – each bought independently of the other. Both remarked how good your Oxford article was, and Lady Rhondda said that your teacher's one you have sent in to *Time and Tide* was most unusually good, so pungent and to the point. Then to read in the train when we went out to the woods at St Remy de Chevreuse today, Miss Bosanquet bought a copy of *Les Nouvelles Litteraires*, which she says is the leading French literary weekly. In it was an article on English women writers – beginning with Virginia Woolf, and dealing with most of the well-known ones. Then it speaks of the young militant Oxford feminist, now critic and novelist, Vera Brittain, specially notable for her novel *Not Without Honour*. Her heroine Christine Merivale has become 'une type et un symbole' of modern English girls and the effect of the war on their circumscribed surroundings. I'll try and get a copy and send it. It is written by the critic Abel Chevalley. He obviously has read *Time and Tide* as he quotes it once, but the stuff about you could only have come from literary gossip and from reading your book. Isn't it interesting?

We walked for miles today in brilliant sun through wintry woods. Very few buds even fat but suddenly we came on a little cluster of anemones. I send you one with love.

I love you – dearest love, Winifred

WINIFRED TO VERA

c/o Jan Smeterlin, 40 Boulevard des Moulins,
Monte Carlo | 9 August 1929

V.s.v.d.l.

Thank you so much for your letter of the 6th and all the
enclosures. Also for correcting my proofs. It is too bad that you
should have to do this as well as all your other odd jobs. It really
is a shame. However, when you get away to Vevey, you will
really be out of London!

I have written to acquaint Rebecca of my presence on the
coast, but heard no more. Not met van Druten or Noel Coward
yet, though both are here. I see Hamilton Forrest a lot. He is
a pussycat of the most vicious kind but has a most interesting
mind and excellent stage ideas – very good to talk to when not
gossiping, and even then amusing but a little alarming – so
dangerously malicious.

People here are the most hair-raising gossipers I ever heard.
Every second person is alleged to be homosexual; their love
affairs are recounted in detail – and probably without any
accuracy at all. Tenors quarrel and threaten suicide, swear
they will have each other's heart out, and are next seen going
off to supper arm-in-arm. Mary Garden makes and unmakes
reputations at a word – but is a much more interesting woman
that I thought last year. When she is talking about her work she
is thrilling. On their own job, most of these musical people are
thrilling. Off it, their ideas are almost exclusively confined to
cannibalism. They eat each other's characters and reputations
daily – a Black Mass. Edith and Jan are different – both so
intelligent and sweet. He is so charming to her now that
she is ill.

I want to write a comedy about Getting On. All the

intrigues and schemes and Important People, which I
never dare write up against a Laski-Academic background,
I believe I could do here, against a Monte Carlo Operatic
background. Call it 'The Industrious Apprentices' after
the old fable – with 'So This Is Music' as a subtitle – what?
And Lady Rhondda modified into an ex-prima donna,
present director of opera house, inhibitions and all – and
quite unrecognisable??? and Laski as an ambitious little
Jewish composer of ultra-modern opera??? What fun … if it
could be done.

 All love to all three v.s.v.d.l.

I do no work. I eat, swim and sleep twelve hours a day. When
women here rave about their lap dogs, I think of John Edward
and giggle. The more I see of dogs, the more I like children.

VERA TO WINIFRED

Canhams, Burgh Heath, Surrey | *10 August 1929*

Darling heart,

 Quite a batch of enclosures this time, tho' none seem very
thrilling. I have just been having quite an eventful day for
August – the interview with Lord Cecil followed by lunch with
Monica and Miss Foot.

 I trembled all last night and this morning about making
the speech on the Treaty for our delegation – but contrary
to expectation the interview was extremely pleasant. Lord
Cecil was *charming.* The delegation was quite a good one –
Mrs Ogilvie, Mrs Gahan, Mrs Archdale and Betty, Miss
Fletcher and me. I made my little speech and he listened
most courteously. He saw us all in a very small study in the

basement of his quite small house in South Eaton Place. He
then talked to us about the Treaty *entirely* without patronage –
took for granted it was important and merely dealt with the
difficulties we should have in putting it across. (For details ask
Lady R. to show you the long typed letter which I am going
to send her giving a full account.) He said that Henderson,
Graham of the Board of Trade, Philip Baker, Mrs Swarmville,
and Mrs Hamilton would all probably be friendly and advised
us to see them all at Geneva. (This is *most* valuable; think
how the attitude of them all will change when we are able
to write and say that Lord Cecil suggested our seeing them!)
But his chief point was that our great difficulty would be in
making the League authorities see feminism as international.
He stressed the opposition which was brought (and which
you and I are well aware of) against the League dealing with
any social questions and emphasized the point that in all
our work and propaganda we should endeavour to show the
international significance of women's inferior status – i.e. any
ways we can possibly think of in which it affects the relations
between countries. This was an extremely valuable tip. He
also said that as the result of asking for the Treaty we might
get a Commission such as the American one – but that as a
matter of tactics it did not much matter whether we asked for
the Commission and went on to the Treaty, or asked for the
Treaty and accepted the Commission, as everyone would be
quite well aware what we were after. He advised us to try to
see the Scandinavian delegates this year, and also promised to
talk the matter over with his colleagues on the delegation!! In
other words he did not turn down the idea as an idea at any
point and when I boldly stepped in and asked if he thought
there was any chance of Great Britain taking up the matter
he said he thought it reasonably possible! He also gave us
permission to make a press statement (which we promised to

show him first) saying we had seen him. Mrs Archdale and I
drew this up over coffee afterwards, and she and Betty, thank
goodness, are undertaking the typing and sending out. The
result of it all has been to make me much keener myself on the
Treaty; as I found when speaking for Monica, there is nothing
like one's own speeches to convert one to a course! What I am
now going to do is to try to draw up a memorandum specifying
all the ways I can think of in which discriminations against
women have international repercussions and send it to Cecil –
also to the members of the British delegation and possibly to
al the delegations. Betty, Mrs Archdale and Mrs Gahan will
be in Geneva and can stay after I have gone.

Monica also will be there. I went on to lunch with her and
Miss Foot after the meeting – they were both delightful and
are coming here on Thursday. The flat really is charming –
especially Monica's little study with its books and crucifix. Miss
Foot treats me with great affection and she had sent to her
bookseller for a list of all our publications most of which she
proposes to order! I think really that she is very conscious of
the fact that, barring accidents, Monica must outlive her, and
with characteristic realism (as over the cremation) is trying
to provide her with younger friends against that time. It must
be rather tragic for both sides when the age gap between great
friends is so large. Monica is very anxious for you to go on a
Committee which Nina Boyle has formed to deal with the
question of native women in Africa, and is going to speak to
you about it in September. By the sound of it I really think you
had better, as Miss Boyle, who has lived for years in Africa,
is capable of doing untold harm with her semi-informed
fanaticism. Monica is on the committee too but she doesn't
know Africa.

Your Privy Council article is in this week's *Nation*. Gordon
actually likes it here and is staying the whole time! – great joy.

Poor John Edward *did* scratch his nose; only the surface but all over it with the result that he looks just like a little toper! or a clown with a red nose.

All love my heart. V.S.V.D.L.

WINIFRED TO VERA

Train, Monte Carlo to Saint Raphael | *17 August 1929*

Darling Love,

Almost all the people here are homosexual and the men have men lovers à la Plato. But they are very intelligent and everyone Edith and Jan know either paints or writes or composes or designs furniture. Mary Garden and her sister Aggie are charming. Aggie wants to come and see us in London. She liked my book. I wish you had been here. I have such a lot to say. But I won't inflict my writing on you. I am just going to Lady Rhondda's.

Jan is sweet. And when he gets cross he is so exactly like you, Vera, that I could kiss him. He says first, the same rampageous things and orders us all to leave the room, and Edith just takes him for granted. They love each other terribly. I think that modern marriage has far more give and take and real tolerance than the old-fashioned sort.

Bless you both, Winifred

WINIFRED TO VERA

25 August 1929

Darling,

I am so sorry about your Father. What a time you seem to be having. And as usual I am away and can't help. I may be coming home earlier than I meant to. Father seems only so-so and Mother very tired. I feel so mean to be in this glorious place.

I will be very careful in the water. I find that though I can't swim at all well, I float like a ball. There are no currents here, so only people who are not floatable could drown. If I get out of my depth I simply turn over on my back and holler till someone tows me in to shallow water. Some people are natural floaters. I think it's a matter of square root.

Only Lady Rhondda and me here so far. Very nice. I think she feels about the Radclyffe Hall like you. We had a long, long talk last night about sexual snobbery. She thinks what you and Gordon are doing supremely important. She says it may happen that you as an artist and thinker won't accomplish as much as you might have done unmarried, because so much of your time will be taken up in fighting for your career, but that only by doing what you are doing will it be possible for people in the future to live normal lives, and that it is immensely important to humanity. She seems to have come to like you *very* much. I think those talks on marriage helped. She said she would not advise me to remain toute vierge always! But that I need not marry! Edith on the other hand said that the whole sex business was overrated and that though it was a good thing to love, sexual relations were neither here nor there. She has become suddenly a feminist. But instinctively and without political implication.

I'll let you know when I'm coming home.

W. v.s.v.d.l.

VERA TO WINIFRED

Hôtel des Familles, Geneva | *5 September 1929*

Darling sweetieheart,

 I had a much more cheerful letter from Mother yesterday.
Have got to the stage when I begin quite acutely to long to see
John Edward again. According to the *Daily Mail* you seem to
have had bad thunderstorms.

 Monica spends all the time with me that doesn't go on
official things. We are going together tonight to the dinner
given by women's organisations to the women delegates. My
days go in one long dream of Assemblies, conversations,
and a tremendous and vehement argument, which never
seems to come to an end, with Monica about feminism and
homosexuality. I am not as you know a shockable person but
her views on the latter subject are revolutionary in the extreme.
She feels men to be such oppressors and such sources of evil
that she says if she had a daughter she would deliberately urge
her to enter into a homosexual relationship with another
woman rather than seek marriage – which is far more likely to
be disappointing and disastrous. I tell her that such views are
dangerous in the extreme and if this is the logical outcome of
feminism, feminists such as she will end by wrecking their own
movement. Last evening she roused me to such a pitch of fury
that I told her she was a dangerous and utterly wrong-headed
fanatic, and banged the door of the Pension Coupier on her.
She only smiled, and turned up at the Stamford party two hours
later as full of agreeableness and equanimity as ever. Gordon
says she is a person of such tremendous passion and fanaticism
that if he saw much of her he would quarrel badly, but she has a
kind of queer fascination for him as he is always looking for her
and asking me where she is.

I hope my dear John Edward keeps well. I have enjoyed
this holiday more than any since you and I went to Italy and
I think Gordon has too – I am so glad I stuck to my guns and
made him go.

All fondest love, my heart, V.S.V.D.L.

VERA TO WINIFRED

6A Nevern Place, London SW5 | *6 December 1929*

Darling girl,

So many thanks for your letter. We are all so glad to know
each day what the news is. My family ring up to hear from
Oakwood Court each day and this morning Mother called
round. So glad you were wise enough to go to the theatre – if
you were able to, that is.

I have not been to Dr Gray yet to find out if it is true about
the infant, as it seems too soon, but shall go in another week to
see if she can tell me anything definite. I think it must be a fact
as my period is ten days overdue which has never happened in
my life except before John came, and also I feel mildly sea-sick
at intervals, though nothing to last time. The end of July won't
be such a bad time – there will be nothing doing in the world
at large for two months and the infant will have three months
of warmish weather before it. I do hope we get St Leonard's
Terrace, as that high bedroom would be so lovely to be in right
in front of the window and no one overlooking – also the
gardens – our own and the big one – to sit in for convalescing
and for the little animal to sleep in. Miss Raynham Smith has
already bespoken a nurse for me.

I had lunch today with such a nice person – Mrs Janet
Chance, who read a paper to the Sex Reform Conference on

her marriage education centre; she wrote to me on the strength
of my *Realist* article. I think she must be rich as she finances
the centre herself, and lunched me most sumptuously at the
Garden Club just off Curzon Street. She is full of most valuable
information on the causes and consequences of sex-frigidity in
women and very ready to pass on the information.

All love, my heart, v.s.v.d.l.

1930

Vera's second child, Shirley, was born on 27 July 1930. Needing a
more spacious home, Vera, Gordon and Winifred moved once again,
to 19 Glebe Place in Chelsea.

VERA TO WINIFRED

19 Glebe Place, London SW3 | 23 August 1930

Darling sweet,

When your telegram arrived yesterday at an astonishingly early
hour, Gordon broke to me the news that you had gone to Paris
by air. You monstrous creature for not telling me – and yet I am
glad you didn't, for I read the account of the Kent accident to the
Le Touquet party about two days before Shirley arrived and was
perpetually haunted by it all the first week I was in bed. So had I
known I should certainly have pictured all kinds of ghastly things
happening to you, especially on rather a windy day. I am most
anxious to know what it feels like and whether you were more, or
less, sea-sick than when you are crossing the Channel. But even if
less I don't see myself doing it, at any rate for the present.

No news at all. I deliberately made Sister go out today from 3.00

till 10.00 and let Nurse go after she had put John to bed, and coped with the infant myself from the 6.00 feed onwards – apparently with success as it is now 8.15 and she is sleeping peacefully. I came down to breakfast this morning too, so I have had a strenuous day and don't feel at all too tired – much better than I did when John was two months old. I even also did a little weeding in the garden this afternoon, and walked back from Peter Jones this morning. So I shall soon be leading an entirely normal life again.

I am still too stupid however to write a letter worth reading. I hope you are safely at Agay by now and will have a really adorable holiday to make up for all the tiresomeness of the past few months. How glad you must be to get out of the atmosphere of nurses, servants and children!

Just got your p.c. from France – so glad you liked it so much and weren't sick, but I still don't see myself doing it.

Ever your V.S.V.D.L.

VERA TO WINIFRED

19 Glebe Place, London SW3 | 31 August 1930

Darling,

Here are all the letters that have arrived in the past three or four days except your contract for 'Poor Caroline', which Curtis Brown have forwarded and I am keeping for you with your cheques.

At last the heat wave has gone, and – remarkably enough for me – I am really thankful. Three days running of 95° was rather hard on John and Shirley, and much as I love heat, a day which begins at 5.30 a.m., ends at 11.30 p.m., and involves a good deal of running up and downstairs with intermittent half hours of playing with John, becomes rather exacting at that temperature.

Sister warned me that during the excessive heat Shirley
probably would not gain, but in spite of the little creature being
bathed in perspiration for four days, she put on 6 oz. in the
week *and* without the aid of tin food. I must admit that I am
really rather enjoying it, just as, when I am feeling perfectly fit,
I enjoy moves and spring-cleaning; if *only* I could eliminate the
constant wish to work, forget I had ever been ambitious, and
cease chasing work-periods which don't materialise because
other claims eat into them, I can imagine nothing much
pleasanter and more satisfying than the care of these little
things – especially as John is a dear and has become intelligent
and left the completely irrational activity stage behind, whereas
Shirley has not yet reached it.

I realise more and more how completely self-indulgent those
women are who make the care of their children an excuse
for doing nothing else. Of course I shall have far more time
to myself when John goes back to school; at present there
are so many little periods when Nurse is bathing Shirley, or
clearing the night nursery, or washing, when John roams
disconsolately about the house; he is bored with the garden and
I don't wonder – it really is so dull and full of weeds; when we
transform it he must have lots of swings and things to play with.
I am proving, much to my satisfaction, the complete truth of my
own contention – namely, the dependence of married women's
careers upon the provision of more nursery schools – and as
much for the middle classes as for the poor.

With all love V.S.V.D.L.

PART III

1931–1935

Triumph and Tragedy

INTRODUCTION

The year 1931 began promisingly for Winifred. In January, she published her fourth novel, *Poor Caroline*, which received enthusiastic reviews, went into a second edition and brought her the offer of a three-novel contract from William Collins. With an advance for her next book, she was able to support herself through the summer, although she did not start a new novel. Instead, that spring she began working on a critical study – the first – of Virginia Woolf. Thomas Moult, a poet who was editing a series of books on modern writers, had invited her to contribute and to pick her own author. Instead of naming Rose Macaulay or Storm Jameson from among the many novelists she knew who had been her literary models, she chose to write on Woolf, 'the author whose art seemed most of all removed from anything I could ever attempt, and whose experience was most alien to my own'.

It was a bold decision. She had never met Woolf, whose high artistry both enthralled and intimidated her. Nevertheless, she confided in the South African writer Sarah Gertrude Millin that she was exhilarated by the prospect of writing a critical book about Woolf, and entering 'even at second-hand, that world of purely aesthetic and intellectual interests'. At first

Winifred consulted a mutual friend, the composer Ethyl Smyth, on biographical details, but Woolf intervened and they had three meetings. In her diary and letters Woolf mocked Holtby as 'poor' and 'gaping' (in reference to a gap in her teeth), 'an amiable donkey'. Winifred was not the only target of Woolf's snobbish insults in her diaries; many came off even worse. Still, when the book came out in October, Woolf wrote to Winifred that she had enjoyed it very much, and joked that 'you suggested so many extremely interesting points of view that I long to write a book on VW myself'. Winifred was always modest about her own critical gifts, but *Virginia Woolf* is a perceptive, wide-ranging and often witty study. One of Woolf's limitations as a novelist, she writes, is that 'she has never understood the stupid'.

Meanwhile, Vera was rereading her diaries and letters in preparation for her war memoir. In August she decided on the title *Testament of Youth*, and she, Gordon and the children went off for a holiday in France. Their plans were overturned in mid-September by Gordon's decision to stand in the general election. He cherished hopes of abandoning academia for politics, and when he was invited to be the Labour candidate for Brentford and Chiswick he grabbed the opportunity. Both Vera and Winifred put their writing on hold to support him. But on 27 October, Labour met an enormous defeat.

Three days after the election, Winifred felt too ill with a 'violent headache' to join Vera and Gordon for breakfast. Vera went to her room and saw that 'there were dark circles under her eyes, and her face was pale with [an] ominous yellowish pallor.' The doctor recommended rest and she went with Clare Leighton – Roland's sister and a close friend – to Clare's cottage at Monks Risborough in Buckinghamshire. On 10 November she wrote cheerfully to Vera that she might be going on a cruise to the Canary Islands as the guest of Lady Rhondda, whom she suspected of conspiring with the doctor to get her to rest. Her headache was much better, but she realised that the headache had been there for weeks; she was so used to it that she didn't notice.

In the event, Winifred did not go on the cruise. For a short time she resumed her busy life in London, but on 23 November she was so ill that her doctor sent her to a nursing home in Earls Court to recuperate. She remained there until after Christmas. Doctors examined her, but could determine only that her blood pressure was alarmingly high. They recommended complete rest for five or six weeks, away from London in a milder climate. In January she and Vera spent some time together at Sidmouth, and then Winifred went back to Monks Risborough.

In March 1932, however, Winifred's blood pressure was up to 200, and she went to see Dr Edgar Obermer, an Austrian specialist in arterial diseases. She did not, however, tell Vera his terrible diagnosis: that she had Bright's disease, a form of kidney failure, and might have only two years to live. Vera spoke to Obermer herself, but he played down the dangers of Winifred's case. He told her that Winifred must come to a nursing home in London for a month while he supervised experimental treatments with diet and drugs. Winifred made light of it, writing that she had been assured of a cure if she was 'sensible' and followed his instructions. For the next year she was resting, at clinics or at home.

Vera was feeling lonely in London, where she had been accustomed to turning for comfort to Winifred; moreover, Gordon had written from Ithaca that he was having an affair with a Dutch girl. She was studying successful war memoirs, but worrying that she might face recriminations if she got facts wrong. But the tide was turning for *Testament of Youth*, which was accepted in January 1933 by Harold Latham of Macmillan for the United States and in February by Victor Gollancz for Great Britain. Winifred rejoiced with her. Although she was helping to take care of her ailing father at home, she made time to compose a long, rapturous blurb for the book. Then Gordon wrote from Cornell demanding major cuts and revisions to the last chapter, in which Vera described their courtship. The manuscript was being edited, and changing the last chapter would leave the reader with no explanation of her reasons for marrying. She was devastated. But Winifred stepped in, and with tact and sympathy negotiated a face-saving compromise: Vera eliminated almost all the details that might identify Gordon, and referred to him only by the initial 'G.', but their courtship and marriage remained in the book as the symbol of resurrection after the horrors of the War.

In June and July, Winifred accompanied Vera, Gordon and the children on holidays in France, and then Vera sat at home and nervously awaited publication and reviews. On 28 August, *Testament of Youth* was published, and became an instant bestseller. It would become her finest book and her greatest success. In December, she signed a contract with the American agent Colston Leigh to give lectures throughout the United States the following autumn. Vera was anxious about leaving her family, but Winifred insisted that she must go, and agreed to take care of the children while Vera was away.

That autumn of 1934 continued a period of triumph for Vera. She had the literary acclaim, respect and fame she had long desired, not just in England but even in the United States. For a week before the tour started in October, she stayed at the Connecticut home of her publisher George Brett and his wife Isabel, and heard about her itinerary: thirty-four lectures in twenty-five cities – in fact there would be more – travelling by train and staying in hotels. The tour was gruelling and exhausting; but Vera was in good spirits, rarely suffering from headaches, and generally uncomplaining.

Her revived energy depended on more than the money and attention. She had become infatuated with George Brett. As her stay in America went on, her attraction to Brett became more intense, and he was leading her on, with flowers and attention. In vivid letters she described the tour and the flirtation to Winifred, who accepted it in her usual loving and non-judgemental way.

At about the same time, Winifred's quietly radical *Women and a Changing Civilisation* was published in London. It was her strongest statement of feminist issues. In her conclusion, she listed her conditions for equality between men and women. First, 'a rational philosophy of life'. Second, advances in mechanical invention. Third, 'effective and accessible knowledge of birth control. So long as women either are forced to remain celibate, or unable to plan their lives because pregnancy may come upon them at any time, so long is it impossible that as workers or citizens they should be as reliable, as efficient, as regular as men.' Her final statement gave her philosophy of life: 'It is no use asking for equality if it is not going to make us happier, wiser, more mature and vigorous human beings. When we talk about emancipation, it is as well to go a little further and ask – emancipation from what?'

On 14 December Vera sailed back to England, arriving a week later in time for a brief reunion with Winifred, who was heading to Cottingham for three weeks. For the first few months of 1935, Vera, Winifred and Gordon were away from London. Vera was on a lecture tour in March, still missing Brett and hoping he felt the same way about her. Gordon decided to give up his academic post at Cornell to pursue a political career in England, and then took off for two months in Moscow. Meanwhile, Winifred was in rented rooms in Hornsea, Yorkshire, finishing *South Riding* and taking care of her mother. She thought that she must be getting better.

Few, including her dearest friends, had realised that Winifred was very ill. She continued to insist that she was perfectly fine and would be going to Liberia when her symptoms cleared up. They planned a group holiday in France in late summer. Vera, the children and the German nanny went first, and Gordon and Winifred were expected to join them later. On 2 August, however, Vera's father disappeared from his Kensington home, and those close to him suspected he was suicidal. Winifred went to France to break the news to Vera, and they rushed back to London together, leaving the children with the nanny. On 5 August, Arthur Brittain's body was found in the Thames near Isleworth. There was no note, but they surmised he had thrown himself into the river. He had long suffered from depression, never having recovered from Edward's death in the war. For all of them it was a nightmarish experience. No sooner was his quiet funeral at Richmond over than Gordon came down with a high fever and an infection they thought he had picked up in Russia. Winifred kept the children in France for a few weeks, while Vera nursed Gordon.

Winifred's last posted letter to Vera was written on 26 August, announcing her return to London with the children. She arrived two days later, but had to leave almost immediately for Yorkshire because of a family crisis. On her return to London, she collapsed in Hyde Park and had to be brought back and put to bed in her room at Glebe Place. Vera and Gordon consulted Dr Obermer, who again admitted Winifred to a nursing home in London. When Vera went to see her, she was horrified by her swollen eyes. Still, Obermer told them she was doing well, and urged Vera to take Gordon on a convalescent trip to Brighton. They were urgently summoned back on 23 September. As they rushed to pack and leave, a bellboy gave Vera Winifred's last telephoned message: 'Do have a holiday. I am much better.'

From this point on, the narrative depends mainly on Vera's account in *Testament of Friendship*, published in 1940, was challenged by some of Winifred's friends, and more recently by Winifred's biographer, Marion Shaw, as well as by Vera's biographers, Paul Berry and Mark Bostridge. The controversy will be discussed in the Epilogue. Here is the part of the story that seems to be undisputed.

After rushing to Winifred's bedside, Vera reported to the

anxious group of friends gathered there that Winifred had wondered if Harry Pearson had ever loved her, and expressed her wish
to be married: 'I feel I *want* to be married somehow – I want some
sort of security now.' Vera resolved that Harry must be persuaded
to propose. Tanned and handsome, he had already visited her at
the nursing home from 24 to 26 September. Gordon was sent to
get him to come back and make a deathbed proposal, and in the
early morning of 28 September Harry returned to her bedside.
When Alice Holtby, the only person who actually talked to
Winifred after Harry's visit, arrived later that morning, she said
Winifred was glowing, and told her that when she was better, they
would get married; 'It's just an understanding between us – no
engagement.'

Soon afterwards, Dr Obermer gave Winifred another injection
of morphine. She fell asleep, and with Vera at her bedside from
the early hours, she died at 4.30 a.m. without reawakening. She
was thirty-seven years old.

LETTERS

1931

VERA TO WINIFRED

Orange Grove, Littleton, Surrey | *29 May 1931*

Darling,

So many thanks for your letter. I hope you didn't have such
a filthy day yesterday. Weather tolerable – but unless it actually
rains the country is delectable now anyhow; everything smells
exquisite and all the blossom is out.

Tell Nurse there seems to be some doubt whether Miss Talbot
can find me a temporary nurse as there are so many demands
for them in July. I don't want to drop my book for 3 weeks, and
apart from that it seems a little unfair to Gordon, when he is
only home this time for 3½ months, to spend nearly a month of
the time absorbed in the children.

It's queer how I miss the children even though longing to

be away from them for a time. I suppose that sub-consciously I
am always looking forward to each next time I see one of them
(rather the feeling that you get when you have a new book or
frock or jewel or something pleasant put away in a cupboard
and all the time there is a secret pleasure in the thought of
looking at it again) and without them life is short of something.
But it is extremely pleasant here and very peaceful.

Very much love, V.S.V.D.L.

VERA TO WINIFRED

19 Glebe Place, London SW3 | 22 July 1931

Darling,

Just a line to send the enclosed. Seeing the signature Doreen
Wallace I read her letter with great interest. Really I think
that a long article or even a book might be written on the
subject of *Married* Women's Work in Modern England and
the way it gets done. How many women, I wonder, are now
(like Mrs Beecher Stowe) stirring that soup or rocking the
cradle with one hand and writing with the other and yet one
doesn't notice that their books are any worse – are often indeed
better – than those of the young males (i.e. Roy Randall and J.
D. Woodruff) who have their lives to themselves and write, as
it were, within sound-proof walls. Alice Meynell wrote as well
as A. E. Housman; Mrs Gaskell though a Vicar's wife with four
children was quite literarily prolific and has at least as assured a
place in literature as Lamb and Leigh Hunt. The only questions
that remain to be answered are: 1) How many married women
don't write at all who, left alone, would? 2) Would the ones who
do write well write *more* if unmarried, and would their place
in literature be better if they did – i.e. with more time would

Alice Meynell have been a Shelley? Or is it really an advantage to be interrupted – because then your work is your play, and you go to it with a zest which soon stales if one thinks of work as work, and works all the time?

Much love V.S.V.D.L.

WINIFRED TO VERA

Pension Rochelle, St Lunaire | 23 July 1931

My darling,

This is a delightful place. Brilliant sun, but coldish evenings and cold sea. I am very sun-burned already. We have a routine that lets one work 7 hours a day and yet not seem busy. I have coffee at 8. Work 8.30–12.30. Lunch. Sit in the sun and drink coffee and smoke till 2. Work 2 to 3.30. Bathe. Work 5.30 to 7. Dine 7.30. Go for walk in the heavenly moon. All the privet hedges and pines smell with a mixture of aromatic and exotic which is divine. We end up about 10 at the place 'Au Petit Beuri', the centre of St Lunaire Night Life – a café and cocktail bar with a big open-air part opposite the Casino, where Lady Rhondda drinks grog and I have chocolate and we watch the Public; English all in evening dress, French all in very smart day clothes, and so to bed.

It is gayer than Agay, and rather smart. I believe you and Gordon might like it sometime. There are no mosquitoes and the sun and colouring are lovely.

Dear love to all the family. v.s.v.d.l. W

VERA TO WINIFRED

19 Glebe Place, London SW3 | *26 July 1931*

Darling,

So many thanks for your long letter. What a delectable sort
of holiday – just what I should so much enjoy myself that I'm
trying to persuade G. to go in for something of the sort at St
Raphael – where I do want to have three weeks for quiet and
sunshine and work on my book instead of cutting it short at ten
days and spending the remaining ten on the exhausting series
of railway journeys that G. so loves in order that he may talk
for ten minutes to the secretary of some Pol. Sci. organisation at
Frankfort!

All love – hope your book is getting on – V.S.V.D.L.

VERA TO WINIFRED

19 Glebe Place, London SW3 | *27 July 1931*

Darling,

Have an idea for a new book – woke up with it – called
'Woman in Transition' – sort of *Woman's Work in Modern
England* in size and type, attempting to estimate just exactly
what the various political and legal changes have meant in
the daily lives of women – starting with the little girl in the
nursery – at school, college, in marriage, in certain professions
etc. etc. Largely a re-hash of articles but something more –
in the Olive Schreiner–Ellen Key tradition which Gordon
likes for me!

All love, V.S.V.D.L.

WINIFRED TO VERA

St Lunaire | August 1931

I like the sound of the new book *immensely*. I believe that
your unique gift of clear sight and unafraid, prescient vision,
combined with an ability to write in champagne of social
changes when most people write in dish-water, might make such
a book as epoch-making as Olive Schreiner's. You have more
common sense than she had, and a better disciplined brain,
and your own experience with all the tedium of combining
domesticity with artistic impulse gives you a right to speak. I do
hope you do it. But the war book first.

I do hope you get a proper holiday.

Dearest love, W.

WINIFRED TO VERA

Villa Roscamare, Cap Ferrat | 16 August 1931

Darling,

I do hope you love St Raphael. The Mediterranean looks too
perfect. We went last night to the new Beach Casino at Monte
Carlo – a real grand Babylon full of celebrities and champagne.
I saw Ursula Filmer Sankey, whose toe nails I used to cut! And
Somerset Maugham (looking very cross, losing heavily at Chemin
de fer) and Peggy Joyce, the original Lorelei of *Gentlemen Prefer
Blondes*, who married in succession five millionaires. She opened
her big baby eyes at Edith and said, 'My! Do you mean to say you
married your husband when he hadn't any money? Waal! You
must have *loved* him? How beautiful! But of course, I never knew
any of my husbands long enough to love them.'

Darling, I love you. I hope you are happy. It seems so mean to be having such a lovely time when you are having a rather grim one. But I can only hope that your lovely time is coming, whereas there are only 3 more days of mine.

My love to all the family, v.s.v.d.l. W.

VERA TO WINIFRED

Ashville, Rustington, Sussex | *23 August 1931*

Darling,

I am rather looking forward now to the end of this 'holiday'. For the first two hours every morning I am occupied in cleaning the top half of the house, doing housekeeping, laundry or running round to shops according to the day. At this part of the day the sun normally shines. I then clean up, collect traps, and about 11.30 set out for a walk on the heath. I have usually been out five minutes when the daily downpour starts. All day long mackintoshes, shoes, stockings, shirts, trousers, etc. – to say nothing of that day's children's washing – steam damply round the small stove where Amy has also to do the cooking. I don't know why we endure it – except for the incurable optimism of the British race, which hopes for three perfect days in the last week to make the whole thing worth while, and the constant fact that in spite of the wet it *is* doing the children good and they are enjoying it.

No – I couldn't bear not to write at St Raphael. For three weeks I have tried to write here in vain – not a stroke have I done. For the previous twelve months I have done the same – only a little more successfully. Heaven for me is now represented by six daily hours of writing with *no* interruptions of any kind. To write at St Raphael from 10 a.m. to 4 p.m. and then have the rest of the day pour s'amuser is the greatest rest I can think of. I want to call my book 'Testament of Youth' – so much more interesting than 'Chronicle' – unless it strikes people as too like Bridges. But the Lord only knows when it will be finished at this rate.

G. and I have decided, for all our hard-upness, to travel to Paris like lords – 1st class by the 10.45 Calais–Dover. After two days of closing a house, packing up, re-packing, changing rooms, etc., I don't feel like a crowd and a rough sea. And my courage wouldn't rise to an aeroplane even if my funds would – and in any case, I want to make as close an inspection as I can of the line between Hardelot and Abbeville, so as to get the main features clear, as I shall be writing about it a few weeks hence. I did think of getting off at Étaples and waiting till the next train to Paris – but G. suggested that that would simply make me remember the country as it is now and forget it as it was in the War – which I think is true.

I asked Mother to find out if you were all right as I thought you might be feeling unduly seasick – and imagined you might not have funds for an air trip at the end of a long holiday.

All love V.S.V.D.L.

WINIFRED TO VERA

19 Glebe Place, London SW3 | *13 September 1931*

Darling Love,

I hated to disturb your holiday, as such a telegram must do, but it seemed worth while. I have had long telephone calls to Monica, who knows the Division well. She says she can pull strings. The last Labour candidate was a dud, who has resigned 'as the result of a bereavement', but I gather really because the constituency was fed up with his lack of energy. Hence the reaction against 'brain' as opposed to 'brawn', which may affect Gordon's chances of adoption. On the other hand, he has a positive policy to put forward, which none of the other six probably has. He will fight on a constructive plan; they will probably go all out simply for denunciation of the government and bankers – a wretched attitude which seems to be spreading.

A heavenly day. John Edward, Shirley and I spent the whole morning in Battersea Park while Nurse went to church. We saw everything, deer, trains, boats, garden, fountain, goldfish. We exhausted the whole magnificent resources of the place!

Just sending off MSS of Virginia Woolf book to Thomas Moult. Have been working all evening removing one entire chapter and distributing the essential bits throughout the book.

Take care of yourself. Don't be lonely. Go over to Agay if you are. Good luck with the book.

Dearest love, W.

VERA TO WINIFRED

Hermitage Hotel, St Raphael | 13 September 1931

Darling,

So many thanks for your various letters and telegrams. Gordon went off this afternoon; I hope he will be home at least in time to be one of the group (one can't call it anything but a group – and *not*, I suspect, a like-minded group) of Labour candidates for Chiswick! It is a fine gesture of availability, which will I imagine be worth what it will cost him – the price of a new dress-suit, which he will make last for another winter; or at any rate, not to have made it would have ultimately cost him more. I wonder whether I shall see him back here on Thursday or not.

Tell Gordon that if when he goes to Ithaca he misses me anything like as much as I miss him here, I'll willingly do anything – daily journalism, dress on 2d a year – to save him from it. My anti-solitude complex, I am sure, is an unhealthy thing; you, being free from unresolved fears and a fundamentally healthy person, have none of it. When I am alone I always remember all the times that I was lonely during and after the War – in Malta, after Roland was dead and it had the effect of making me feel that everyone in the hospital was 'down' on me; in Oxford, when I had the same feeling, after everyone else was dead and before I met you. Is it, I wonder, the War, or is it children, that gives such an enhanced and altogether exaggerated value to companionship and security? Memories of the long time when no one – neither others nor one's self – was secure? Or the queer thraldom of having had children and always, the moment one is alone, feeling them tug at one, wondering whether they are all right, whether they are wanting one. I can wish Shirley nothing better than the solitary, bold explorer's temperament.

Have written 50 pages of book since I came; it's *very* bad but I'm going on the principle that it's psychologically better to get it down somehow; even though one has solidly to write the whole thing out again it's a stage further than having it all toiling and moiling in one's head.

All love, dear heart V.S.V.D.L.

In the autumn of 1931, Gordon ran unsuccessfully for a seat in Parliament. Winifred, who had campaigned strenuously on his behalf, collapsed immediately afterwards, and went to convalesce in a cottage in Monks Risborough belonging to Clare Leighton.

WINIFRED TO VERA

c/o H. N. Brailsford, Icknield Cottage,
Peters Lane, Monks Risborough,
Buckinghamshire | 10 November 1931

My Darling,

I too have received a solemn letter from Dr Gray which I
enclose. Do you think that she and Lady Rhondda have been
conspiring? Because last night I had quite a pathetic letter from
Lady R. saying that *she* had been overworking and that *her*
doctor had ordered her a sea voyage at Christmas – and that
she was thinking of going to the Canary Isles from December
18th or 19th for three weeks (all told) but could not possibly
go alone, and would I come as her guest to keep her company?
It looks strangely like collaboration to me, and I hesitated at
first – knowing how much there is to do round Christmas and
feeling it a shame to leave you – and my family. But now with
Dr Gray's letter, I think I may go. Better a short sharp cure than
a long convalescence, say I.

I *do* feel better. Have had *no* headache for two days now.
Suddenly realise, not having it any longer, that I haven't really
been quite free of it for weeks, but was so much used to it that I
didn't notice it.

I am quite alone except for the char-woman in the morning,
and *loving* it. I play their glorious gramophone nearly all day,
and eat fruit and sleep. Clare comes back tomorrow night and
we both go up to Town on Friday morning. I'll let you know
later if I'll be in to lunch.

I *loathe* my glasses. I look a *hag* in them. I think I must have
my hair curled and my nails pinked if I am to disfigure my face,
such as it is, like this.

I'm afraid I shan't see Brailsford again to ask about Chiswick.

Personally, I don't think there is much hope in the seat. Give Gordon my love, and to yourself, much and much.

So sorry to have been such a nuisance the week after the election. *You* really needed the rest. I feel perfectly fit now. But I will be careful.

Dearest love W.

1932

VERA TO WINIFRED

19 Glebe Place, London SW3 | 22 February 1932

Darling,

Alas and alas! I have got chickenpox – at least practically for certain; Dr Gray is coming tomorrow morning to make sure; can't see spots at night. Only about 10 spots so far but a terrific ache all over – neck so stiff I can hardly hold my head up. Shirley apparently hasn't got it this time. I suppose she'll get it from me in another fortnight. We shall have to fumigate the whole house!

I suppose my book *may* be finished in about 1950.

Darling, I didn't want £8 for housekeeping and won't take it; I refuse to let you pay just because I choose to write a book instead of doing journalism – which is really why I am poor. I can manage; I merely am not flush! Don't send any more as I shall just tear up the cheque if you do! I may have to borrow large sums from you eventually if a few more people get ill; so hang on to it!

Father is urging me to urge you to take your £1,000 out of the house. I don't know if now you'd like to reconsider doing so but if you don't you ought to let us pay you interest as for an investment.

All love, my dearest dear, keep well – *so* fed up I can't see you for such ages.

V.S.V.D.L.

VERA TO WINIFRED

19 Glebe Place, London SW3 | 24 February 1932

Darling,

So many thanks for your letter and for sending the lovely nectarines – they came first thing this morning and as they said it was a post order I guessed they might be from you. But you shouldn't be so good to us, my darling sweet, and in such expensive ways, too. But it is a great joy to have such nice fruit. I don't really want anything else.

I am covered with enormous spots which drive me nearly mad; I'm rather glad you're not here to see me.

So sorry to hear your father is ill again but don't let them persuade you to go home; get Dr Leverkus to forbid it. She wrote to Dr Gray that you looked much better than she had expected to find but apparently your blood pressure is still about 180 and you have to be very careful.

Gordon writes that he has been having an affair with a Dutch girl in N.Y. and fills one page of a large block wondering whether he has a sensual nature!! At the present moment I don't care two damns whether he has a sensual nature or not!! He comes to the solemn conclusion (I do assure you that there is no irony) that after all his morals are better than Luther's! I laughed helplessly till the tears ran down my cheeks but alas! there was no one to share such unseemly mirth. He justifies his little escapades rather elaborately on the ground that it does his psychology so much good to feel he is attractive to women! Apparently the fact that I selected him as a husband is no guarantee of his attractiveness; apparently I was ready to put up with someone of quite dubious fascination, so my affection is no compliment!

I do wonder if all wives appear to men to be so awfully alike as all husbands appear to women!

All love my sweetieheart and thanks. V.S.V.D.L.

WINIFRED TO VERA

The Double Cottage, Monks Risborough,
Buckinghamshire | 25 February 1932

Dearest little Love,

I am delighted that you have a nurse. Do keep her long enough to get really well. I am so glad that she brushes your hair and does things. I had a letter from your mother this morning saying that your spots are very bad. Do take care of them, and don't let them get septic by scratching. My poor sweet. And don't bother to write me letters. You have enough to do writing to Gordon and forwarding my stuff. A line on a card is enough from time to time to say that you are well.

About money. I don't know what to do. You are actually out of pocket now on that transaction over the tax. I *do* want to pay something. And I do *not* want to withdraw any money from the house. Why should I? However, we need not argue now. We can discuss it some time.

There is one good thing about your not coming this week-end. The weather is very cold and grey, and Dr Leverkus is very firm about my not walking any distance yet. She came in yesterday as she was visiting Clare (who felt she was taking too

long over her 'flu recovery), and said my b.p. was not down at
all, in fact, a few points up, and I must cut down work to two
hours a day, and spend longer in bed. So I am being very good.
Dr Leverkus says that what I really ought to do is wool work!
And listen to the wireless!! I *have*, for a diversion, written to
Harrods about portable sets and prices. It might be rather nice
to have one. But I fear that mine would always be going wrong.

I do love you so. My thoughts only dwell on you with such
rest and gladness. Do take care of your most precious self.

Bless you, bless you, v.s.v.d.l. W

VERA TO WINIFRED

19 Glebe Place, London SW3 | 25 February 1932

Darling,

I sent you a *Week-end Review* because it contained a copy
of the Family Life Questionnaire and I thought you might be
interested to read Beveridge's articles on it and perhaps to fill
it in with regard to your own parents' marriage. It says that
unmarried individuals can do this if they like, and I do think it
is important to get a few facts about non-highbrow marriages –
so many highbrows will fill it in. I am doing one for Gordon and
myself. Despite the absurd strictures of the popular press I do
think it is an important and useful investigation.

I am keeping the nurse for a week as my spots are *appalling*; I
can't possibly get up and dress till they moderate a little. They
are not only all about my back, front, neck and face, but on my
nose, inside my ears, under my hair and in the corners of my
eyes; covered with calamine lotion from head to foot, I look like
a long-buried corpse! I sympathised with you and your bromide
rashes last night, for the effort not to scratch made me nearly

desperate; I couldn't sleep and spent hours dabbing myself with lotion, and trying to read and forget the tickle!

All love. V.S.V.D.L.

WINIFRED TO VERA

The Double Cottage, Monks Risborough,
Buckinghamshire | *1 March 1932*

Darling,

I'm worlds better this week. Last week's curtailment of work was from the complicated cause that when Father was ill, I sent for Dr Leverkus to vet me to see what I should reply about going or not going. She found my b.p. up over 200 again (which may have been a temporary result of being worried about what to do) and forbade me to go up, as I told you, while Father was ill and put me on a rigid time-table. The time-table or something has done me worlds of good. I felt rather rotten, constant small headaches, till Saturday, and since then, worlds better – and am trying to work a little longer.

When you're better, couldn't you possibly get to a night here in my cubbyhole?

One thing you must let me do is to partly pay for the spring cleaning. That *is* my job. I am still most unhappy about our financial arrangements, which leave everything to you.

Faber and Faber have turned down 'Virginia Woolf' – they don't say why. Higham wants me to alter it. But I can't do that, *and* my novel *and* a little journalism. This present régime gives me less time for work than I ever had! It is very agreeable, but *not* good for work.

I am longing to show you my cottage and the lambs.

W.

VERA TO WINIFRED

19 Glebe Place, London SW3 | *2 March 1932*

Darling,

I was so glad to get your letter last night and to learn that you are feeling a bit better. I was desperately worried and miserable when you were getting headaches and your work was cut down for I *knew* that your blood pressure was up again; I could curse and damn this wretched chickenpox which prevents me from coming every week to see how you are; if I had had appendicitis don't think it would have held me up so long.

Don't your family realise even *yet* that you can't go tearing up and down to Yorkshire; that your illness is, potentially at any rate, as serious as your father's and should be treated with even more respect and care, since you are not only younger but, without any disrespect to him, so much more valuable? I do hope your mother and Lady Rhondda won't tire you; both of them, it seems to me, still persist in regarding it all as partly psychological – the kind of thing you could 'throw off' if you wanted to – whereas it is so utterly beyond your control.

If your time-table has put you right, for heaven's sake stick to it as far as possible. Are you satisfied with Dr Leverkus? Do you think she takes enough trouble? Has she been to see you again to take your b.p. since it was over 200? Do you think the place suits you? Or is it too high and would you be better by the sea?

I often wonder whether we have taken quite enough trouble over doctors – after all, Dr Ironside himself is a nerve specialist rather than anything else. I feel London may have other possibilities – and if not London, perhaps Paris, Berlin, Vienna? If we heard of a great specialist on the subject, it might be at least possible to arrange a postal consultation through the London doctors and find out what the treatment is. I don't feel prepared to sit down under the prospect of your living as a semi-invalid always under the threat of a blood pressure which may rush up at any moment. I don't feel satisfied that there are drugs which will take it down when it has gone up; I feel that there ought to be something to prevent its going up at all.

I am asking Gordon to inquire through the Cornell Medical School whether there is a specialist of this kind in New York; I feel sure it is a disease that America, through its high-speed mechanised life, would be more likely to develop than England and therefore they may be experimenting more than we are with methods of treatment.

No news here at all. I really think that after the middle of March, if I don't get any more spots, I can begin to think of coming to see you; it's not as if I should be meeting any children. I do nothing but refuse invitations; some I am sorry about, but I have got out of one or two very mouldy meetings at Chiswick and elsewhere; that's some little compensation. All love my sweet, and don't let anyone tire you or make you do more than you want. I am sorry about the Virginia Woolf book – that's the worst of a book written for a series – but I should leave it now till your novel is done and perhaps re-write after; Higham could try other publishers meanwhile.

Always V.S.V.D.L.

VERA TO WINIFRED

19 Glebe Place, London SW3 | 5 March 1932

Darling,

Have just finished the Malta chapter – a month behind schedule – but as it's 108 pages and all written since Jan. 20th, at least the last 5 weeks despite all their illness have not

been entirely unprofitable. But alas and alas! the book is now
535 pages and 5 more chapters to go (7 written); I fear some
drastic cutting will be required, but I can't estimate what is
most valuable until it is all down. I can hardly shorten the
'remembered' part much, so I fear a good many contemporary
letters will have to go.

Odette's letter is *delicious* – can I send it on to Gordon?
What vitality! To think that the great Wells is so like the rest
of human husbands! No doubt Gordon's next stage will be to
do the same thing to me – or tell me he feels 'middle-aged' and
wishes he could marry Ethel Mannin! The latter's contributions
to the *New Leader* certainly are the only bright things in it,
but I do get rather tired of her perpetual 'charming youth',
considering she is exactly the same age as yourself – not that
you're not young but you know what I mean; too many of these
permanent kittens and puppies about.

I am interested in Odette's dislike of autobiographies and
cannot see her objection to the values in it being consistently
the author's values; this need not make it dull if the author is
not dull, and surely the same thing is true of a novel – precisely
true of all Wells' novels, surely. But I do agree that the great
difficulty is to make enough of an autobiography objective to
give sufficient variety to the prolonged subjectiveness; this is
where Sassoon is so good; I have been studying very carefully
his two Memoirs.

All love, my dear one V.S.V.D.L.

WINIFRED TO VERA

The Double Cottage, Monks Risborough,
Buckinghamshire | 5 *March 1932*

Darling sweet,

I really am getting better – though still can't do as much as
I did at Sidmouth. I can't think why. Did I tell you Dr Gray
was trying out Ellen Wilkinson's 'Hypotensyl' on an older
patient, and is coming here on the 19th on her way from
High Wycombe, and will start me on it if she finds it good?
I'd try anything. This is a pleasant life, a charming, peaceful,
happy life. But I don't want to be charming and peaceful and
happy. I want to work! Still, it might be so much worse. And
I do *adore* the country and the lambs and the little fattening
buds. I'm never lonely and never bored. Indeed – I'm not lonely
enough. I've acquired a new swain – Ernest Rhys, the editor
of the Everyman's Library – an absolute darling – 75, white
beard, eye-glass, friend of Swinburne and Watts-Dunton, who
escorts me from the Bell at night over dark fields and reads his
poems aloud in a lovely rolling voice, and manifests all signs
of rising interest in my very plain, untidy, unhair-washed self.
He has written a really lovely poem about an old tree's spring
burgeoning! So I'm not dull. No, no, not dull. And Harry
announces his intention of coming to stay for next week-end.

I am doing *no* work. That's the worst of it. I don't get up till
11. Then I go out till lunch time. Then I rest till tea. Then I
talk to someone till dinner. Then I go to bed!!! I am trying to
think how I can stay in bed as long as my physique seems to
require and yet work. When quite alone, I can work between tea
and dinner. But now that I have callers, that goes. When this
week-end is over I shall really retire from the world and work.

I sent Gordon a *very* self-pitying letter the other day. Not

that I felt very sad, but that I thought it would be good for him!
Told him how I am tied in a Tantalus trap of feeling capable of
good work and not being able to do it. I really am having a very
happy time. And wish I could share with you half my pleasures.
I can't describe to you the intensity of my enjoyment of the
pink-eared lambs, and music in the dark. I wish, I wish, I wish –

a) You could be care-free, finish your book soon, and be
   as famous as you will be.
b) You could come here – You *shall*.
c) I could work 6 hours a day – I *will*.

I am being very, very careful. Oh, did I tell you Dr Leverkus
has put me on a very strict diet that sounds sensible? No coffee,
not more than one egg, or one piece of cheese a day – very
weak tea – and heaps of fruit, vegetables, and to make warmth
and energy, sugars instead of so many milk and egg things?
Anything that makes blood or stimulates knocked off – she says
as I'm not taking much exercise, that does not matter, and sugar
will keep me warm without making blood.

Bless you, my dear, my sweet, Winifred

WINIFRED TO VERA

The Double Cottage, Monks Risborough,
Buckinghamshire | 7 March 1932

Dearest,

I'm so glad you've done the Malta chapter – never mind if
you are behind schedule. I am coming to believe that much
of the best work is done in spite of time, circumstance and
discomfort. I wrote back *passionately* disagreeing with Odette

about autobiographies. But we disagree on almost everything. Witness her letter on *Brave New World*. She can't think that the book is about states of mind. Nor can she see that the subjective can be as interesting as the objective. What about St Augustine's *Confessions? The* most subjective of works – *morbidly* egocentric – yet immortally interesting and valuable.

I am lying now in bed almost out of my bedroom window, with only one of those very lacy nightgowns of Edith's on – sun-bathing – otherwise bare to the waist. Would be quite bare were I more sure that the whole of me is not visible from the road.

I've done no work except revise an already written *Radio Times* article since Mother came. But when I have visitors I can't manage them *and* work! And I *must* get on with my book. You are the only person I know in the world who does not prevent one working.

Otherwise I've felt better again yesterday and today. *Very* fit this morning – no headaches.

Much love – v.s.v.d.l. W.

VERA TO WINIFRED

19 Glebe Place, London SW3 | 7 March 1932

Darling,

The Lord knows when I shall get to see you, for it seems almost certain today that Shirley has got chickenpox – the usual group of little spots on her back and we are waiting for them to develop. Why wouldn't she have started when I did? Now we have to add another fortnight (she will have it concurrently with me for one week) to the time of infection, which means the middle of April. Add on another fortnight for fumigating and spring cleaning and I shall have had a dose

of illnesses lasting unbroken from the end of Jan. to May! And
Gordon thinks himself the unlucky one!

About your work – your day *does* seem full but couldn't you
do an hour before you get up in the morning? Again, when the
weather gets warm enough for you to sit out, instead of walking
about from 11 to 1, you could take your reading or writing on to
the Downs.

Here it is so strange – writing always about the past in a
present that has become a kind of vacuum, without friends,
without incidents, without conversation. I seem to have the
children all day on and off – now they can be together I shan't
have to have them so much – but still, through seeing no one
and going nowhere, I seem to get quite a fair amount of work
done. The country sounds adorable and I do look forward to
coming when I can.

All dearest love, V.S.V.D.L.

VERA TO WINIFRED

19 Glebe Place, London SW3 | 14 March 1932

Darling,

If Harry is with you, could you please ask him if he
remembers what month of what year the Étaples mutiny was?
It was either Oct. or Nov. 1917, or February 1918. I must know,
and can't think how to find out. Obviously it is not the kind
of thing that would be in any of the war histories (which, like
Pollard, always make out our *morale* to be *so* splendid!) *and* of
course I couldn't mention it at that time in my letters home – so
in the war relics of the France chapter I can find no trace of it,
yet I particularly want to include it. I believe you said once that
you found it mentioned in one of the war books but I couldn't

remember which one, and have been through all the likely
ones – Graves, Blunden, Sassoon, quite in vain. Can't think
who else would know whose address I still have. Can you?

WINIFRED TO VERA

The Double Cottage, Monks Risborough,
Buckinghamshire | 17 March 1932

Dearest,

Harry leaves tomorrow. I have thoroughly enjoyed him. He
is ridiculous and quite irresponsible and won't or can't take the
future seriously; but he is charming, considerate, and funny,
makes me laugh, gets on with all the neighbours, and has done
me a great deal of good instead of tiring me. He, I, Mr Rhys and
Mr Rhys' daughter picnicked yesterday in Clare's garden, and
they seemed to enjoy it so much they have invited themselves
again for today. I *am* looking forward to Monday. I may come
and meet your train at Monks Risboro' or may not, so just come
straight here.

Sun-bathed yesterday in nix but spectacles and bedroom
slippers for 2 hours!! before tea.

Dearest love – longing for Monday. W.

VERA TO WINIFRED

19 Glebe Place, London SW3 | 17 March 1932

Darling,

Some *lovely* things came from Harrods today – three pots of
heavenly paste, smoked salmon in oil and two lovely bottles of

olives! But, my sweet, you *shouldn't* regale me with delicacies like this; I've done nothing to deserve them, and it isn't Christmas or my birthday or anything. Why spoil me so? I'm still drinking your beautiful sherry, too; it has been a perfect joy all this bitter cold month. But don't spend your money on me, my sweetheart, especially now, when your power to earn it is so limited; if you do it any more I shall be forced to suppress *Harrods News* instead of forwarding it.

Just been reading Graves' Postscript to *Goodbye to All That* in *But It Still Goes On*. He seems to have spent about a year in answering correspondents, writing to newspapers, repudiating libel actions, quarrelling with his family, etc. I suppose if my book *ever* is finished and published I shall have a similar fate – fury from the Brittains, from Buxton, from Oxford, from St Thomas's, from all dons, from all nurses, and so *ad infinitum*.

All dear love my sweetieheart and so many thanks for the delicious things.

V.S.V.D.L.

VERA TO WINIFRED

31 March 1932

Darling,

I thought you would like to see this excellent review by Priestley of Phyllis Bentley's book. It should make its fortune, I should think. P. B. I suppose is certain to get it with her press-cuttings. Could you let me know her address; I should like to write to her.

Dr Gray has just this minute phoned to say that she has fixed your appointment with Halls Dally for 5.00 next Thursday. This seems a splendid time; you can stay in bed all morning

and come up in the afternoon; can you find a good train which
leaves High Wickham about 3.00? Dr G. has asked me to
meet you and take you to the specialist as she can't get there
much before 5.00 owing to a clinic. We could have some tea
somewhere first. Then you can come back here and have dinner
in bed, and I will take you back next day.

 All love, V.S.V.D.L.

WINIFRED TO VERA

The Double Cottage, Monks Risborough,
Buckinghamshire | 2 April 1932

My little love,

 What am I to say to you, you naughty, extravagant, darling
creature! The most exciting box brought the postman struggling
to the door at 7.30 this morning. It's a perfect morning and I
woke up without a headache *at all*, feeling splendid. So I popped
down and Mrs Calcraft made us both a cup of tea while I went
'up the garden' (where daffodils are now blooming) and opened
it right away. Asparagus, salted almonds, figs, dates. All the
things I *adore*. Mrs Calcraft has never handled out-of-season
asparagus before, and is quite excited. Then I opened your letter
and the lovely hankies appeared. That's a sort I particularly
love – such good washing kind and such pretty colours. You are
a sweet to send me such lovely things.

 I entirely agree with your 'report on my position'. I expect
Dally is an expensive cure, but I must see him. After that I'll try
radical cures. I'll let you know for certain about trains etc. So far,
the idea is to come by the one arriving at Paddington at 1.40, if
Dr Halls Dally can see me at 2.15. But I'll let you know later.

 Dr Leverkus was coming today in any case, to take a '24

hours urine test' – I've been weighing and measuring since
8 a.m. yesterday morning.

I can't think why I felt so mouldy yesterday. Woke up with
a headache – felt, but was not, sick, and rather dizzy. I should
have sent for Dr L. if she were not coming today. And now
today I feel magnificent – not a trace of headache, dizziness
or sickness. I ate practically nothing yesterday. So query – *Is* it
starvation I want? I've always been rather *fed* in the places I've
been to – egg flips, Ovaltine, etc. etc.

Phyllis Bentley's novel arrived yesterday. By night I'd finished
it, feeling unlike any work of my own. It is *magnificent*. Strong,
human, abounding in vital characters, passionate, rich, *really*
something worth praising. I'll bring it up when I come to you.
Her address is 8 Heath Villas, Halifax. She takes one valley in
the West Riding and traces it from the industrial revolution
through the war, the post war slump and the failure of the mills
and the hope of reconstruction from your man who carries in
his veins blood of both agitator and master. All so lively and
vigorous in its story. I am really excited over it.

But work.

Bless you, darling, I am feeling splendid today. W.

WINIFRED TO VERA

The Double Cottage, Monks Risborough,
Buckinghamshire | *4 April 1932*

Dearest,

You need not read the enclosed, but they may amuse you to
look at. Violet Scott-James and Edith Shackleton brought me the
Telegraph cutting on Saturday. They motored out here for tea –
only stopped an hour and were very nice. Rebecca is *most* unfair

to Phyllis Bentley. But I am sure that she dislikes her work, as one
of the most sarcastic passages about an unnamed woman writer in
Ending in Ernest clearly refers to Phyllis' last book *Trio*. Of course, P.
B.'s style does not sparkle. She has no wit and little humour – but
she has power, courage, nobility and immense creative resource.
Did you see the *splendid* notice in the *Observer* yesterday?

Darling, I should much prefer to be in a nursing home if I am
to have lots of tests and things done. It's so nice to have a nurse
do them all for you and Courtfield Gardens is not expensive. I'll
bring all necessary things.

I'm *very* pleased with the sound of Obermer; and if under
him, I should certainly like to be in a home just while he is
doing the tests. His tests on Clare are so elaborate that they
take all her time while she is having them. *E.G. Every* piece of
food, even marmalade, has to be weighed separately! It's a life's
work and in a home they have to do it for one.

Dear love, I'm not at all devastated. I'm *enjoying* it all.
I'm so egotistic that I am enchanted at all this ego-centric
consultation upon my symptoms. I've never felt so important in
my life!! Also I *must* get to a state where I can write better. I am
becoming less and less capable of an idea. My novel is *awful*.

Mr Rhys came to see me in the evening and brought me
some papers. Did I tell you he was a great friend of Havelock
Ellis and used to know Olive Schreiner well? He is one of the
most delightful companions I have met and so considerate
and tactful.

Darling I'm afraid I add tremendously to all your cares and
jobs. But I do love you and am so much looking forward to
seeing you on Wednesday.

Of course if I don't have to have a lot of elaborate tests etc.,
I could stay a night or two at Glebe Place before coming back
here. But we'll see what happens.

Bless and bless you. W.

VERA TO WINIFRED

14 April 1932

Darling,

Spring-cleaning progressing but ladders, men, dirt and paint
are all over everything and I ache all over. My hands are like
nutmeg-graters – have tried working in gloves but it's no good.

I have now *filed* all your letters and shall continue to do
so whenever they are of interest so will you please *date them
properly* – day, month and year, and not just put 'Sunday'. Spent
about 10 mins. this morning adding the year to them all. Army
plus school training makes me put the year even on a p.c. I have
clipped all your 'letters from the great' together and put them in
your Miscellaneous Letters file.

I forget if I told you that Phyllis Bentley accepted my
invitation with enthusiasm! She wants to come down for 5
days round about May 11th when Gollancz has an At Home.
She seemed to take for granted I should be going to this, but
of course I'm not invited – in Golly's eyes I'm tarred with the
Time and Tide brush, so in a way I fall amusingly between
two stools, having quarrelled with the Viscountess – no, not
quarrelled – merely both remaining at a polite distance. Don't
feel guilty about this, tho' it was over you, for after having
disliked Margaret Rhondda for so long (no, not disliked, felt
uncomfortable in her presence) it's really rather a relief to own
it to one's self and others, and have done with pretence and not
have to meet!

I must get Phyllis Bentley somehow to put over to Golly:
(a) The Autobiography; (b) that I *don't* write for *Time and
Tide* any more.

Forgive writing – hand tired and sore.

All dear love V.S.V.D.L.

WINIFRED TO VERA

The Double Cottage, Monks Risborough,
Buckinghamshire | *15 April 1932*

Darling,

I'll try to date my letters properly. Often I don't know the date; but I can find out!

Yes, Phyllis must put over the autobiography. By the way – would you like *me* to talk to her about it, or can you do it quite easily? She's a very easy person to talk to about one's work. I should think you could without effort. But I will if you like.

I have met *such* a nice old man – a Norfolk rat-catcher now working here on the roads. He told me wonderful tales of fleets of rats migrating by night under the moon to find new water. He has seen them travel like a river down the road in thousands. You can hear them squeaking nearly a mile away.

No news at all. I expect Edith and Margaret tonight. Rather wish they weren't coming. I shall have to hear all about the endless discussions of my 'case', I suppose.

Dearest love always v.s.v.d.l. W.

VERA TO WINIFRED

19 Glebe Place, London SW3 | *17 April 1932*

Darling,

You will by now have heard both from Clare and Dr Gray (with whom I have just been having a long telephone conversation) that Dally and Obermer want you to go into Courtfield Gardens for three or four weeks while they put you through a new series of tests, experiment with new diets, new drugs, etc. both to reduce your b.p. and to neutralise the kidney trouble at the same time. I said, why couldn't you come here? which would be perfectly possible by Friday or Saturday, but Dr G. said that only a trained nurse can carry out the experiments and that you have to be observed by night as well as by day, which would mean both a day and a night nurse; also Dally definitely said he wanted you in a home where you can have the necessary 'special conditions' – whatever that may mean. They want to start at once without delay and want you in the home by Tuesday evening (or earlier on Tues. if it suits you better) so I told Dr G. that I would be responsible for seeing you got there, and she will make the arrangements with Matron.

I told Dr G. I would go down to Monks Risboro on Tuesday and fetch you up by train but Clare, to whom I have just been telephoning, says she is coming up anyhow on Tuesday and will bring you with her. If you will let me have a p.c. I will meet the train and take you on to the home. Dally and Obermer say you not only can work at the home but will be much better if you do; they are very emphatic that you are not to behave as an invalid. I can't imagine what the tests are that make it so urgent for you to be in a home instead of here; you will know better when you have been there a few days; if it really isn't necessary for you to be there you could just refuse to stay, and come here.

At the moment we are still in unutterable chaos; of *course* the men didn't finish on Saturday either in the nursery or on the stairs, so we can't get the ground floor rooms finished or the stair-carpets down until Tuesday or Wednesday.

I do hope these new arrangements don't bother you too much – at least something is being done, and anything is better than the state of mere acceptance of the situation into which people seemed to be drifting before you saw Dally and Obermer. Don't forget to let me know your train.

If you don't want to go straight to Courtfield Gardens could

we have lunch out somewhere and then you could come here
and rest in my room (which is quite finished) and we could have
some tea here. You don't have to be in Court. G. till about 6.00.
Let me know this and the train.

Dearest love V.S.V.D.L.

WINIFRED TO VERA

3 Courtfield Gardens, London SW5 | 6 May 1932

Darling

Forgive hurried scrawl. Yes, I'd love to see Phyllis tomorrow
morning, and I may now see as many people as I like unless I
tire, and I may go out to tea when fine.

What *is* a bore is that they can't yet say when I may leave
here. Quite definitely my blood pressure is down and my pulse
steadier. But my kidneys are not doing their work, and there is
a danger, if I don't have them put really right now, of getting
one of those urinal poisonings, or Bright's disease or something
foul like that. To stop any of those things and make me
100% well (which he thinks he really can) means drastic and
continual measurements, injections, medicines and diets. He
says that I *must* be under trained observation the whole time. I
rather gather that some of the pills may upset me, and that the
injections quite probably will.

I told him the financial position more or less (Dr Gray was
there too) and he promised me to let me out the moment
he dare. But apparently I need watching night and day after
certain kinds of treatment, and he can't say yet how long these
will take.

On other days, I may get up, go out, work, spend a whole
day at Glebe Place if I like. But at present, I may not go to the

lavatory anywhere but here as every drop has to be kept and measured, so it rather puts a limit to my activities!

He really was very nice. He was nearly 1½ hours here, and seemed really interested. He did quite definitely say that there was nothing to worry about *at all* if I was sensible and had this treatment now; but he said I might get really ill if I didn't, as I was poisoning myself a little all the time.

I do see that it would be impossible to do these things anywhere but a home. Some days I do nothing but take pills, but on others I [do] not have to be in bed all the time, but may quite suddenly get wildly ill for about 3 hours, as after the nitrates. No one can tell *which* thing I react to, and honestly, it's not a question of you're being ready to wait on me for £3.3.0. It's a question of possibly needing at any moment a night or day nurse.

It may only last a week or two if they find the right treatment at once. But he says he would simply be foolish to give a date.

What I *beg* you to do is to let me pay my share of the gas, light, telephone, rates etc. I can – and am miserable at this financial let-down to you, if I don't.

One day I'll try to pay you back for all this trouble and expense – though I can never repay your patience, and your sweet bright darling face round the door.

Bless you, Winifred

VERA TO WINIFRED

19 Glebe Place, London SW3 | 26 August 1932

Darling,

My book is making me unutterably miserable. Still, for good or ill, it must be finished; I suppose from the point of view of reputation it's better to produce something that everybody curses and derides, than just not to produce. But I am *bored* with it, and have lost heart.

Yesterday Phyllis (whose capacity for being concerned over other people's problems really *is* remarkable) sent me a copy of Ruth Holland's *The Lost Generation* (which she had been reviewing for *The Observer*), together with a most distressed letter fearing that R. H. had used my theme, cut away all my ground, etc. etc. and feeling that at least I ought to know! As a matter of fact the book is so utterly unlike mine that I was relieved to read it – it is a *beautiful* novel, but if it were not for its title one would hardly think of it as a war novel at all.

Her chief character had an emotional history rather like mine – lover killed in War, short marriage to man who died after war of War wounds, final second marriage which looked like lasting – but no ambitions, occupations or interest in the outside world. Some of her conclusions about war etc. are rather like mine, but, as I told Phyllis, any woman (or man for that matter) who brings a normal degree of courage to bear on a life overshadowed by disaster is *bound* to come to more or less the same conclusions – and they are conveyed quite differently.

What I do however feel is that if I don't hurry up some woman or other like Ruth Holland (whose novel obviously has an autobiographical basis) *will* do an autobiography instead of a novel – and then mine will have no merits or originality at all, will merely be more long-winded and 'explanatory'. Oh dear, oh dear! it's hard to 'hurry up' when one's completely lost confidence in what one's doing!

All dearest love. Hope you're still feeling better, V.S.V.D.L.

WINIFRED TO VERA

Bainesse, Cottingham, East Yorkshire | *27 August 1932*

Dearest, dearest child,

What can I say to make you believe in your book as I believe
in it? You know that I really am a very critical judge of the
work of people I love – and always a little afraid that they may
not come up to any high standard set for them in my mind. (I
want my friends to be perfect. That's the trouble.) When I read
your novels, I thought them good, but not the work I felt you
would one day do. They were a promise; a guarantee; but not
themselves of importance. When I read those early chapters
of the *Testament* I felt 'This is *it*. This is the thing she has
been waiting to do. This is the justification of those long years
of waiting.'

That you are bored, I'm not in the least surprised. If you
could have gone ahead writing without looking up fact, it would
have been all light. This looking up, verifying and copying
would always bore a creative artist.

The dear Phyllis has even sent *me* a postcard. Personally,
I'm not in the least afraid of other people's books being like
yours. What other woman writing has *both* your experience
and your political training? But I do want you for *your* sake to
get it finished soon, so as not to be bored and depressed by it
any longer.

Don't go and scare yourself with reviews by other people of
other people's work. In Virginia Woolf's 'Letter to a Young Poet'
she explains how difficult it is for the successful and for those
who *feel* successful to write good poetry. I think it's really the
truth of the 'How hard is it for a rich man to enter the Kingdom
of Heaven.' When driven against time, against fear, against
interruptions, against debt, like Scott and Dr Johnson, against

madness and death, like Virginia Woolf (who, in a *charming*
letter forwarded here, explains that she has been ill again),
against sorrow and neurosis (I imagine) like Sassoon, against
loss of manuscript, like Carlyle and T. E. Lawrence (funny
couple), one throws aside every superfluous phrase and thought.
One is stripped like a wrestler fighting for life. And it is *good*.
You write with your heart and nerves and sinews. You write
of what you must. You have *paid* for your material by grinding
work, and broken youth and sorrow. No, my dear, nobody is
going to produce a book just like your book. There is brain in
it, as well as memory – good, hard, disciplined intellectual work.
And there is experience, deeply scored into the memory.

I have, now that I have read it, no fears at all. It is a book of
flesh and blood and intellect. No one else can do just the same.
I wish I could think that I could ever do so *real* a thing.

I expect to come by the noon train from here on Tuesday.
Shall be back in time for supper, having had tea.

Bless you, darling love. W.

VERA TO WINIFRED

*8 Heath Villas, Halifax, West
Yorkshire | 1 December 1932*

Darling,

Should be enjoying this and Phyllis's society very well if I
didn't feel so unutterably mouldy. Toothache for the moment
has subsided but I have light colo-cystitis all the time and *can't*
get warm. This country is just like that round Buxton; am
coming to conclusion that part of reason I hated it so much is
that I was always cold. We motored part of the way to Haworth
today and walked the rest over the moor – lovely day, beautiful

colours, frosty sunshine, Haworth v. interesting but it was spoilt for me by fact that I felt sick and half frozen all the time. P. did her best with innumerable stops for cups of tea but I now feel half dead.

Mrs Bentley I think is quite terrifying; she is very pleasant to me, liked the lecture and we get on all right, but quite obviously she is without compunction and has steadily drained Phyllis's vitality for her own purposes for the past 30 years; it is a *shame*. P. is starting on the *Evening Chronicle* job and had a huge poster about her splurged all over Manchester yesterday. How she has kept her intellectual freedom and vigour in this atmosphere is a miracle.

She obviously likes having me and I shan't come back before Tuesday unless I get to feel worse.

All love to John and Shirley and to you. V.S.V.D.L.

WINIFRED TO VERA

27 December 1932

Darling,

I'm so sorry you have lost your voice – do take care, darling, You really do need a holiday so badly. I wish you could get quickly for a long week-end at Rye.

Here all is psychologically peaceful if socially tumultuous. Harry came over on Christmas Eve, but I never saw him except across a crowd of people. He says he is going to walk over today. But it's a filthy day. I don't know if he will come. He was charming to me in the way of small impersonal attentions – treats me as a cross between a queen and a prize pekinese – but I never had a chance of one word of reality.

Bless you always W

VERA TO WINIFRED

> 19 *Glebe Place, London SW3* |
> *28 December 1932*

Darling sweet,

So glad to hear from you. Have felt since Christmas completely cut off from everybody and everything – a feeling increased not only by a slightly ailing tooth but by this vile laryngitis which makes even telephone conversations impossible. You certainly haven't missed anything attractive by being away from here!

Gordon writes me a long dissertation from Oxford on the strategic importance of Constant Entertaining! I expect the upshot will be that Nurse has to give up her work for the time being and I shall have to get someone else – but quite who or what type of individual to get if she does, what to look for, God only knows.

My dear, I am more than ever convinced that I ought *never* to have married, or at any rate never to have had children, and *certainly* not just at the age I did, if I ever wanted to achieve anything in this world. It's no good, I *cannot* organise a household; the management of maids simply paralyses me, the least thing wrong, the feeling of 'atmosphere', makes work impossible; my relations with Gordon seem all wrong because he completely disregards the extent to which it all worries me, wants instead to add to the burden of domesticity (why can't he entertain at restaurants? I should love that myself, and would gladly pay for it all), and imagine that I am cold or unresponsive to him when all that is really wrong is that I am secretly meditating how to prevail on Amy to clean the steps without a devastating row. Instead of doing my work I am obsessed with a possible change of nurses; I know I can write, I know I can

get through more literary work in a day than almost anyone I
know if I have simply that and nothing else to think about –
and instead of that, the one thing I can do gets dissipated
and lost in a maze of small worries. I am perfectly convinced
that Storm Jameson has never written a really great book for
just this reason – she's too talented not to produce good work
under any circumstances, but with those gifts and that rich
and rather wild personality, she could have done far, far better.
Why isn't there some way in which people like herself and
me can have marriage and children without this incongruous
burden of household and servants being piled on our defenceless
shoulders!

No line from Phyllis. I dare say she'll be furious that I should
dare to write, even as a stranger, about the beloved West
Riding – such a presumption, when it belongs only to her! Keep
off my grass, you hysterical and unreliable little urban artificial
creature; it's sacred grass and I won't have your impertinent feet
treading down one consecrated green blade!

Well, I don't suppose I shall have much of a birthday
tomorrow, but at least I can look forward to seeing you back,
which is better than anything.

All dearest love V.S.V.D.L.

1933

WINIFRED TO VERA

Bainesse, Cottingham, East Yorkshire | *19 February 1933*

Darling,

It is a marvellous morning – thick white snow and brilliant sun and huge pale clouds leaping up in a completely cobalt sky. I have sent Edith out and am sitting with Father. Edith looks thoroughly tired; but as usual when aware of being the pivot of the house is happy and sweet and cheerful.

I had a long talk by myself to Dr Innes last night. He says that both kidneys and liver have now begun to fail, and the coughing is very bad. He does not think it can be more than a week or two and might end any time, so I told Mother I would stay till the end of the week, then, if there was no change, return to London for the next week – come back for the week-ends. By the end of the week he should be rather more settled and less collapsed if he is going to live for some time longer. So I shall probably come back on Monday, the 27th.

Do let me know what Gollancz says whenever you hear. It is maddening to be away just now, but so like life. However, I still feel that it is somehow better, more fruitful, more *enriching*, to be bound up with the exasperating complications of people and things than to enjoy a dry rootless immunity.

We have a night nurse, so I get good nights. And I have the big room with the gas fire, so can work. I am as comfortable as can be in the circumstances. Bless you, dear child – give my love to my little darlings.

v.s.v.d.l. W.

In January 1933, Vera submitted the manuscript of Testament of Youth *to the publisher Gollancz, and was anxiously awaiting his response, while Winifred had gone home to Cottingham to help care for her dying father.*

VERA TO WINIFRED

19 Glebe Place, London SW3 | 20 February 1933

Darling,

So glad to hear that you at any rate got safely home and for once are tolerably comfortable there. I've been on tenterhooks all the weekend for fear you too were ill. I'm sorry about your father but I suppose it is inevitable now; one can only hope it will be over soon rather than late. I long for you here but naturally understand that everything must be indefinite.

John is improving but poor Shirley is very poorly this morning after such a bad night of coughing; I fear it'll mean another infection. I'm just now waiting on tenterhooks for the doctor. She looks so pale and is such a little thing; it does seem a shame.

No news about book whatever; I've quite given up hope of Golly, though my legs turn to water every time the telephone goes or the doorbell rings. Phyllis writes a blithe p.c. advising me to 'rest' and take an expedition into the country!! She really *hasn't* any imagination, that woman; ought to have had six children and an ailing husband; might then have just faintly grasped the fact that we can't all live to ourselves, or even to our books! A *charming* letter from Margaret Storm Jameson, who's *had* whooping cough, and asks me to spend the evening with her tomorrow so as to get a change. If Shirley is well enough, I shall go. M.S.J. is very pleased about

Macmillan and says she knows they will give the 'Testament'
a good show.

All love, V.S.V.D.L.

WINIFRED TO VERA

20 February 1933

Both doctors last night seemed pretty hopeless. We are getting
a day nurse in too. Thick snow and bright sun, looks lovely,
but very slippery for cars. Just as it was while Grace was so ill.
I'm wondering and wondering how soon Victor Gollancz will
let you know. Blessings – Do hope the children are better.

W.

VERA TO WINIFRED

Telegram | *21 February 1933*

GOLLANCZ WRITES READ TESTAMENT WITH
GREATEST ADMIRATION GREAT BEAUTY EVEN
GREATER COURAGE VERY PROUD TO PUBLISH.

VERA TO WINIFRED

19 Glebe Place, London SW3 | *21 February 1933*

It was the queerest breakfast, here all by myself with such mixed
feelings. Gollancz's letter and your sad little postcard; it seemed
so wrong to feel so rapturous about anything when your father

is dying, and yet I knew that if you'd been here you'd have felt it too. My dear love, how can I ever find words in which to thank you for your faith in my book? If it hadn't been for you and your persistent belief and charity and patience, my own courage would have failed again and again, and I should never have finished it.

Somehow when I got up this morning – a lovely morning, mild, sunny and benevolent, so different from the dark snowy days of the week-end – I knew that Gollancz's letter was on the hall-table, and almost what was in it. I *made* myself get dressed just for the sake of discipline, but during my bath felt almost breathless with excitement (the water was hot, too, another absurd little omen!) and when I got into the dining room and opened it, this is what I read:

'Dear Miss Brittain, I have read *Testament of Youth* with the greatest admiration. It is a book of great beauty, and even greater courage, and I shall be very proud to publish it. In places, I confess, it moved me intolerably. As you ask, I am returning the manuscript under separate cover; and I am writing to Higham about the business side. Yours very sincerely, V.G.'

I have already spoken to Higham – who phoned me – about not being over-exacting and tiresome about terms; and Golly's secretary has already been on to me to know the exact length of the book.

Alone here all day I've had the utmost difficulty from time to time not to burst absurdly into tears! But luckily dear Margaret Storm Jameson, having had whooping cough, has asked me to dinner tonight, so I shall be able to work off my pent-up feelings on her and she won't mind! Mother dropped in for a few minutes and brought me a darling pink primula (not laconica!) in a pot.

I hope you're not having too bad a time, my sweetieheart. I don't know what to say or hope about your father – except for peace, I suppose, and a tranquil crossing.

All love and gratitude, my darling, Always your V.S.V.D.L.

Shirley rather better; no chest or heart trouble or temperature, just the cough.

Just got terms for contract by 'phone from Higham – £200 advance, 10% up to 10,000, 15% up to 20,000, 20% after. Golly wants to bring it out at 8/6 at the end of August so as to get start on autumn publishing season – with possible modifications in case of a Book Society choice of which he seems to have great hopes.

WINIFRED TO VERA

Bainesse, Cottingham, East Yorkshire | 24 February 1933

All the time, whatever I am doing, I am conscious of a note of happiness and relief because of your book. So often when I have been up here, I have been aware that in London you were being worried by your parents, by children ill, longing to get to you and anxious. It's so lovely now to know that even if driven between Shirley and revision and maids and chores and coping, you are facing happiness rather than care. I have become so much accustomed to feeling you part of me that every line of happiness in your letter – your newly done hair, Higham's terms, everything – lights up the candles on my Christmas Tree. I am so glad because my judgment is justified too. I know now that all my hopes for what you may do with the book are going to be justified. It will be the instrument to give you that power you need to work for the things you care about and fulfil your destiny and yourself. That is the only security and the only happiness. If Latham and Golly see the book as I see it – then that is the way it will be seen and can be used.

Father is now very little conscious – under morphia most of the time. I am sitting by him now. He looks more like a corpse than a person, and only the faint groan of his breath makes me know he lives. But I had a long talk to Peter yesterday, and he may linger on like this for *weeks* and while he does, though I may run up to town for a day or two, I can't go further. Surely, surely, it won't last till April. Everyone here is getting worn out – except me. I do no nursing – very little can be done. I sit here a few hours a day, I amuse Mother at meal times, and I live in a detached dream world of books, reviews, etc. My new novel is taking shape all the time. I had thought of running up to town, but Mother does not seem keen for me to go. I think she is frightened herself of collapsing when the end comes and wants me by her. After all, I do understand her better than anyone, and am prepared therefore to stand more from her strained nerves than anyone else.

I'm feeling fine. The new calcium tonic Obermer gave me is the first tonic I have had since I began to be ill. I sleep well and eat well, and am full of perfectly happy inner activity – which may be incongruous, but just does happen.

VERA TO WINIFRED

19 Glebe Place, London SW3 | 24 February 1933

I do wonder how you are and how everything is. Are you keeping warm? It's *bitter* here – snow, wind, general bleakness.

How I wish you were here to be told some of the amusing things that are happening! Do you know, even getting *T. of Y. taken* seems to make an extraordinary difference to one inside the *Inner Circle*! Several of them were at Rebecca's party last night, at which Rebecca herself looked charming in a moonlight-blue evening dress with a long rope of green jade twisted round her neck. (She herself was delightful to me; actually put her arm round my waist when introducing me to someone). Amongst others was

Mrs Gollancz, whom you may remember cut me dead at Dr Stella Churchill's garden party last year! She came straight up to me, beaming, practically clasped my hand and said: 'I must congratulate you on having written such a wonderful book. I couldn't get Victor away from it; he was reading it and crying over it for most of two days.' I felt quite overwhelmed but managed to say with great presence of mind, 'Well, *I* cried when I read his letter.' Then Rose Macaulay sauntered up, and instead of the usual distant nod, said: 'I hear you've written a very good autobiography.' I was positively flabbergasted this time, because as you know she disapproves of autobiographies on principle and I hoped she wouldn't find out for some time. However, I gasped out: 'How *do* you know? It was only taken two days ago.' She said: 'Oh, its publisher told me. I saw him last night and he kept on talking about it.' Well, at least it's cheering to know that Golly likes it enough to talk about it outside his office to people like R.M. Saw R.M. and Mrs Gollancz again at Naomi Royde-Smith's tea-party this afternoon; both as agreeable as if I'd been their bosom friend for years. As it was snowing violently, Margaret Kennedy took me home in her taxi and dropped me at my door; most cordial all of a sudden.

Everybody last night at Rebecca's asked after you and how you were – Rose said again how good she thought 'Mandoa'.

V.S.V.D.L.

WINIFRED TO VERA

9 March 1933

Darling,

He died quietly at 5 this evening. Mother and I were both in the room. The funeral probably on Saturday but not sure yet.

Bless you, W.

VERA TO WINIFRED

10 March 1933

My darling girl,

Your little note has just come. I'm so very, very sorry – not
for him because I know it is best – but for all of you and the
long strain you have had, and for the shock that comes when
something, however long expected, actually does happen. Your
mother will feel this very much even though she may often
have prayed for it in a way; the long culmination of years is a
deep grief, however much for the best their end may be. Isn't it
almost the anniversary of Grace's death five years ago? What a
sad time the spring always is! Life seems to end in it as often as
to be renewed.

I am so very glad that you have finished your book; that at
least is a weight off your own mind, and you can accept the
sorrow of these days without the tearing fret of the feeling
that they are preventing the completion of something that
belongs to life.

My best and dearest love, dear sweetieheart V.S.V.D.L.

WINIFRED TO VERA

12 March 1933

Darling,

I have no time but a hurried note. House full and letters
pouring in. I am doing all the answering for Mother, writing
reports for the local press, etc. Your sweet note, your telegrams
and your mother's, the maids' letters and your most lovely
flowers, were a great comfort. Mother particularly loved your

gay springlike bunch and the palm which means, she says, 'peace'. She asked me to thank you most warmly and for your loving message.

Really an impressive funeral. All the old farm servants came, and crowds of people. A thirty-mile drive to Bridlington on a gorgeous spring day.

Mother stoical and full of organising ability as usual, but arranged a perfect memorial service, with *Nunc Dimittis* sung as they carried the coffin down the church between banks of flowers into the spring sunlight. All very touching.

Dear love, vsvdl W.

VERA TO WINIFRED

19 Glebe Place, London SW3 | 14 March 1933

My darling girl,

I hope you really aren't overdoing it. Your account of the funeral was most moving; you will all feel better now that it is over. It's a very good idea to take your mother to Scarborough and if only it goes on being fine like this it will do you good too. Shall you come here when your mother comes to London or stop with her at the hotel? I'm glad you'll be at the Lady Rhondda dinner. I had arranged to go with Violet Scott-James and Edith Shackleton.

I had a long conversation with Violet Scott-James over the phone about getting a notice about your father into the *Yorkshire Post*, I hope it got in and that the various details I gave were correct. V.S.J. seems to have a 'down' on Lady Rhondda to which my own slight antagonism is a grande passion in comparison! She could see no merits in her autobiography at all – said there was 'nothing in it' – and has apparently given it quite a scathing review in the *Yorkshire Post*. I thought it interesting, and full of ideas – or rather, perhaps, suggestions for ideas than the ideas themselves.

All dearest love, V.S.V.D.L.

WINIFRED TO VERA

16 March 1933

Darling heart,

All my letters have been so scratchy in comparison with your sweet and interesting ones. But life is a chaos. We have in the house (a) electricians; (b) painters; (c) upholsterers; (d) chars spring-cleaning. A chorus of relatives, lawyers, friends, undertakers, inquirers in the background – a sort of factory of post-mortem activity. I've been helping Edith to pack Father's clothes and possessions most of the morning. I've written over 300 letters – all different! since Monday – and have just got my *Schoolmistress* article done in a room seething with people! But Harry came over yesterday and took me out for a walk and made me play bagatelle for an hour, and is here today licking stamps and running errands and being a general lamb. I'm perfectly well except for a roaring cold in head and everyone is quite cheerful.

I'm so pleased about Golly and your book and everything.

Give my love to your darling children. Yes – the work and discipline you put into them *was* worthwhile.

No time, no time, but *lots* of love. W.

VERA TO WINIFRED

19 Glebe Place, London SW3 | 17 March 1933

Darling,

So many thanks for your letter and enclosures. Your description of your activities makes me think, in a slightly different interpretation, of Emily Brontë's words: 'There is no room for death.' No time for it, anyway, among the really active living. But I suppose part of these activities – the house-decorating, at any rate – is what *should* have been done by the living ages ago if only it had been possible.

You must be feeling rather as I am – so confused by all the things you've done and have to do, that you're not quite sure whether you're yourself or not. After that nightmare week, which ended on Monday, of revising my book against time at the expense of both meals and sleep, followed on Tuesday by the rush to get the publicity material for America together and typed so that it could go by the *Europa* too, and on Wednesday by the day of interviews at Oxford, I am still feeling confused and distraught – rather as if I'd come back to normal life after a period of lunacy or a nervous breakdown! There are tons of things to do and I feel lost and don't know which I should do first. Actually I suppose I ought to take a complete rest of some sort and do nothing but read and eat and walk for about ten days, but it's very difficult to do this by one's self and in London.

The worst of it is that – having no other immediate thing to get interested in – my mind seethes with plans for future work and I can't make it lie fallow. I suppose I oughtn't to call this the 'worst of it' for it's really the 'best of it'; in other words, the praise I've had from Gollancz and Mr Latham has given me what all these years I've longed to have; namely, the confidence

that in future there'll always be publishers (and therefore
presumably a public) for what I want to write. Suddenly sure
(because people I so much respect have assured me) that I *can*
write well, and write what matters, I feel that in another decade
I could get myself the reputation of a female H. G. Wells – if
only I hadn't a husband, and parents, and a father-in-law, and
children, and maids, and a house, etc. etc. And then I realise
that if I hadn't these things my writing wouldn't have that
quality of humanity which both my publishers seem to think its
chief element of beauty – and then I don't know what I *do* want,
more time or not? – and so *ad infinitum*. What I suppose I *do*
want is more people to whom to delegate, not the responsibility,
which is valuable, but the small jobs connected with all these
things which take up so much time. And that means, I suppose,
one more maid or nurse-housemaid, and a good secretary, which
means more money, which again means more time to make it –
and so we start another vicious circle!!

I want to do a lot of reading the next few weeks – I feel
terribly empty and in need of replenishment in spite of all this
seething of ideas.

Now what I want to ask you is this. I'm up against a real
practical problem. I think I may, in the near future, have quite
a measure of success, but if Gordon doesn't get it too (and I see
no reason to suppose that he will) he will put it down, not to
hard work on my part, but to my having sacrificed his interests
to my own, and the less successful he is, he more he will feel
this, if only to justify his failure to himself! (You know the
kind of thing – if only I had entertained more, if only I'd been
a sort of glorified secretary like Mrs Laski, if only I had crowds
of students to tea as Laski does!! *Nothing* will ever persuade
him that all this is irrelevant to one's real work!) But he is also
quite untouched by the argument that I seem somehow to have
succeeded without *his* doing propaganda for me. And he'll get

more angry with me, and *more* insistent on my wasting my time entertaining his acquaintances who don't *want* to come, and it'll be increasingly difficult to get time for my increasing work without quarrelling with him – and yet I don't *want* to quarrel with him, for I'm really very fond of him in a way that is, I think, quite obvious in the last chapter of *T. of Y.*, and I adore the children, and don't want them to grow up with parents who are antagonistic to one another.

Do you think it would be right, or honourable, to act as G's permanent collaborator without having my name on his books and articles? (I don't want it on; I want to be entirely myself in my own books, not associated with him.) For the sake of maintaining a peaceful marriage I feel I *am* prepared to collaborate secretly – and if I only have *time* I feel my own capacity for good and lucid work to be for the present unlimited. But I've still to convince myself that this form of unobtrusive collaboration would be right – right from an ethical, or literary, or a feminist point of view. What do you think?

All dearest love V.S.V.D.L

WINIFRED TO VERA

Crown Hotel, Scarborough, East Yorkshire | *18 March 1933*

Darling,

At last I have time to answer your dear letters – though very little brain. All I really want to do is to sit on the cliff and watch the great waves, in curves three miles broad, sweeping into the bay. For physical beauty, Scarborough really is lovelier than any seaside town I know. Of course your mind is teeming with projects. It's a glorious condition. I hope you will just let it *teem* though, for the present, and make yourself drop all except essential work for a few weeks. Make working a time for reading and frivol a bit, as you seem to be going to do, before you go up.

I think your plan of making money by lectures and articles until your book comes out is really sensible. Lie fallow *imaginatively* until the summer passes, and make money and get publicity. The publicity will help you to sell *Testament*, and the money will enable you to engage a secretary to help with the next book! And I do think the idea of discussing the order of books with Golly is sound. Unless an idea comes and 'drags you by the hair and compels you to assent', I think his flair and his shrewdness, combined with his genuine admiration of your gifts, should make him a most helpful counsellor.

On the question of collaboration, I can give you Mother's opinion, I'm sure, before even asking it (though I will ask it when I can get her alone. Do you know that while writing this letter alone, we have had 3 callers, here in Scarborough?) I am sure that she would say that the *morality* of silent collaboration is perfectly defensible. Most men – even Wells – have admirable secretaries who help, even, I imagine with their prose. It's a purely practical question. How far can you do it without wearing yourself out, if you produce all your own work? *Certainly* don't sign your name to his – a great mistake from the point of view of both of you. But if you can help a little, and make things easier like that, I see no more reason against your helping in that way, than if you were a social genius and helped by entertaining. If his ambition were to be a poet or stylist, *then* your help might be immoral. But the thoughts would be his own and he is a Herbert Spencer, not a Keats – and if you can help him to make his thought more articulate, I can't see that you will be doing any injury to him, or to 'absolute integrity'. The question is a practical one of your own energy.

Physically I feel well, apart from my cold, and delighted at
having got through all this without a collapse. I am obviously
much better in spite of that collapse in June. But mentally I am so
tired and stupid that it took me hours to write my utterly dull and
stupid 'Notes on the Way' this week, and I find I can't take in the
doings at the Geneva Disarmament Conference though I read
Ramsay's speech for it three times! It's only the result of dealing
with incessant swarms of people, all strung up and tired, without
being able to take complete responsibility even for a telephone
call. I never mind what I do when I am my own mistress. I should
enjoy running anything from a charity ball to a Crown Colony;
but to be the tactful go-between and lieutenant, never to be able
to say *just* what one thinks, to compromise between conflicting
interests, to talk to relatives with whom I have not one thought
in common – to write letters to people who are vague names
to me. All this, combined with a blind, streaming cold, a small
succession of quite trivial headaches, and the knowledge that if
the heavens fall, my *Schoolmistress*, *News Chronicle*, and 'Notes on
the Way' articles must be got off to time – have left me no ounce
of energy for personal feelings. I have been an institution not a
person – never alone except in bed – writing usually in a room
full of people so that I can be on the spot if needed. Incidentally,
I should like to go somewhere in Yorkshire, where I can plan out
my novel, or at least think about it, in the right atmosphere. But I
may have to postpone that for weeks.

    v s v d l W

19 Glebe Place, London SW3 | *20 March 1933*

Darling sweet,

You *do* sound as if you'd had a perfectly ghastly time, and I
feel most ashamed of myself for having impelled you to write
such a long letter. I didn't mean you to at all; I only write you
rapid screeds myself because talking to you in some form or
other is second nature, and my activities and preoccupations
are at least a change from the dull and exasperating exactions
with which you are faced at home. *Don't* write to me again. I
suggest, as soon as your mother has gone, two days in bed here
without seeing *anybody* – even me. You can get your publicity
stuff together there, and I can type it. Don't bother about my
problems, which are not urgent, and presumably, alas! quite
permanent. Gordon sent me only this morning an article for
the *New Clarion* which *may* take it, and *another* review, to be
lodged 'where the last one was lodged', but preferably in some
journal with lots of influence and publicity value!!!

You know, in spite of all the efforts I've put in on G.'s behalf
in various ways (I've really given much more thought to his
career than to my own, and have five years of correspondence
to prove it!) I believe he still feels I never do a thing for him,
and if I were to die to-morrow, everything I've done in the way
of running the house, and bringing up the children, and writing
books, and paying for everything (I haven't, in any year since
the children came, had more than £100 from him), and seeing to
his father, and saving him every kind of worrying responsibility,
would all be as if it had never been, and he'd settle down quite
happily with one of his Kirks or Somerskills or Wishermanns,
and thank his stars he'd found such a comfortable substitute!
Apart from the lame and limited affection of parents and the

dependent, demanding, baby affection of the beloved children, I don't believe that a soul in the world except you really cares a pin for me.

All love – so looking forward to Thursday. V.S.V.D.L.

PS. Just had a 'phone call from Clare inquiring after us all – she tells me amongst other things that although her mother was at first so benevolent about my book, she never really thought much would come of it, and now that Gollancz and Macmillan's are publishing it is furiously jealous! Last week-end she said to Clare that the time for writing war books was long past, that nobody wanted to read that sort of stuff nowadays, that she was astonished I'd had it accepted at all, and couldn't possibly have got two such good publishers unless they'd been paid to take it, and she supposed that Lady Rhondda was paying for its publication!! This reduced me to complete hysteria. Think of all the implications! Imagine Lady R. – quite apart from her normal attitude to me nowadays – paying for my book to be published by the American firm which turned down her own!!

But somewhere below the mirth a burst of obscure rage smoulders – the injustice of humanity and its determined refusal to recognise merit is sometimes too much for my sense of humour. I have rather a feeling too – since I have published, and attempted, nothing on this scale before – that quite a number of people may say that you have helped me to write it – or Phyllis, who *has* worked on this scale, that *that* was why I had her here so long last summer, gave parties for her, introduced her to editors, etc.! Does it constitute libel, I wonder, to say that a person hasn't written their own book? Much as I hate the law, I really think that after the anguish, and heavy labour, the book has involved, I'd bring an action, with you and Phyllis as chief witnesses – not to get damages, but just to prove my complete integrity!

I think I'd better lie low and write nothing more about the
book to the old Leightons till it's actually out.
V.S.V.D.L.

WINIFRED TO VERA

19 *Glebe Place, London SW3* | *2 April 1933*

Darling,

I'd give almost everything I possess to do this so well that
everyone in Europe for generations to come would want to read
your book, and now, this is all that my atrophied imagination
seems able to produce. It has to go off tonight, for Golly says
he must have it tomorrow – but oh, what a lame and halting
version it is of what I feel I could write about your book.
I rush to the post.
Oh, a lovely, lovely book.
With my homage, Winifred

WINIFRED HOLTBY TO VICTOR GOLLANCZ

2 April 1933

Dear Mr Gollancz,

Here is my version which I, having so confidently
volunteered to do it, now feel to be quite woefully inadequate.
Please use or discard it exactly as you think fit.
Having thought the matter over, and re-read a good deal of
the book, I cannot help feeling that for me to sign this would
be a little indecent, considering how often and how intimately I
am referred to in its pages. But as I have come to the depressing

conclusion that I am as congenitally incapable of observing the rules of good taste as I am of detecting the limits of obscenity, I am still prepared to leave the decision in your hands.

Yours sincerely, Winifred Holtby

Jacket Description. TESTAMENT OF YOUTH. An Autobiographical Study of the Years 1900–1925. By Vera Brittain.

'There was a need to write this book, but little assurance that it ever would be written. Never before was a period so pregnant with great issues, so crowded with significant change, as the first twenty-five years of this century. These issues and those changes affect all of us; we cannot hope by the unpretentious obscurity of our lives to escape their impact; yet only by the honest chronicle of individual experience against that large background of political and social movement can we be fully shown just what was happening. And such a chronicle could only be adequately made by a writer who was a poet, with a poet's heightened intensity of vision, by a writer who had personally endured the experience of those who in 1914 were young and vulnerable and whose imagination had the informed and disciplined power to portray in their true proportions the huge sweep of world events closing in upon a generation.

'There are not many such. Others have borne witness to the horror, the wastage, the pity and heroism of modern war; none has yet so convincingly conveyed its grief. But here, too, courage testifies, not only the passive courage which endures beyond desolation and defeat, but the active courage which determines to understand the causes of its misery and to rebuild for future generations a new and finer life out of the ruins of the old.

'The book contains, in the first place, an almost intolerably

poignant personal record. By the use of contemporary letters, diaries and poems, Miss Brittain has recaptured, with
amazing fidelity, the changing moods of those half-forgotten
years. Reading her pages we can live again through the days
of untroubled or rebellious immaturity before the war, when
in their comfortable middle-class homes and carefully chosen
schools the unsuspecting future soldiers and nurses were growing to meet their hidden destiny; we live again through the days
and nights of nagging and unrelieved suspense, and the months
and years of work through which we passed from exultant
bewilderment to satiety and from satiety to a blind and dogged
persistence without hope or comfort; we remember again the
swift irrelevant humours, and still swifter, still more irrelevant
crashes of disaster, which the war brought to all those whom it
most directly affected. And in her final chapters we relive the
painful struggle towards resurrection of those who survived the
inconclusive irony of the Armistice.

'These personal experiences are set against an immense and
heroically sustained panorama, culminating in three superbly
written historical documents: a description of the penultimate
voyage of the doomed hospital ship *Britannic* through the
submarine-infested waters of the Mediterranean in the summer
of 1916; an eyewitness's account of the Americans swinging
confidently forward to victory through the driven and desperate chaos of the retreat of 1918; and an unforgettable picture of
postwar Europe during a journey undertaken in 1924 to study
the varying attempts to recreate a civilisation from the wreckage of catastrophe. The form of the book has been so planned
that the individual stories illuminate with their fortuitous
symbolism the great march of European tragedy.

'But though deeply tragic, *Testament of Youth* is not depressing. Its mood is rich in colour, swift in movement and eager
in response to all manifestations of beauty and adventure; a

response often expressed in the direct and musical lyrics scat-
tered through the grace and irony of its flexible prose. Out of
the cruelties of circumstance arise the memories of personal
relationships, lovely and touching in their innocent devotion:
the romantic passion between a young idealistic and articulate
boy and girl; the loyal hero-worship of young men who were
friends, and an almost perfect intimacy and understanding
between the sister and her brother who survived until the
summer of 1918. The whole book is controlled by a philosophy
of life which, with its nobility, intelligence and courage, challenges our cynical lethargy and ignominious despairs.'

VERA TO WINIFRED

Worthing | *3 April 1933*

Oh, my darling sweet,

What a joy, what a love, what a *genius* of insight and
intelligence you are! What supreme piece of good fortune gave
me, I wonder, the miracle of your friendship – a miracle that I've
done *nothing* to deserve? (Wrote she, weeping so hard that she
couldn't see the page.) No wonder Lady Rhondda feels a little
grievance towards me for having so much of you – I don't blame
her at all!

Your notice of *Testament of Youth* is beautiful and *so*
understanding. Do you really see all this in my book? If so, it
must be there – and my confidence in it is restored. Our poor
Phyllis's petty and parochial notice almost made me feel that my
book was petty and parochial. I didn't feel petty when I wrote
it – I always felt that my story was a universal story, beginning
with the Trojan women and repeated through all ages and
all generations. And now has come your *lovely* description to

restore my faith in myself and in the possibility of succeeding
in what I set out to do and to make other people *see*. And I
began to feel that poor Phyllis is not exceptionally intelligent or
infinitely superior at all – but simply a well-meaning but narrow,
self-righteous, bigoted, egotistical and quite stupid woman
who happens to have the semi-conscious, half-mechanical
gift of the *raconteuse* – rather like a gift for ventriloquism or
for walking on one's toes! I can't help shedding a few tears of
regret for the genuine love, the genuine attempts at generosity,
thrown away on such a person. But I can't go on trying to give
her what she needs and won't take. It costs too much in time
and hurt sensibilities! Henceforward I've *done* with her as a
friend. As an acquaintance towards whom I feel a little wary
but entirely benevolent, yes – I'll go on with that. But she can't
matter any more.

Why should she matter, when I've got you! To revert to the
far pleasanter subject of your notice, there are some lovely
sentences in it for which I should like specially to thank you.
'The huge sweep of world events closing in upon a generation' –
'the active courage which determines ... to rebuild for future
generations a new and finer life out of the ruins of the old' –
'that universal quality which makes the story of the fall of Troy
still relevant to our daily lives' – such sentences as these say
exactly what I meant my book to convey, and the final sentence
about 'stricken but unbroken youth' is just what I hoped people
would feel.

What really matters is what you *have* got with such
miraculous, almost uncanny perception – the peculiar quality
of the youth of our generation – its naïve idealism, its gallantry,
its dogged, unbroken persistence even when faith was lost and
hope was gone. Bless you, my dear, for being part of this youth
yourself and for understanding its quality.

My blessings on you – dear, dear love. V.S.V.D.L.

WINIFRED TO VERA

Cottingham, East Yorkshire | *4 April 1933*

Darling,

Darling, I *loved* doing your book, I really think it is a great book. In the bus yesterday evening, I amused myself by an imaginary conversation with somebody, Golly perhaps, Siegfried Sassoon, perhaps, or Rose Macaulay – about the years in which you had been looking after babies and relations and writing a long, long book and doing meticulous research, and how you sometimes had thought that I was the one who was going to count – so many books, so much activity, *Time and Tide*, *Who's Who* etc. And all the time I had known and chuckled inside myself, 'You wait. You wait. Wait till you see what Vera was really doing.' And now you've done it. And soon everyone will know. And I'm so wickedly and jubilantly triumphant. Because it's just what I expected, and I feel so pleased. I know that this book is going to make a tremendous difference to you, to the opportunities you will have for doing those things you want to do.

But don't let this make you feel that what you gave to Phyllis wasn't worthwhile. It's always worthwhile to love people, because love is, I think, an art, and the practice of an art is never futile even though it seems to have little or no effect. And Phyllis *is* a tragic person, whose limitations call for far more love and patience and understanding than – say – the warm rich natures like Storm Jameson's. She will need your friendship, as you have foreseen, more and more as the years go on. And though she has not much imagination, she has intelligence, integrity, and power of a queer, dark, twisted kind. Only don't expect too much and hurt yourself with her, as you have done before. One gets, after a time, accustomed to the limitations of otherwise loveable people, and often one doesn't expect too much.

Bless you, my dear and sweet and splendid love. v.s.v.d.l. W.

VERA TO WINIFRED

19 Glebe Place, London SW3 | *5 April 1933*

Darling sweetest,

Last night I was reading Lady Rhondda's autobiography and loving it, and thinking what a really charming and honest and honourable person emerged from it, and puzzling over why I'd never liked her and she'd never liked me when we have almost everything in common except, perhaps, my faculty as an artist and her business experience – and of course the more superficial differences of wealth and social standing. Then, this morning, came your letter about being able to love and appreciate Phyllis just the same so long as one didn't expect too much, and recognised her limitations and refused to be hurt by them.

I really am resting quite a bit and should be completely if it weren't for the shoals of letters involved by my book – can't leave as it will mean so much delay over proofs – so many are to American publications.

Take care of yourself – all I can love V.S.V.D.L.

WINIFRED TO VERA

Bainesse, Cottingham, East Yorkshire | 7 April 1933

Darling,

I'm *so* glad you like Lady Rhondda's book. She really *is* like that – 'charming and honest and honourable' – and I feel that she too some day will learn to understand you.

I had an exquisite day yesterday – the sort of thing one only expects in youth, and never hopes for at Cottingham. I had to go to the funeral – (that was rather fine too, in a way. A very popular, respected, kindly man – crowds of Hull employees – and an April showery day, and music I love – 'Oh, Rest in the Lord' – and the 23rd psalm, and Chopin's Funeral March.)

Then Harry took me by train to Beverley, and we arrived too early for tea, so went to look at the carvings in St Mary's – and he told me absurd stories of what all the carvers were thinking about when they made the pictures on the pews – then to his cousins. The girl was a teacher who paints, the boy is a seed-merchant but plays the piano beautifully and their house is full of books and flowers and two adorable little boys of 5 and 7.

We had tea over a big open fire in a book-lined room, then went for a walk on the Westwood to an oak wood I never knew existed, full of wood anemones – lovely – and stayed till the moon rose and talked nonsense. Then went back for supper (H. had told them I was vegetarian) and then Wilfrid, the boy, played the chorals from the *St Mathew Passion*, which he saw was being sung at Leeds, and played most beautifully. And they brought me home by car. Nothing in it, perhaps, but a lovely and happy time – perfectly at ease, and Harry completely himself. They love him there and he is completely at home with them.

Much love vsvdl W.

VERA TO WINIFRED

19 Glebe Place, London SW3 | *8 April 1933*

Darling,

What an exquisite day it sounds – and yet I feel as if I could shake Harry sometimes; why not just complete such exquisite experience in the way that seems indicated? Why let your best years, and his, go on without it? – but I expect he seems even *more* exasperating to you for this! Anyhow it *was* a lovely day; one of the kind that one remembers for years. I should have adored the music and the wood sounds heavenly.

All dearest love, V.S.V.D.L.

VERA TO WINIFRED

22 Navarino Road, Worthing, Sussex | *10 April 1933*

Darling sweet,

I found this morning an almost extinguishing blow in the shape of my last chapter returned by Gordon, with alterations and omissions indicated that will mean re-writing the whole of its first twenty pp. and incidentally rendering them quite dull and meaningless. Although he has now read the whole of the book, he sends me no word of comment or appreciation to show that he understands what I meant it to do and be. Instead, he scores whole pages across, and writes beside them such comments as 'intolerable', 'horrible', 'pretty terrible'. If he does want me to alter my book, I don't know why he can't ask me to do so without insulting it. I didn't mean any of the things I wrote to be 'horrible', and I didn't – and don't – think that any of them are. He is supersensitive about his own work,

and incidentally expects me to work pretty hard on its behalf;
why should he expect me, after three years' hard work and
some periods of almost intolerable strain – to be less sensitive
about mine?

The result of all this, coming on the top of a month's
incessant worry about copyrights, and all the bother about
Phyllis, has been to make today a complete nightmare. I
suppose I am seeing everything out of proportion as the result of
being too long alone (or rather, too long closeted with prattling
non-adults – Nurse's conversation is like that of a Fifth Form
schoolgirl and I find John's infinitely less exhausting) during a
period of strain and worry. But something in me seems to have
broken – some element of faith and hope and confidence that I
had, at least in some measure, achieved by my book what I set
out to do for my own generation. It is bitterness itself that this
book – which I meant to be a *Lamentation of David* over my
generation's dead and a brave *Odyssey* of its survivors – should
appear, to two of the people most dear to me, to be nothing but
a source of wounding and exasperation. Are they blind, or am I?

From the practical point of view of the alterations G. wants,
I do think he might – knowing how important it is to avoid
delay – have cabled asking me to hold up chapter 12. I have
sent an urgent letter to Victor Gollancz Ltd. asking if they
can possibly return the last chapter to me before it is printed;
otherwise the alterations involved will be most costly both in
money and time. Also, say what he will, I *cannot* make them all.
He wants me to remove every statement which could possibly
identify him, all references to his politics, religion, profession,
friends, academic achievements, family background, etc. In
other words, to make him, in comparison with Roland and even
with Victor, a complete cipher and supply the reader with no
reason whatever why I should decide to marry him! I am sorry,
since he objects so much, that I couldn't have left him, and our

marriage, wholly out, but this would have utterly doomed the book – in which, as you saw so clearly, my method has been to illustrate the tragedies of Europe and the story of our generation by the fortuitous symbolism of my own life. My marriage to G., my resurrection from the spiritual death of the War, into the new life and new personality which came to me so largely through him, are absolutely essential as illustrating Europe's struggle after a similar self and new life, and the resurrection with different personalities of all those who suffered in, and survived, that War.

Moreover, I think that even from the crudest tactical point of view he is wrong to want the few personal details that I have given of him removed. The circumstances of our marriage do him nothing but credit; it could do him no harm that it should be told, and might do a great deal of good. Nobody would fail to admire him for his delicacy, and lack of jealousy, over my previous relationship with men long dead, and for his understanding of the feminist point of view (he actually asks me to delete the bit in which I say how much I was attracted by the feminist bias of his letters; does he then repudiate all his feminism now?), of my work and my peculiar difficulties about marriage, while his attitude towards religion and politics, his early vote for Labour, the deep human basis of his determination to study the theory of Politics and find out the reason for civilisation's periodic fractures, could do him nothing but good by being better known.

What am I to do? I cannot remove all these details, and make utter nonsense of the indirect and very careful references to him and his career in earlier chapters. I feel I ought to cable my disagreement, but what could I cable: 'Cannot agree to all modifications but will eliminate all direct identifying details' or 'Too late for fundamental modifications . . .'? Would that do? I can't wait a month for his reply – don't think V.G. would agree to hold up proofs so long. Why, oh why, do these things always happen when I'm away and have no one to consult?

Why is it that a person as sensitive as Gordon seems quite unable to realise what it has meant to write a book like that, or to have had to take so long over it?

What am I to do about G.? (Another non-adult in some way, I fear!) I can't, without *another* row in which I don't feel I can endure to involve my book, point blank refuse to make most of the changes he want – and yet I can't bear making nonsense of so much of it. Suggestions for a tactful course of action? Damn the distance to America.

Must stop this. I really think I should have committed suicide long ago if I hadn't got you with your confident faith and understanding.

All dear love, V.S.V.D.L.

WINIFRED TO VERA

Bainesse, Cottingham, East Yorkshire | *11 April 1933*

My sweet girl,

First about Phyllis. Do you know, I honestly believe her letter may mean little more than it says? She may be simply incapable of seeing what your *Testament* means. It sounds incredible, but people are so strange; she is such an egoist (the allusion to her own experience while Scarborough was being bombarded, for instance, seems so odd) that she may merely regard the whole incident as of no more importance than that she wrote a rather inadequate puff for one of Vera's books, as you might have written an inadequate one for *Trio*. And her reaction to the War part may have been envy rather than sympathy – envy for your experience, the love and admiration of four such fine young

men, which was yours. After all, that's an understandable point
of view – to envy the rich emotional experience of tragedy as
well as of love.

There will be many women reading your book who will
hunger for your pain – just as some hunger, not for the joy of
children, but for the pangs of childbirth. It is our human destiny
to need suffering, to need our enemies, to need loss and need
death, as well as we desire love, life, joy and creation. The whole
motive of asceticism, martyrdom, and masochism is a testimony
to this; and those for whom life provides the scourge, as in
your case who have known love and loss and tears and agony,
are envied more than pitied by those who have known only
the nullity of frustration. It may be possible that this is what is
affecting Phyllis.

Gordon is a much more serious proposition. I have been
writing him a long, long letter – perhaps unavailingly – in
reply to one I had from him too this morning. He wrote to me
saying he was most anxious not to hurt you, but quite clear that
he found your references to himself not tolerable. He dreads
that they will be regarded as voluntary and conscious publicity
by his colleagues, bring ridicule upon himself, and wholly
destroy forever his opportunities of doing the work which is his
life-blood.

I have written to say I think him wholly wrong. Only the
irredeemably vulgar could regard with ridicule so poignant
and dignified a record. And what is said of him could only
do him good.

But as he *does* feel like that, it is possible that others,
reared in the desiccated, inhuman, suspicious atmosphere of
the academic world may so regard it; may laugh at him; and
may cause him to believe your point of view wrong and his
right. Which would be quite intolerable and destroy your
future relationship for good perhaps. He *is* hypersensitive; the

academic world has its amazing and inhuman code; its perverse
vulgarities; and he has to live in it.

Therefore I think that you had better accept his suggestions
as far as you can, and cable 'Will eliminate all direct identifying
detail and modify as far as possible.' Actually, apart from the
trouble, I do not think that this will spoil the chapter, and
certainly not spoil the book. Actually, it is *your* resurrection,
your attitude towards marriage, your decision to 'take up the
exquisite burden of life' as Arnold Bennett says, which makes
the book; it does not matter aesthetically that his should be
a somewhat shadowy figure. He did not, when he read them,
apparently disapprove of the earlier references to himself. Keep
those in. But he feels so strongly about the possible effect of the
further details upon his future career that I think (however false
I consider his reasoning to be) that you would be wise to modify
the chapter. It is not worthwhile, and would, I think, be quite
intolerable to you both, to have a quarrel over this. He is most
anxious not to hurt you (though how he expects his attitude
and comments can avoid that, I don't quite know!). And, as
an outsider, I can see that to leave his figure shadowy will not
detract from the strength of your argument, and your resolution.

I have written telling him all the reasons why I think him
entirely wrong in his judgment of the effect upon himself. I
think he needs these details to break down the legend of his
inhumanity. But it is of no use to expect that my letter may
change his feeling, and still worse to do anything that would
make him more self-conscious and more unsure of himself than
he is already. That would be to do him irreparable harm.

So I should make this further concession to the limitations of
your friends and hope it will be (as I think it must be) the last
to be made.

Listen, darling, you must hold on. I think it *is* true that you
may see things out of proportion now. But knowing how much

the book has meant and means to you, what this spring has been, and what the failure of both Gordon and Phyllis means to you, I'm not surprised. The truth is that both are so profoundly preoccupied with their own work that they think first of that. Gordon alone, hyper-sensitive to ridicule, wounded in his vanity as keenly as ever you have been wounded in your affections, flinches at possibilities of ridicule that nobody else would see. Phyllis, I honestly think, may *not* be wounded or disturbed in any way, but simply blind to what the incident has meant to you.

And you, my dear, my sweet. You have written a great book, one that may live, as I told Gordon, with Newman's *Apologia* and Thoreau's *Walden* and all other self-revelations which have enriched the human spirit's own understanding of its purpose. And because you have put into it every particle of yourself, your strength and your purpose, everything that touches it will touch you. It *is* yourself and you cannot help being wounded through it. But also, I believe that you will be enriched beyond measure by it. You will make friendships and opportunities by it beyond all dreams. I am absolutely sure of this.

Darling, darling, I wish I could come to you. I feel torn in half; but I know that I must stay. You are strong; you are brave; you have a thousand ties to life; your spiritual awareness has given you weapons to meet exasperation, wounds and disappointment. Mother is old, tired, surrounded by the menace of death, which seems to be attacking all her near and dear friends, part of a dying generation, and anxious for the future. I must stay till after Easter – then I'll come directly I can.

Hold on to the knowledge that you have done a splendid thing. Hold on; keep faith. We need your faith and courage. Bless you.

    Winifred

WINIFRED TO VERA

Bainesse, Cottingham, East Yorkshire | 24 April 1933

My very dear,

I was glad to have Golly's notice. I certainly did not want
it to be known that I wrote it. When I re-read the M.S. (in
its original version too!), I came to the conclusion that the
portrait of myself was so noble that really I couldn't possibly
sign the description of the book containing it, and told Golly
so. After all, this book is probably the only way in which my
memory may live, so it really would be hardly proper for me to
tell people to read it! I certainly need no 'recognition' for what
was a *joy* to do. I spent that Sunday with the book in a white
heat of excitement trying until final post-time by re-writing and
re-writing to get on to paper something at least of what you
had achieved.

Went a heavenly walk yesterday through wet woods with
Harry. Came back with *armsful* of cowslips and young green
branches. He cycled home last night. He has been completely
sweet to me. I feel so extraordinarily at rest when he is here –
as though something about him were a support and stay. The
sexual philosophers would say our relationship was wrong and
unnatural. At the moment it is all I want, and seems to be all
he wants. If I really were treating him badly and he wanted
more, surely I should feel some strain or restraint or impatience
in him? I feel none. He says he is taking the Pearl Assurance
job. I'll wait and see.

Bless you, darling. v.s.v.d.l. W

*A joint visit to Hardelot-Plage had intervened between the April letters
and the following letter.*

VERA TO WINIFRED

19 Glebe Place, London SW3 | 21 August 1933

I was so sorry to miss you yesterday morning – especially as
I thought afterwards it was really rather silly of me to be so
hurt about *Time and Tide*. But as it happened I met Cicely
Hamilton when I was out early paying the books yesterday
morning, and she told me that she too had felt very hurt when
Lady R. told her Pamela Hinkson was doing it, as she had
imagined that it was an understood thing that she was doing
it unless Ellis Roberts wanted to do it himself. Thinking that
she was pretty certain to have it, she made no effort to get
it for anything else and is now rather disgusted because she
seems to be doing it nowhere. She wrote off at once to the
Morning Post to ask if she could have it, but fears it may be too
late and that Delafield or someone else has got it. I *do* hope
not E.M.D., as she was so silly about Storm Jameson's book –
said it was all *vieux jeu*, etc.

I imagine that the book has not only gone to P.H. but that
she has actually written the review. If so, the only thing that
could be done which would be of any help to me would be
not only to put in the review in the week of publication but to
advertise it on the cover as one of the week's features, as the
Week-end Review did for my review of Storm Jameson.

It is very kind of Lady Rhondda to say I can use her letter.
Though its general tone is appreciative I don't think there's
anything specially quotable in it, but I will send Gollancz a
copy and let him judge for himself. He probably will think that
people would discount what she said because of a supposed
prejudice in my favour!!!

All dearest love – V.S.V.D.L.

VERA TO WINIFRED

19 Glebe Place, London SW3 | *23 August 1933*

Darling,

I never dreamed this week would be so tedious and depressing. I look forward to the week-end, yet dread it unspeakably, and spend my whole time in mental argument with imaginary critics who abuse me for this, that and the other! I can't settle down to a damned thing and am quite glad when there is something to do for the children. The 'fun' starts with Beatrice Kean Seymour's review in the *Woman's Journal* on Friday; then there is Cecil Roberts on Saturday, and I suppose one or two of the Sunday papers may review it. I was in the West End yesterday being photographed again, and every bookshop I passed had a 'display' of *Wonder Hero* in the window.

Selfridge's had a huge window dedicated to Priestley alone; there was an enormous photograph of his bull-nosed countenance, about the size of the dining-room table, in the middle, a placard beside it giving the details of his sales (*Faraway*, 60,000; *Angel Pavement*, 142,000; *Good Companions*, 300, 000) and ranged round the lot at least 100 copies of the book itself. I fear that none of us will ever compete with that . . . How are these things *done*? Even the dignified Bumpus's had cleared two shelves for him. I hope that by next week a few will have been sold to make a modest space for one or two little copies of *T. of Y.*

It gives me a cold feeling down my back to think that, after all that reading of contemporary documents, verifying, reading of war history, visits to British Museum etc., the whole book may still be full of blunders because of the queer tricks that memory plays, shuffling facts and confusing real episodes with imagined ones until one is not sure which is which. Did I really dream the whole thing, I sometimes ask myself? Will some adverse reviewer accuse me of having perpetrated a gigantic fake ... ? But then there are the letters, etc. At least I can show any disbeliever the original documents upon which the whole thing is based and they can be compared with the extracts quoted.

Gordon is at Oxford today, so I am all alone, conducting imaginary arguments with hostile relatives. G. made a remark the other day of considerable psychological acuteness with reference to the friction between myself and Phyllis which precipitated our final quarrel; he said that when she was here I patronised her and treated her like a country cousin, so she sub-consciously compensated herself by persuading herself that I was a negligible writer!

How objectionable I am, aren't I! No wonder St J. Ervine and Cecil Roberts (and no doubt numerous others who aren't quite so honest) had such a contempt for me! Too depressed to work so I am just off for a walk round Battersea Park. Hope Scarborough is doing you good; it must be rather cold.

All love, V.S.V.D.L.

WINIFRED TO VERA

Crown Hotel, Scarborough, East Yorkshire | *24 August 1933*

My dearest Love,

I was so sorry to have your sad little letter, my own sweet girl – as though you were not a splendid friend to have, on whom we lean constantly. I do. Gordon does. Your mother does. Storm Jameson does. Phyllis will again. There may be something in Gordon's shrewd analysis of inferiority on her part. People do resent any implication of naïvety or innocence far more than any accusation of immorality, you know!

Darling, sweet, don't worry. Your book is a grand piece of work. It will endure. I feel that it may even have repercussions upon opinion which will cause thousands to bless your name and existence. I shall never do anything like that; but I am proud to be your friend.

v.s.v.d.l. W.

Testament of Youth was an immediate and enormous success. In the months between the previous letter and the next, Vera was invited to lecture all over England.

1934

VERA TO WINIFRED

1 April 1934

Feel considerably better today. Throat and back are less persistent and yesterday's crashing headache has departed. However, it is something to have done all the 74 lectures without abandoning one, in spite of feeling like death over a good many. The nurse said my throat was quite as much fatigue as flu.

I have decided to go to one small quiet place and stay put for the whole fortnight. Tonight I suddenly remembered that Henry and Rebecca went for their honeymoon to a little place near Genoa, so I rang him up. He happened to be there because Anthony is still ill, and told me about the place, which is called Portofino and does sound enchanting. He says it should be ideal now, and the little hotel is called the Albergo Nationale, simple but very clean, running water and excellent cooking of the local fish, chicken, vegetables, spargetti kind. He talked a lot about its simplicity, but if it is comfortable enough for him and Rebecca it should certainly do for us!

All dearest love V.S.V.D.L.

WINIFRED TO VERA

Delma, Waxholme Road, Withernsea,
East Yorkshire | 7 April 1934

Darling,

Of *course* I will pay my share of the spring cleaning. I have *masses* of money, and living here costs me about 30/- a week! – (except that I spend a bit travelling round the country). I should think we had better go halves, wouldn't you, as Gordon can't pay you back? And it is we who like new paint! I am only too glad to have it done.

I have at last begun to think of my own novel. I think I shall call it 'South Riding' – it's a pretty name and ambiguous and rather romantic.

Much love, darling v.s.v.d.l. W.

VERA TO WINIFRED

9 April 1934

Have had a wire from Gordon saying he will meet me at Sta. Margherita on Thursday; have also got all the tickets and paid for them, so if you don't hear from me to the contrary I shall set off on Wednesday morning. Taking children to Oxford by myself tomorrow. Only pray that Shirley isn't sick!

Poor Phyllis! I am still *sure* they could have managed without her and that her mother's hand wasn't as bad as all that. Did she write to you here or know your Withernsea address? I have a feeling that she'll never write to me, even now – especially since this recall home will have destroyed all her sense of triumph in America. I am accepting the fact now that I must write down Phyllis as one of my failures. There haven't up to date been *many* personal ones, thank Heaven! I do know, too, that I have come to the end of the amount of white sheet-wearing I am prepared to do for her – I was in the wrong, but she wasn't altogether blameless, and I don't quite see why I should play the penitent any longer. A year ago I think I was still dazzled by her prestige. Now that my own has equalled and in some personal ways even exceeded it, I see her in rather a different perspective, and don't see why I should go round any longer trying to propitiate or console her! I make no move towards her, ever again, unless she makes one first.

I *love* your title of 'South Riding'. I do hope that you'll make it a big book – something that will do for Yorkshire agriculture as a saga what 'Inheritance' did for Yorkshire industry.

Dear love, V.S.V.D.L.

WINIFRED TO VERA

Delma, Waxholme Road, Withernsea,
East Yorkshire | 10 April 1934

Darling,

I'm so glad you like the 'South Riding' title. As I see it now, it's going to be an immense spread book. In time occupies only from July 1932–July 1934 – and in space only a few score square miles; but every possible kind of family comes in. All the county councillors and all the parents of the children at the High School. The Headmistress of the High School and the most conspicuous Conservative councillors are still the chief protagonists; but the whole comedy-tragedy of local government comes in, and each part is called by the title of a committee of the council, e.g. Education; Mental Deficiency; Public Assistance. And each part treats of some aspect of administration as it affects a human life – or several human lives, while all the time a fight is going on between the people who want to plan and change things by deliberate will, and the people who just want to 'let things happen'. (It's a more profound cleavage than between mere Conservatism and Socialism to my way of thinking.)

Yes, I think you may well leave Phyllis alone. I am desperately sorry for her. She needs you far more than you ever needed her. But if she is so neurotic and egotistic and hysterical, that you merely frighten and upset her, it is no use trying to do anything about it. The loss is hers; but there are some losses one can't help. I shall go on being friendly with her; but my relationship has never varied much. She's never been particularly interested in me, only quite mildly affectionate. One day you and she will probably meet quite unconcernedly. I shouldn't call it a failure on your part. It was one on hers. And she *may* one day come to sense.

I found a new tea place today, right out on the cliffs north of Withernsea. Almost every day I go out to tea somewhere two or three or four or more miles away, walking one or both ways, or busing so far. It's a good objective. I'm getting to be a splendid walker. Did I tell you I did 17 miles one day with an ex-sergeant major? And I sleep 10 hours some days, and I am so well. Just loving every minute of it.

Do have a good time. v.s.v.d.l. W.

WINIFRED TO VERA

Delma, Waxholme Road, Withernsea,
East Yorkshire | 7 May 1934

Darling –

I think you must go to America. You may never have quite
such another chance. I knew your father had tried to kill
himself, but not the details. Your mother let it out in one of
her quick, nervous expressions, then withdrew again and said
she would tell you all about it, so I said no more. In his nervous
condition, it was almost inevitable that he should try it. But you
can't stop him. You can't really even help your mother much.
It is probable that he won't even try again. And if he does . . .
What is life to him, poor man? I promise that if anything
does happen while you are away, I will do everything I can to
help. But I know that really no one, not even you, can do very
much. You will be far more use, I feel, not only earning money
but propagating ideas in America, than waiting in London for
something that *might* possibly happen.

Mother loves your poems and has been round the Hull shops
telling them to get in lots of copies. She has also told the East
Riding to order *Preface to Action* for the County Libraries. (She's
on the committee.) She has also just been made a member of the
North Regional B.B.C. 'Week's Good Cause' committee, which
she has to attend at Manchester and advise on speakers and causes.

I must get on. Returned after the week-end to the usual *pile*
of letters. People have now begun to pester me to speak again,
and I am straining my brain to invent excuses.

v.s.v.d.l. W.

VERA TO WINIFRED

19 Glebe Place, London SW3 | *8 May 1934*

What a splendid publicity agent your mother is – and really
what a marvel. Mrs Sidney Webb – a very incisive old lady
who has *all* her faculties, plus an ability to walk 2½ miles after
an operation last January for the removal of one kidney –
nevertheless seems much older at 74.

I *did* like Mrs Webb. So downright, so witty, so easy to talk
to for all her slight alarmingness: I'm afraid I'm not really a good
democrat, for there still doesn't seem to me anything quite equal
to complete intelligence *plus* complete well-bredness. If one has to
choose, one of course prefers the intelligence without the breeding
to the breeding without the intelligence, but there's something
in thorough-bredness which makes for the self-confidence and
dependability that you never quite get without it. What snobbish
reflections! – but Mrs Webb makes them inevitable.

I agree with what you say about America. There are so many
invalids and dependents in my life, and so many vague disasters
that might happen to them all, that the only thing is to
disregard the lot and behave as if they weren't there. By doing
this I have had a good many adventures in my life already, only
I used to disregard people with anguish, and that is so nervously
expensive that I'm trying to learn to disregard them with
equanimity. It is, as you realise, largely a question of how much
other people will help. I could never disregard the children with
equanimity, but can leave them to you feeling you will treat
them as your own.

All dearest love V.S.V.D.L.

WINIFRED TO VERA

Delma, Waxholme Road, Withernsea,
East Yorkshire | 19 May 1934

Darling,

I have no plans; come how and when you like. Simply send a
wire and I will be at the station with a car.

Harry is in Cornwall, writing, and for the first time really
placing articles, and happy, I think. After all, what all decent
men and women really want is the thing, whatever it may be,
which they feel is justifying their existence. That, I suppose,
is why you now face dental extractions like a lion – and why
unemployment is so much more of a spiritual than even of a
material tragedy.

I am going over to Cottingham tomorrow and shall probably
now stay till Tuesday as you aren't coming, though I grudge
every minute from my book. I see I am going to have no time
at all for it when I get back to London, as *Time and Tide* wants
lots of me, and Ballinger is coming to England, and Howard
Pim, who supported our funds in S. Africa, is dead. And life
altogether is going to be full of Africans and Armaments!

Did I tell you I did go to the Fascist meeting and distributed
Dorothy Woodman's abusive pamphlets as the audience came
out? I'm not at all brave. I was terrified, I lost two days' good
work through sheer and quite unnecessary funk. When it
actually came to it, nothing could have been milder. I stood on
the steps in my best clothes, fur coat, white gloves, and handed
out pamphlets, with a Blackshirt beside me. As I looked such
a lady, as the pamphlets look so innocuous, and as both he
and I were strangers, he thought I was a local lady helping the
meeting, I suppose. *Very* impressive meeting from the stage
management point of view. Forty imported Blackshirts stood

at attention throughout a speech so bad I yearned to get up and make it for the poor man (not Mosley, of course. A Major Billington. Extremely handsome, perfect male figure, nervous, charming, mentally defective, Adonis of face and fourth form boy in ideas.)

I don't know if he or I did any good or harm. Probably neither of us had the slightest effect.

Au revoir, little love. v.s.v.d.l. W.

VERA TO WINIFRED

19 Glebe Place, London SW3 | 22 May 1934

Darling,

I am rather worried at this moment by a 'phone message from Curtis Brown reporting a cable offer from U.S.A. of $10,000 for the film rights of *Testament of Youth*. They seem to think me mentally defective because I don't jump at the idea of selling my soul (to say nothing of other people's) for £2,000 – but just think what Hollywood might do with *T. of Y.*! Of course a dignified, woman's *Cavalcade* film *could* be made of it, but would it, by America? On the other hand, think what £2,000 could do for the children, for G.'s career, for the various institutions like the Union of Democratic Control which are working to rescue civilisation. I have sent a temporising cable back to U.S.A. saying that the offer is financially acceptable provided I approve of the treatment of the film. What are your own reactions, particularly in view of the fact that you yourself might be personified by Tallulah Bankhead or someone even worse!!?

I feel so perturbed that I almost hope the whole thing will end in smoke as so many film offers seem to do.

Colston Leigh writes that he has already booked $3,000

worth of 'business' for me; of course as I only get 35% of the total takings (since his share and Curtis Brown's 10% have to be deducted) this isn't as much as it sounds – only just over £200, though I suppose there will be further bookings. Have you any idea what people reckon normally to make on these tours? So far opening date is Oct. 11th. What with films, lectures and correspondence, I sometimes feel like praying as in *Tawny Island*, 'Oh God, give me back that enchanted obscurity . . .' but I suppose I shouldn't really like it now if he did!

Always, V.S.V.D.L.

In September, Vera and Gordon sailed to the United States, leaving Winifred in charge of their children.

VERA TO WINIFRED

Fairfield, Connecticut | *24 September 1934*

Darling,

The night before the boat got in I stayed up till 3 a.m., chiefly due to G.'s desire to dance, and the wish of Lord Latham and the producer of the *Man of Aran* (separately) to talk to me; we then got up at 6.30, had breakfast early and docked about 10.00. I didn't get interviewed by a reporter, as to do that I should have had to remain in my cabin in order to be found, and I felt I should probably get all the publicity I wanted, and would much rather watch the boat go up the Hudson and see the marvellous outline of New York appearing through the morning mist. However various people (strangers) who read *Testament of Youth* on the voyage over came up to me and said things about it.

The Bretts were on the dock. We had the usual hunt for luggage and customs officers – worse than usual, indeed,

owing to the packed boat. The docks were *sweltering* – it was
somewhere in the 80s all the time last Friday, Saturday and
Sunday, and I was there for about 2 hours in my best travelling
clothes before everything was collected. Then began a day
from which I am only now beginning to recover. I am writing
this from the Bretts' country house in Fairfield, Connecticut,
where they have most wisely and kindly taken me for a week's
complete peace before the racket begins with their reception for
me, Macdonell and Sean O'Casey on Friday. (S. O.'C.'s *Within
the Gates* is just about to be produced in N.Y.)

Well, after lunch (then about 3.30) I signed my letters,
telephoned to my cousin Dr Chard, and then was dashed up
(in so far as one can dash at all in Fifth Avenue) by Major Brett
in his car with the Macmillan sales manager to see Colston
Leigh. We then – on the 37th floor of the building, which
still appeared to me to be going up and down like a rough
sea – discussed my tour for two hours. At first it all sounded so
appalling that I concluded that the real point was not *whether*
I should break down, but simply *when*. Later, however, when
I went through it quietly with George Brett, it seemed – and
seems – quite manageable, and nothing like as bad as yours in
S. Africa.

My itinerary – of which I am having copies made, and will
send you one – so far includes 34 lectures at 25 towns; Leigh
proposes to put in 6 more lectures which will make an average
of 4 a week and 3 days' rest (tho' these include some travelling).
He is billeting me almost entirely at hotels, as this does enable
one to have breakfast in bed, go for walks, and get to bed early,
which is *never* possible with hostesses.

Today the Bretts both went to N.Y., leaving me here in
complete peace, having nobly got me out of a luncheon and a
dinner to which I was invited in the neighbourhood. Hence I
have got all my letters done; this is the tenth and last. I am, as I

said I would, using my letters to you as a diary, as I can't sit down
to write a diary at length nowadays, it's too deadly impersonal.
At last, for the first time since I went on the boat, I have got my
suitcases unpacked and my papers and small clothes straightened
out, and am beginning to feel less dazed. I got two walks today
as well as all the letters; this country is gorgeous, rather like
Gloucestershire but much warmer, damper and more luscious.

My poems were published here a fortnight ago and have
gone into a second edition today. *T of Y.* is about in its 35th
thousand. I just can't get over all this being the result of it.

I told George Brett about *Truth is Not Sober* going into 3
editions in England in spite of Collins' pessimism, and about the
interest taken in it by the B.B.C. They are probably publishing it
here the end of this month, but this is not quite settled.

I do wonder how you all are; this terrifically alien, rushed life
makes you all seem so far away, and I feel desperately homesick
every time I think what a vast amount of work lies between today
and the time when I see you and my darling babes again! I wonder
how poor Father is. I've got a terrific job in front of me but think
I can get through it if only all goes well at home. If I can survive
last week-end on top of the voyage, I should be able to manage
trains and lectures. Do take care of yourself, my sweetieheart; you
look after everybody and no one really looks after you.

All dear love, my sweetieheart, V.S.V.D.L.

VERA TO WINIFRED

60 Fifth Avenue, New York | 29 September 1934

Your lovely long letter of Sept. 17th came just before the party;
I burst it open but never got down to reading it till 1.30 a.m.
that night.

   This life would be quite incredible if one weren't living it and
knew it to be true. I thought I knew New York; I do know what it
is like to be a celebrity in London – but being a celebrity in New
York is like nothing else on earth. I *never* have time allowed me
for such minor details as getting dressed, or packing, or unpacking,
or reading my letters (even business ones have to be gone through
at express-train rate), or for changing into the elaborate toilet
expected of one at the smart hotels or restaurants to which I am
invited. When I first arrived a maid partly unpacked for me; the
rest of my trunks are still half packed. I don't know where she has
put all the things she has unpacked and have never had time to
look; I don't clearly know what I have got in Connecticut and what
in New York. When I do have to change into smart clothes (always
in 3 minutes or less) I hopefully seize the nearest gloves, stockings,
bag that I can find – and never yet, I think, have worn all together
the etceteras so carefully chosen to go with each get-up!

   Party began at 4.00 and lasted till 8.00; one or two newspaper
men got rather tight. I was supposed the share the rôle of guest
of honour with Sean O'Casey (a darling) and A. G. Macdonell,
but O'Casey had to leave for a rehearsal at 5.30 and Macdonell's
boat was late and didn't dock till 5.00 so he didn't get here till
6.00; hence I bore the brunt of the whole thing. Fashionable
New York, literary, social, academic, streamed in; for four
hours I shook hands with 250 people, made polite responses to
flattery, was photographed, stood most of the time, coped with
people who wanted me to do things.

At the end of the party about 16 people were left; we put on
the smartest hats we had and were all taken off to dine at a very
gay mid-town restaurant with shrieking decorations – quite new,
only opened this spring. I never learnt its name but standard and
expensiveness were that of the Savoy. I couldn't eat much of the
marvellous dinner after snacks all afternoon, but I danced quite
a lot (George Brett, whom I find more attractive than is entirely
convenient, dances divinely), and all the time felt astonished that
I wasn't more tired. George says that the first time he danced with
Phyllis she trembled like a jellyfish and held him at arm's length –
so I said: 'Well, I can't dance, but I won't hold you at arm's
length' – which was perhaps a provocative request for about the
closest dance compatible with decency; anyhow I got it! He gave
me a gorgeous spray of mauve orchid to wear at the party, which
queerly enough looked lovely with the flame chiffon. We got
home about 1.30 a.m. and I read your lovely letter about my darling
babes and could see you all as I read. *Do* write more like that.

Dear love, your letters and cables save my life. God knows
when I shall get letters written to anyone but you and Mother –
especially as G. writes almost every post wanting consolation
because he hates Ithaca!

Always V.S.V.D.L.

WINIFRED TO VERA

19 Glebe Place, London SW3 | *6 October 1934*

Odette came to lunch today and stayed till after tea, reading
to me the unfinished chapters of her essay on Wells, her voice
detached and steady, the tears pouring down her cheeks. It is
a brilliant piece of work, incisive, penetrating, profound. It has

cost her nearly a nervous breakdown to write it; but I think it is worth while.

She says she is going to America to finish her maternity training almost at once. I think she may be in New York before you return. She is a superbly courageous, indefatigable, tormented seeker after salvation.

My *Women* book came out yesterday. The *Daily Sketch*, of all papers, gave me a full column on the day of publication, very complimentary – nothing much else.

Monday Oct. 8th 7.45 p.m.

I went and saw your father this evening. He had been to the dentist, was rather tired and complaining of pain; but quite interested in between about things – chiefly my new clothes. I had been at Foyles Lunch and went straight round in my new navy things. They really are quite pretty.

Your mother, Aunt Florence and Ruby Williams came to the lunch and all had good places just under the top table. Sir Josiah Stamp was ill, and James Agate took his place. He stared at me hard (he sat next but one to me), and after the affair when I was signing books, went off and spoke to the *Sunday Times* man who afterwards approached me and said that Agate had specially requested – would I take the chair when he speaks at the *Sunday Times* book exhibition? Well – of course I said I would, especially as your friend Eric Gillett seemed to think that you and I would henceforward cut Agate for life! I'll have fun with him though, somehow, especially as in his speech he confessed that between that lunch and a dinner he had to go off and review *seven* still unread books for the *Daily Express*. He's a fat bald man with bad teeth. *I'll* have him somehow.

I do hope you are happy and well, my dear, dear little love, v.s.v.d.l. W.

VERA TO WINIFRED

Hotel Windsor, Wheeling, West
Virginia | 6 October 1934

At last I have time to write you something better than a
postcard. Where was I when I left off? Just going back to
Fairfield from New York, I think, a week ago.

It was a very pleasant weekend, which I spent (except for the
usual teas, cocktail parties, etc., given by people in the district)
chiefly in the company of George and A. G. Macdonell, and
sometimes of George alone, as Bruce (the younger boy) was down
with a slight attack of grippe and Isabel Brett was largely taken up
with him. (One of the things you notice the moment you enter
this country is how many men of your own age there seem to be
compared with England. I suppose other English generations have
been like America in this respect. She lost so few.)

Macdonell and George and I walked through lanes and
woods and swamps (owing to the fact that there had been a
terrific rain-storm during the night). They wore shirts and
flannel trousers (George sometimes discarding even the shirt)
and I a short-sleeved blouse and white linen shorts. Whenever
we came to a swamp, George picked me up and carried me.
Macdonell remarked laconically: 'I believe he takes you where
there *are* swamps, so that he can carry you over them.' I could
easily be a little in love with George Brett if I liked, but it
probably wouldn't be a good idea as the author–publisher
relationship is complicated enough without that. Also, it
is so difficult to know whether one attracts as well as being
attracted. After a fortnight in his company I still don't know
whether George's habit of holding my hand and taking my arm
at frequent intervals is due to reciprocal attraction or merely to
American *joie de vivre*. I keep telling myself that he probably did

exactly the same to Phyllis – who does seem, my goodness, to have been a *devoir* to the Bretts. After the first few days in New York so many people telephoned to Isabel Brett saying: 'What's the matter with Miss Bentley? Why doesn't she dress properly?' that Isabel was obliged to take her round the shops and help her to buy a completely new outfit.

Wednesday's interviews were terrific; each of them took an hour, and it was worse than giving three lectures, because in a lecture you do know what you are going to say, and in an interview you have to make it up as you go along. Between the interviews George took me out to lunch and then to the top of the Empire State Building, the highest skyscraper of all.

On Thursday night I came here (a twelve-hour journey) by night train for my first lecture. In appearance the hotel is much what you might see at Hull or Stoke or Derby, but how different is the plumbing and the food!

The Club greatly admired my frock and hat (the ones I wore at Foyles), and the two superb mauve orchids which George gave me just before he saw me off at New York, but the lecture was very tepidly received, reminding me of the audience at Bolton. It was the one on 'Why I wrote *Testament of Youth*', which is always received with such acclamation in England, but the trouble was that apparently hardly anyone had read the book (this is not exactly a literary town). I *know* I gave the lecture if anything better than usual, and I did get a clap for the passage (which I read aloud) on seeing the American troops enter the War, but since *T. of Y.* is my only title to fame, I can't think why they chose either me or the subject, since I offered several others.

Colston Leigh, who appears to regard me as a little gold-mine, is pushing in ever so many extra lectures at colossal fees, and I can't be sure of my itinerary for more than a week ahead. He has done his best to persuade me to stop till January 1st and do

another four lectures at $200 each, but not for $10,000 would I
extend my tour or abandon the attempt to get home for John's
birthday. If I get through this tour all right I shall have all the
cash I want for the present, thank you, and after the few spring
lectures are over I go into cold storage, quite definitely, for a
least a year and probably two. I shall have had quite enough of
being a celebrity to last me for a very long time. A quiet life is
much pleasanter than anything else in the world, really, though I
suppose one needs to have been a celebrity at least once to find it
out, and that is why misguided people hanker foolishly after fame.

All dearest love to you and my babes, V.S.V.D.L

VERA TO WINIFRED

Wade Park Manor Hotel, Cleveland,
Ohio | 26 October 1934

I got in this evening to another great city of skyscrapers and
crowds and parallel streets after a lovely run along the edge of
Lake Erie from Toledo – but how alike the cities themselves
mostly are! After four annihilating though glorious days in the
Twin Cities, Minneapolis and St Paul, which face each other
across the Mississippi near its source in Minnesota, and 18
hours of travel via Chicago here, I arrived at this hotel to find
17 letters awaiting me, all requiring some sort of answer, and a
huge pile of books to be autographed from a local store! A note
from Storm Jameson says that my tour 'sounds just like hell
opened', and tonight it did seem rather like that, especially as
I had spent about 9 of the 18 hours in the train answering the
accumulation of letters I never got down to in St Paul! Hence

your letter is more scrawled than usual; I always leave it till last as it rests me to write it.

Monday I arrived in St Paul to enter upon 4 days of glorious, amazing, annihilating pandemonium. My hostess, Mrs Woodard Colby – a charming, young, frail-looking doctor's wife who writes poetry and is a great worker for peace and who reminded me a little somehow of Storm Jameson – was kept answering the telephone all day by organisations and schools, etc., wanting to get hold of me. The Twin Cities are strongly anti-war (the University of Minnesota is one of the only two in U.S.A. to abolish compulsory drill) and the enthusiasm with which I was received was beyond my wildest dreams.

Next day the Women's Club (the ordinary social town one) to which I had to speak on 'Autobiographies' had their auditorium, which holds 700, crowded to the ceiling. When I had finished the lecture, they asked me to read them the passages from my book about the German offensive and the Americans coming into the War, which I had read the previous evening. When I had finished them the tension was so great that half the audience seemed to be in tears and I was nearly crying myself; swarms of them came up and greeted me afterwards with wet eyes and seem almost speechless.

Yesterday morning I spoke to an audience of 5,000 (faculty, students and townspeople – it was thrown open to the public) at University Convocation in a huge auditorium as large as Queen's Hall. I talked on 'How War Affects Women' and my speech was broadcast all over the State of Minnesota (which is larger than England), a lovely state of lakes and forests, so different from the flat, dusty Middle West.

In fact I was treated more like a prophetess than a human being – and only wish I possessed that imperviousness to strain and fatigue which prophetesses traditionally appear to possess!

It is queer indeed the rôle that life seems to be forcing on me since *Testament of Youth*. Twenty years ago it would have seemed like a wild fantasy. I pictured myself then as writing, but never as the centre of cheering, exalted, wildly excited crowds.

All dearest love V.S.V.D.L.

WINIFRED TO VERA

*19 Glebe Place, London SW3 | 27
October 1934, 10.15 p.m.*

I am just going to bed, before I go must describe to you Shirley teaching John his exercises. In her little green knitted frock, very short, bare footed, she dances on the nursery floor, her fat, serious face ferociously concentrated. 'Now jump – Keep in the same place. Lightly. *Spring!*' she chants. She makes him lie on his back and 'bicycle'. If he does not stretch his legs to her satisfaction, she flings herself on the floor beside him and ferociously pulls his feet down, smacks his knees straight, and, without compunction, puts him right. Only when completely exhausted does she lie down on the ground beside him, collapsed with bubbling laughter, and pulls his face down to her rough kisses, rolling over and over with him as though they were young otters in a wood.

I have just been up to see them – John on his side, asleep with dignity as usual; Shirley a rolled tangle of silvery-gold hair and rose-flushed cheeks.

Whatever the effect on Shirley's already pedagogic disposition, the result of her attentions on John's legs is admirable!

The account of your tremendous journeys reminds me almost of St Paul – in journeyings oft, in perils oft, in dangers by land and water, in dangers among false brethren. But I hope that

your fragile body, like his, overcomes sweets, fatigue, banquets
and alternate fastings; for I am sure that your gospel, like his,
has power – even if it is delivered to Mid-West townships that
have never heard of anything. I am very glad that Latham was
there to strengthen your hand with Colston Leigh, who sounds
a born exploiter.

Lunch yesterday with Shaw and Stamp very enjoyable. Shaw
and I sat next each other and discussed Wells, Prayer and
autobiographies. Prayer the most illuminating. Also Poverty – a
relative affair. The real handicap being a *limited* rather than
a frugal life. Shaw could agree to Buxton being worse than a
Dublin slum. He loves O'Casey. Everyone does. He ended up
by trying to learn how to play the piano-accordion. Can you
imagine the *Time and Tide* staff gathered round cold relics of
a lunch in Lady Rhondda's office, while one of them, very fat
and blushing, solemnly played the 'Blue Danube' on a piano-
accordion, in order that Shaw might explore a new musical
instrument? Sir Josiah Stamp, a genial fellow with a bold and
rolling eye, kept quiet and let Shaw tell him that there was no
Money Problem. I wonder.

I must go to bed. Off to Blackshirt meeting in Albert
Hall tomorrow night 'Investigating' for Council of Civil
Liberties again.

Monday morning.

I went to the Blackshirt meeting. Albert Hall completely
surrounded by police. My taxi stopped in Exhibition Road –
had to produce ticket. Hall packed. Lime-lights, banners,
band, massed Blackshirt chorus. Such excellent technique of
showmanship. For what? For a tirade against the Jews as nasty
and uncivilized as any Hungarian could devise. Hilda Reid, two
rows from me, stirred to her gentle soul, hissed like a kettle.
No one even heard her, for the ringing bursts of applause. She,

I and another Conservative friend of hers marched out after
the meeting singing the 'Red Flag'. But so tuneless and word
imperfect were we that no one molested us. Gosh, gosh, gosh,
gosh, gosh! as Shirley would say.

Bless you, my dear, v.s.v.d.l. W.

VERA TO WINIFRED

Train, Toronto to Boston | *31 October 1934*

Well, Toronto was *terrific* – the most annihilating place yet,
even worse than Minneapolis; thrilling to the spirit but rather
devastating to that ass, the body. In 3½ days (I arrived early
Sunday morning by night train from Cleveland and am now
leaving, Wednesday afternoon) I was put into contact with
every organisation, group or individual which could possibly
help *Testament of Youth* (the consequence of having an
enthusiastic and efficient publisher on the spot).

It was all so exciting and exhausting that in a few minutes
at my hotel between engagements the second morning I
found that tears were pouring down my face – partly from
tiredness, partly from a feeling that I hadn't got the right sort
of impressive presence for all this publicity and could never
live up to it.

Amongst my engagements I forgot to mention 4 visits to
bookshops and the autographing of 100 copies of *T. of Y.* Before
my big lecture for the Metropolitan Memorial Church, I went to
a State dinner at Government House, and later the Governor of
Ontario (the Hon Dr Herbert A. Bruce, the first medical man
to occupy the position) took me down to the lecture and took
the chair for me. He is a perfect *darling*, with penetrating blue
eyes and curly white hair; during the War he was in France as

an operating surgeon with the Royal Army Medical Corps of
Canada, and, curiously enough, I distinctly remember seeing
him at Étaples, as the Canadian hospital, 26 General, which he
used to inspect, was next door to ours. His wife, much younger
than he and *very* charming, was an English V.A.D.; he met her
at Wimereux, though how he was ever allowed to see enough of
her to marry her is an unexplained mystery!

The auditorium was packed; every seat was sold, chairs
were placed in the passages, outside, I had a microphone, and
the church organisation to its great delight made a profit of
about $1,000.

Well, now I have to climb down and tell you that as the
result of all this I disgraced myself by nearly fainting at the
Empire Club President's dinner (quite a young man, post-war
Balliol and very good-looking); fortunately besides himself and
his wife there were only 3 guests to be inconvenienced by my
idiocy, so it wasn't very serious; thank God it didn't happen
at the Governor's dinner the previous evening before the big
lecture! It was most odd; as I was sitting at dinner (in a very
hot room, with the steam heat full on and a blazing fire, it must
have been about 100°) the room suddenly began to whirl round;
I kept up as long as I could, but when I knew that I should have
to be sick or fall down and probably both, I had to ask to go out,
and spent the rest of the evening till midnight in a deep sleep
on my hostess's bed instead of entertaining the guests asked to
meet me. Don't tell the family this. I don't take it as seriously
as I might because I know that though of course partly due to
fatigue, it was also the consequence of injudicious champagne!

Tried to find time to send my darlings some absurd little
ribbons and feathers from my various bouquets, but will try to
send from Boston instead.

All dearest love, V.S.V.D.L

WINIFRED TO VERA

Bainesse, Cottingham, East
Yorkshire | 4 November 1934

Dearest,

I spoke at an East Yorkshire League of Nations Rally at
Hessle yesterday. Hall well filled. Bishop in chair. Tonight I
preach in the parish church on the arms trade.

Harry met me in Hull yesterday and was waiting here for
me when I got back from the lecture. We sat talking over
the fire till he caught a late train back to Driffield. I wish I
could do anything to raise him from the lethargy of complete
hopelessness. I seem to beat with all my energy against a barrier
of despair. He is so sweet, so generous, so gentle, so anxious to
cause no trouble, and so impossible to help or comfort. It is like
loving the dead to love someone whom you can't touch or help.

We are so extremely entangled now in people's minds that
Lady Steel Maitland, my chairman at Thursday's meeting,
introduced me as 'Miss Vera Holtby!' to loud laughter
and applause.

v.s.v.d.l. Love W.

VERA TO WINIFRED

Train, New Haven to New York | 12 November 1934

I am just on my way back to New York from my 23rd lecture.

When the train did arrive in N.Y. and I got out into the cold
early morning, there was George on the platform to meet me!
We drove to the house and had breakfast alone together (Isabel
always has hers in bed!); either the unusually early hour or

seeing one another again after several weeks caused us to drop immediately into a very intimate conversation. Part of it was about Phyllis, who seems to fascinate him by her very alien and troublesome qualities. He is very worried about her next book – fears that she included in *Inheritance* the only real contact with life she has ever had; he finds her love scenes incredibly naïve and says – very rightly for a person who is himself more or less unliterary, though a publisher – that he doesn't see how a person can go on making books without having had the life experience from which to make them. 'It would do her a world of good to have someone sedooce her,' he said vigorously, and added in a ruminative tone: 'I guess she'd give rather a different impression if you saw her in the nude.' I suggested that he had the strongest possible economic motive for doing the job himself. He only smiled and said: 'I could've taken her that day she fell in the pond – she was all shaken to pieces!' then shook his head and added: 'No, Vera – it would take more than that . . .' At a later stage in the conversation he said he wasn't worried about my next book even though he knew that no one could twice write a *Testament of Youth*. 'You see, Vera, you've lived the life. You're not a maiden lady. I guess you'd need to go pretty far back to find the time when you were?'

I said vaguely that it seemed a long time ago, and didn't enlighten him about dates!

George drove me to Morristown and stayed for the lecture; unluckily I wasn't able (as I so often have been) to rise to the occasion and lecture well just when I wanted to; partly I was very tired, but chiefly the audience was of the small-town tepid type, and the hall a small place of the village hall variety, with a poor little platform. On the other hand I was my best self at the lecture for Mr Latham's organisation and he seemed quite entranced; this *would* happen, though in any case he is far the more capable of the two of understanding the point and

purpose of the lecture (the *T. of Y.* one) which was the same in
both cases!

Far more interesting have been the Armistice-tide
ceremonials. Gordon came up for the weekend, and on
Armistice Eve I was invited by the New York Women's Overseas
Service League to be their guest and bring him with me and
give them a message from England. It was at the Waldorf; I wore
my medals (George with considerable trouble found a place on
4th Avenue where English service medals could be bought)
and the flame-coloured taffeta which the Bretts like best of
all my evening clothes and insisted on my wearing. Even for
this small speech we had quite a struggle with Colston Leigh,
but George overcame him in the end. He wasn't a guest at the
dinner himself, but took me there already dressed in his Victory
Ball get-up – gold braid, navy full-dress, navy cloak lined with
pale blue, looking so handsome that my heart ached not only
with a kind of baffled longing and regret, but with a renewed
realisation of just *what* the peace movement is up against unless
it can somehow create its own pageantry.

When the time came for me to make my little speech
I was almost put off it by the sight of George and Isabel
hovering round the doorway listening to it, but afterwards he
congratulated me on it very warmly and said it struck exactly
the right note. Then he took me along to their box at the
Victory Ball and the show began – crowds of people in and out
of the box all the time and the usual constant round of drinks
which nobody in the N.Y. publishing circles seems able to live
without (chiefly 'high balls' – i.e. pure whisky poured over ice;
very intoxicating). Below in the huge ballroom followed the
trooping of the colours in which George took part – banners
and pennons of all kinds – Stars and Stripes, the American
Legion, Daughters of the American Revolution, War of
Independence, Napoleonic War, Civil War, Spanish American

War, etc. etc. It was all very colourful and magnificent, and a
series of National Anthems were sung while everyone stood
to attention. In my mind all the time two distinct points were
hammering:

1) This is what the peace movement is up against.
2) This has nothing *whatever* to do with modern war as it
   is waged today.

If only you could convince the peace movement of (1) and
the readers of jingo newspapers of (2) you would have got
somewhere; this, I feel, is something for us to concentrate on
here and now. Later dancing began and in spite of the tiresome
American cutting-in habit (men just come up and seize you at
will from the partner with whom you are dancing and he has
to give way), George and I achieved one long and divine dance
together; he is one of the few people with whom I can shut
my eyes and not even look where he is taking me. He never
drinks as much as his guests, and later when we were both
rather tired he came and sat with me in the front of the box
and as we looked down upon the dancers (many of whom were
now getting rather tight), talked soberly and seriously about
bayonet fighting – how wildly patriotic he was when America
went into the war, how eagerly he learnt bayonet fighting and
instructed other people, and then the mixture of disgust and
sheer insanity which seized him when he was face to face with
the real thing. He was overseas nearly two years and at the front
without a break from April 1918 to November 1918, which is
quite a good record for an American. He was never hit at all but
was gassed; a gas shell burst at the door of his dug-out and he
became immediately choked and unconscious; his life was saved
by his orderly dragging him into the open air just in time but
it affected his lungs for 3 years afterwards. All this was related

to me at the ball – also his theory that the best way to stop the
next war is to announce beforehand that you will conscript
everyone, both men and women, up to the age of 90.

We got back at 4 a.m. and stayed in bed on Sunday morning,
and in the afternoon saw the marching of troops in Fifth
Avenue, and the parading of colours and finally an Armistice
Day Service in St Thomas's Church (the largest Protestant
church in New York, the cathedral being Catholic). George
was parading again, this time in the same khaki uniform that
he wore in the War. In the gallery of St Thomas's Church I sat
just above him, and with his black hair and slim figure among
the greying heads and developing paunches he looked not a day
more than 28 though he is actually 41 on Dec. 9th; I didn't see
anyone else whose uniform still fitted them! Many had to leave
buttons undone, which I am sure wouldn't happen at home;
American men seem to get stout earlier than English – due,
I suppose, to so much car-riding. Again as I saw the flags and
pennons looking so gorgeous and brilliant against the austere
grey walls of the church I felt sick at heart, but the service was
a surprise; it began with 'O Valiant Hearts', but after that the
prayers, collects and address by Governor Whitman (the wartime Governor of New York State) laid a most emphatic stress
on peace; the ex-Governor even alluded to the demonstration
of colours, the navy and white and scarlet of the Stars and
Stripes – as a gesture on behalf of the dead who died in the
belief that they were ending war.

Gordon went back on the night train last night; I came back
from my Newark lecture to find a silent house (except for the
very nice maid who brought me some Ovaltine and biscuits).
It was a cold windy night, and I slept uncomfortably, dreaming
about George Brett. But it wasn't altogether a waste, however
futile, for I woke with the sudden knowledge that what I want
for my novel, to make it absolutely different from *T. of Y.*, is for

Ruth Alleyndene's gallant young war-time lover, whose mistress
she is at Hardelot and who is killed in the last advance, to be
an American with whom she will have several conversations
about what modern America wants and where it hopes to go.
This will not only give the book an added pull over here, but
will prevent the young man becoming Roland all over again –
which he inevitably would do unless I deliberately modelled him
on a quite different type. So I'm going to model him upon the
twenty-three-year-old George Brett whose portrait in uniform
stands on the mantelpiece of the living room in Fifth Avenue;
this way I shall be able to utilise instead of having to fight
against the overwhelming impulse to think about him all the
time when I am not working. The trouble with me is that I fall
in love much too easily and always have! I ought to be getting
over it at my age but I don't seem to be. Why it had to happen in
this particular way I can't imagine – except as part of the normal
heavy cost of life. Nothing could be more absurd and hopeless,
for even if we weren't both married, George as my publisher is
morally bound to maintain a 'correct' attitude which he couldn't
possibly modify except as the consequence of an indication so
clear that no self-respecting woman could give it! This of course
is exactly your own situation with Harry. He can't make a move
unless you do, and you can't unless you are convinced he wants
you to; it's a real vicious circle in both cases.

Well, thank God for books. In *Mandoa* you gained, I suppose,
some measure of peace from your description of Bill's fate
and psychology. In *Testament of Youth* I sought – and to some
measure have found through its influence on other people – a
kind of peace and reconciliation with the War. But three things
in my life remain unreconciled – the failure of my friendship
with Phyllis; what Colonel Hudson told me about Edward's
last week in Italy (involving such fundamental doubts and
speculations which can never more be answered); and now this

involvement, unexpected and mainly (though not entirely) physical attraction to an American with whom I can never even correspond except about business. How I can reconcile two of them by drawing a portrait of George 20 years ago (not so difficult, this, as psychologically he is still 25, which probably partly accounts for his attraction to someone who has always been attracted by men slightly younger, even though in actual fact he is slightly older) and of Phyllis twenty years hence, and then killing them both off, only another writer could know; but you will understand. I'm getting sick of this lecture tour, for I long now for a little peace and quiet in which to think out the whole situation.

November 15, 1934

Yesterday I had one of the worst headaches I ever had in my life. It was due, I know, not just to lecturing and travelling, but to the queer strain of two serial conversations with George about my next book. He says that so much depends on it – that I've had a wonderful rush to fame with *T. of Y.* (as no one realises better than myself, nor how much of it is due to his business ability, and his decision to stake the reputation and money of his firm so much upon it) and should have a marvellous career before me in this country if only the next book can be carried on in the same spirit. 'I can't produce a work of literary genius to order,' I told him, and he said earnestly: 'Forget all that. Forget what I've said about the business and the reactions of the booksellers. The genius of authorship that marks *Testament of Youth* is in you; it's part of you and it became part of the book because you lived it so intensely while you wrote it. What matters now is that you should live this next book in the same way – really care about it while you're writing it.'

We talked on in this way till nearly 1 a.m.; I had another

bad night going over what he'd said and wondering how on earth to get in the American scene and background into my portrait of the young American lover of Ruth Alleyndene. Yesterday morning when he was going over the final part of my itinerary with me I suddenly decided to take a chance of getting material from the most direct and best possible source, and said: 'George, I've got to have the portrait of a young American in my book, and I don't know many Americans at all intimately. What would you feel if you found a portrait of yourself in my book? How would you like to be reincarnated as the young American lover of my heroine, during the War, and to die in the last advance?'

He looked at me in such a queer way – almost as if he were too overwhelmed to speak – half smiling and half as if he had had a direct blow in some vital spot, and then burst out: 'Do whatever you darn well like with me, Vera. I don't give a damn so long as the book is the book *you* want to write; that's the way it will be great.'

So I said: 'Very well, as there's nothing like making my publisher write my book for me, will you answer me these questions?' and I gave him a list I had roughly prepared on a train journey about what Americans did in the War, where they fought in the last advance, where they were killed and were buried, and what young Americans hoped for their country just when he left college twenty years ago. He forgot all the morning's business, got suddenly thrilled and exclaimed: 'Look here, Vera why don't you use my experience in the 77th Division and my own fighting in the Argonne?' and proceeded to rush up and down the house and the office pulling out photographs, war maps, souvenirs, etc. (all the things I rather guess that Isabel Brett, who told me herself that she refused to live with him for about two years after he came back from France because he was so 'queer' and she didn't want to be

married to a maniac, has probably never cared to see – what
comforts the spoiled young American wives must have been
to their returning soldier husbands!). Then after about half-an-
hour's excited conversation we were both reluctantly recalled
by the usual sense of obligations, engagements, work, etc., and
George said: 'Look here, I'll get all my official war histories and
maps and things together for you, and we'll have a 3-hours talk
about all this when you come back from Kansas City on Dec.
9th and the work connected with this damned tour of yours is
nearly all done.'

So it stands arranged. As I say, there's nothing like making
your publisher write your book for you and draw his own
portrait. But the situation in itself is material for a short story!
Of course I shall give myself away completely, because when
I write of what Ruth feels for Eugene I shall be telling George
Brett what I feel about him – but I don't care, because I more
than half suspect that by his excited readiness to cooperate in
the idea, he is telling me what he feels about myself.

Poor Harry! Yes, I suppose it is really sadder to be in love
with someone essentially dead, than with someone inaccessible
but very much alive! And my experience has to be temporary,
whereas yours is too, too permanent.

Au revoir, sweetieheart V.S.V.D.L.

WINIFRED TO VERA

19 Glebe Place, London SW3 | 14
November 1934, 9.45 a.m.

Darling,

Your letters from Toronto and Cambridge were fascinating
and horrifying. I am far from surprised that you had a collapse

at Toronto. As usual you did things neatly so that they
inconvenienced as few people as possible! I do hope that the
time before you is not quite so strenuous, but obviously your
own success creates its own problems. The better you do in
one place, the more people want you to do in the next. The
Toronto episode reads more like the Prince of Wales having
allied himself with the Salvation Army than anything else! The
mixture of enthusiasm and prestige, hustle and discomfort, with
moments of what must be very real enjoyment and satisfaction.

Your ribbons and feather have come and delight the children.
Shirley spent this morning before school learning – with
passionate impatience – how to fold up ribbons. Her desire for
efficiency is something really admirable and is exceeded only by
her persistence.

Don't worry about me and my work. It certainly is not the
household which has prevented it. I never knew (touch wood)
how little trouble they could be. The children are so good and
Amy and Charlie so helpful. My only bother is my sense of
the importance of getting Ballinger settled, the Peace Ballot
supported, and all the people who seem to want assistance of
some kind adequately disposed of.

I don't want to go away till Feb. or March, when I shall
go to Hornsea or Withernsea and finish 'South Riding'. The
News Chronicle wants me to do a 'five-day serial'. I may if I can
think of one.

E. M. Delafield asked after you on Monday. She was at
the *Times* Book Exhibition and Lord Camrose's luncheon. A
gorgeous lunch – champagne, brandy, etc., etc. James Agate was
there and came up to me, bubbling all over with champagne
and enthusiasm for my Foyles speech, and I didn't recognise
him!! A little fat bald man. Well, well. I am taking the chair
for him today and have fortified myself by re-reading his review
of *T. of Y.* And if I can pray to the God of Pussycats, I shall

just let the claws out from under the fur. But my trouble is that when I want to be catty I so rarely succeed – or if I succeed I overbalance everything, as in the famous Somerville Debate Speech (which I shall regret till I die, and which has cramped my malicious style ever since – to my great sorrow).

Later.

   I *was* catty – referred to 'by bluestockings for bluestockings' – but he disarmed me a little by having bad neuralgia and being obviously under the weather. I never can retain a good hate.
   Au revoir, my very dear v.s.v.d.l. W

VERA TO WINIFRED

Richmond, Virginia | *18 November 1934*

My last lecture in New York was really my first in N.Y. proper, as it was at Columbia University. You'll be amused to hear that two days before it I was rung up and invited to dinner beforehand by Dr Philip Stimson who was the doctor who attended G. when he had measles in 1926, and was so kind and reassuring to me; he is now on the staff at Columbia, had read and admired *Testament of Youth*, and had only just been told by our mutual friends the Bruce Blivens that the author of the book and the 'charming little wife' (as he phrased it) of the young Cornell man who got measles were one and the same person.
   I went down on Friday evening to North Carolina; it was a little tiring there at the Women's College as I didn't get much sleep on the train, and I was enthusiastically entertained by students and faculty from 11.30 with scarcely a break till my evening lectures ended, with 20 minutes of questions, at 10 p.m.

But they were charming people, and the country with its
rust-red earth (more scarlet and less pink than Devon), its pine-
forests and vivid red-brown autumn trees against the evergreen,
is perfectly lovely; and it was so warm this morning that I was
able to have my breakfast out of doors without a coat on a
sunlit verandah.

All dear love to you and my sweet babies V.S.V.D.L.

WINIFRED TO VERA

19 Glebe Place, London SW3 | *23 November 1934*

Darling Vera,

I think I do understand about George. What I don't know
is whether it is better in such circumstances to keep apart and
do nothing about it, or to have your weekend and get it out
of the system. Only sometimes that means getting it *into* the
system. Physical fascination can be so powerfully increased by a
really adequate lover. I don't know. I have no advice to give and
no wisdom to share. But of course it is queerly stimulating to
fascinate and be fascinated.

Apropos – James Anderson is not going to marry Ivy
Cayley. And we spent yesterday afternoon walking round
Battersea Park in the fog and sitting over tea in the twilight
here. I don't find him quarter so physically attractive as Harry.
No one I have met yet is so, to me. But I find his personality
extremely moving. I feel sorry for him and interested in him,
flattered by his interest in me (though he finds aspects of
me forbidding, he obviously likes others) – and altogether
concerned with him. He is so much a person, so powerful and
yet so forlorn. He can't bear the thought of going alone to
China. He can't bear the thought of marrying someone who

is not Stella. He does not want to love and leave a mistress, and can't take a mistress to China . . . I often think that men have a much more difficult biological burden to bear than women. To be passionate yet fastidious, monogamous yet easily attracted, dignified and exclusive, yet lonely and affectionate . . . What remedy?

All very interesting, and very difficult.

Bless you, my dear, W.

WINIFRED TO VERA

19 Glebe Place, London SW3 | *26 November 1934*

Darling,

Well, well. I can see that the *affaire George* will turn out to be ultimately very useful. I can't help feeling a little glad about it. a) You will receive further insight into American male psychology. b) You always write better when you are emotionally excited, in actuality or in retrospect, by a situation, and the *affaire Phyllis* really did not seem adequate stimulation for a whole long novel. c) The thing itself, painful as it may be, must have its good moments. Pain and passion are inseparable, but to live completely without both over a long period when one is still comparatively young, is a little depressing.

No. The situation with Harry has none of those maidenly hesitations about it that you mention. We had a complete crisis at Withernsea – my doing. I decided that the time had come to abandon pride, convention and all the rest of it. I am glad I did. It's very different from a new relationship with a married man. Ah, well. Don't break your heart over it, my love. But so fine and attractive a young man – of George's generation too, and of his war experience and on Armistice Day – I'm glad. Vive l'amour et vive la bagatelle. Only don't take it too seriously and hurt yourself too much.

The asset to the book really sounds most opportune and might be the making of it.

I opened the Green, White and Gold Fair on Saturday, and was extremely touched by the extraordinary welcome given to my little woman book by all those old suffrage societies. Apparently they have decided to favour it. They had a stall filled with it, and I autographed copies for half an hour.

John has learned some new tunes at the piano and practises well. Mother is in love with Shirley. Edith vehemently favoured John. I think both are very sweet, and I love them dearly. Shirley flew into one of her real roaring tempers on Sunday and quite scared your mother, but it was really very funny. She had a little woollen rabbit with her. On the way to the bus – your mother was walking with us – Shirley said she had dropped it. It was past six and dark. Your mother went running back to the hotel for it, though I implored her not to, knowing my Shirley. Meanwhile I questioned Shirley and discovered that she had the rabbit, a tiny thing, hidden in her glove all the time. So, as your mother was out of breath and fussed, I said, Shirley, that is very naughty, *very*! To play a trick like that and make Granny go running about in the dark. Madame Shirley gave one roar and flung herself on the pavement. I picked her up and carried her towards the bus. She roared. She screamed. Your poor mother was quite alarmed. I went on carrying her, while she kicked – really aware of her wickedness and furious with herself, with life probably, with what she had hoped to be a really funny joke which had not come off. Then we came to a shop all decorated with the flags and whatnot that today are smothering London for the Royal Wedding. 'I should like one of those flags,' said the philosophical John. 'Auntie, will you get me a flag?' Shirley pulled herself short in the middle of a frenzied roar

to gasp: 'And me.' And thereupon completely forgot her fury
and beamed upon us. The ruling passion had ruled her lesser
passion. Darling silly stormy Shirley. I feel I know so exactly
what she feels like when her jokes go wrong.

Dear love, v.s.v.d.l. W.

VERA TO WINIFRED

*New Willard Hotel, Washington
DC | 28 November 1934*

Darling girl,

I am here in Washington, having arrived by the night train
from Pittsburgh. On Monday I lectured in Pittsburgh at Mellon;
then took the afternoon train to Cleveland (3½ hours), and
spoke there in the evening in a *mammoth* auditorium with
no microphone. It was packed with at least 2,000 people (it
was a McBride Foundation Lecture sponsored by the Western
Reserve University) and there wasn't a vacant seat anywhere.
After having had a morning lecture I was terrified that my
voice would go and I shouldn't make them hear; but I gathered
they all did, and there was tremendous enthusiasm. The effort
however nearly burst my head and I haven't felt quite normal
ever since.

I imagine all this will eventually get to George – which
does not displease me; but oh God! how tired I get, and what
an anguish it is to be so much in love with someone! I realise
now that my interest in most of the men whom I have known
since 1916 has been originally provoked by *their* interest in me.
It is difficult not to be moved by a man being in love with you;
but I had forgotten how different this is (and in Gordon's case
too it was that way round) from falling in love with someone

independently of whether he loves you or not. Because I was
in love with George Brett for weeks before I knew whether he
returned the feeling or not, the sudden mutual abandonment of
our defences is still all but unbearable in its results.

God knows what opportunity all this will give for seeing
anything of George. I could slaughter Colston Leigh (who is
even threatening to put in a lecture on Dec. 10th, when George
and I had planned to have a last evening of dancing together)
for working me like a machine in the way he has. Phyllis's light
schedule was a comedy, but my packed one is a tragedy.

I just hardly know how to bear being so much in love with
someone whom in years upon years I shall probably only see for
a few days at a time, though our business connection will, I now
hope and believe, endure to the end – for besides telling me what
he thinks of me as a woman, he has spoken of what he calls my
'genius of authorship', and he said the other day: 'Go on writing
about the War as much as you wish; you write of it so beautifully.'
This morning, feeling so tired when I arrived and knowing that
I shall probably have next to no chance of seeing or speaking to
him when I get back to New York, I sat down alone in my hotel
room and cried and cried – and had just got my eyes thoroughly
swollen and nose thoroughly red, when the Washington News
Service photographer (who has somehow discovered my presence
here in spite of the Macmillan secretaries and George himself
faithfully addressing my letters as 'Mrs Catlin' in the hope of
giving me a few days' peace here) rang up to know if they could
photograph me in a few minutes' time! I don't know whether I
cursed love or fame the most at that moment – but somehow I
got my nose powdered and my hair tidied, and went along to their
studio with an agreeable smile and rage in my heart.

I rather suspect George may be feeling *something* like as bad
as I am, for he continually finds excuses to write me business
letters which require replies.

How odd it is to work so hard for fame and to long for it –
and then get it and find it an intolerable nuisance because one
has fallen hopelessly in love!

This evening Gordon will arrive here – full of his plans
which, God forgive me, I don't want to hear about at all! I am
willing to pay for them but oh, I don't want to listen to them! In
another way, of course, I want to see him, because I'm so lonely,
and he does love me dearly in his own preoccupied way – which
will never permit him to perceive how tired or preoccupied I
am myself!

I rather think I am not, after all, going to tell him about
George for the present; not in the least because I want to
deceive him or think he wouldn't understand, but because I
don't want to complicate for him the business relationship with
Macmillan upon which his plans so largely depend. Thanks to
my intervention with George and Mr Latham (but don't tell
Gordon this, as he thinks it's entirely due to the merits of his
work), I have persuaded the Macmillan Company to publish
his next two books and give him quite a decent advance. He
is delighted about this, but I'm afraid that if he knew about
George his delight would be spoiled by embarrassment and he
might feel he didn't want to publish with Macmillan any more;
he might even think that I was paying for his opportunities by
offering myself physically to George – though the arrangement
I did make with George was something of quite a different and
purely business nature. And what happened between us that
last night in New York was far too spontaneous, God knows, for
any thought of Gordon or his work to come within a mile of us!
What a mix-up it all is, isn't it!

I am torn between the reluctance to make any more demands
on you, and the feeling that never before have I needed you
so badly! The only immediate compensation, I think, will be
my novel, which will offer not only a vehicle for describing

vicariously this absurd and forlornly hopeless passionate
obsession, but also something I can do for George in which he
will be at least as interested as I am.

This is my 12th letter today. I'm going to stop now and walk
frantically round Washington's Memorial!

All dearest love, V.S.V.D.L.

VERA TO WINIFRED

Train, The Milwaukee Road, *Chicago
to Winona* | *2 December 1934*

Darling sweet,

I am inspired to write yet another letter because there is a
comfortable little writing table on this beautiful air-conditioned
train, where I have a seat in the observation car – enormous
windows at back and sides from which one sees the flat fields
of Illinois spread all round one like a map. It is one of the most
famous American railroads and I look forward to going through
the State of Wisconsin – all lakes and forests, one of the
loveliest in the Union – by day; each time I passed it before, on
my way to and from St Paul, was at night. By the time I arrive
at Winona this evening I shall have been 1,000 miles from
south to north within 48 hours.

I wonder how many miles I have travelled altogether; one
day I must work it out on the map. I have been altogether in
17 States – New York, New Jersey, Connecticut, Massachusetts,
Pennsylvania, Virginia, West Virginia, North Carolina,
Kentucky, Ohio, Indiana, Illinois, Missouri, Iowa, Michigan,
Wisconsin, Minnesota – so I know a little more about America
than I did in 1927!

Before going to my train I dashed out for a 20 minutes' walk

along the shores of Lake Michigan. Chicago was rapturous with
sun and frost and the lake was radiantly blue, with little waves
lapping the sides of the promenade. It must surely be one of the
loveliest cities in the world.

I thought as I walked of this lecture tour and what had been
its chief characteristic – and came to the conclusion that,
owing to the number of lectures and the amount of travelling,
never at any point had there been enough *time* for anything.
No time really to see places properly or to meet the people
I wanted to meet; no time, even, for love to reach its logical
conclusion. (Will the exasperating irony of the bedroom on the
New Orleans train remain with me all my life, I wonder – to be
unexpectedly alone together, and then to have *no time!*)

And now it's all nearly over. In a week I shall have all but
finished travelling from north to south and east to west; in a
fortnight I shall be on the Atlantic; in three weeks taking the
children to tea with Mother, as though all this had never been.
And hardly any of it has been recorded; my letters to you are
the only record, and they don't contain half of all I wanted
to remember.

It will come back to me afterwards, I think, chiefly as a
series of pictures – the skyline of New York as the *Berengaria*
sailed up the Hudson; warm summer evenings on the verandah
in Connecticut with George and myself sitting opposite each
other at a little table 'talking business', as Isabel put it; in other
words, as I realise now, holding endless serial discussions over
my schedule in order to be together. A warm dark evening on
a boat, with the lights of Long Island Sound trembling in the
distance; and when we got back the crickets in the Fairfield
garden shrilly chirruping: 'Katy did, Katy did, Katy *didn't!*'
Another warm summer evening, with the rain coming down
as heavily as in Somerset Maugham's play; Archie Macdonell
taking Isabel off to dance at the country club, while George and

I were left behind because he was recovering from an attack of grippe and I felt too tired to dance. The two of us, standing, later that evening, alone in the house at my bedroom door, with the rain teeming down outside – looking intently and rather mournfully at each other and then with the utmost correct propriety shaking hands and saying Goodnight! The train at Pennsylvania Station, leaving for West Virginia – George and Isabel seeing me off and George giving me a curly purple orchid to wear as I left.

Two people in a dark upper room with the moonlight shining brilliantly through the window and queer black shadows across the floor – two people clasped forlornly and desperately in each other's arms, away for only a brief quarter-hour from publicity and gossip and suspicion.

Maybe I shall have time to write of them; maybe I shall only be able to tell you when I get home. But it has been all worthwhile, I think – in spite of this underlying pain and sadness of regret which will take, I think, a long time to disappear. Indeed if I go on writing, and the Macmillan Company goes on publishing for me, perhaps it will never go, but will be constantly revived and constantly unfulfilled. 'Out of this nettle, danger, we pluck this flower, safety' – the strange, poignant safety of a spirit that has known love and farewell and grief and beauty and fame and excitement and adventure. Above all adventure, which one must be prepared for, bring what it may, if the questing, experimenting, creating spirit is not to die.

All dear love, my sweetieheart, V.S.V.D.L.

WINIFRED TO VERA

19 Glebe Place, London SW3 | 3 December 1934

My dear Love,

This is, I suppose, the last letter I shall write before I see you again. It seems so odd. The time has flown. It hardly sems a week since I stuffed with tissue paper the loops on your flame-coloured taffeta.

I hope you find us all well – as we are at present. Fräulein, who returned very wan and with a fearful cold (How colds follow funerals!), seems to be recovering. Shirley, who caught her cold in spite of many precautions, has already recovered. John is practising the piano with deliberate, though distasteful, concentration. I do admire that boy's persistence. He also does his exercises with commendable regularity. Routine is in his blood. Oh, they *are* darlings.

I hope you don't come back to a whirl of worries. Your mother is house-hunting again, but the doctor, whom I saw today, does not favour any immediate decision. Your father is distinctly improved physically. They even went to a cinema last week to see the pictures of the Royal Wedding, but he still has his nerve pains and gets fed up with everything.

I shall have to go home for Christmas; but I shan't stay many days, and shall be back before the New Year, and then *You Must Go Away*. You will probably be glad to be by yourself for a little, to sort your impressions and rest from the fatigue of so much travelling, working and emotion.

I hope you have a good and restful journey. I hope my flowers arrive in your cabin safely, to welcome you on board. I hope you will be pleased to be back, my very dear love.

In spite of everything, I expect it was all very well worth while, wasn't it? I should have been glad of it all – if it were I.

Odette asked me what you were going to do next. I told her in rough outline the plot of 'Honourable Estate'. She said: 'But that might be superb. That has a sweep – a range! That is a great theme.' You will know all the better now how to deal with the irony of so-called 'honourable' and 'dishonourable' estates. Perhaps before you had lived almost too rigidly. It may be a great book.

1935

WINIFRED TO VERA

Bainesse, Cottingham, East Yorkshire | *13 February 1935*

Dear love,

You will be at Leeds, and I hope not too bored and tired. I hated leaving you. I should like to be with you always. But I knew I did right to come here. Mother really has been ill. Angina. She hasn't been told and is much better and has no more pain, and is taking it all with her usual cheerful philosophy. She comes down on to a couch in the afternoon and goes out in a car. But, but, but. Of course, it is inevitable. Bodies are mortal and must wear out. But I don't want her to be an invalid. She has resigned from seven of her committees, and she will have to go quietly; but she can do a little work, and meant to retire in two years anyway. But a shadow falls across the day every time I think of what may be in store for her. We both know that pain too well. However, as I said, she is by no means an invalid yet.

I have taken rooms. I went to Hornsea this morning. The

rooms are kept by three sisters, the Misses Brooks. Theirs is an ugly little house, but the estate agent and the shop at which I called both told me that people who went there always liked it. As soon as I saw the woman at the door, I felt I could live with her. She seemed to know what I wanted at once, and I am to have the back sitting room and the bedroom above it. And I have already ordered a fire in your room on the 22nd. I long for you to come. I wish you could stay all the time. Never for a moment think I don't want you. I should like always to be with you. Only I must sometimes come away from London. I feel better already for that walk along the sands.

Bless you my heart. And I do think that your novel can be a great book.

Till the 22nd and with all my love. v.s.v.d.l. W.

VERA TO WINIFRED

19 Glebe Place, London SW3 | *13 February 1935*

I got back this afternoon and read your sad little note. Alas! for human mortality! I do at least hope that your mother will be able to keep some of her work going for the rest of her days; I don't somehow feel that she would ever allow herself to be a complete invalid. Of course you must be near her and the others – though I wish for your own sake that your relatives weren't all of an age to be (quite apart from your own health) a burden to you just when *you* are at the age in which work and responsibilities are heaviest.

Please give my dearest love to your mother and say how sorry I am that she has not been well. I wonder whether the incessant conflict between the urge to work and the limitations of one's capacity for doing it ceases at all when one gets old. I mean does the urge and necessity get less?

WINIFRED TO VERA

*Bainesse, Cottingham, East
Yorkshire* | *17 February 1935*

Dearest,

I read your letter when I returned from Harrogate yesterday evening, and have been thinking what I can do to make things easier for you. I don't like those headaches. I'm not surprised you have them, but I do wish you could shake off some of your mixed burden of responsibilities. I have come to a few conclusions.

1) I am writing to Gordon, urging him to leave you alone, and suggesting other means of getting on, i.e. when I am away he can have my whole share of Miss Moore except for her forwarding of my letters and about an hour a week or less that she does for the Friends of Africa Committee which runs Ballinger. I am going to advertise for a shorthand typist in Hornsea who can come sometimes and help me with letters and type the articles I should have sent to Miss Moore. It will really be much more convenient. For instance, this is my seventeenth letter this morning, only answering those which came since I went to Manchester on Friday. If he feels he is having more of Miss Moore, it may help him psychologically. He must not worry you.

2) If you like Hornsea and feel you could work there, why not come up in March for 3 weeks or so and bring your work. While Gordon is in London and when you have no lectures, surely you could work here. We could turn that upstairs south bedroom into a workroom for you,

with a fire and table in the window. I am sure I shall
find a typist who could come in and do your letters
for you so that you would not have the awful feeling
of their accumulation. It is very cheap – 30/ a week
for the rooms and service, and just our food, whatever
we order, on top of that. It would do you good. The
London Library can send books to me (for you) there,
and there is a first-rate reference library in Hull, to
which I am going tomorrow for old papers. You could
work and walk all day. The sands are splendid for
walking on.

Don't you think you could? Gordon must take his
share of the children, and the household can get on
all right. When you are not there to be grumbled to, it
doesn't grumble!

But one piece of real luck. I had a letter from Obermer
in which he says that my last kidney test actually shows
improvement. Originally he said that he could keep my kidneys
from losing any more power of action, but he did not see how
he could get the scarred tissue to work again. But if they are
working better, something must be happening. I felt myself that
I couldn't possibly be feeling so much better if I actually was not
better. So now perhaps in a year or two I really may be almost
normal. I stood the really quite strenuous two days on Friday
and Saturday very well, in spite of an entirely sleepless night
on Friday. I was tired, but no real headache – and that was
unthinkable a year ago.

I have two more letters and a *Schoolmistress* article to do, so
must stop.

But *do* consider Hornsea.

v.s.v.d.l. W.

George really is clever and quite conclusive, I should say, about
his feelings. He seems to make every possible business excuse
to see you alone. Oh, June should be All Right, my dear my
very dear.

VERA TO WINIFRED

19 Glebe Place, London SW3 | 18 February 1935

How *ghastly* of me to have made you write a 17th letter
yesterday! But I'm glad, at least, that it provoked a reply
telling me the good news from Obermer. It sounds queer and
unbelievable that you could actually have *improved* in spite
of all the work you do – almost perhaps as though you were
still young enough for part of the lost tissue to be reendowed
with life. You are such a pathological eccentricity anyway, that
almost anything seems possible. This is quite the best news that
I have had for ages.

   I don't, deliberately, worry you about your health more than I
can help or discuss it with you, because I know that this would
only irritate you and would do no good; but I think about it
constantly. Not only on your account, but for the most selfish
possible reasons! The mainsprings of life for me – i.e. the things
that make it really worth having – have always, I believe, been
people rather than things; I seem to be typically feminine in
this way. (Or is it that getting the things is in my own power,
more or less, whereas helping the people is not? – that one can
to some extent control one's self, but fate is a Juggernaut beyond
one's power.)

   For the past ten years – ever since I married – I have believed
that if I could once be famous I should be happy for the rest
of my life, and want nothing more (in a sense I think I have

always suffered from this illusion, except during the brief period when I was in love with Roland and he was alive). Well, I became famous; and George taught me in a fortnight that what I had believed about fame by itself conferring happiness simply wasn't true. I don't ache for his presence any less because I draw record audiences at Leeds and Bradford!

And the same is true of you. I don't believe even my work would give me much pleasure now if I hadn't you to share its success or failure with. But the real point is what you can do with your *own* work if you only have time. You *must* have time – and if only you take reasonable care of yourself, there seems to be, now, no reason why you shouldn't have. It's marvellous to be as you are after such a complete smash-up only 3 years ago.

All dearest love V.S.V.D.L.

WINIFRED TO VERA

Hornsea, East Yorkshire | *5 March 1935*

It certainly is not a good time to begin a novel. Yet I know that, both from your experience and mine, the only thing to do is to stick to one's work and plough doggedly ahead. You know from *Testament of Youth* how little your mental condition when you wrote affected the work. I know that the same is true of mine. This persistent effort is a terrific labour, but I know of no other way of getting through life.

I too am not getting on very well with my book. I had a very disturbing week-end which lasted till Tuesday noon. I returned to find a letter from Harry inviting himself down for the day on Thursday. I never asked him. I want and don't want him. I want to WORK. And I have to go off to my uncle again on Saturday. But in between I get on to some extent. I am really in

love with my people. I have a feeling that if only I can do what
I want to do, it might be good. But I know I shan't do half of
what I want to do, not through lack of opportunity, but through
lack of power.

And all the time the news in the paper is so disturbing that
I feel I ought not to be sitting here comfortably writing a novel.
I ought to be stumping the country against re-armament. I
think MacDonald's White Paper on Rearmament is one of
the most ignoble, injudicious and dangerous documents this
Government has published. I read it with a fury not diminished
by my memory of the Cecil–Amery debate which I listened into
last night on the wireless. Amery's assumption that the British
Government had done everything possible to promote peace,
that Cecil was (a) an unpractical dreamer, and (b) a fire-eater
who would keep Great Britain perpetually engaged in League
wars, made me so wild that when Cecil cut in quietly after one
of Amery's outbursts with 'Why so violent?' it was almost like a
reproof to my own fireside indignations.

Do come on the 16th.

Letters are so exasperating. I say little because I feel that all
I say may be beside the point when this letter actually arrives.
But I do love you. I wish I could help you. Whatever happens,
I love you and will stand by you. If you are going to have a
baby and need someone, I can easily put off Lybaria [sic]. I love
you dearly.

v.s.v.d.l W.

P.S. Sticking to *Mandoa* and to other work with me is not
courage. It may be a kind of superficiality. Pain, sadness and
regret *bore* me so that I would rather think of anything else. I
welcome work as something positive and real that one can get
a grip on. I have made far too much of a fool of myself over my
personal affairs to find much thought about them exhilarating.

A nice letter from Virginia Woolf asking if I would like to write an autobiography for the Hogarth Press. I take this to be an indirect compliment to *Testament of Youth*, which we know she loved.

VERA TO WINIFRED

19 Glebe Place, London SW3 | *6 March 1935*

For one who is supposed to be away working, you do seem to be having a mouldy time. I really think that visiting the sick is one of the most vitality-absorbing occupations that one can have. I do hope I never have a long illness and feel tempted to absorb the time of the active. Harry's visit will inevitably be disturbing, I suppose. I wish he would either be satisfactory or leave you alone. I agree with you too about the news. I feel I ought to be doing fierce propaganda instead of writing a novel.

My interest in 'Honourable Estate' has been revived by Mrs Catlin's diary which is fascinating and will provide, I think, more than enough material for Book I with the ideas for it I already have. At present I am still in her childhood (1889: she began keeping a diary at 13). She was obviously much beloved and spoiled. She was a clever child too as she constantly reports at the end of term that she was top in 9 subjects; she also (which I didn't know) continually went in for and passed exams, including the Senior Cambridge, and was working for Matric. when she met Gordon's father. The later diaries are full of passion, turbulence and introspection. I know I shall sympathise with her all through.

WINIFRED TO VERA

5 Clifton Terrace, Hornsea, East
Yorkshire | 7 March 1935

I can't help thinking that your physical condition is due to nerve-
strain. Because this has never happened before does not mean
that it is unlikely to happen now. I hope it is only that, and that
iron and tonics will put you right; but if not I entirely agree with
you that you must have every possible help. Of course I would do
anything I could to make your 1936 American tour possible. As a
matter of fact, unless I can be of convenience to you there rather
than here for any reason, I am not at all sure that I want to go to
the U.S.A. myself. The exasperation of wanting to do things and
being unable to do them would probably outweigh any financial
advantages. But that can wait. In any case, I am ready and eager
to co-operate, my very dear, in anything that can help, not only
you, but all that you stand for.

The diary sounds superb. The little extract you quoted
provides exactly the kind of touching, intimate *uninventable*
detail which makes a book vital and convincing. I really believe
that 'Honourable Estate' may be a great book.

I hope my letter on Tuesday did not sound depressed. I took myself
vigorously in hand that evening, and decided that if I could not have
what I wanted, I would want what I could have. It is undignified and
ridiculous to regret or complain, and I am damned if I won't enjoy
everything. I walked by the sea. Great sea planes like gulls were
zooming over the town and dropping depth charges into the North
Sea. Rehearsal for pandemonium. Life is so short. The menace of
horror is over us all so completely, that to waste time on self-pity
seems extremely unintelligent. John Middleton Murry's maudlin sensibilities have made me out of love with the wistful introvert.

Oddly enough, after these bracing if rather repulsive

conclusions, I came home to find myself called upon a) by the
Vicar's wife; b) by a young reporter who had motored from
Leeds to ask me: Are Women Still in Chains? The evening
became so chaotic and comical that I abandoned any hope
of work. I haven't opened my novel since last Friday; but have
hopes tonight after Harry goes. Yesterday I was doing *Good
Housekeeping.* I have found a typist here called Miss Boast.

Bless you, my love. I long to see you a week on Friday.

I am very well. A doctor, whom I saw last week, as Obermer
wanted him to take a blood test, said he was quite certain my
whole trouble started when I had scarlet fever, mumps and
quinseys together when I was 15. Apparently, he heard from
people up here that I had it very badly, with a sort of poison
symptom (which I never knew of) and scarlet fever can always
start kidney trouble. He is an intelligent little man and most
optimistic about my general condition.

I must go and meet Harry's bus. The sun shines. The air is
full of a fine frosty brightness. I have written across my heart,
'I will not be dismayed.' And the curious result is that, at the
moment, I am not. After all, it is loving and not being loved,
which is the vitalising experience. I will give him anything that
he is prepared to take, though I think that this is very little,
and be thankful that at least I have known what it is to love.

WINIFRED TO VERA

10 March 1935

Darling,

I wish you did not feel so ill. But you shall certainly rest in
the weekend as much as you like. I shall come into Hull with
you on Sunday and come out here for supper.

Harry really was so sweet that he made everything easy. It was by chance the one really warm and glorious spring day. We walked 11 miles and sat and smoked on a rifle range and watched aeroplanes bombing a target in the sea. It was curiously like being back in the War. He is going to Spain.

Dear love. vsvdl. W.

WINIFRED TO VERA

Cottingham, East Yorkshire | 24 March 1935

Darling,

I have just been discussing with Mother her plans for Easter and all, and now all is clear.

You could come to Hornsea before Easter, we would keep the rooms on, and you could stay as long as you liked.

I can't get away before Easter anyway; but I could quite well come immediately after. I told Mother you weren't well and *might* be going to have a baby, and she said that she didn't really think Hornsea a good place if you were feeling ill, and said she could perfectly well manage after Easter, and advised me to go down South, unless you would prefer to come up here.

Yes, I would like a Jubilee ticket. We ought to see that, I suppose.

I had another note from Harry. He has not apparently got the job, and is neither going to Evesham nor Spain, but wants to come over to Hornsea and see me soon. I will make no more arrangements about him ever, unless I feel sure he can fulfil them.

Yesterday I was in Hull, Leeds, Stalybridge, Ashton-under-Lyne, Harrogate, Leeds and Hull again. Haven't been so tired for weeks, but all right today.

The Hull University lecture was packed out – people standing – result of local curiosity, I suppose. I must say it is half the work to lecture in a big crowded hall that it is in a small meeting.

Open Door Council very pleased with their conference. Room in Town Hall *full*. Lots of local cotton and wool women. Frolein [*sic*] Anna Westergaard, second head of Danish State Railways, the chief guest, grand woman, superb grey head like a handsome man's, beautifully waved grey hair, most witty speech in clear but attractively funny English, and smoked *cigars* – to the amazement of the Mayor and Councillors of Ashton, who were present. Met Margaret Ashton too – now over eighty and nearly blind, who started the birth control clinic in Manchester which put Stopes and Roe on to the idea. A little beaky-nosed, red-faced, sweet woman. Really rather a little duck. Said: 'I'm an old nuisance and no use to anyone but I do like it when these younger women let me come to their meetings.'

Bless you. Do take care of your dear self.

v.s.v.d.l. W.

VERA TO WINIFRED

19 Glebe Place, London SW3 | *25 March 1935*

Your journeyings last week sound just about as bad as my last expedition to Chester, Liverpool, etc. Please *don't* do any more of this kind of thing for a bit. It must have been thrilling to have that packed audience at Hull University – rather like mine at Liverpool – but such things are even worse for you than they are for me. One doesn't fully realise how much such expeditions tire until about a week afterwards. I'm beginning to think that the six months of that kind of thing that I have had will take at least another six months to recover from.

I am seeing Dr Sharp again on Wednesday. I don't suppose Dr S. can tell me anything definite any more than she could before, but I shall take my rubber cervical pessary and make her tell me if it still fits. If it doesn't that may account for everything. It is the size fitted by Dr Gray after the birth of Shirley and my anatomy has probably changed again since then. And I shall ask her if she knows of a country convalescent home for the overworked.

I saw Gordon off at Liverpool Street on Saturday night and felt rather desolate. It was like seeing him vanish into the Ewigkeit for 2 months. All I have is the Intourist address in Moscow, and whether they forward my letters to him or his get through to me seems a matter for pure speculation.

I have sudden flashes of hope about 'Honourable Estate' and a sense of its significance just as I used to have about *Testament of Youth* If only I could feel fit and get on with it!

WINIFRED TO VERA

*5 Clifton Terrace, Hornsea, East
Yorkshire | 3 April 1935*

I'm awfully pleased you feel better. I shall enjoy Tenby enormously, I am sure, and, apart from everything else, it may get me away from this persistent bombing. The aerodrome here is training our young air force men, and they have now taken to dropping real bombs into the sea which boom, boom, boom all day. A war may be coming but I find it difficult to finish my book among sounds that make me imagine that it has started already!

I was at Dowthorpe yesterday and met there for the first
time since the war a man called Tuke Hosdell with whom I was
violently in love when I was about thirteen (before I met Harry
properly). He reminded me of this fact and says he still has a
copy of my poems which I inscribed for him during my first
year at school! He is now grey, stout, middle-aged, dyspeptic –
(he was badly wounded in the stomach, poor lad) – and has
two different grown-up families. It made me feel most aged. He
motored me back to Hornsea. It was like meeting a ghost. He's a
corn-dealer, and quite well off.

All blessings and congratulations, you gallant creature,
v.s.v.d.l. *W.*

VERA TO WINIFRED

19 Glebe Place, London SW3 | *3 April 1935*

Darling,

So glad about the rooms. Of course I'll take the top one if it
is as high as the 4th floor – don't want you always marching up
and down stairs, and I like being high. The place does sound
nice, doesn't it? Glad we don't have to bother to dress much.

By the way, I wonder if among your or your mother's
possessions at Cottingham you happen to have anything (book
or magazine) of the nature of pious talks to girls (period 1908–
12). I want my headmistress at Playden School (where 'Ruth'
goes before the War) to preach a sermon to the girls on 'Purity'
and would like an authentic model if possible. I thought I had
a copy of Miss Soulsby's *Stray Thoughts for Girls* which would
be just right, but can find no trace of it or of anything similar.
I don't think the London Library would be likely to have
this, do you?

Don't take time over it, but I seem to recollect that
Cottingham had some examples of this type of literature.
    In haste, V.S.V.D.L.

WINIFRED TO VERA

*5 Clifton Terrace, Hornsea, East
Yorkshire | 8 April 1935*

Dearest,

I do hope you aren't too disastrously tired after your
Newcastle lectures. It's the journeys that are such a bore.

I only have two more talks to give too, both on women.

I'm afraid Purity doesn't seem to have been a very fruitful
subject in our household. Nor have we any actual *Talks to Girls*.
But dear Miss Soulsby seems suggestive, especially the chapter
'a missing link'. Dean Farrar's talks may give the peculiarly
'Christian' atmosphere – and I suggest a quotation or two from
Sesame and Lilies.

This seems the best I can do at Cottingham, but I think you
should get the tone from these. I looked through old *Quivers*, but
the fact seems to be that Purity in girls was so much taken for
granted that it was not discussed much. I never remember hearing
one single school sermon (and we had two a week!) on such a
questionable subject. The only possible temptation against which
we were warned was 'listening to nasty jokes' made by other people!
    v.s.v.d.l. W.

VERA TO WINIFRED

19 Glebe Place, London SW3 | 9 April 1935

So many thanks for the pious books. I can manufacture a talk from these, I am sure. Probably you are right in thinking that no headmistress would give a direct talk on Purity in 1910; it would probably be called 'The Beauty of Holiness' or something.

Got back from Newcastle yesterday afternoon. It really was a most interesting week-end. Angus Watson turned out to be not only the 'Skipper Sardine' millionaire (with a very comfortable but not ostentatious house) but also the founder of Ivor Nicholson & Watson (his son, aged 28) and the next chairman of the Congregational Union – a really charming, kindly, thoughtful man of about 57.

Since Sept. 18th, 1933, when I addressed the Newcastle Luncheon Club (my first lecture after *Testament of Youth* was published), I have given exactly 170 lectures and speeches. Odd that I should finish in Newcastle where I began. Besides my lecture on *T. of Y.* at the St James Forum in the afternoon I gave the morning sermon by request at the local Unitarian Church on 'Youth and War', to a crowded congregation.

Somehow it was all very moving – the prayers, the hymns, the political circumstances of today, and the queer sense of being a little minority group gathered together in the face of almost certain disaster, yet not giving up all hope of preventing it. They all, including the Minister, seemed to have such confidence in me, little knowing how little faith or confidence I had in myself. So doubtful am I of the quality of my next book, and of my ability to do anything further, that I always feel now that someone else really wrote *T. of Y.* and that I am speaking about the work of a stranger. Literally, now, I cannot remember writing any of it or how I did so.

Yet again, when I recall the number of churches up and down

this country in which I have spoken since *T. of Y.* came out, and especially this year, I wonder whether I am really entitled to interpret morality in my own way and act upon the interpretation. How far when one becomes a public character is one entitled to do things which one does not believe one's self to be wrong or evil, but which if known would vitiate one's message for one's listeners, because one's conduct would seem wrong to *them*? How much private life does one's public responsibility permit one? It's all too, too difficult. I am not a less efficient, or a less convinced, advocate of peace and reason because I have loved and may love someone in an unorthodox way – and yet if most of them knew this, they would not want to listen to me in a world where Heaven knows there are already too few who can get people to hear them.

A letter from Gordon tonight – seems to be living in a terrible rush and finding Moscow extremely cold.

All dearest love V.S.V.D.L.

WINIFRED TO VERA

5 Clifton Terrace, Hornsea, East Yorkshire | 11 April 1935

I too find questions of morality extraordinarily difficult. Impossible at least to advise other people about. There are always the big permanent values which nothing can affect – courage, loyalty, caritas in the Latin sense of love, responsibility. But how far each person must interpret these according to orthodox rules seems to me so much a matter of individual personality. The law 'Thou shalt not be found out' seems so disastrously ignoble, and yet is what, in a world of such varying standards, common sense dictates. I should have thought that you were a better speaker, better writer, certainly a better interpreter of America

to England and England to America, because you, so fastidiously
and energetically English, happened to love an American. I feel
sure that you have a more profound sense of the complexity
and difficulty of human life because you have had your own
experience. All your former problems were so intrinsically
straightforward (even if agonising) and so completely honourable
and decorous. I believe that *Honourable Estate* will be a far better
book, and I think it possible that your speeches are far better
speeches, because of what you have endured and known.

Harry went off this morning. I am a fool to want more than
I get from him. What I have is so gay, foolish and charming –
something everyone needs – a frivolity, an enchantment, a
relaxation. Then, in his black moods, he revolts both against
and towards me – does and does not want me.

Took me to Hull, to the Tivoli. We heard an idiotic music hall
show. He introduced me to a bar maid of 57, a friend of his, and
the assistant manager of a 3rd rate provincial music hall. Well, I
have got out of the episode a red rose and another scene for *South
Riding*, and a further understanding of how people behave in
bars after a football match (which is, after all, something). I can't
pretend I don't owe him far more than he owes me. I love every
tone of his voice, every movement of his hands. I wouldn't *not* love
him for anything. But it is, I suppose, a humiliating and ridiculous
situation for a woman of my age, intelligence and interests.

Anyway, he's an antidote to these committees and speeches.
A formal invitation from Liberia arrived this week – to be the
guest of the Government any time between November and
March 1935–6. If there's really going to be a war, I shan't go. But
otherwise it's something that would be useful if ever a Labour
Government got into power again. I could be a better general
adviser and assistant on imperial affairs – and hardly any
socialists know a cure for those.

v.s.v.d.l. W.

VERA TO WINIFRED

19 Glebe Place, London SW3 | 11 April 1935

I seem to be quite well again. Usual function returned this
week – perfectly normal, no unusual pain or fatigue – though
whether this was due to the injections or merely to the
cessation of dashing about and a fortnight of comparative peace
and regular living no one can say. I had been feeling, physically,
a different person for some days beforehand.

It's very bad for me to be too long alone; I am obsessed as
usual with the idea that my book will involve me in libel actions
and other troubles of all sorts, and that the greatness of the
theme (which *is* there, I think) will somehow fail to get over. I
am perpetually troubled, too, about how to behave to George P.
Brett in June, which seems to be getting so horribly near. If he
would give me a lead, if he would make it clear that *he* no longer
wanted anything but a friendly business relation, it would be
so easy – painful, but not a problem. But he'll wait, I think, for
me to give it; in his position it would be difficult for him to do
anything else, and what am I to give? Do I want to terminate
the whole thing – or rather, *ought* I to do so? And if I do, how
difficult to do it without conveying the impression that he no
longer attracts me as a person – a more humiliating suggestion
to a man, I think, than even to a woman, who is more used to
humiliation – and so profoundly untrue! What I really want is to
talk to him (which I've never been able to do) for two or three
uninterrupted hours, and such are our lives when we meet, that
an interval for discussion is ruled out by the rush of obligations
and engagements. I don't fear unconventional morality so much
as the undercurrent of antagonism, the desire to hurt, which is
in all passion – a volcano constantly threatening to erupt. But
can one ignore passion when it is there, and behave as though it

didn't exist? Can one avoid its complications by merely refusing
to express it? Did your two days with Harry teach you anything?
Oh, I am all at sea – blind, confused, uncertain, incapable of
seeing my way! I don't wonder really at the persistence of the old
morality, for though rigid, unimaginative, cruel, unenlightened,
it offered, however unconstructively, peace and safety; a set of
narrow, exact rules for conduct which spared the individual the
disturbing necessity of thought. Once you leave those beaten
paths, the responsibility for decency, dignity, generosity, becomes
your own; society protects and guides only those who uncritically
accept its standards.

I am following in her diaries Mrs Catlin's conflict of
intelligence against traditional expectations with sympathy and
a growing sadness that so much fighting should have ended
only in failure and death. In her habit of going over some
philosophical or religious matter over and over again, discussing,
rending it, tormenting herself over it and never coming to a
final conclusion, she was extraordinarily like Gordon. Do you
know that her diary ends (on Dec. 9th 1917) a fortnight before
her death (she must have been taken ill within the next day
or two) with the entry 'Jerusalem captured'! What a strange
symbolism – which I must certainly use in my book.

Dear Gordon! How incessantly and exasperatedly, supposing
I were married to a person like G.P.B., I should miss that
sensitive understanding, that sympathetic perception of
nuances and shadows, of conflicts in values and standards. He
understands everything, and G.P.B. (in this shadow-world of
the spirit) almost nothing. Why is there this strange divorce
between one's mind and one's flesh – why does one's flesh refuse
to respond where one's mind loves and admires, yet is kindled
to flame by someone without tenderness or compassion? Or is
this a biological fact of life – *must* passion involve antagonism
to so fundamental an extent that where there is absolutely no

antagonism of the spirit (as between Gordon and myself there is
not) there can be no passionate response of the flesh? 'Behold, I
show you a mystery . . . ' it seems to be the only just comment.

All dear love V.S.V.D.L.

WINIFRED TO VERA

*5 Clifton Terrace, Hornsea, East
Yorkshire | 12 April 1935*

Dear Love,

I *am* so glad that you are so much physically better. Sorry it
took injections which you so much hate, to put you right; but
certainly that does seem to have been the proper treatment.
I am so glad too that you no longer have the psychological
uncertainty of not knowing quite what was wrong.

My long and often painful experience has taught me this, that
passion can become friendship. I don't say without heartache –
yes, and *physical* ache. But then one never expects life to be
without heartache, and I personally have never known it to be
without some humiliation. That is a quality which you have
rarely had occasion to experience, but I assure you that one need
allow it only to affect a very small area of one's consciousness,
and need not affect the relationship to the person involved at all.

I do not think that, if you want to stabilise your relationship
with George Brett on to a basis of friendship that you
need humiliate him at all. You have shown your love and
your courage. You could talk things out. You could allow a
considerable elasticity for *his* feelings. If he desperately needs
you, a need is a real obligation. If he does not, but can 'manage'
as they say, and you would find the publisher-friend relationship
easier, more permanent, and more secure, I don't see why you

should not both accomplish it, with the added intensity and tenderness of remembered passion. I do at least know that this is possible. Of course it is painful at times. But so is almost every close relationship in the world.

Still, I have not made so much success of my own affairs that I can pose as a safe guide.

The meeting tonight is for 'Purity and Social Welfare'!! I shall wear Harry's red roses. That, at least, I owe my sense of humour.

Dearest love v s v d l W

Between the previous letter and the one that follows, George Brett came to London in June and disappointed Vera by showing no inclination to renew their dalliance. Gordon returned from Russia, suffering from an infection that would trouble him all summer. At the end of July, Vera and her family went to France on holiday, while Winifred went to the Malvern Festival. Their plans were interrupted by the suicide of Vera's father.

WINIFRED TO VERA

Malvern Hotel, Malvern, Worcestershire | *29 July 1935*

Darling,

I'm working hard here on the last draft of my book. The actual Festival starts today.

The Shaws live in a whirl of reporters, visitors, rehearsals, etc. We hardly see them, except for a minute when George Bernard Shaw called us on to the balcony to be photographed with him. It was in the *Sunday Graphic*.

We went on Saturday to Tewkesbury to hear Shaw, Masefield and Francis Brett Young make an appeal for the preservation of the Abbey.

v.s.v.d.l. W.

VERA TO WINIFRED

> Grand Hôtel des Anglais et des Bains,
> Wimereux | 31 July 1935

We all got here without mishap at 1.30 – lovely crossing; John a perfect angel, enjoyed everything, and Shirley not too bad. Hotel excellent; very nice top-floor rooms.

Could you bring over a half-pound packet of china tea; the one I bought today cost 13½ francs, i.e. 4/6! Next time Gordon wants the children to have a holiday in France he can pay for it himself!

In great haste to catch post,
V.S.V.D.L.

The body of Vera's father, Arthur Brittain, was discovered on 5 August, floating in the Thames at Isleworth.

WINIFRED TO VERA

> c/o Miss Garbutt, 27 Cavendish Avenue,
> Harrogate, North Yorkshire | 6 August 1935

My darling,

I think of you constantly. I wish there were something I could do. I wish that you had not all this business of inquest and funeral; but I know it is inevitable, and I know that you will be your strong and valiant self.

I am sending some flowers from Harrogate. I hope they arrive in time. I shall always think of that gay, handsome, kindly man I first knew, who was always so sweet to me.

I expect to be in Harrogate by about 4.15. Norman is driving

me a roundabout way to Derby via Dovedale. He is very, very
sorry about your father.

I have brought Shirley's photograph up with me.
Everyone loves it.

My blessings and my love. I'll ring you up on Friday evening.
Winifred v.s.v.d.l.

VERA TO WINIFRED

37 Edwardes Square, London W8 |
7 August 1935, 1.30 p.m.

Darling sweet

Just a brief line (no time for more now) to say that your
beautiful pink carnations came quite safely this morning and
in plenty of time; the funeral is this afternoon in Richmond
cemetery at 3 o'clock. Your flowers are *lovely*, and I am so glad you
chose just those, for pink and red were Father's favourite colours
for flowers. I am giving him the usual Ophelia roses that I carried
at my wedding when he looked so spruce and debonair and
Gordon's one red rose and Mother's red and white carnations.
I'm *very* glad you sent your flowers, for owing to Mother's feeling
about it to begin with we haven't many; at first she said she would
have no flowers and no one at the funeral but I was sure Father
would hate that; he liked people to pay their respects and he was
a decorative person to whom flowers are appropriate. So at last I
persuaded her to allow it, but that was why there was no funeral
mentioned in the *Times* notice. I wrote the notice myself. I was
determined that *nothing* should be done to suggest that we are
in any way ashamed of what Father did; after all, it was only the
logical consequence of his illness and the state of the law which
prevents people who wish to die from doing so easily.

We are just back from the inquest – on the upper-floor billiard
room of an inn at Isleworth over a most lovely reach of the river –
just such a place as Father was found. I can't speak too highly of the
decency and co-operation that we have had from the police and
the public authorities as well as the officials at Richmond cemetery.

Once again my dear love and thanks for your beautiful flowers
and your dear little note with it, which Father would have loved.

always V.S.V.D.L.

WINIFRED TO VERA

Grand Hôtel des Anglais et des Bains,
Wimereux | *14 August 1935*

Darling,

I am so sorry that poor Gordon continues to be ill and that
he must miss a week of Sunderland, and most of all that you
are having such a mouldy time. I wish there was anything one
could do. When I get back, you *must* have a holiday.

Mother has written to me to ask if it would be of any help if
she invited your mother to Cottingham. I don't somehow feel it
would, though, do you??

I shall be all right for money. All very well here. Yesterday
everyone but Shirley and I went to Boulogne for the afternoon.
It stopped raining but was rather cold and windy. John *adored*
Boulogne! All the adults went to see Josephine Baker in *Zouzou*
last night, except me again; I looked after the babes and went
early to bed. I feel worlds better for the rest here.

John actually put his arms round my neck and kissed me
yesterday. I felt so flattered. I do think he is a well behaved little
boy, and does get the discipline he needs in his usual environment.

vsvdl W

VERA TO WINIFRED

19 Glebe Place, London SW3 | 15 August 1935

Darling,

We've just got settled in here with our quantities of luggage, etc. Gordon's temp. is still 101°, and another gland is beginning to be affected now, so I'm afraid we're not out of the wood yet. Thank Heaven I still seem to be so framed, as in the War, as to be able to stand a large measure of grief and anxiety without collapsing; I should hate to be unable to look after him, as he looks really ill and doesn't *want* to do anything; has even ceased to worry about his book, which means he must feel pretty bad, I fear.

I feel guilty about last week; if only he could have gone straight to bed when the trouble started he would probably have been all right by now, but of course he carried on with all the business and didn't admit he was ill.

It is *very* good of your mother to offer to take Mother, but really I don't think it would do at all; their temperaments are so antipathetic, and anyhow, Mother is in such a tense difficult mood that she might upset your mother quite considerably – she is better with her sisters. Do thank your Mother very much however, it was sweet of her to offer.

Love to my sweet babies, Always, V.S.V.D.L.

WINIFRED TO VERA

Grand Hôtel des Anglais et des Bains,
Wimereux | *15 August 1935*

Darling,

How perfectly wretched. I am so sorry, both for you and
Gordon. The only thing we can do is to see that you both get
a proper holiday when all this is over. I am sure of one thing –
that Gordon will get better quicker at Glebe Place than at
Edwardes Square, if part of the need is rest and quiet. And you
shall get away when he is better and I am back. I suppose that
the best thing I can do is to stay here. As a matter of fact, it is
making a different person of me. I really was rather a rag by the
end of the summer – nothing to do with your affairs, but simply
that it's no use pretending I don't need constant holidays more
than a normal person does. The air and rest and doing nothing
for even these few days have set me up and I feel quite different
and much more able to cope with things, so that when I come
back I can do anything at all to help – quite different from the
worm who went to France!

The children are lovely and seem very happy. They both
send their love. I haven't told them that Gordon isn't so well,
because they get so easily upset by illness, and love both you
and Gordon so much.

Dear love – vsvdl W.

VERA TO WINIFRED

19 Glebe Place, London SW3 | 16 August 1935

I think on the whole it is better that you should tell anyone
you happen to write to, and whom I am likely to meet, the
real truth about Father – not only because I am anything but
ashamed of it but because it saves the possibility of subsequent
embarrassment in conversation. People feel they must utter
some word of sympathy, and say they hope his end was
peaceful – and what can I say? Everyone who has written to us,
not knowing, has said this, and I have judged it better to tell
them. In the end it saves people embarrassment and the feeling
that they have caused pain unintentionally.

There *was* one notice in the Press – in a Brentford paper we
had forgotten – splurging my name in large headlines, but it
didn't come out till Aug. 10th. But it was an indication of what
would have happened if we hadn't taken the precautions we did.

Gordon doesn't seem much better and his doctor says he fears
it will be a long job before he is quite fit. When he recovers the
doctor is going to give him a long talking to about his general
mode of living; he asked me several questions about it as he says
such an infection could only so thoroughly get hold of someone
very run down. G. has got to see a specialist on Monday, not
because he is *necessarily* any worse but because the doctor very
sensibly wants to make sure that the infection is not spreading
to yet other glands and that the treatment is right. I see myself
doing G.'s Sunderland campaign yet! Actually his temperature
is not so high this evening as it has been all the week (102° the
day before yesterday), and I am sure this is due to the change
from the perpetual nag, hurry and tension at Edwardes Square.
If only each of them had married someone else, both might now
be sane, and Father alive. No wonder really that I am sometimes

queer, neurotic, inconsiderate. No, often. At Edwardes Square, empty, dark and shuttered today, I seemed to keep hearing Father's voice saying: 'Is that you, Jack?'

Just got your letter. I'm so glad the sea and air and rest are making you better; of course really you're just as bad as G. about holidays; you wouldn't have gone to France if I had not urged you and the children hadn't needed you! Although G. hasn't a great deal of treatment – not nearly enough to justify a nurse – and is patience itself, I seem to be on the go all day and never to get out.

So glad dear John and Shirley are well. Give them my love and a kiss; will try to send more Comics tomorrow.

All love, V.S.V.D.L.

WINIFRED TO VERA

Grand Hôtel des Anglais et des Bains,
Wimereux | 17 August 1935

Darling,

I was so glad to have your letter of the 13th this morning. But I have been thinking all the time that you ought to get a nurse unless Gordon shows very rapid signs of improvement.

Would you like me to keep the children here longer? I could do so easily and there are plenty of rooms. Would that help you at all? I have no urgent reason for recall myself, and could send for some more money. I will do *anything* at all that you feel most helpful.

When Gordon is better you *must* have a holiday, whether you feel like one or not. It almost seems as though you had one of those temperaments so full of nervous energy that in crises your whole metabolism is keyed up to concert pitch and acts well,

but in between crises your vitality is too much for your body
and you get ill and run down; great organisers and leaders and
men like General Booth were such. But that doesn't mean that
you or they or anyone can go on forever.

Bless you, dear love – and anything most helpful to you,
I will do.

vsvdl W.

VERA TO WINIFRED

19 Glebe Place, London SW3 | 18 August 1935

Darling,

Gordon has to keep as quiet as possible and rest all he can;
apart from the douches and poultices this is the most important
part of the treatment. So will you warn Fraulein that the
children must be kept on the ground floor, and as quiet as is
possible to expect of children. She must take them to the Park
or Burton Court – they mustn't be left hooting up and down
the stairs and in and out of the front door, while she dawdles
over the washing! Perhaps you could tell them too that they
must be as quiet as they can. I have racked my brains to think
of anywhere I could send them till the end of the month, but in
vain. What does worry me is the length of time it seems likely
to take before G. gets right; I don't think there's any question of
danger but I am concerned, not only with the inevitable delay
for my own book, but with the repercussions in Sunderland,
espec. if the election is soon. It looks as if I may have to go up
instantly myself if they are not to get utterly fed up; and God
knows I haven't time to add this to everything else, nor at the
moment do I feel I have the energy. But I quite visualise six
weeks elapsing before G. can really work again.

I am also concerned about G.'s book – more so than he
realises. If only I could write it for Gordon I would, but so much
of it relates to experiences I didn't have. At present his temp.
has fallen from round about 101–102 to 99–100, but any work,
even proof-correcting, immediately sends it up. As for the book
in England, it seems to have been abandoned to its fate. He
couldn't have been ill at a worse time, when I so badly wanted
to leave all our business affairs in someone else's hands and
have them run smoothly.

Made myself go for a walk by the river yesterday evening. I
was beginning to feel I could never go near it again, but decided
that this must be overcome.

Hope all is still well with John and Shirley; I long to see
them again.

All dear love, V.S.V.D.L.

VERA TO WINIFRED

19 Glebe Place, London SW3 | 19 August 1935

Just got your letter of Saturday and have wired to say that if it
really is convenient, and won't upset your mother or anyone, it
will be much the best solution to keep the children in France
for another week, i.e. till Aug. 28. To try to keep them quiet
here would be very hard on both Gordon and them (to say
nothing of myself!), and then London is so stuffy and airless;
the garden here so cramped and scrubby, the Parks burnt out
and full of dust and torn papers. And – incidentally – I'm not
sorry on your account to give you another enforced week by
the sea! Ten days holiday in a year isn't much and if only you
are strong-minded enough to go on treating it as a holiday it

should do you a world of good. Let me know however if there is anything I can do on your novel or any other piece of business.

There really isn't so much to do for G. now – his treatment takes 2 hours in the morning and ½ an hour at night only – not nearly enough to occupy a nurse and keep her quiet. Now that I have at last caught up on my business correspondence I can have all the rest of the day for writing if I like, but I haven't yet felt like tackling my novel again. My mind keeps running on Father; I feel I am partly responsible for his melancholia and the way he died; that I ought to have gone to see him oftener; that to be left so much to Mother's unbenevolent and grudging conscientiousness was enough to drive anybody to suicide in the end. I think he must have been fonder of me than anyone really, or he wouldn't have left me all his personal belongings; and of course he adored the children and was proud of me for having such nice ones. It is so intolerably difficult to assess one's obligations in this world. It makes me indescribably miserable to feel that after all Father's kindness and generosity to me and the children, he may have thought I neglected him; it seems so unfair that he should be asked to pay the first price of success and public obligations which meant nothing to him. I keep wondering whether he called for me or wanted me when it was too late to go back or make anyone hear. I have been re-reading several of his charming letters about the children, which I kept.

But I remember that you managed to write *The Astonishing Island* when your father was dying of angina, and have decided that somehow, tomorrow, I will go back to my novel.

Yes, I will take a holiday as soon as I can. I don't actually feel very tired except that I know I am by my legs, which feel exactly like lead – so heavy that I can't take a longer walk than quarter of an hour without getting dead weary.

All dearest love and thanks, V.S.V.D.L.

WINIFRED TO VERA

Grand Hôtel des Anglais et des Bains,
Wimereux | *23 August 1935*

Darling,

The children are splendid and Fraulein's cold better.

We have loved looking after them. Hilda has a natural genius
for children, and I have found a quite revolutionary difference
between child-care while trying to work, and the same exercise
while doing nothing else. It has done me all the good in the
world to abandon myself to infantile amusements for a few days.

As for the future. Do go away to the Cotswolds. I have to
be in London then. I have no objection to visiting and being
visited by your mother. She probably irritates me less than
anyone, because I am naturally placid and because, as a matter
of fact, she is generally quite nice *to* me. She may find me
irritating and criticise me behind my back, but I never mind
that if people are nice to my face! I don't think I shall be very
busy before I go to Africa, and really there could not be a better
time for you to go away. Do take the opportunity and go. Really
to plunge yourself into your book in perfect peace and privacy
would do you good. It is no more than I did at Hornsea and
Withernsea. So *do* take the chance and go! I promise you that if
ever I find it too much, I will tell you.

At the same time, I am all for encouraging your mother to
assume responsibility as much as possible. It will be something
to fill her empty life. But you can count on my co-operation
when I am in England. It is not a burden. I *love* the children.
They warm my heart and refresh my spirit, and who knows
what sort of an academic busy-body I might be without them?

v.s.v.d.l. W.

VERA TO WINIFRED

19 Glebe Place, London SW3 | *25 August 1935*

So many thanks for your wire, but really there is *no* necessity
for the children to stay longer than Wednesday – noble though
you are to suggest it. For one thing, I shall not now send the
children to Edwardes Square to stay. Gordon is so much better
that it is not necessary, and Mother seems very much relieved
that she need not put them up. So we'll expect you back on
Wednesday by the time arranged.

I feel a good deal better owing to the fact that G. is
improving so rapidly – there is so little to do for him now that I
can get to a little work of my own. My mind works badly and I
am very slow, but even to get *something* done is invigorating.

All dear love and many thanks for offering to stay longer.

WINIFRED TO VERA

Wimereux | *26 August 1935*

Very well, we will come back on Wednesday as arranged. We'll
come straight to Glebe Place.

I'm so very glad dear G. is so much better.

I shan't write again, but shall wire if there is any change of
plan. It's a lovely day again, and two more days on the sands
won't hurt the children, as well as giving you a few more hours'
peace. So expect us on Wednesday; 5.21, isn't it?

Dear, dear love, W.

In late August, Winifred returned from France with Vera's children as planned. Vera and Gordon – the latter still recovering from the infection contracted in Russia – went for a holiday in Brighton. While they were away, Winifred suffered a severe attack of illness and went into a nursing home, from which she wrote the following note, the last letter of the correspondence.

WINIFRED TO VERA

[23 September 1935]

Darling, why not move to the Metropole if plush bores you? Had lovely supper last night, two chicken sandwiches and slept all night and Obermer says I can have tomato-juice cocktails and biscuits every morning. Sorry to be so gastronomic but this is news for *me*! Do have a holiday. I am *much* better. Overwhelmed by offers of visits. Edith will do everything. Give Gordon my love, I wish you both shared my passion for the Pavilion. Funniest institution in the world, I think. Love. W.

Winifred died in the Elizabeth Fulcher Nursing Home, Devonshire Street, in the early morning of 29 September.

EPILOGUE

Immediately after Winifred's death, newspapers and magazines were inundated with remembrances, saluting her as both an inspiring feminist, pacifist and anti-racialist leader, and a lively, approachable and lovable woman. *Time and Tide* needed two special editions to contain all the tributes. Harold Laski, the prominent Marxist economist, took the high road, writing of 'her passion for great causes', and seeing in her 'what Mary Wollstonecraft must have been'. An obituary in *The Times* paid respect to all the serious facts of her life and influence. As a director of *Time and Tide*, it pointed out, Winifred had a significant platform from which to present her political interests and progressive opinions. On a different note, it also credited her exuberance and informality as equally 'essential to an understanding of her character'. No haughty intellectual, she could 'give rein, when occasion arose, to the reckless humour and Falstaffian gaiety which she liked to call her "farmer's daughter" sense of fun'. Winifred's blend of innovative thinking and approachable warmth made her a symbolic figure of her period, a woman of her time.

A large crowd of friends attended her memorial service on

1 October 1935 at St Martin-in-the-Fields. The next day Vera, Gordon, Lady Rhondda and Hilda Reid travelled to Rudston for Winifred's funeral. In the village churchyard, a simple gravestone identified her as the daughter of David and Alice Holtby, with the verse 'God give me work / till my life shall end / and life / till my work is done'. It said nothing about her writing and literary identity. Vera was reminded of both another Yorkshire woman writer, Charlotte Brontë, and her modest grave, and the dilemma of the woman artist in the twentieth century that Winifred had examined in her book on Virginia Woolf.

Vera was named in Winifred's will as literary executor, a responsibility she took with the deepest seriousness, and would carry out devotedly for the rest of her life. Her first challenge was to persuade Winifred's mother, the general executor of the estate, to approve the posthumous publication of *South Riding*. An epic chronicle of an imagined Yorkshire province like Hardy's Wessex, with 167 characters listed in their order of appearance at the beginning of the book, it was Winifred's masterpiece. But Alice Holtby feared that its plot about local government, and a central character based on her work as alderwoman, would be embarrassing. When it came out on 6 March 1936, however, *South Riding* was a huge critical and commercial success, winning the James Tait Black Memorial Prize. Alexander Korda produced the admired film version in 1938, and there have been many adaptations since.

Vera's more demanding task was Winifred's biography, titled *Testament of Friendship*. She spent three years researching and writing it, slowed down in part because of her guilt for ignoring the signs of Winifred's decline. Too late she felt remorse for taking advantage of Winifred's generosity. As she wrote to St John Ervine, 'I know I exhausted poor Winifred's vitality. Rereading my letters to her and hers to me has been like a bitter self-revealing indictment of me. But I wasn't the only one; we all did it between us.' Nonetheless, she defended her unique value to Winifred and the intimate bonds of trust they shared. 'We were completely at ease with each other ... When she was with me ... she didn't have to play any part, keep up any appearances, conceal any feelings. She could, so to speak, completely unbutton her personality.' That made a huge difference when she was dying, because 'when you are in pain, the only person whose society is tolerable ... is the person with whom you can be completely unbuttoned'. Yet Winifred *had* concealed the seriousness of her illness from Vera, and Vera had not grasped it. For this failure she would try to atone, beginning with the biography. As she wrote to Sarah Gertrude Millin, if it could 'suggest even a dim reflection of the glowing, radiant, generous creature whom we have lost, it will be the best way of returning all that she did for me'.

Testament of Friendship was a best-seller – selling more than *Testament of Youth* initially – when it came out in 1940, although reviewers felt it was more about Vera than Winifred. Subsequent biographers and critics have particularly objected that Vera imposed her own idea of a heterosexual romance on the narrative of Winifred's life and death. Marion Shaw comments that 'Vera's intense desire to write a love story for Winifred led to a definitive version which imposes a romantic ending on Winifred's life, but also depicts her as deluded in her final hours and dying in a kind of sanctification which it is difficult to believe she would have approved of'. At best the story of Harry's deathbed proposal feels like a diminishment of Winifred, a sentimental postscript to her life of courage, adventure and independence. As her semi-autobiographical heroine Sarah Burton thinks in *South Riding*, 'I was born to be a spinster and by God, I'm going to spin.'

Overall, Vera's loving account of their relationship also stresses its hidden benefits to Winifred, rather than its huge and obvious benefits to herself. In *Testament of Experience*, the final volume of her memoirs, Vera summed up Winifred's life as vicariously dependent on hers: 'None of her books published in her lifetime had sold remarkably so she helped mine to sell magnificently. The only man whom she really loved had failed her, so she identified herself with my married happiness. Her burdens were great and intolerable, so she shouldered mine which were often trivial. When she learned that she must never have children, she shared in the care of ours.' From this perspective, Vera's generosity in sharing her family and celebrity justified her acceptance of Winifred's services. In *Testament of Friendship*, Vera highlighted the moments when Winifred expressed her love and appreciation. Just a few days before she died, she told Vera: 'Remember that I love you dearly . . . I'm intensely grateful to you – you're the person who's made me.'

The idealised image of a perfect reciprocal and sisterly friendship was a fiction both valued, but Vera was the one who created and maintained it. Their Oxford contemporaries and many of their London friends generally viewed Winifred as a victim of Vera's selfishness. They were indignant that Winifred always gave and Vera always took. In her obituary of Winifred in *Time and Tide*, Lady Rhondda noted that people might think she was 'describing a saint'. And, she added, 'I am.' She was not the only person in their circle who saw Winifred as a saintly figure. Vera also called her 'a young saint' with a profound social conscience and a limitless need to serve. Behind that metaphor is a view of Winifred as an immature artist who let herself be distracted by her compassion and died with her promise unfulfilled.

But the image of a saintly and incomplete Winifred is also reductive. It erases the earthier woman friends recalled, and underestimates the esteem Winifred earned in her short lifetime as a prolific journalist and productive novelist. Marion Shaw argues that Vera's view of Winifred reflected the areas she herself valued and played down the others. Winifred was no pale shadow of Vera; she was 'livelier, more famous, more heroic and less pathetic than Vera paints her, and also fun to be with and to know, with a public presence which commanded respect and affection in literary and political London'. Beyond sainthood, Shaw maintains, 'a more robust, humorous, independent, active, and innovative person, even a more dislikable person, waits to be recovered'.

When Vera's three Testaments were reissued by Virago between 1978 and 1980, at the height of the women's liberation movement, the friendship became a legendary tale of ideal feminist sisterhood. Since then, however, interpretation has swung from uncritical acceptance to a more sceptical analysis by biographers and scholars. As the letters amply reveal, Vera was the dominant member of their partnership, and Winifred accepted and perhaps even enjoyed the subordinate role. This was not the fairy-tale story of an equal partnership, but it was also more interesting, raising questions about female friendship, rivalry, love and power.

Their relationship was co-dependent, with each partner combining munificence with need, and the balance shifted during their fifteen years of friendship. When they first became friends, the age difference was important and gave Vera a legitimate advantage. Her seniority and her personal history had given her a profound sense of the horror of war, and a determination to fight against it. That task, among others, could not be realised without challenging the disempowering of women and, implicitly, the privileges of men. Vera had read more purposefully about feminism and peace. She had sought out and joined organisations promoting international cooperation and world peace, especially the League of Nations. She introduced Winifred to feminism, and the post-suffrage campaigns for women's rights to equal citizenship and leadership. Winifred needed and learned from Vera's more developed political engagement, and from her experience of war. She had not grown up with a sense of women's subordination, and Vera's fierce feminism opened her eyes. Ironically, in many respects she became more radical politically than Vera, more attuned and dedicated to issues of class and race.

When they met, Winifred was also uncertain in her ambition to become a writer, a profession she worried her mother might not respect. But Vera's conviction, that writing novels was an important kind of intellectual and cultural work, gave her licence to take her fiction seriously. Moreover, she overcame her tendency to underrate herself, and gained the confidence to independently assert her own voice and technique. Vera originally had attempted to micromanage her writing, but by 1925 Winifred rebelled. As she wrote to Gordon, 'knowing my very great faults as a writer, she tried to cure them by analysing and criticising my ideas before they became books ... It nearly drove me crazy until I had to set a complete taboo upon her discussion of my work save after it was done.'

Winifred also needed security, stability and companionship. She needed to live in London to pursue her political and literary work, and she needed to express and receive love. She had been prepared to step down and surrender her life with Vera to Gordon. But it was Vera who invented the idea of an expanded marriage, argued for it as a progressive model and persuaded both Winifred and Gordon to accept it. Winifred recognised the rivalrous aspects of their relationship, and there are certainly moments when she even felt superior, but she was neither as competitive nor as ambitious as Vera. Throughout her life she moved away from criticising the stultifying practice of traditional marriage, especially for women, towards imagining utopian communities of choice and love.

They pioneered a way to live together that worked for them both. Winifred loved children and a family, and a home. Vera needed Winifred for much more than childcare, and Vera was the one who insisted on their staying together, although she knew they would be the targets of speculation and gossip. For Vera, unhappily unsuccessful at making women friends, Winifred was a miraculous combination of friend, mother, sister, reader, editor, comrade. Still, their relationship, however freighted, was only one part of their lives. We would have a different perspective if we could read what they were each writing to others during these fifteen years and after. Vera had a regular and affectionate correspondence with Gordon; they discussed their sexual histories, their marriage and especially their children. Winifred was writing to Jean McWilliam, Lady Rhondda, Stella Benson and Sarah Gertrude Millin among many, offering thoughts about her dedication to Africa, feminism and humanitarian causes, and about her life with Vera.

After Winifred's death, Vera asked herself how she would move on. 'Winifred in dying took with her that Second Life that she initiated for me after the war; can I make a third? Can I, once more, begin again? Are children and books enough incentive for living?' She kept on writing, but she would never again equal the power of *Testament of Youth*. In 1937 she committed herself to the pacifism of Canon Dick Sheppard, the leader of the Peace Pledge Union, the largest peace movement in Britain at the time. During the Second World War, at a time when pacifism was not just unpopular but suspect, Vera was even more uncompromising in her stance. The decision came with high costs. First, her readership in the United States (though not in Britain) dramatically declined. Then, when she and Gordon sent their children to Minnesota to stay with an American family Vera had met during her book tour, she was forbidden by the British government to travel to see them. The separation later took a toll on her relationship with her son John. However, she took pride in the brilliant political career of her daughter Shirley Williams, who became a prominent Labour MP. Vera rejoiced to see Shirley continue the feminist line that ran from Olive Schreiner to Winifred Holtby.

Vera Brittain died in 1970, and Gordon remarried the following year. In some ways, he was a disappointed man. He had, to a large extent, sacrificed an impressive academic career to his ambition to be a politician. But he never succeeded in becoming an MP. Latterly, he blamed Vera's involvement with pacifism for his problems. When Virago republished *Testament of Youth* in 1978, he was suspicious of this new feminist press: 'I have no interest in Virago,' he wrote. 'I think it an extremely bad title (!! Lesbian).' Yet the publication launched a revival, not only of *Testament of Youth* as a feminist classic and enduring memoir of the Great War, but also interest in Vera's life, her friendships and her relevance to women beyond her generation and even her century.

In her will, Winifred left the royalties from her writing to Somerville College, with the stipulation that if it came to more than £3,000 it should go to a scholarship for a mature student. No one would have supposed that her writing could make that much money. But *South Riding* has survived and flourished. It has never been out of print. Somerville has received nearly £500,000 from the bequest.

NOTES

ABBREVIATIONS

B&B   *Vera Brittain: A Life* by Paul Berry and Mark Bostridge
         (London: Chatto & Windus, 1995)
Gorham   *Vera Brittain: A Feminist Life* by Deborah Gorham
         (Oxford: Blackwell, 1996)
Shaw   *The Clear Stream: The Life of Winifred Holtby* by Marion
         Shaw (London: Virago, 1999)
SL   *Selected Letters of Winifred Holtby and Vera Brittain*,
         edited by Vera Brittain and Geoffrey Handley-Taylor
         (London: A. Brown and Sons, 1960)
ToF   *Testament of Friendship* (1940; reissued London:
         Virago, 2012)
ToY   *Testament of Youth* (1933; reissued London: Virago, 2018)

PART I: 1920–1925

INTRODUCTION

37   'would rather share this pilgrimage': ToF, p. 129.

'shared working existence': Ibid., p. 117.

39   'it seemed to me that the correspondence . . .': ToF, p. vii.

'a gay, grateful, infinitely responsive letter': ToF, p. 110.

'grew mature together': Ibid., p. 1.

40   'provincial narrow inhabitants': B&B, p. 39.

'Strange how one can feel as I do': Gorham, p. 73.

41   engaged 'for three years': B&B, p. 83.

On the morning of 26 December: Ibid., p. 92.

'only ambition held me to life': Ibid., p. 136.

42   'she must be careful': Shaw, p. 26.

'on the fringes of the war': Ibid., p. 82.

43   'How can I know': ToF, p. 88.

'a piece of wartime wreckage': ToY, p. 490.

'gawky and weird', 'a stuffed Amazon', 'Not in that size': Gorham, p. 166–7.

'superbly tall, and vigorous', 'vitality smote': ToY, p. 487.

44   'the contrast between': ToF, p. 93.

When the Somerville debating society: ToY, pp. 488, 489.

'ironically inauspicious beginnings': Ibid., p. 495.

45   'strenuous, independent, enthralling London existence': ToF, p. 117.

'educated women of the post-war period': Gorham, p. 169.

46   'The really awful thing has happened': Shaw, p. 107.

'*we are not equals any more*': VB to WH, 21 August 1922. See p. 71.

'*was the satellite*': Shaw, p. 7.

a subsidy . . . paid, or at least advanced, by Winifred: B&B, p. 181.

47 '*Amongst our friends*': ToY, p. 578.

'*was not for me*': Gorham, p. 580.

48 *mocking her '*intellectual pretensions*'*: B&B, p. 191.

'*In June, Vera will go*': Shaw, p. 120.

49 '*I like, respect [Gordon]*': Ibid., p. 125.

'*When you return to England . . .* ': Ibid., p. 126.

'*the child*': Ibid., p. 199.

LETTERS

Summer Vacation 1920

51 *Anlaby*: a local name, later changed to Anderby (SL). WH's first
novel, *Anderby Wold*, was published in 1923.

'*The Dead Man*', '*The Amateur*': titles of other early works by WH.

15 December 1920

52 *Mr Leighton*: Robert Leighton. A well-known journalist and the
author of popular stories for boys. He was the husband of Marie
Connor Leighton, the novelist, and father of three children, including Roland (killed in the First World War) and Clare, a woodcut
artist (SL). See Dramatis Personae.

The Outlook: a British weekly periodical, 1898–1928.

Chambers's Journal: a British weekly periodical, 1832–1956.

Christmas Vacation 1920–1

53   Bainesse: the house where the Holtby family lived in Cottingham, a
      village near Hull. It has since been renamed Holtby House.

      Harry: Harry Pearson. See Dramatis Personae. The occasion of this
      letter was the news that he was engaged to a piano player named
      Irene on a ship to South America.

55   'Dead Manish': 'The Dead Man' was a poem by WH published in
      the 1920 number of Oxford Poetry; according to Marion Shaw (p.
      53), it is the poem she sent to Harry Pearson.

      Driffield: town in Yorkshire, a short distance north of Hull.

      Carlo Rosa: an opera company active in the late nineteenth and
      early twentieth centuries.

Easter Vacation 1921 [c. 27 March 1921]

56   Boar's Hill: village about five miles from Oxford (SL).

27 June 1921

58   Potterism: novel by Rose Macaulay (1881–1958), published in 1920,
      satirising the newspaper industry. The Potter family are newspaper
      magnates. Arthur Gideon is the head of the Anti-Potter League.

      The Lee Shore: novel by Rose Macaulay, published in 1912. Peter
      Margerison is the central figure, an upper-class Englishman who
      drops out to lead a simple life in Italy.

      Hilda: Hilda Reid. See Dramatis Personae.

30 June 1921

59   Maude: Maude Clarke, history tutor of VB and WH at Somerville
      College, Oxford (SL).

59–60 Mrs Tulliver, Aunt Glegg, St Ogg's: characters and a town in The
      Mill on the Floss.

60   Miss Heath-Jones: Louise Heath-Jones. See Dramatis Personae.

Grace: WH's sister, who later married Peter Tolmie. See Dramatis Personae.

Carysfort: a Royal Navy ship.

Captain Carpenter: Alfred Francis Blakeney Carpenter (1881–1955), VC; he ended his career as a vice admiral.

5 July 1921

61   Crantock: a seaside village in Cornwall (*SL*).

Between Viva and Schools July 1921

63   *Cruttwell:* C. R. M. F. Cruttwell, dean of Hertford College.

16 August 1921

64   *Leighton family:* see Dramatis Personae.

65   *so delicate:* in a letter of 7 March 1935, WH will tell VB that a doctor she has just seen attributes the origins of her soon-to-be-fatal health problems to 'when I had scarlet fever, mumps and quinseys together when I was 15'.

'*Daphne*': VB's first novel, published in 1923 as *The Dark Tide*. Daphne is a character, and both VB and WH use 'Daphne' as a provisional title.

18 August 1921

The manuscript that WH reads to her mother is a version of *The Dark Tide*, VB's first novel. Virginia Dennison, who makes the speech quoted, is one of the two main characters; the other is Daphne Lethbridge. Daphne is closely based on WH, and Virginia on VB.

66   *Dowthorpe:* Dowthorpe Hall, a Holtby family residence in East Yorkshire; it is thought to be the model for Maythorpe in WH's best-known novel, *South Riding* (1936).

Mrs Jameson: Annie Edith (Foster) Jameson (1868–1931), botn in Hull, author of some forty novels under the pseudonym J. E. Buckrose.

20 October 1921

WH and VB had just returned from a holiday together in France and Italy.

4 November 1921

No text of the letter that VB seems to be answering was among the surviving manuscripts. It must have told her WH's sister Grace found WH's lecture on 'Frederick' dull, and it must have included some accounts of WH's dreams.

68   *in bed a week:* VB was suffering from a severe attack of jaundice.

       Sheila Kaye-Smith (1887–1956): a prolific and popular English novelist.

5 November 1921

69   *'petty, parochial':* WH was answering VB's letter of 4 November, an excerpt from which appears in the present volume, but these terms do not appear in the sources available.

11 November 1921

70   *Asiago and Louvencourt:* sites in Italy and France, respectively, where VB's brother Edward and her fiancé Roland Leighton were killed.

21 August 1922

In this letter, VB is reacting to the news that WH's first novel, *Anderby Wold*, has been accepted for publication.

71   *Bumpus:* a famous bookstore in Oxford Street, London.

       Dot: WH's friend Dorothy McCalman, who was then at Somerville (SL).

       'The Wallflower': published as *The Crowded Street* in 1924, WH's second novel (SL).

24 December 1922

73   *Siena and Assisi:* cities in Italy visited by VB and WH in 1921. The other proper names are famous sites there.

      Hilary Deane: VB's biographers do not comment on this pseudonym and VB did not use it.

74   *League of Nations Union:* organisation formed in the United Kingdom in 1918 to promote the ideals of the League of Nations. VB and WH were enthusiastic supporters of the LNU.

      Doughty St.: VB and WH shared rooms in Doughty Street in Bloomsbury until autumn 1923.

      Barbellion: Wilhelm Nero Pilate Barbellion was the nom de plume of Bruce Frederick Cummings (1889–1919), an English diarist who was author of *The Journal of a Disappointed Man.*

      '*Little Dog*': in the manuscripts of VB's letters, on the fifth page of her letter of 23 December 1922, one finds the following editorial note: '"Little Dog" was our nickname for the selected extracts from my diary which I was typing out under the title of "Chronicle of Youth" for a competition in autobiographies offered by an obscure firm of publishers named Philpots. It did not get a prize.' The diary was published after VB's death as *Chronicle of Youth* (1981).

      '*Man on the Crucifix*': probably a provisional title for *Not Without Honour.*

      Hugh Walpole (1884–1941): popular and prolific novelist.

      '*Elizabeth*': this name is in quotation marks as if it were a title, but Hugh Walpole did not write a novel with this name, and it probably refers instead to Elizabeth von Arnim (1866–1941), another novelist whom VB admired, author of *The Enchanted April* (1922), set in Italy.

25 July 1923

75   *your clothes and Grace's . . . bridesmaids' dress:* the Holtbys were preparing for the wedding of WH's older sister Grace to Peter Tolmie.

76   *The American girl:* her name was apparently Miss Foster, but she is not further identified.

Lord Waring: Samuel James Waring, 1st Baron Waring (1860–1940), industrialist, public servant and benefactor. See also VB's letter of 28 July 1923.

'*The Prophet*': later published in 1924 as VB's second novel, *Not Without Honour* (SL).

V.S.V.D.L.: very small very dear love. In the letters we have seen, this is the earliest occurrence of this abbreviation. After this date, both VB and WH will use it frequently as part of a closing formula, sometimes in lieu of a signature.

25 July 1923

76   The Dark Tide: VB's first novel, published on 16 July 1923 and greeted with 'tumult and criticism'; see B&B, p. 182.

Sylvester: Raymond Sylvester, a character in VB's novel *The Dark Tide*, apparently modelled on C. R. M. F. Cruttwell, d VB and WH's tutor.

28 July 1923

77   Robert E. Lee: a play by John Drinkwater (1882–1937) which opened at the Regent Theatre, London, on 20 June 1923. The cast included John Gielgud and Claude Rains, with Felix Aylmer in the lead role.

Sir Harry Brittain: Sir Harry Ernest Brittain, KBE, CMG (1873–1974), journalist and Conservative politician.

28 July 1923

79   *Grant Richards*: See Dramatis Personae.

'*The House in Raymond Passage*' and '*The Creditor*': according to VB, these were never more than ideas (SL).

'*The Crowded Street*': title of WH's second novel.

31 July 1923

80   Holehird: Holehird Gardens is now the home of the Lakeland

Horticultural Society. The house was formerly a care home for the elderly. In 1923 it was the 552-acre estate of VB's uncle Henry Leigh Groves, heir to a wealthy brewing family, who married Muriel Brittain, the youngest of VB's father's sisters.

24 December 1923

81   *Mr Catlin:* George Edward Gordon Catlin, whom VB would marry. A political scientist, he held a lectureship at Cornell University in Ithaca, New York. See Dramatis Personae.

Basil: Basil Henry Blackwell. See Dramatis Personae.

27 December 1923

83   *the near approach of thirty:* VB was born on 29 December 1893.

1 January 1924

86   your *Dr Jackson:* VB had met Dr Jackson, a friend of Peter Tolmie's, on a visit to WH.

3 January 1924

87   *Aunt Muriel:* Muriel Brittain, wife of Henry Leigh Groves. See Dramatis Personae.

Sir Roger de Coverley: an English country dance.

Hassan: Hassan: The Story of Hassan of Baghdad and How he Came to Make the Golden Journey to Samarkand (1922), a verse play by James Elroy Flecker (1884–1915).

The situation here: in July 1923, during a stay at Holehird, VB thought that her uncle Leigh was making advances to her.

10 April 1924

88   *John Donne,* Problems and Paradoxes: Donne published *Juvenilia, or Certain Paradoxes and Problems,* in 1633.

16 April 1924

88   *Von Gerlach:* Helmut von Gerlach (1866–1935), German journalist
      and politician; during the First World War he became a pacifist
      and generally supported liberal and internationalist causes. He fled
      Germany after Hitler came to power in 1933 and died in Paris.

89   *Pinoli's:* Italian restaurant on Wardour Street in London,
      1890s–1949.

      Cicely Hamilton: See Dramatis Personae.

      Lady Rhondda: Margaret Haig Mackworth, Viscountess Rhondda.
      See Dramatis Personae. A friend and supporter of WH, but never
      close to VB.

19 April 1924

89   *my book: Not Without Honour,* VB's second novel, was published in
      February 1924.

90   *Christine:* Christine Merivale, another self-portrait of the author in
      her pre-war, Buxton days, heroine of *Not Without Honour.*

      deal Leigh a more or less knockout blow: (Henry) Leigh Groves, hus-
      band of VB's father's sister Muriel. He and VB engaged in a flirtation,
      which VB feared was getting out of hand, and she planned to end it.
      He, however, wrote her a charming letter and she relented somewhat.

22 April 1924

92   *Turgenev, On the Eve:* Turgenev's third novel, published in Russia
      in 1860, translated into English in 1895, was set during the Crimean
      War.

20 August 1924

94   *Grace and Peter:* Grace Holtby and her husband Peter Tolmie, WH's
      sister and brother-in-law. See Dramatis Personae.

      Harry: Harry Pearson, WH's reluctant suitor. See Dramatis
      Personae.

95   *Dawes:* unidentified.

'her engagement': Gordon Catlin landed in England on 10 June, proposed marriage to VB on 15 June, and she accepted on 5 July.

27 August 1924

96   The Lay Anthony: first novel (1914) by the American novelist Joseph Hergesheimer (1880–1954).

Wycliffe: John Wycliffe (c. 1330–84), radical English theologian and philosopher. WH was writing a novel based on his life, titled 'The Runners', but it failed to find a publisher.

28 June 1925

99   *La Grave:* small French ski resort in the Hautes Alpes, near the Italian border; VB and Gordon will arrive there on 19 July 1925.

100   *Mrs H. Shaler Williams:* widow of Henry Shaler Williams (1847–1918), an emeritus professor of geology at Cornell at his death; she was born Harriet Hart (1849–1932). Gordon had probably lodged in her house before his marriage. Mrs Williams extended hospitality to VB, who regarded her as a 'lion' of Ithaca society.

Lord Stamford: See Dramatis Personae.

2 July 1925

105   *Venusberg:* i.e., 'mountain of Venus', a motif in folk tales in which a mortal man is seduced by Venus and visits the other world.

7 July 1925

109   Les Désenchantées: a 1906 novel by Pierre Loti.

14 July 1925

112   *Plateau:* the Asiago Plateau, where Edward Brittain was killed and buried.

20 July 1925

114   *Edith:* Edith de Coundouroff, WH's stepsister. See Dramatis
       Personae.

       Hilda: Hilda Reid. See Dramatis Personae.

       Bucolic Comedies: a 1923 collection of poems by Edith Sitwell.

1 October 1925

128   *Prescott:* F. C. Prescott (c. 1872–1957), professor of English at
       Cornell, known for early application of Freudian ideas to literary
       criticism.

129   *Cushman:* Robert Eugene Cushman (1884–1969), professor of
       government at Cornell; his wife was the novelist Clarissa White
       Fairchild (1889–1980).

Monday [5 October 1925]

130   *Stonepits:* a manor house in Kent occupied by Lady Rhondda and
       Helen Archdale.

       Mrs Archdale: Helen Archdale. See Dramatis Personae.

21 October 1925

132   *Mr Macdonald:* Ramsay MacDonald (1866–1937) WH later calls
       him 'J. Macdonald', and his first name was actually James; in his
       youth he was called Jaimie. He was a leading Labour politician, and
       had served nine months as Prime Minister in 1924 in a minority
       government.

       Philip Baker: Philip John Noel-Baker, later Baron Noel-Baker,
       PC (1889–1982), British politician, diplomat, academic, amateur
       athlete and renowned campaigner for disarmament. He received
       the Nobel Peace Prize in 1959.

25 October 1925

134 *Miss Hull:* Mary S. Hull (born *c.* 1868); she was living in her brother's household in Ithaca, NY.

Hull: Charles Henry Hull (1864–1936), professor of American history at Cornell.

Preserved Smith (1880–1941): distinguished historian at Cornell, 1923–1941. His second wife, née Lucy H. Humphrey, was the author of three books: *The Poetic New World, The Poetic Old World* and *To Arms! An Impression of the Spirit of France.*

PART II: 1926–30

INTRODUCTION

146 *Meek wifehood:* B&B, p. 222.

argument for 'semi-detached marriage': Evening News, 4 May 1928; in Paul Berry and Alan Bishop (eds), *Testament of a Generation: The Journalism of Vera Brittain* (London: Virago, 1985), p. 131.

147 *'to carry a weak man':* B&B, p. 223.

'stupid not to realize', 'produce a baby': Ibid.

148 *'many times during the early part':* ToF, p. 227.

review of Radclyffe Hall's The Well of Loneliness: 'Facing Facts', *Time and Tide,* 12 August 1928.

149 *'I am a markedly heterosexual woman':* Paul Berry, 'A Marvellous Friendship', in *Testament of a Generation,* p. 13.

'wholly a heterosexual person': B&B, p. 274.

'the partnership between Holtby and Brittain': Kennard, pp. 8–9.

the term 'lesbian' should be: Gorham, p. 163.

'My predominant concern': letter to Gordon, 1929, in ibid., p. 198.

150　'*bloodsucking friend*', '*liked having her blood sucked*': B&B, p. 276.

'*imagine anything that will*': Ibid., p. 234.

In his mind: Gorham, p. 196.

151　'*in case she ever had to describe a childbirth*': B&B, p. 243.

'*How tremendously we gain*': Gorham, p. 219.

152　'*was the nearest thing to complete happiness . . .*': ToF, p. 291.

'*for my brother and me*': Shirley Williams, *Climbing the Bookshelves* (London: Virago, 2009), p. 8.

LETTERS

10 January 1926

This letter was addressed to London and forwarded to South Africa.

154　*Henderson-Livesey:* Captain A. H. Henderson-Livesey, writer of anti-feminist books and articles (SL). In 1926 he published *Sex and Public Life*.

155　The Harp: 1924 novel by Ethelreda Lewis (1875–1946), an English-born writer who moved to South Africa in 1904; in 1925 she came to London with an introduction to WH, who introduced her to VB. VB admired the novel, a story of interracial conflict and romance set in South Africa, and sent a copy to Gordon, who did not like it. Her best-known work is *Trader Horn* (1927–9).

24 January 1926

156　*The Sheik:* a famous silent film of 1921 starring Rudolph Valentino.

24 January 1926

157　*Jonathan Cape* (1879–1960): founder of the publishing house Jonathan Cape.

18 February 1926

160   *Alan Cobham* (1894–1973): a pilot in the First World War, afterwards a pioneer in long-distance aviation. In 1926, he flew from London to Cape Town.

     League of Remembrance: an organisation founded in 1920 to provide support and social services to widows and dependents of British military veterans.

161   *Mrs Millin:* Sarah Gertrude Millin. See Dramatis Personae.

24 February 1926

162   *Klu Klux Klan:* the correct form of the name of the American racist secret society is Ku Klux Klan, but like many people, both VB and WH write the first word as 'Klu'. First founded at the end of the Civil War and suppressed after a few years, the Klan was revived in 1915 and flourished until the Second World War, and was then revived again in 1950.

26 February 1926

166   *Manilal:* Manilal Mohandas Gandhi (1892–1956) second son of Mohandas Gandhi; joined in his father's protest activities but remained in South Africa.

     Champion: Allison Wessels George Champion (1893–1975), Zulu campaigner for racial equality, trades union leader.

28 February 1926

167   *'The Incidental Adam':* one of the many fictional versions of Vera's war experiences that preceded *Testament of Youth*, 'The Incidental Adam' was to be a narrative of a woman's development over a decade.

8 March 1926

168   *Mrs Lewis:* Ethelreda Lewis (1875–1946), South African writer.

South African Party: political party of Jan Smuts, later merged with two other parties to form the United Party, which ruled South Africa between 1934 and 1948.

8 March 1926

170 *Chards:* VB's American cousins (SL). Standish Chard, a lawyer, married in 1914 Daisy E. Ashmun (1881–1963). See Dramatis Personae.

Hedda Gabler: this revival of Ibsen's play was being staged at the Comedy Theatre in New York. The actress playing Hedda was Emily Stevens (1882–1928).

'grippe': a term for influenza, originally French, from the 1740s, adopted in English in the late eighteenth century and old-fashioned today. 'Flu' came into use in the mid-nineteenth century.

15 March 1926

173 *Clements Kadalie* (1896–1931): South Africa's first black national trades union leader.

28 March 1926

VB is answering WH's letter of 26 February.

174 *Prohibition:* The 18th amendment to the US Constitution, banning the manufacture, sale and transportation of intoxicating liquors, was ratified on 16 January 1919. It was repealed on 5 December 1933.

5 April 1926

176 *May 25th:* WH did not sail from South Africa until late June, but this remark led VB to stop addressing her letters to South Africa prematurely.

30 April 1926

182 *Grace:* WH's sister; her daughter Anne had just been born.

183 '*Confessions of an Ex-Feminist*': article published anonymously in the *New Republic*, 14 April 1926.

2 May 1926

184 '*Hungarian Rhapsody*': title of an article by VB; this idea eventually became WH's third novel, *The Land of Green Ginger*. 'The Runners' was the provisional title of WH's novel about Wycliffe, which was never published (*SL*).

East Witton and Wensleydale: localities in the western part of North Yorkshire.

18 May 1926

186 '*The Land of Green Ginger*': name of a street in Hull, used as the title of WH's third novel, published in 1927.

4 June 1926

188 *Kegan Paul*: English publishing company, founded 1877, taken over in 1903 by George Routledge and Sons, which kept the imprint.

Mr C. K. Ogden: Charles Kay Ogden (1889–1957), British linguist, philosopher, writer, editor.

189 *H. J. Laski*: Henry Joseph Laski (1893–1950), English political theorist and economist.

Sir John Marriott (1859–1945): Conservative MP, historian and the former Secretary of the Oxford Extension Delegacy who had encouraged VB to apply to Somerville in 1914.

invitations to travel and lecture come of themselves: VB later inserted this note in the top margin of the holograph: 'My God, don't they just (1939)'.

29 June 1926

196 *on the way back*: WH wrote to VB on 24 May that she would sail from Cape Town on 19 June, on the *Barrabool*. On 20 June,

however, she wrote that the *Barrabool* had not yet arrived and that her departure would be delayed. By 29 June she was at sea, bound for England.

197   *'I will meet you at Southampton if possible'*: this line appears in WH's letter of 18 May. She had received no mail from VB for several weeks, because VB had begun addressing her letters to England in the belief that WH would sail much earlier.

17 July 1926

This letter was written over several days; the first part, dated 17 July, was written on board the *Barrabool* as it neared port in London, while the second part, dated 18 July, was written from VB's parents' home in London, after WH had read VB's letters of the past two and a half months. VB began early in May sending her letters to London to await WH's return.

204   *Heineman:* Heinemann, the English publishing company founded in 1890.

20 August 1926

212   Town Crier: the *Town Crier* was the Royal College of Art's trade magazine in the 1920s.

c. 6 December 1926

This letter is unusual in several respects. Although it begins with a salutation, 'Sweetieheart', it has no date. It is certainly incomplete, as it ends 'On the other hand by going out to America I should not only ...' There is of course no signature. It was written on lined paper, not stationery, and it begins with a numbered list of fairly trivial requests to WH ('Will you please ...') which have been cut in this edition, but item 3) begins 'Have had the most wretched weekend ...' and quickly becomes a lettered sub-list; sub-item b) goes on for several paragraphs and the surviving text does not go as far as item c). Was this perhaps a draft, VB's effort to organise her thoughts, and never sent? VB and Gordon had an acrimonious quarrel toward the end of 1926, in which Vera suggested 'a formal separation, "based not on incompatibility of temper but on incompatibility of occupation'" (B&B). That idea is echoed in the present text. Gordon, alone in Ithaca, felt on the verge of a complete 'smash-up'. WH helped avert a disaster by cabling him, and he responded promptly, dropping his demand that VB come to America immediately. VB's letter to Gordon, thanking him for 'having made, and with apparent success, this effort, this very real effort, to pull through', was dated 8 December 1926 (B&B). In the collection at Hull, the manuscript of the present document is classified with the letters of 1927, but it must have been written before this reconciliation and so it has been given here the approximate date of 6 December. There are no other letters between VB and WH between August 1926 and the Christmas holiday, when WH returned to her family home. In those end-of-year letters, VB talks a great deal about her plan to have a baby, suggesting that the rift with Gordon had been fully mended.

2 April 1927

221 *Mrs Scott-James:* Violet Scott-James. See Dramatis Personae.

Kathleen: Kathleen Byass, publicity agent and Somerville contemporary of VB and WH (*SL*).

Martha Harris: presumably a staff member at Heinemann.

Guy Chapman: (1889–1972), historian and author, married Storm Jameson in 1926 as her second husband.

222 The Lovely Ship: part of a trilogy by Storm Jameson about Yorkshire shipbuilders: *The Lovely Ship* (1927), *The Voyage Home* (1930) and *A Richer Dust* (1931).

7 April 1927

222 *John Lane* (1858–1925): publisher, founder of the Bodley Head, also published under his own name.

Rebecca West: already a well-established author and part of the *Time and Tide* circle; she and WH had cordial relations afterwards. See Dramatis Personae.

19 April 1927

224 *Dewey:* John Dewey (1859–1952), celebrated American philosopher, wrote and reviewed for the *New Republic.*

Mr G. *Stirling Taylor:* George Robert Stirling Taylor (1872–1939), English barrister and historian.

14 May 1927

229 *Two Old Men:* VB's father, Arthur Brittain, and Gordon's father, the Reverend George Edward Catlin, whom WH was tending to while VB, her mother and Gordon were all in America.

15 May 1927

232 *Miss Dainty:* probably a nickname for their housekeeper, Mrs Walker. In a letter of 17 July 1926, not included in this volume, VB wrote: 'I arranged with Mrs Walker to meet me at Wymering Mansions, & have engaged her.'

3 July 1928

238 *the child:* VB's six-month-old son John, whom WH was looking after.

239 *Vice-Provost of King's College, Cambridge:* Arthur Berry (1863–1929), mathematical economist and astronomer.

The Dynasts: an English-language closet drama in verse and prose by Thomas Hardy about the Napoleonic wars, 'in three parts, nineteen acts and one hundred and thirty scenes'. The three parts were published in 1904, 1906 and 1908.

The Four Horsemen of the Apocalypse: *Los Cuatro Jinetes del Apocalipsis,* a Spanish novel by Vicente Blasco Ibáñez, whose English translation by Charlotte Brewster Jordan was a best-selling novel in 1919.

21 August 1928

240 *Jan:* Jan Smeterlin (1892–1967), Polish concert pianist who in 1925 married WH's friend Edith Mannaberg, thereby become a friend of Winifred's.

Andrews: Henry Maxwell Andrews (1894–1968), a banker, who married Rebecca West in 1930 as her second husband.

Arthur Symons (1865–1905): prolific poet and essayist; his *William Blake* was published in 1907.

Henderson: Arthur Henderson (1863–1935), Labour,L Party leader, cabinet minister, winner of the Nobel Peace Prize in 1934.

241 *Radclyffe Hall* (1880–1943): author of *The Well of Loneliness* (1928), which VB reviewed in *Time and Tide*; VB was later called as a witness in the notorious obscenity prosecution.

25 September 1928

241 *6A Nevern Place:* in September 1929, VB, Catlin and WH rented the first and second floors of 6 Nevern Place, near Earls Court.

242 *Treviglio:* a restaurant in Church Street in London W1.

Open Door Council: a British organisation pressing for equal economic opportunities for women, founded 1926; Lady Rhondda was one of the founders.

26 December 1928

243 *feeding not one but two infants:* WH's sister Grace had died in March 1928 after giving birth to her second child; WH was with her family over Christmas and helping care for the babies.

Undertones of War: memoir by Edmund Blunden, published in 1928.

Johnnie: VB and Gordon's son John, born in December 1927.

30 March 1929

244   *National Union of Societies for Equal Citizenship*: an organisation of women's suffrage societies.

245   *Theodora Bosanquet* (1880–1961): literary editor of *Time and Tide* (1935–41) and Lady Rhondda's partner from the early 1930s.

     Abel Chevalley: (1868–1933), French critic who wrote on English literature.

9 August 1929

246   *Hamilton Forrest* (1901–1963): American composer.

     Mary Garden (1874–1967): Scottish operatic soprano; sister of Mrs Walsh.

247   *'The Industrious Apprentices'*: named for the virtuous figure in Hogarth's series of prints on 'Industry and Idleness'.

10 August 1929

247   Canhams, Burgh Heath: country house belonging to St Monica's School, where VB was educated (*SL*).

     Lord Cecil: Edgar Algernon Robert Gascoyne-Cecil, 1st Viscount Cecil of Chelwood (1864–1958), known as Lord Robert Cecil from 1868 to 1923, was a British lawyer, politician and diplomat; one of the architects of the League of Nations, for which work he was awarded the Nobel Peace Prize in 1937.

     Monica: Monica Whatley (1889–1960), feminist and Labour parliamentary candidate (*SL*).

     Miss Foot: unidentified; from context, partner of Monica Whatley.

     the Treaty: an equal rights treaty, for which League of Nations sponsorship was thought possible (*SL*).

     Mrs Ogilvie: Maria Matilda Gordon (1864–1939), known as May Ogilvie Gordon, geologist and politician, delegate of the Six Point Group.

248   *Henderson, etc.*: British delegates to the League of Nations meeting.

249 *Nina Boyle:* Constance Antonina Boyle (1865–1943), British journalist, campaigner for women's suffrage and women's rights charity
and welfare worker, and novelist; a pioneer of women police officers
in Britain; in April 1918, the first woman to submit a nomination to
stand for election to the House of Commons.

17 August 1929

250 *Aggie:* Mary Garden's sister Agnes, born *c.* 1882, married in 1911
Edward DeWitt Walsh, a Wall Street broker, who died in 1917.

25 August 1929

This letter was dated 'Sunday'. 'Aug. 1929' seems to have been added later
by VB, probably while preparing texts for *Selected Letters.* On 17 August,
WH was on the train from Monte Carlo to St Raphael; on 19 August
she wrote that she had arrived at Agay; the 25th was the first Sunday
following.

6 December 1929

253 *news:* of a family illness at Cottingham (*SL*).

Dr Gray: see Dramatis Personae; VB's diary entry for 5 December
1932 says that she is getting married.

254 *Janet Chance* (1886–1953): British feminist writer, advocate for sex
education and women's health reformer.

Realist: a monthly magazine, published by Macmillan and subsi-
dised by Lord Melchett, of which Gordon was a co-founder. Arnold
Bennett and H. G. Wells served on the editorial board.

23 August 1930

254 *19 Glebe Place:* the Chelsea house off the King's Road to which VB,
Gordon and WH moved in May 1930.

the Kent accident: on 21 July 1930 a small aircraft flying four passengers from Le Touquet to Croydon crashed near Meopham. All

on board were killed, in what became known as the Meopham Air
Disaster.

Shirley: VB's daughter. See Dramatis Personae.

PART III: 1931–1935

INTRODUCTION

259 *'the author whose art seemed':* ToF, p. 308.

'*even at second-hand':* Ibid., p. 308.

260 *'poor', 'gaping', 'an amiable donkey':* Marion Shaw, preface to
Winifred Holtby, *Virginia Woolf: A Critical Memoir* (London:
Continuum, 2007), p. viii.

'*you suggested so many':* Ibid., p. xviii.

'*she has never understood the stupid':* Ibid., p. 17.

'*violent headache', 'there were dark circles . . .':* ToF, p. 315.

264 *'Do have a holiday':* ToF, p. 496. See also WH to VB, [23 September
1935], p. 418.

265 *'I feel I want to be married . . .':* B&B, p. 325.

'*It's just an understanding between us':* Shaw, p. 63.

LETTERS

29 May 1931

267 Orange Grove, Littleton, Surrey: the home of Florence Bervon, VB's
aunt and former headmistress at St Monica's.

Miss Talbot: unidentified; from the context, ran an employment
agency for nurses and nannies.

22 July 1931

268 *Doreen Wallace* (1897–1989): prolific novelist and, like VB and WH, an alumna of Somerville College, Oxford.

Roy Randall: an 'extremely cultured young acquaintance' of VB's who had literary ambitions but died young. While she was writing *Testament of Youth*, Randall made the tactless remark to her that 'I shouldn't have thought anything in your life was worth recording.'

J. D. Woodruff: John Douglas Woodruff (1897–1978), editor of the *Tablet* and later chairman of the Catholic publishers Burns & Oates, graduate of New College, Oxford, friend of Evelyn Waugh; wrote under the name Douglas Woodruff.

23 July 1931

269 St Lunaire: seaside village in Brittany, in the Ille-et-Vilaine department.

26 July 1931

In August, VB and Gordon did in fact go to St Raphael, and had to cut the stay short because Gordon had put his name in to become a Labour candidate for Parliament and received an invitation from the nominating committee.

27 July 1931

270 'Woman in Transition': This eventually became VB's book *Lady Into Woman: A History of Women from Victoria to Elizabeth II*, published in 1953.

Ellen Key (1849–1926): Swedish feminist writer.

August 1931

This letter replies to VB's letter of 27 July 1931.

16 August 1931

271   *Ursula Filmer Sankey, whose toe nails I used to cut!:* as a pro-
      bationer in a nursing home during 1917 (*SL*). Lady Ursula
      Filmer-Sankey (1902–78), formerly Lady Ursula Grosvenor, daughter
      of the Duke of Westminster.

      Peggy Joyce: Peggy Hopkins Joyce, née Margaret Upton (1893–1957),
      an American showgirl who married six men, all millionaires and/or
      nobility, and is thought to be Anita Loos' model for Lorelei Lee in
      Gentlemen Prefer Blondes.

      Edith: Edith Smeterlin. See Dramatis Personae.

23 August 1931

272   Ashville, Rustington: small communities on or near the south coast
      of England in Sussex, slightly west of Brighton.

273   *Bridges:* Robert Bridges (1844–1930), Poet Laureate 1913–30; he pub-
      lished his *Testament of Beauty* in 1929.

      Hardelot, Abbeville, Étaples: small towns in France near the English
      Channel, and close to where VB had served as a nurse in 1917–18.

13 September 1931

273   *such a telegram:* see VB's response, also dated 13 September 1931.

      Monica: Monica Whatley.

      MSS of Virginia Woolf book: WH's book, *Virginia Woolf: A Critical
      Memoir,* was published in October 1932.

      Thomas Moult (1893–1974): versatile British poet and journalist;
      probably a reader for Faber and Faber, which declined to publish the
      book.

13 September 1931

WH had offered to take care of the Brittain-Catlins' two small children
so that they could have a holiday in St Raphael on the French Riviera.
Gordon had put his name in to be a Labour candidate for Parliament, and

was unexpectedly summoned back to England to be interviewed by the selection committee for a by-election in Chiswick. He was in fact chosen, but the election turned out to be a general election, and he was soundly defeated. Vera was just beginning to write the final version of *Testament of Youth* (B&B, pp. 244–5).

10 November 1931

276 Icknield Cottage, Monks Risborough: the cottage in the Buckinghamshire village, later renamed Four Hedges, home of Clare Leighton, who was living with the writer Noel Brailsford.

Canary Isles: WH was too ill to make this trip with Lady Rhondda.

22 February 1932

277 *chickenpox:* caught from her son John, who picked it up at his nursery school (SL).

24 February 1932

278 *Dr Leverkus:* see Dramatis Personae.

25 February 1932

279 The Double Cottage, Monks Risborough: WH went to stay at this cottage when her doctor, believing that her illness was due to overwork, ordered her to rest in the country (SL).

25 February 1932

280 *Beveridge:* William Henry Beveridge, 1st Baron Beveridge (1879–1953), economist, known for his 1942 report 'Social Insurance and Allied Services', known as the Beveridge Report, which was an important influence on the post-war welfare programmes in Britain.

1 March 1932

281 *Higham:* David Higham (1895–1978), VB's literary agent, and part of the London agency Pearn, Pollinger & Higham from 1935.

2 March 1932

282   *Dr Ironside:* Redvers Noel Ironside (1899–1968), distinguished London neurologist.

5 March 1932

284   *Odette:* Odette Zoé Keun. See Dramatis Personae.

Ethel Mannin (1900–84): prolific novelist and memoirist.

Sassoon: Siegfried Sassoon (1886–1967), famous as a war poet, published two autobiographical novels in 1928 and 1930.

5 March 1932

285   *Ellen Wilkinson* (1891–1947): socialist campaigner and Member of Parliament for the Labour Party, Minister for Education (1945–7), author of books including the novel *Clash* (1929).

'*Hypotensyl*': still in use as a medication for high blood pressure.

Ernest Rhys (1859–1946): founding editor of Everyman's Library (*SL*).

Watts-Dunton: Theodore Watts-Dunton (1832–1914), poetry critic, friend of Swinburne.

14 March 1932

288   *Étaples mutiny:* a series of incidents in September 1917 at the British training camp at Étaples, where newly arrived troops were trained for trench and gas warfare by men who were thought to have avoided such service themselves. For VB's highly misleading account of the mutiny in *Testament of Youth*, see Mark Bostridge, *Vera Brittain and the First World War: The Story of Testament of Youth* (London: Bloomsbury Continuum, 2014), pp. 150–1.

Pollard: Alfred Oliver Pollard (1893–1960) served in the First World War with exceptional bravery, and was awarded the VC. In 1932 he published *Fire-Eater, or Memoirs of a VC*. He went on to be a prolific author of fiction.

31 March 1932

290   *Phyllis Bentley's book:* the novel *Inheritance* (1932). See Dramatis Personae, and on Bentley's complicated relationship to VB, see B&B, pp. 247–54.

   Halls Dally: John Frederick Halls Dally. See Dramatis Personae. He published a book on high blood pressure in 1923.

2 April 1932

291   *Calcraft:* the couple who were WH's hosts or housekeepers at Double Cottage.

4 April 1932

292   *Edith Shackleton:* Edith Shackleton Heald (1885–1976), bisexual British journalist, later the mistress of W. B. Yeats.

   Rebecca: Rebecca West, 'then doing "star" reviews for the *Daily Telegraph*' (SL).

293   *Courtfield Gardens:* nursing home in London, to which WH moved for further treatment.

293   *Obermer:* Dr Edgar Obermer. See Dramatis Personae. He lived and worked in England, and took his training at Lausanne.

14 April 1932

294   *Gollancz:* Victor Gollancz. See Dramatis Personae.

   the Viscountess: Margaret Haig Mackworth, Viscountess Rhondda.

6 May 1932

The doctor WH refers to as 'he' is Dr Edgar Obermer.

26 August 1932

299   *Ruth Holland:* novelist and collaborator of J. B. Priestley, and sister
      or kinswoman of his second wife; she published *The Lost Generation*
      in 1932.

27 December 1932

WH did not give a place in dating this letter, but she was at home at Bainesse.

19 February 1933

305   *Edith:* Edith de Coundouroff. See Dramatis Personae.

      Dr Innes: Ian G. Innes (1890–1964), GP in Hull.

20 February 1933

306   *coughing:* both children were ill with whooping cough (*SL*).

307   *Macmillan:* owing to a series of chances the Macmillan Company of
      New York accepted *Testament of Youth* before it was submitted to an
      English publisher.

24 February 1933

      The manuscript of this letter is missing in the microfilms available
      to us, but an excerpt from it appears in *Selected Letters*, on which the
      present text is based.

309   *Latham:* Harold Latham. See Dramatis Personae.

310   *Peter:* Peter Tolmie, WH's brother-in-law.

24 February 1933

310   *Rebecca:* Rebecca West.

311   *Mrs Gollancz:* Ruth Lowy (1892–1973), daughter of Ernest Daniel
      Lowy, a stockbroker, was an artist and architect and a suffragist; she
      married Victor Gollancz in 1919.

Stella Churchill (1883–1924): British medical psychologist and psychoanalyst.

Naomi Royde-Smith (1875–1964): British writer who published nearly four dozen novels, biographies and plays, and was the first woman literary editor of the *Westminster Gazette*.

'Mandoa': WH's *Mandoa, Mandoa*, published in January 1933, a comic novel about the conflicts and misunderstandings between Africans and Europeans.

10 March 1933

312   *Grace's death five years ago:* Grace Holtby Tolmie, Winifred's sister, died 11 March 1928.

14 March 1933

313   *her autobiography:* Lady Rhondda's memoir, *This Was My World*, had just appeared.

20 March 1933

320   *Kirks or Somerskills or Wishermanns:* from the context, female students of Gordon Catlin's.

2 April 1933

323   Jacket Description: The typed copy of this jacket description that appears among the manuscripts of the letters contains a few hand-written edits, which were included in *SL*.

11 April 1933

333   *inadequate puff:* Phyllis Bentley had written a jacket blurb for *Testament of Youth*, which was so feeble that Gollancz rejected it and asked WH to write the blurb instead. See WH's letter of 2 April 1933.

21 August 1933

338 *Pamela Hinkson* (1900–82): daughter of Katharine Tynan, the novelist, and the barrister Henry Albert Hinkson. 'Doing it' was reviewing *Testament of Youth* (SL).

Ellis Roberts: R. Ellis Roberts (1879–1953), author and critic, then literary editor of *Time and Tide* (SL).

Delafield: E. M. Delafield (1890–1943), author of the 'Provincial Lady' series, and a *Time and Tide* contributor (SL).

23 August 1933

339 *Beatrice Kean Seymour* (1886–1995): well-known popular novelist and the first wife of William Kean Seymour, a writer who was also VB's bank manager.

Cecil Roberts (1892–1976): English journalist and author.

Wonder Hero: 1933 novel by J. B. Priestley.

1 April 1934

341 *Henry and Rebecca:* Henry Maxwell Andrews (1894–1960), a banker, and the writer Rebecca West; they were married in 1930 after being introduced by the Catlins (Andrews was a New College, Oxford contemporary of Gordon's). Anthony was Rebecca's son from her affair with H. G. Wells, born in 1914.

Portofino: an old fishing village near Genoa. It began to attract tourists in the late nineteenth century, and Elizabeth von Arnim's 1922 novel *The Enchanted April* is credited with making it fashionable.

7 April 1934

342 *Withernsea:* a seaside town in East Yorkshire. WH went there in 1934 to restore her health.

'*South Riding*': this will be the title of WH's final novel, published posthumously in 1936.

9 April 1934

342   *Gordon:* he was attending a sociological school in Rome (*SL*).

      Sta. Margherita: Santa Margherita Ligure, a municipality bordering Portofino.

343   *Phyllis:* Phyllis Bentley; in a letter of 6 April, VB reported hearing the news that Mrs Bentley was ill and that Phyllis had been 'telegraphed for by her brother to come home at once without finishing her tour' in the United States.

7 May 1934

345   *I knew your father:* in April 1934, while VB was in Italy, her father Arthur Brittain attempted suicide. He had been in poor health for a long time and was subject to depression. He took his own life in 1935.

      poems: Poems of the War and After (1934), in part a reprint of VB's earlier *Poems of a VAD*.

      Preface to Action: a book by Gordon Catlin, published in 1934.

19 May 1934

347   *Howard Pim* (1862–1934): a South African businessman, active in Johannesburg municipal affairs.

      Dorothy Woodman (1902–70): British socialist and journalist.

22 May 1934

348   Cavalcade *film: Cavalcade* is a 1933 American film based on the 1931 play by Noël Coward. The story presents English life during the first third of the twentieth century from the point of view of well-to-do London residents Jane and Robert Marryot, their children, their close friends and their servants. Several historical events affect the lives of the characters or serve as background for the film, including the First World War.

      Tallulah Bankhead (1902–68): an American actress, who performed on the London stage between 1922 and 1931, then went to Hollywood.

Colston Leigh: See Dramatis Personae.

349 *Curtis Brown:* VB's British agent; the company, founded in 1899, is still a major agency.

Tawny Island: Chapter VII of *Testament of Youth* is called 'Tawny Island', that is, Malta, where VB was 'sorrowful, anxious, frustrated, lonely – but yet how vividly alive', and she writes: 'Take away this agreeable London life ... and give me back that lovely solitude, that enchanted obscurity ...' (p. 291).

24 September 1934

349 Man of Aran: 1934 film about the Aran Islands by Robert J. Flaherty.

The Bretts: George P. Brett, Jr, president of the Macmillan Company, and his wife Isabel. See Dramatis Personae.

350 *Macdonell:* A. G. Macdonell (1895–1941), author of *England, Their England*, a popular book in 1933; his *A Visit to America* in 1935 was less successful.

351 Truth is Not Sober: a collection of short stories by WH, published in London by W. Collins in 1934 and in the USA by Macmillan in the autumn of 1934

6 October 1934

354 *Ruby Williams:* not identified, but from context a relative or family friend.

Sir Josiah Stamp (1880–1941): British economist, a director of the Bank of England.

James Agate (1877–1947): writer and critic; wrote a negative review of *Testament of Youth* in the *Daily Express*, which used the phrase 'a book for bluestockings by one of them'.

Eric Gillett (1893–1978): writer and literary critic. He and VB had acted together in Buxton.

6 October 1934

356   *Empire State Building:* built 1930–1, the world's tallest building until
      1970.

26 October 1934

358   *Mrs Woodard Colby:* Ruth Gage Colby (1899–1984), wife of a pro-
      fessor of medicine at the University of Minnesota, suffragist, peace
      activist; she and VB became lifelong friends, and VB sent her chil-
      dren to live with the Colbys during the Second World War.

27 October 1934

359   *in journeyings oft:* adapted from 2 Corinthians 26.

31 October 1934

361   *Herbert A. Bruce* (1868–1963): lieutenant governor of Ontario
      1932–7, later a Conservative member of the Canadian Parliament;
      married Angela Hall in 1919.

362   *unexplained mystery:* this refers to the segregation of officers and
      VAD nurses in the First World War (SL).

4 November 1934

363   *Lady Steel Maitland:* Mary (1871–1944), daughter of Sir James
      Ramsay-Gibson-Maitland, 4th Baronet, of Barnton
      and Sauchie, since 1901 the wife of Sir Arthur Herbert
      Drummond Ramsay Steel-Maitland, 1st Baronet (1876–1935), a
      British Conservative politician.

12 November 1934

363   *Bretts' house in New York:* the Bretts' residence was attached to the
      building where Macmillan was located.

364   *'sedooce':* probably to suggest George Brett's American
      pronunciation.

365 *constant round of drinks*: the amendment repealing prohibition was ratified on 5 December 1933. A highball was actually whiskey with a mixer, usually club soda.

367 *Governor Whitman*: Charles Seymour Whitman (1868–1947), Republican governor of New York State from 1 January 1915 to 31 December 1918.

368 *Alleyndene*: the name of a family central to the novel VB was writing, published in April 1935 as *Honourable Estate*.

Colonel Hudson: Charles Hudson (1892–1959), commanding officer of the unit in which VB's brother had served. In 1918 VB had tried in vain to persuade him to give her details of Edward's death in battle in Italy, and she wrote *Testament of Youth* believing that Hudson withheld information that would have confirmed his heroism. After the publication of *Testament of Youth*, which depicted Hudson in a very unfavourable light, he offered to tell VB the facts, warning that she would be saddened. The truth was that Edward had been accused of homosexual acts with his subordinates and was facing court martial; Colonel Hudson warned Edward the day before the battle in which he was killed. Facing disgrace, Edward may have exposed himself to enemy fire, though there is no firm evidence to this effect. See B&B, p. 129ff, and Mark Bostridge, 'The Tragedy of Edward Brittain', in *Vera Brittain and the First World War: The Story of Testament of Youth* (2014).

14 November 1934

372 *Prince of Wales, Salvation Army*: an allusion to General Booth, founder of the Salvation Army, being invited to the coronation of King Edward VII in 1902, after decades of being regarded as an eccentric troublemaker

Amy and Charlie: Charles Burnett and his wife Amy, née Francis. See Dramatis Personae.

Lord Camrose: William Ewart Berry, 1st Viscount Camrose, DL (1879–1954), newspaper publisher.

James Agate, Foyles: see WH's letter of 6 October 1934.

18 November 1934

373 *Dr Philip Stimson* (1889–1971): served in the Army Medical Corps in the First World War, wounded with British forces in Flanders; paediatrician and later a leader in the fight against polio.

Bruce Bliven: probably born *c.* 1890 in Iowa; in 1930 living in Manhattan with wife and child, profession: editor (US census of 1930).

23 November 1934

374 *James Anderson* (1893–1946): British consular official in China and husband of Stella Benson, who had died in 1933. WH became friends with James and Stella in 1925.

Ivy Cayley (1903–36): a cousin of Stella Benson.

26 November 1934

375 *Well, well:* WH is answering VB's letter of 12–15 November 1934.

the affaire George: refers to VB's attraction to George Brett.

Vive l'amour . . .: French phrase meaning 'long live love, long live frivolity', popularised by Laurence Sterne in *A Sentimental Journey*.

28 November 1934

377 *get to George:* one of George Brett's relatives was in the audience.

2 December 1934

381 *New Orleans train:* VB did not go to New Orleans, but the train she took to North Carolina on 17 November had New Orleans as its ultimate terminus.

13 February 1935

384 *Hornsea:* a small Yorkshire seaside town on the east coast (SL).

17 February 1935

We have no manuscript or other version of the letter from VB, dated *c.* 17 February 1935, which WH is answering. In it, VB must have complained of headaches and of overwork, partly because of Gordon's demands and his reluctance to assist in caring for the children.

5 March 1935

This letter responds to letters of VB which are in the manuscript scans but incomplete, and even less complete in *SL*. VB talks about working on her new novel, *Honourable Estate*, and mentions WH's plan to go to Liberia. She also suggests coming to visit WH on 16 March, the only time she has free because of lectures. There is no specific mention of a possible pregnancy in the existing pages, but VB stresses that Gordon has just returned from America and is entitled to some companionship as a husband.

390   *MacDonald:* Ramsay MacDonald, Prime Minister 1929–31.

White Paper on Rearmament: a document published on 4 March 1935 by the War Office, which asserted the failure of the League of Nations and the need for British rearmament.

Amery: Leopold Charles Maurice Stennett Amery (1873–1955), usually known as Leo Amery or L. S. Amery, Conservative politician and journalist, noted for his interest in military preparedness and for his opposition to appeasement.

Lybaria: Liberia; WH wrote to Phyllis Bentley on 26 August 1935 that the Liberian government has asked her to visit its republic as an official guest and write a report.

6 March 1935

The manuscript for this letter is not included in the manuscript scans. The text is taken from *SL*.

391   *Mrs Catlin:* Gordon's mother, Edith Kate Catlin (*c.* 1874–1917), dedicated suffragist and political worker who died in 1917 after separating from Gordon's father, Revd George Catlin.

7 March 1935

392   *letter on Tuesday:* the letter of 5 March.

24 March 1935

395   *Anna Westergaard* (1882–1964): Danish railway official and influential women's rights activist.

Margaret Ashton (1856–1937): suffragist, politician (the first woman city councillor for Manchester) and pioneer infant welfare worker.

Stopes and Roe: Dr Marie Stopes (1880–1958), birth control specialist, and her husband, Humphrey Verdon Roe (1878–1949).

25 March 1935

396   *Dr Sharp:* unidentified; from context, VB's doctor or gynaecologist.

saw Gordon off: on a journey to Russia, to cover Anthony Eden's visit for the *Yorkshire Post* (SL).

Ewigkeit: German for 'eternity'.

3 April 1935

396   *Tenby:* town in Wales.

397   *Tuke Hosdell:* John Tuke Hosdell, a corn merchant in East Yorkshire.

3 April 1935

397   *Miss Soulsby:* Lucy Helen Muriel Soulsby (1856–1927), headmistress of Oxford High School for Girls, published *Stray Thoughts for Girls* in 1893. It was reissued several times, and she published many other similar edifying works, several titled 'Stray Thoughts for . . .' She opposed women's suffrage and higher education for women. VB was working on *Honourable Estate*.

8 April 1935

398   Talks to Girls: by Eleanor Augusta Hunter, published by the
       American Tract Society in 1891.

       Dean Farrar: Frederic William Farrar (1831–1903), Dean of
       Canterbury Cathedral 1895–1903, prolific author of books on reli-
       gious topics.

       Sesame and Lilies: by John Ruskin (1865), a classic
       nineteenth-century statement on the natures and duties of men and
       women.

       Quivers: *The Quiver* (1861–1956), weekly magazine published by
       Cassell's, was designed for the promotion of biblical truth and the
       advance of religion.

9 April 1935

399   *Angus Watson:* Sir (James) Angus Watson (1874–1961), founder
       of Angus Watson and Company, a major importer and canner of
       sardines.

       Skipper Sardine: a trademark of Angus Watson and Company.

       Ivor Nicholson & Watson: a London publisher, active in the 1930s.

11 April 1935

403   'Jerusalem captured': British forces took Jerusalem from the Turks on
       9 January 1917.

       'Behold . . .': 1 Corinthians 15:51.

29 July 1935

405   *Festival:* first held in 1929, the Malvern Festival ran annually until
       1939; devoted to modern theatre and especially the work of George
       Bernard Shaw, who was the festival's patron.

       Francis Brett Young (1884–1954): British writer, novelist, playwright,
       poet, composer.

6 August 1935

On 3 August, WH travelled to France, where VB was on holiday with her children at Wimereux, to bring the news of VB's father's disappearance. WH and VB returned immediately to London. Arthur Brittain's body was later recovered from the Thames. By 11 August, WH returned to France, where she remained to care for the children while VB was occupied with her father's funeral, an inquest, her bereaved mother, etc.

406 *Norman:* Norman Maclean Leys (1875–1944), a British Africanist and critic of imperialism. His daughter, Nannice, was a friend of WH's.

7 August 1935

407 37 Edwardes Square: the house in Kensington that VB's parents took after leaving their Kensington hotel.

14 August 1935

408 *Sunderland:* Gordon was missing an event related to his effort to win a seat in Parliament there.

Josephine Baker (1906–75): entertainer and film star, born in the USA and naturalized French; *Zouzou* (1934) was a French film in which she starred.

16 August 1935

411 *Gordon doesn't seem much better:* he was ill, owing to an obscure form of poisoning possibly due to the infection he had picked up in Russia.

19 August 1935

415 The Astonishing Island: a satirical work by WH, published in 1933.

26 August 1935

There is no manuscript for this letter in the manuscript scans; in its place, there is a handwritten note by VB: 'Her last letter to me (August 26) taken out for safe keeping.' A note at the end of *Selected Letters* says: 'Winifred appeared to be much better in health when she first returned home, but two weeks later she went into a nursing home owing to the final onset of her illness, and was unable to correct the recently typed manuscript of *South Riding*. She died on Sunday morning September 29th, 1935, aged thirty-seven.'

[23 September 1935]

Unlike almost all the other letters in this volume, this letter was not sent by post, but was handed by WH to VB when the latter rushed back to London from a holiday in Brighton on receiving a message from Edith de Coundouroff that WH had taken a turn for the worse. VB cited it in the closing pages of *Testament of Friendship*, and the text is transcribed from that source.

418　*Metropole*: a famous hotel in Brighton, now part of the Hilton chain.

Pavilion: Originally a royal residence, built between 1787 and 1823 for William IV, it was sold by Queen Victoria in 1845 to the city of Brighton for development as a tourist attraction, which it remains today.

EPILOGUE

422　'*I know I exhausted poor Winifred's vitality*: Letter to St John Ervine, 8 February 1939, Winifred Holtby Collection, Hull History Centre.

423　'*when you are in pain*': B&B, p. 335.

'*suggest even a dim reflection*': Ibid., p. 333.

'*Vera's intense desire to write a love story*': Shaw, p. 64.

424　'*Remember that I love you dearly*': B&B, p. 327.

'*describing a saint*': Quoted in Carolyn Heilbrun, introduction to ToF, p. xx.

'*a young saint*': ToF, p. 506.

'*livelier, more famous, more heroic*': Shaw, p. 292.

425 '*a more robust, humorous, independent*': Ibid., p. 10.

426 '*knowing my very great faults as a writer*': Ibid., p. 124.

427 '*Winifred in dying took with her* . . .': Hilary Bailey, *Vera Brittain* (London: Penguin, 1987), p. 105.

Vera rejoiced to see Shirley continue: B&B, p. 510.

428 '*I have no interest in Virago*': B&B, preface, p. 1.

LIST OF ILLUSTRATIONS

INDEX